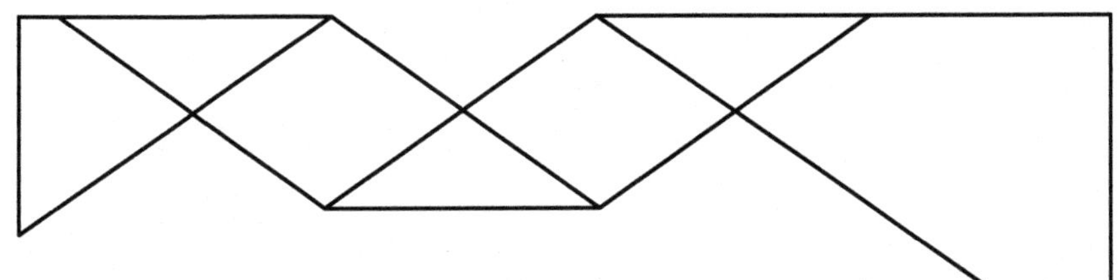

Instructional Analysis and Course Development

Third Edition

atp

American Technical Publishers
Orland Park, Illinois 60467-5756

Howard D. Lee
Orville W. Nelson

American Technical Publishers, Inc. Editorial Staff

Editor in Chief:
Jonathan F. Gosse
Vice President—Production:
Peter A. Zurlis
Project Editor:
Catherine A. Mini
Copy Editors:
Catherine A. Mini
Jeana M. Platz
Cover Design:
Melanie G. Doornbos
Book Design:
Jennifer M. Hines
Illustration/Layout:
Jennifer M. Hines
Melanie G. Doornbos
Bethany J. Fisher

3 4 5 6 7 8 9 – 10 – 9 8 7 6

Printed in the United States of America

ISBN 978-0-8269-4063-6

 This book is printed on recycled paper.

Contents

Introduction

Instructional Analysis and Course Development, 3rd edition, integrates the two topic areas of instructional analysis (determination of what is needed through needs assessment, task analysis, etc.) and course development (building the content of the course using outlines, syllabuses, performance objectives, etc.). Its main focus is on choosing a needs assessment technique, what content to teach, and how to gather data to make appropriate content choices. These choices are then used as a base on which to develop a course or program.

The text is an invaluable resource for academic educators, corporate and industrial trainers, supervisors, and human resource development specialists. On a practical level, topics such as performance and task analysis, how to write effective reports and presentations, and how to evaluate courses and programs are covered. The text uses graphics and charts to reinforce these fundamental concepts.

This edition covers information on distance learning and how to adapt instructional materials for use in an LMS (learning management system). Expanded examples of the three learning domains: cognitive, psychomotor, and affective are given, and information on how to put together an LAP (learning activity packet) for classroom use is included.

To obtain information about related learning material, visit the American Technical Publishers website at www.atplearning.com

The Publisher

About the Authors

Howard D. Lee is a professor emeritus at the University of Wisconsin-Stout. Dr. Lee has served as dean and associate dean, as department chair, as executive director of Stout Solutions (the university's extension and research arm), and as the graduate program director for the M.S. and Ed.S. degrees in career and technical education. He has taught industrial arts at the high school and technical college levels and has worked as a training evaluator in business and industry. Dr. Lee is a UW-Stout University Scholar and presently supervises technical college student instructors for the University of Wisconsin-Stout.

The late *Orville W. Nelson* was a professor emeritus at the University of Wisconsin-Stout. Dr. Nelson served as graduate program director, associate dean, and director for the Center for Training and Technical Education. He wrote numerous grants and contracts and presented at local, state, and national conventions. Dr. Nelson was the author of numerous evaluation and outcome reports and held a Ph.D. from the University of Minnesota. Before his passing, Dr. Nelson served as a consultant with the Northwest Wisconsin Manufacturing Outreach Center.

Acknowledgments

The authors and publisher are grateful for the assistance provided by the following individuals:

Content Review

Dr. Thomas Erekson, Eastern Kentucky University

Assistance in Manuscript Preparation—University of Wisconsin-Stout Staff:

Diane Longsdorf

Amy Gullixson

Mary Weber

1 Instructional Analysis and Course Development Principles

INTRODUCTION

OBJECTIVES

DEVELOPING A TRAINING OR EDUCATION COURSE

MODEL/CONCEPTUAL FRAMEWORK

Need for a Model

Essential Elements for a Training/Education Curriculum Model

Base or Foundation • Needs Assessment and Analysis • Business and Industry Input • Content Identification • Instructional Development • Delivery • Evaluation and Assessment • Changes

SYSTEMS APPROACH

SETTINGS

REVIEW QUESTIONS

REFERENCES

INTRODUCTION

The key to developing effective training courses and curricula is valid content. Needs assessment provides the rationale for the course, and task analysis identifies specific content to be covered in the training or classroom setting. Content is what is taken to the next course and what is applied on the job. Needs assessment and task analysis determine content, and evaluation revises it.

In this book, needs assessment and content identification are paramount. The needs assessment must be conducted and the content decision must be based on data from jobs that actual workers perform, or what they will need as technology changes. These data on needs are the primary source of content and assist the instructor in making good decisions on what should be taught. Other training and educational issues arise after the needs assessment is conducted and the content decision is made for a training or education course. In all cases, learner characteristics, background, age, and learning styles must be considered in this process.

OBJECTIVES

After completing this chapter, the reader should be able to do the following:

1. Identify the main focus of this book.
2. Identify the role of needs assessment and analysis.
3. Explain the need for a model when performing an analysis and developing a course.
4. Illustrate the essential elements of a training/education curriculum model.
5. Describe the difference between a system and a model.

DEVELOPING A TRAINING OR EDUCATION COURSE

One of the main focuses of this book is to provide strategies for making decisions about needs assessment techniques, what content to teach, and how to gather data to make appropriate content choices. Content choices should be based not only on the needs in the present work setting, but also on emerging trends, technology, and competencies. This book discusses the analyses necessary for developing a training or an education course. "Is there a training or education need?" is a basic question that must be answered. If there is no training or education need, then there may be no need for the training or education course. If there is a need for the training or education course, then content decisions must be made.

Many instructors train or educate on what they know, based on their experience, or what they enjoy, and not necessarily on what is needed to be successful on the job. Yet the content decision is one of the most critical for training or education outcomes.

In a training setting, decisions to offer a course or training are often made by fulfilling a management request; that is, a manager comes to the training department, sends a communication, or expresses a need for training at a management meeting. Sometimes the request for training is made without first checking to see if there truly is a need, or if the problem is one that training can address and correct. In some cases, training may not be the answer. In other cases, content decisions on training are made without much thought and under tight timelines, limiting the input of relevant data.

In an education setting, such as a two-year technical or community college, needs assessment and content decisions may also be made based on limited input from those that matter. Those that matter may be the business and industry that hires the course or program completer or the instructor of the next course that the student will take. Frequently, decisions about content are made by an instructor based on the course title, interest, or expertise. In some cases, content needs have already been determined, but in many cases it is simply left up to the instructor.

This book will only take the trainer or educational instructor so far. Needs assessment, content identification, curriculum design and development, and course and program evaluation are covered. In addition, task analysis and writing reports on the needs assessment are also covered. The actual delivery of the instruction, evaluation of the instruction, and assessment of changes are not covered in this book.

Basic assessment and analysis techniques are covered in Chapter 2. Many of these techniques can be applied to needs assessment as well as to task analysis. The basic techniques are essential for any instructional developer and should be selected based on the specific project requirements and setting. Essentials of needs assessment are covered in Chapter 3. Reasons a needs assessment should be performed before starting any instructional development, data needs, and a time-tested procedure are noted. Performance and task analysis processes and procedures are covered in Chapter 4. A research method using the mail is also covered.

Developing effective presentations, reports, and proposals is covered in Chapter 5. Dealing with the message and the audience, determining the information to be presented, analyzing the audience, selecting the best communication channels, and monitoring the feedback are essential for any presentation. Report writing, oral presentation, and proposal writing are key elements addressed in Chapter 5. Chapters 6, 7, and 8 deal with the curriculum design and development and actual instructional development. These three chapters are based on the need and task analyses performed to ensure that correct content is delivered. Chapter 9 deals with benchmarking and program evaluation. Evaluation is critical to any instructional development program and must be planned for before the training or technical education programs are delivered.

MODEL/CONCEPTUAL FRAMEWORK

Instructional development in a training setting or education setting requires some kind of organizational schema or model. A model provides the conceptual framework for looking at phenomena or, in this book, instructional development in training and technical education. Models give the instructional developer a place to start and provide a path to follow to complete the analysis (Oliva & Gordon, 2013).

A model is no more than a plan or an organized way of thinking. It can be a pictorial that shows relationships among different parts. Models help in visualizing a complex process and seeing how component parts fit together. Training or instructional curriculum models are viewed as all-encompassing and cover need and content identification, instructional development, and evaluation.

Need for a Model

Using even a simple model will help determine if there is a training/education need. See Figure 1-1. If the existing problem is not a training/education problem, it simply needs to be solved. If it is a training/education problem, then a task analysis needs to be conducted. The model used can vary depending on the setting. In *Figuring Things Out,* Zemke and Kramlinger (1987) discuss the need to "always work from a model . . ." (p. 8). Zemke and Kramlinger feel that working from a model facilitates the process of selecting the factors to study and the method to employ. Furthermore, they feel that the model "provides a framework for analyzing and reporting results" (p. 8). Models can provide the conceptual framework for making decisions as to what needs to be done and when it needs to be done.

FIGURE 1-1

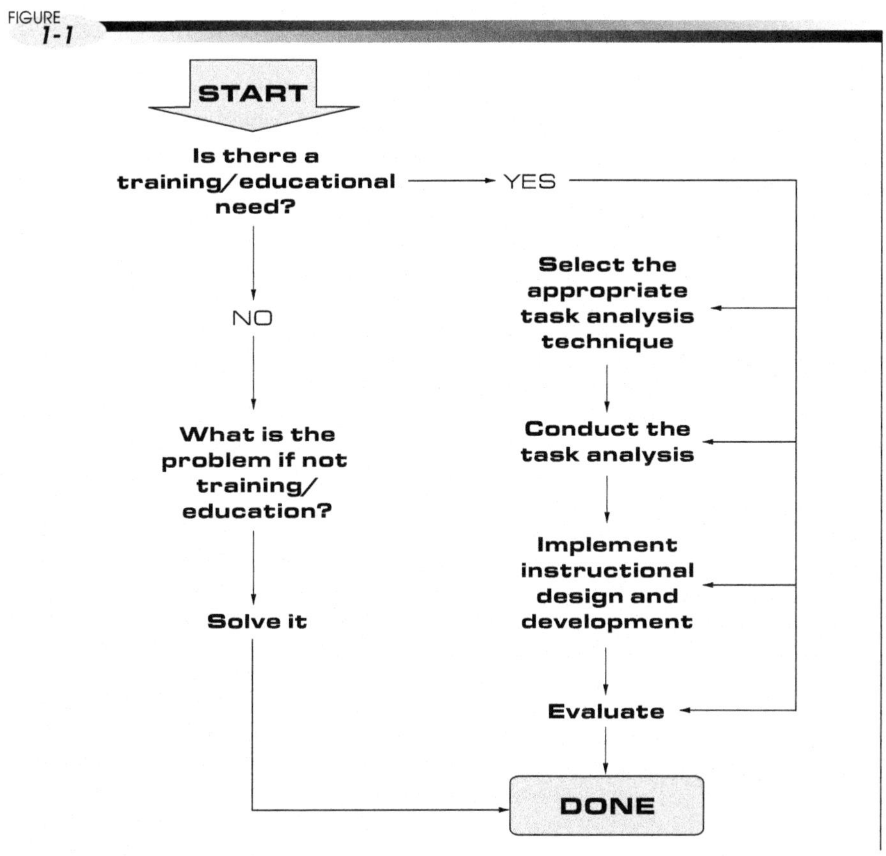

Is there a training need?

As in any model, it is important that the implementation of the model be based in the context of the setting. Instructional settings in business, industry, and school differ greatly. Models should always be adapted to the setting, never adopted. The process of instructional development will vary according to the interests, skills, and concerns of the parties involved. The backgrounds, philosophies, knowledge, and interests of industrial trainers, managers, educators, and administrators all contribute to the selection of one or more instructional-development processes and models over others. A review of the relevant literature is also useful. Before going any further, it is important to discuss where instructional development fits within the whole training and education enterprise.

Essential Elements for a Training/Education Curriculum Model

Curriculum is the planned educational experience offered by a training department within a company, or offered by a school or institution anywhere at anytime. In practice, curriculum consists of a number of plans in written form and of varying scope that delineate the desired learning experience. Following a training and education curriculum model will increase the probability of producing content and curriculum that is useful and meaningful to students. A functional model also speeds the development process, which is increasingly important. Furthermore, a model provides consistency. See Figure 1-2.

FIGURE 1-2

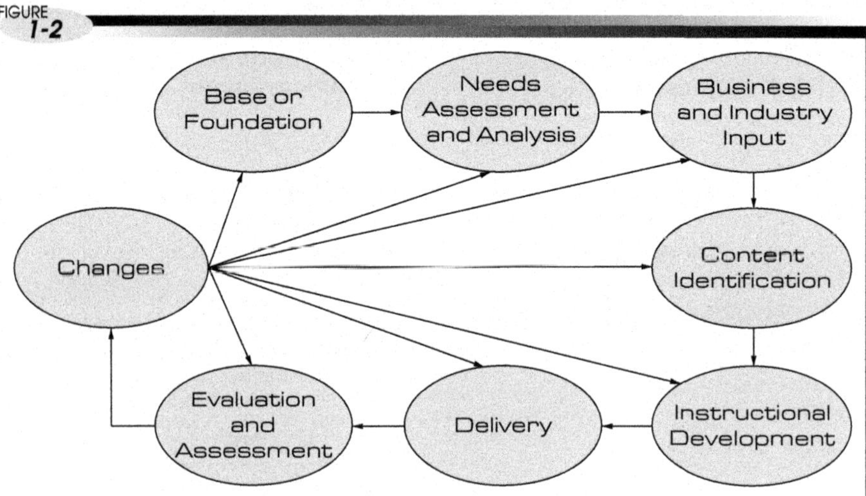

The training/education curriculum model identifies eight essential elements.

The training and education curriculum model identifies essential elements: base or foundation, needs assessment and analysis, business and industry input, content identification, instructional development, delivery, evaluation and assessment, and changes. Each is an essential process step for implementation and delivery of good instruction.

Base or Foundation. The base or foundation speaks to the company or educational institution that is addressing a perceived training need. What kind of company is it, what is the core business, and what is the relationship of training and development to the core business? Are there already established processes for training/education decisions? If it is an educational institution, does it serve a small area or a large region? What processes are used to develop a program and how is it determined if the course or program fits with the other offerings. The kind of business and industry, or educational entity, determines the processes used for deciding on the training or education curriculum.

Needs Assessment and Analysis. Needs assessment and analysis deals with the need for a training/education program. What is the gap between the knowledge and skills required to perform a job and what is known by the worker? Is there really a need for the training/education program? If there is, how was it determined? If there is not a need for a training/education program, then what is the problem? What went into deciding on the technique selected to gather the data, and are data sources appropriate for the decisions that need to be made? Needs assessment and analysis will answer these questions.

Business and Industry Input. Input is solicited from business and industry to understand needs and ensure that content will be relevant. In a training setting, the question, "How will training impact the bottom line?" should always be asked. What is the return on the training/education investment? What is the possibility of business and industry certification in the area under discussion? In an educational setting, how will business and industry input be solicited? How will the content task listing be validated?

Content Identification. Task analysis is a process of identifying appropriate content. Many techniques can be employed to determine content to cover in the training or education setting. The result of content identification is a listing of appropriate duties and tasks. Content identification is one of the primary focuses of this textbook.

Instructional Development. Instructional development is comprised of the activities and processes used to plan training and/or educational experiences offered by a training department or educational institution. What process will be used to finalize the course scope and sequence, syllabus, description, objectives, and units of instruction? Where does evaluation fit in and how will the learning be assessed? Writing performance objectives, developing content outline, developing instruction sheets, planning activities to reinforce learning, and measuring performance are all examples of instructional development. In instructional development, detailed lesson plans are developed.

Delivery. Delivery is the process of implementing the instructional development plan. The course can be delivered on-site or off. Technical instructors, if available within a company, can conduct the sessions or consultants can be hired. Will web-enhanced instruction be used or will it be an online course? Will the training/education course or program be delivered within the company or educational institution or will it be outsourced? How will information about the course or program be communicated and how will screening for prerequisite knowledge occur?

Evaluation and Assessment. Evaluation is the process of assessing students' competencies against course or training objectives. Evaluation also takes into account the learning styles and the expectations of the students. Formative evaluations (assessment during the instructional process) and summative evaluations (assessment after instruction) are necessary for any course or program. What did the students know when they entered the course or program and what did they know when they completed the course or program? How can the gain in learning be attributed to the course or program? Now that data has been collected, what will be done with it and what mechanisms need to be in place to ensure changes? Were students able to apply the appropriate knowledge and skills in either a business or educational setting?

Changes. No element in the model is immune to changes. The evaluation and assessment data may indicate that the way the training/education program has been conducted is no longer effective for the people receiving it. Needs assessment and analysis methods employed last year may not be as effective as techniques not previously tried. Likewise, how business input was solicited, or the methods in which clients were contacted to provide input, may no longer be appropriate. New methods, procedures, and technology employed in business and industry require an examination of content. Feedback from students and clients that utilize the knowledge from the completers may indicate that different instructional strategies, delivery, and evaluation methods are needed.

These are the elements of a training/education curriculum model. This text will cover the process from assessment and analysis through program evaluation. However, it does not cover delivery of the training or program. The actual delivery methods are more adequately covered in other textbooks.

SYSTEMS APPROACH

The model just discussed was developed using the principles of systems design. A system is comprised of input, processes, output, and feedback. Also, a system functions in an environment that can influence its effectiveness. Most of the content in this book is presented using a systems approach. This implies that there is input, process or transformation, and output in each stage of the curriculum model. The input may take many forms, such as data, decisions, prerequisites, or students. The process or transformation is action taken with the data, decisions, prerequisites, and students. The output could be a table of data, a decision, a prerequisite cut-off score, a selection of students for a workshop, or students with additional competencies they did not have prior to the workshop, training, or education.

Systems consist of subsystems that contribute to the whole system. There is a system for training and instructional development. One subsystem is task analysis, which is used to identify content. Inputs might be the result of a needs assessment that indicates a need for workers or students to know certain content. The process might be a DACUM, a focus group, or a research questionnaire that identifies the essential content for the training program. The outputs are the specific competencies, task statements, or task listing to be used in the training program.

The systems approach can easily be used for a lesson, which is another subsystem. The content has already been selected through a task analysis process, thus, for a lesson, the content is the input. The process or transformation is what the trainer or technical educator goes through to prepare the lesson. Writing lesson objectives, selecting and planning appropriate activities, matching methodologies to the activities and expected outcomes, and determining the prerequisite knowledge students will have are all part of the process. Assessment instruments to measure product and process are also developed during the process stage. The output is the completed lesson plan.

A system can then be applied to the actual delivery of the lesson. Students would be the input, along with the lesson plan. The actual implementation of the lesson plan and assessment would be the process. Through the process the students are transformed. The output would be students with competencies they have acquired as a result of the lesson. Evaluation provides feedback on the effectiveness of the system and input for the next round of program and instructional development. The whole process starts again.

Systems thinking will assist any trainer or technical instructor in carrying out the tasks of assessing and analyzing need, identifying content, preparing and delivering lessons, developing evaluations, and making necessary changes. Since systems follow the same natural rules, the knowledge from one system is transferable to another system.

SETTINGS

This book is intended for two main audiences, industrial trainers and technical educators. Industrial trainers work in business and industry and perform actual training or coordinate training outside the company. They typically move into their positions through human resources, or have some training in their background. Technical educators are typically those teaching in a postsecondary educational setting and are responsible for specific technical content. Technical educators are usually hired for their technical expertise and may teach the whole program or portions of it within a technical college. Likewise, technical/vocational education program coordinators at the secondary level will find the content in this textbook very useful. General education instructors will also find that the techniques covered may be used to make their content more relevant to students.

For the industrial trainer or the technical educator, the task of deciding on the elements of a training/education curriculum model are a reality. Each stage must be accomplished to deliver a credible training or education program.

Review Questions

1. Explain why needs assessment should always occur prior to task analysis.

2. From your perspective, how should content be determined? Explain why.

3. What factors might affect content decisions?

4. Identify several advantages of using a model in a training or education setting.

5. Identify and explain the essential elements of a training/education curriculum model.

6. Explain the difference between a system and subsystem.

7. What are the intentions of this textbook?

References

Oliva, P. F., & Gordon, W. R. II (2013). *Developing the curriculum* (8th ed.). Upper Saddle River, NJ: Pearson.

Zemke, R., & Kramlinger, T. (1982). *Figuring things out: A trainer's guide to needs and task analysis.* Reading, MA: Addison-Wesley Publishing.

Data Collection and Analysis Techniques 2

INTRODUCTION

One of the basic elements in the curriculum and instructional system presented in this book is the use of data from workers, supervisors, students, and other stakeholders to make decisions. Needs assessment, job analysis, and program evaluation require valid and reliable data collection techniques. Several data collection techniques are presented in this chapter. An attempt has been made to provide techniques that will work in a variety of situations. Each one has some unique strengths and weaknesses. For example, DACUM is effective in identifying the current skill content of jobs, but does not identify trends. In contrast, the Delphi Technique can be used to predict future developments, but is not used to identify the tasks in current jobs.

While there are many technologies used to deliver surveys, such as the Internet, interactive voice response, smart phones, tablets, or mixes of these, this chapter will mainly focus on data collection techniques and analysis of the data collected. The discussions of techniques that are well-known and used extensively, such as interviewing, focus on how to use the technique in a needs assessment. For techniques that are not well-known, such as DACUM, the discussion also includes a brief history. The concluding section presents information on instrument development, demographic measures, and cover letters.

OBJECTIVES

After completing this chapter, the reader should be able to do the following:

1. Describe interviews, focus groups, DACUM, and the Delphi technique.
2. Identify situations when the interview, focus group, DACUM, and Delphi technique would be used.
3. Explain how a data collection technique is selected.

4. Outline the differences between Pareto charts, process flow charts, and cause-effect diagrams.
5. List advantages of the nominal group technique.
6. Describe the criteria for selecting different instruments.
7. Explain the instrument design process.

DATA COLLECTION TECHNIQUES

A list of certain factors must be considered when selecting a data collection technique. Each of the data collection techniques presented in this chapter is evaluated against these factors. See Figure 2-1. For those who are using this book as a course text, Figure 2-1 will provide a framework for studying and comparing the techniques. Readers who are looking for an appropriate data collection technique for a specific situation should find the table helpful in narrowing their selection process.

Interviews

An interview is typically a conversational interaction between two people, the interviewer and interviewee, formulated to gather data. In many situations, an interview involves only two people; however, more than one interviewee can participate in an interview if the interaction between interviewees does not hamper the interview process. For example, it may not be productive to jointly interview a line employee and the employee's supervisor. Interviews can be conducted by telephone although this limits the opportunity to observe nonverbal behaviors.

Interviews can also be used to gather information at the beginning of an assessment and to cross-check or validate the data from surveys. On-site interviews provide an opportunity to observe the job being studied and the context within which the need occurs. Also, in some situations, interviews can gather more detailed data on sensitive problems and situations.

The interview process provides great flexibility. It is especially useful when the researcher has little or no structured knowledge on the problem being studied. When a new or unexpected factor is brought up by the interviewee, the interviewer can pursue the new direction and come back to cover the rest of the interview questions.

FIGURE 2-1

Problem/Purpose	Current State of Knowledge	Sources of Information	Location of Sources	Technique(s)	Cost Level of Technique
a. Explore a situation or problem area to – identify problems/ factors – identify needs	a.1. No reports or documentation available a.2. Some organizational information available	a.1. Stakeholders in the problem a.2. Stakeholders	a.1.1. In local area a.1.2. Spread in wide geographic area a.2.1. Local a.2.2. Dispersed	a.1.1. Interview a.1.2. Questionnaire a.2.1. Interview or records a.2.2. Questionnaire and a few interviews	a.1.1. High a.1.2. Low a.2.1. High a.2.2. Low to moderate
b. Develop a detailed description of a situation or organization – variables, interactions, climates	b. May range from none to some information	b. Stakeholders in the organizations	b. At the organization	b. Case study	b. High
c. Identify a list of problems, needs, or opportunities 1. general list 2. prioritized list	c. Little or no documentation	c. Stakeholders have firsthand experience	c. Where stakeholders are	c.1. Focus group c.2. Nominal group technique	c. Moderate
d. Identify factors and/or developments that will impact programs in the next 10–15 years	d. Dispersed with experts	d. Individuals who have expertise related to potential factors	d. Dispersed	d. Delphi	d. Moderate
e. Identify and sequence job tasks	e. Current task list not available	e. Individuals who do the work or supervise it	e. In local area	e. DACUM	e. Moderate
f. Develop a prioritized list of job tasks for course design	f. Task list is available	f. Individuals who do the work or supervise it	f. Dispersed	f. Questionnaire	f. Low to moderate
g. Evaluate program effectiveness	g. A variety of in-house data on students and the program are available	g. Program stakeholders (instructors, students, graduates, employers, etc.)	g. Dispersed	g. Interviews; student, graduate and employer surveys; records and reports; case study	g. Moderate to high

A number of factors go into determining which data collection techniques to use.

The authors have effectively used interviews in a variety of situations. Interviews have been used to identify needs. In some situations, these needs were used to develop statements for a formal survey instrument that was distributed to a large group of employees. Interviews have been used to validate the results from mail surveys when response rates were low. For example, in a statewide study of dropouts, interviews may be the sole source of data because typically, dropouts do not respond to other methods.

Although the interview is a very effective tool when used appropriately, it has some significant disadvantages. Interviewing is time-consuming and costly. Telephone interviews significantly reduce travel costs but also result in an important reduction in nonverbal data. In addition, interviewers must be careful to avoid introducing a bias. Sometimes the conversational nature of the interview lulls the interviewer into minimizing planning and preparation for the interview. This can have serious negative effects on the quality of the interview. The interview must be planned to meet specific objectives.

Interview questions have to be identified and written. When possible, potential responses should be listed with the interview questions so they can be checked if given during an interview. Also, the interviewer may want to probe to determine if one or more of these responses are correct.

There are three major stages in using the interview technique: (1) planning, (2) interviewing, and (3) concluding activities.

Planning. Careful planning is essential to successful interviews. Some of the information for planning, such as the purpose and objectives of the study, will come from the overall study design. However, it may be necessary to clarify these statements. Valid sources of data for the study will have to be identified. Would employees or their supervisors be the best source, or are there better sources?

The interview questions and process can be developed next. These should be pilot-tested with a small sample of the population used in the study or with two to three colleagues to identify any concerns. This will also provide an opportunity to determine the amount of time needed for the interview.

Once the time needed for the interview is known, interviews can be scheduled. To allow for some flexibility in an interview, it should be scheduled for 20 to 30 minutes longer than the time required in the pilot test. It is better to finish early than to run over. Approximately 15 to 20 minutes should be included between interviews to complete interview notes and prepare for the next interview. The interview appointment should be confirmed by mail or e-mail.

Opening and closing comments need to be prepared. Opening comments are very important in setting the tone of the interview. They are designed to inform the interviewee about the purpose of the interview, gain rapport, and establish a conversation related to the interview questions.

A process for closing the interview also needs to be planned. The closing should be friendly, positive, and express appreciation for the interviewee's time and input. Let the interviewee know what will happen with the input given. Sometimes the interviewer will finish before the interviewee is ready to stop. The interviewer should have a contingency plan for this. Once the interviewer has the data needed, any interruption, pause, or comment that the interviewee has no additional information is a good opportunity to move into the closing comments. Although it may seem unnecessary to plan proactive ways to close an interview, the issue of time allocation needs to be closely considered.

Interviewing. The interviewer should be on time for the interview. The interviewer should use the opening comments to complete the introductions, note the purpose of the study, and learn more about the interviewee. The interviewer should start with easy questions, such as what the person does and save the more difficult and sensitive questions for later.

During the interview, it is important to stay on task. The interview questions are the main tool for doing this. They do not need to be covered in the sequence listed, but all of them will have to be answered before the interview is completed. If the interview moves off track, it should be moved back by asking a new question or repeating the previous question. One way or another, control should be maintained in a positive manner. Negative feedback should not be used to change the topic being discussed.

If more information is desired, a probe should be used. One of the most effective probes is silence. This gives the interviewee enough time to compose a response. Some interviewees will respond faster than others. The interviewer should identify the pace and adjust the interview to it. The interviewer should give positive feedback when the comments are on target. A smile, nod of the head, and a look of interest are positive nonverbal feedback. Comments such as "good," "interesting," and "that is helpful" reinforce the confidence of the interviewee. If more information is needed, questions such as "Could you expand on that?" or "Could you clarify that?" are helpful. If a more definitive statement is needed, the interviewer's comments should be rephrased, for example, "Do you feel that the problem is really ___?"

During the interview, the interviewer will take notes to record the comments made. Often there is not enough time to write complete sentences and phrases, so symbols, words, or notes will be used. Also, the flow of the conversation may not follow the sequence of the interview questions, and there may be relevant comments that are not related to the interview questions. It is a good idea to have extra notepaper in addition to the interview survey form.

When the interviewee has provided the data needed, the interview should be skillfully moved into its concluding phase. The interviewee may comment that they have no additional information or the interviewer may perceive that no new information is being given. At this point, the interviewer should begin the closing process.

INTERVIEWS

Strengths

- Interviews are flexible. The interviewer can follow-up on comments and new ideas.
- The interviewer has an opportunity to observe nonverbal behavior and study related activities at the interview site.
- There is a high response rate. Most people follow through with their interviews.
- When good rapport is established with interviewees, they are often willing to provide information they would not write on a survey.
- Usually, an interview will allow more in-depth exploration of an idea or topic.

Weaknesses

- Interviews are time-consuming.
- Because of the time involved and travel for face-to-face interviews, interviewing is expensive.
- Most interviewer data is in the form of notes and requires more time to analyze. Also, the interviewer must make use of consistent terminology when making interview notes.
- Interviewer bias can affect the interviewee's responses and the interviewer's interpretation of them.

Concluding Activities. There are two phases in the post-interview process. The first occurs immediately after the interview has been completed and consists of reviewing, editing, and completing the interview notes or record. This is also a good time to write summary impressions of the interview. If another person is to be interviewed, some of this time should be used to prepare for it.

The second phase in the post-interview process involves analyzing and reporting the data. Also, a thank you letter should be sent to each interviewee. The purpose of the interviews will direct the analysis. If a needs assessment is being done, the analysis should identify needs and problems.

To facilitate analysis, each need or problem will be identified with a one- or two-word descriptive label. For a job analysis, duties and tasks will be identified. The format for these statements should be defined before the analysis is initiated. See Appendix A. (Additional information on interviews can be found in Chapter 4.)

Steps in the Interview Process. The following steps summarize the activities used in planning, conducting, and completing the interview process.

1. Preplan.
   a. Review study objectives.
   b. Develop interview questions.
   c. Identify the population from which the interviewees will be selected.
   d. Select the sample to be interviewed.
   e. Pilot test the interview.
   f. Schedule the interviews.
   g. Confirm interview schedule with interviewees.
   h. Prepare opening and closing comments for the interview.
   i. If multiple interviewers are used, train them on the purpose of the study and the interview process.
2. Conduct interview.
   a. Use prepared opening comments.
      - introductions
      - purpose of the study and interview
      - general questions on the interviewee's work and interests to establish rapport
   b. Continue with the interview questions.
   c. Record comments on interview form.
   d. Probe to obtain more data.
      - nonverbal
      - verbal

   e. Redirect interviewee to interview questions as needed.
   f. Conclude interview when questions have been answered.
      - start at a natural ending point
      - thank the interviewee for the time and information given
      - indicate what feedback will be given
3. Follow up interview.
   a. Immediately after the interview, edit and summarize notes.
      - clarify notes where needed
      - check to see that the information is complete
      - include date and name of person interviewed
   b. Later after the interview, analyze and report data.
      - send thank you letters to interviewees
      - compile and analyze the interview responses
      - prepare report of the results

Focus Groups

The purpose of a focus group is to collect qualitative data related to research questions. For example, focus groups are used to obtain qualitative data (data that does not have a numerical value) on a specific topic. These data are in the form of comments that convey the perceptions, feelings, and ideas of the group members. The group does not attempt to develop consensus. A focus group is especially useful in identifying problems and needs.

A focus group is usually comprised of 7 to 10 stakeholders, people who have knowledge and interest in the problem area. This group size is based on establishing effective group dynamics. If it is important to involve more participants, additional groups can be formed.

Many of the articles and books on focus groups suggest that group members should have similar backgrounds but not be familiar with each other. This can be accomplished in some instructional and curriculum development projects, but is difficult in others. To solve this, the facilitator should use good group technique, stay on target, involve everyone, and defuse competition. When input is sought from instructors in a department or school, most, if not all, of the focus group members will know each other. The authors have successfully used this method with both types of groups.

Also, both homogeneous and heterogeneous groups have been used successfully. For example, in a school evaluation, the authors used homogeneous groups based on departments and heterogeneous groups comprised of participants from several departments. In the latter groups, a question on interaction between departments was added.

FOCUS GROUPS

Strengths

- A wide range of qualitative data can be gathered from stakeholders.
- Focus groups are useful in obtaining information on topics and problems that lack structured information.
- The process can be completed more quickly than with some alternative techniques.
- Participants interact and generate spin-off ideas.
- Focus groups are an effective way to acquire stakeholder input.
- Focus groups are not dependent on participants' writing skills.
- The researcher interacts with stakeholders and gains a more comprehensive understanding of their feelings, needs, and ideas.

Weaknesses

- Group participants may represent a biased sample and may not represent the total group or population.
- The process does not produce statistical data.
- If the moderator is not skillful in the use of group techniques, one or two participants may dominate the discussion.
- Analysis of the data is time-consuming and relatively judgmental.

The director of the study will need to exercise some judgment in selecting group members. It may not be wise to mix supervisors with their staff members. Also, there may be other combinations in an organization that would not be conducive to a free flow of ideas in a focus group.

Group members are asked to respond to questions related to the study. For example, graduates might be asked to identify the strengths and weaknesses of the educational program they completed. These comments are recorded on a flip chart and later analyzed by the researcher. Participants are encouraged to make comments that spin-off from earlier comments. (Additional information on focus groups can be found in Chapter 4.)

Steps in Using the Focus Group Process. The following steps summarize the focus group process:

1. Identify people to participate in the focus group. Keep group size from 7 to 10. Use additional groups to accommodate more participants and to create the type of group desired (homogeneous/heterogeneous, strangers/colleagues, employee/management).
2. Prepare questions for the group(s).
   a. Use open-ended questions to stimulate comments.
   b. Ask for feelings, perceptions, and experiences.
   c. List four to seven questions. (Focus group should complete its work in two hours.)
   d. Start with general questions and move in a logical manner to more specific and/or sensitive ones.
3. Select a moderator who has experience working with groups, understands the study objectives, and is knowledgeable about the focus-group technique.
4. Schedule a room that will be conducive to discussion and group interactions. Participants should be seated around a table so they face each other and the moderator.
5. Make provisions to record with a tape recorder. Also, have an assistant to the moderator who can take written notes on a flip chart.
6. Pilot-test the process and revise as needed.
7. Conduct the focus group session.
   a. Give a general introduction to the purpose and format of the session.
   b. Moderator and participants should introduce themselves. (Each person should have a name placard.)
   c. Use the first question or two to establish rapport in the group and set context for questions that follow.
   d. Have the assistant record comments on the flip chart. If possible, also record on audiotape for later review. Moderator should also make brief notes if possible. Flag ideas that are emphasized, especially those noted by several participants. Link spin-off comments to their original idea with an arrow.
   e. Probe if more information is desired in an area.
      - a pause encourages responses
      - look at other participants to encourage responses

- try to involve everyone and recognize shy members first when they want to comment
- ask participants to clarify or expand on their comments

f. Use the last 20 to 30 minutes of the session to summarize.
- ask participants if there are any other relevant questions or comments
- ask each participant to write down what they thought was the most important point, present it to the group, and hand it in
- summarize the session and thank participants for their input

8. Debrief with assistant immediately after the session and record the participants impressions.
9. Analyze the comments from the participants.
   a. Review study objectives and determine what to look for in the comments.
   b. Listen to the tape of the session. A transcript can be made if time and resources are available.
      - record words or terms related to objectives
      - try to identify what stimulated/caused these comments to be made
      - look for reoccurring ideas, thoughts, and themes and record their frequency
      - identify when comments are supported by other participants
      - look for major ideas or themes that encompass major portions of the comments
   c. Review debriefing notes and written notes and contrast these with the results from step b. Check for unique ideas, inconsistencies, and common themes.
   d. If two or more focus groups were used, look for common themes and unique ideas.
10. Report the results.
   a. Report by objective.
   b. Describe the nature of the participants.
   c. Identify the themes or ideas.
   d. Clearly identify any interpretations made.

DACUM Process

The DACUM process was developed to identify competencies and tasks required to perform a specific job or cluster of related jobs. DACUM is an acronym that stands for "develop a curriculum." The end product of a DACUM analysis is a map or chart with a sequenced list of tasks that are required in a job. These tasks are prioritized or sequenced based on their importance in performing the job. See Appendix F.

The DACUM process uses the knowledge of the individuals who perform and supervise the job being analyzed. A committee of 8 to 12 people who either perform the job or supervise it is convened to identify the competencies required. Committee members may have a working knowledge of the total set of tasks required in the job being analyzed, or they may be knowledgeable about a portion of the work performed. Committee members are selected so a knowledge of all of the tasks performed on the job is available in the committee.

Committee members do not have to do much preparation to participate on a DACUM committee. They may be asked to review some information on the DACUM process and jot down some of the critical tasks involved in the job prior to the time the committee meets.

The DACUM committee meets for one or more days depending upon the nature of the job analyzed and the specific approach being used. If the DACUM committee meets for only one day, it is usually necessary to have the committee members review draft copies of the DACUM chart after the DACUM session has concluded. This can be done by mail and thus save the time of the committee members.

There are five major phases in the work of the DACUM committee:

1. Review the nature of the job to be analyzed.
2. Subdivide the job into functional areas.
3. Analyze each functional area and identify the tasks required within it.
4. Sequence the tasks within each functional area.
5. Review the draft copy of the DACUM chart and recommend changes.

The initial portion of the DACUM committee meeting will focus on discussing the nature of the job to be analyzed. A job description may be reviewed, or the participants may discuss the work performed on the job.

The second step is to break the job down into 7 to 12 major functional areas. In DACUM, these functional areas are called general areas of competency, or GACs. Some people also call these duties. The following are examples of jobs and functional areas:

- manager—planning, directing, evaluating
- secretary—scheduling, information and records management, word processing

- auto mechanic—repairing electrical systems, repairing drive train, tune-ups

The purpose of identifying GACs is to divide the job into smaller components that are easier to analyze. This allows the DACUM committee to focus on a specific area of work within the job. Any one of the GACs can be selected to be analyzed first. However, it is usually best to start with one with which all of the committee members are familiar.

In step 3, tasks encompassed in each GAC are placed on 3 × 5 cards. This is done so their sequence can easily be changed. Usually the coordinator of the DACUM committee will ask the committee members, "What task would have to be performed first in this general area of competency?"

After the first task is identified, committee members will be asked to identify the next task. This process is repeated until all the tasks for a GAC have been identified. During this phase of the DACUM analysis process, the committee brainstorms the tasks required. All tasks identified will be recorded and displayed. The room selected for a DACUM session must have one clear wall where the 3 × 5 cards can be posted. An adhesive that is strong enough to hold the cards on the wall, but not damage the surface, is used on the back of the cards. Removable adhesive putty that is sold in art stores works effectively for this.

Later these tasks will be reviewed and those that are redundant or inappropriate will be combined or deleted, respectively. No attempt is made to contrast tasks across general areas of competency at this point in the process.

After tasks have been identified for each GAC, it is time to review the sequencing of all of the tasks. This process starts with a review of each GAC. There are several ways to sequence tasks. The one used in the original DACUM process was "What task would be most useful as a new employee starts on the job?" Tasks might also be organized on logical or psychological bases.

The last step in completing the DACUM chart or map is to compare the tasks in each of the columns in the chart. In other words, take a look at all of the tasks that are in the first column of the chart to see whether they have the same priority. This review process will be done by column to determine if tasks that are related to each other, but come in different GACs, are placed in the appropriate sequence. This process is called a vertical scan.

At this point the initial copy of the DACUM chart or map is complete. The committee's work for this stage of the process has been completed. The DACUM coordinators will number the cards that represent the tasks and have them typed. The numbering system will represent the GAC and column location for each card or task. These will then be placed on a chart and duplicated. Committee members have an opportunity to review the draft copy of the DACUM chart, and their input on the draft copy is used to develop the final DACUM chart.

The final product from the DACUM process is a DACUM map that identifies the GACs and tasks for a job. The map or chart lists the tasks in priority sequence within each GAC. The basis for prioritization depends on the intended use of the map. If it is going to be used for short-term training to make people job-ready quickly, it will be sequenced on "what is needed to get started on the job." If the purpose is to design a two- or four-year technical program, the tasks could be sequenced logically. (Additional information on the DACUM process can be found in Chapter 4.)

DACUM PROCESS

Strengths

- Firsthand job knowledge is used to create the map.
- Consensus is achieved from experts' knowledge and experiences.
- Process can be completed in a relatively short period of time.
- DACUM map organizes job tasks and identifies priorities.
- DACUM map gives a graphic description of job content.
- GACs in the map are useful in writing job descriptions.

Weaknesses

- One or two participants in the process can dominate the discussion. In some situations it may be better to place supervisors in a separate group and reconcile the maps developed by the workers and supervisors.
- A DACUM map presents a picture of the job content at the time the committee met. This can be a problem when job content is changing, even at a moderate pace. The authors have combined the DACUM and Delphi processes to overcome this weakness.
- A trained coordinator is needed. The training is not lengthy, but the coordinator must know the process, terms, and structure of the map. Also, it is important to understand how a group functions, how to coordinate its work, and how to involve all the participants.

Steps in the DACUM Process. Steps in the DACUM process include the following:

1. Identify the job to be analyzed.
2. Select the DACUM committee of 8 to 12 individuals. Approximately one-half of the committee should perform the work, and one-half should be supervisors.
3. Convene the committee members and orient them to the process.
4. Develop the DACUM map for the job.
   a. Identify GACs.
   b. Identify tasks for each GAC.
   c. Sequence tasks within each GAC.
   d. Sequence tasks across the GACs (vertical scan).
   e. Label the cards to identify row and column locations. For example, A-1 is task one within GAC A.
5. Process and edit the map.
   a. Process a draft copy of the map.
   b. Review the draft copy with the DACUM committee.
   c. Make final changes.
   d. Duplicate the final map.
6. Use the map in curriculum development and evaluate its validity.

Delphi Technique

The Delphi technique was developed for the Department of Defense after World War II to provide a process for predicting future events. Since the technique was released to the public in the early 1960s, it has been applied in a number of ways for a variety of purposes. Business and industry, education, and health care are the three fields in which the Delphi technique has been used most frequently. Typically, it has been used in one of two ways. Either it has been used to gain consensus on future events, or it has been employed to derive consensus on specific problems or priorities.

The Delphi technique was designed to collect expert thinking and provide a process for achieving group consensus. The process was designed to minimize the impact of personalities on the thinking and decisions of the group or panel of experts. The panel members do not meet face-to-face. Keeney, Hasson, and McKenna (2011) cited Olaf Helmer, one of the developers of the Delphi Technique, who wrote the following:

> Its objective is to obtain the most reliable consensus of opinion of a group of experts. It attempts to achieve this by a series of

> intensive questionnaires interspersed with controlled opinion feedback. (2011, p. 4)

Panel members must have expertise related to the study. They can be located anywhere since the process is conducted by mail. The panel can be large; however, the volume of responses to be processed must be considered when determining the size of the panel. A panel of 20 to 25 members is sufficient for most studies. A smaller panel can be used when the topic studied is very focused and the panel members are likely to respond to all of the surveys.

Usually, the Delphi technique begins with a brief survey that contains one or more open-ended questions related to the problem or topic being studied. This survey is mailed to panel members. Members of the panel of experts write comments in response to these questions. It is important that these questions be general so they do not direct the thinking of the respondent. For example, a question might read, "What new technology will be used to improve technical education and training in the next ten years?" Some argue that use of these general questions can change the thinking of the members; however, some stimulus is needed to direct them to the area being studied.

The responses to the 1st round of the Delphi study are synthesized into a series of statements related to the problem or topic being studied. These statements are placed in a rating scale or survey and sent back to the members for their evaluation. For example, if a statement predicts the likelihood of events at some point in time, the respondents would indicate the probability of occurrence, or they might predict the year or date by which the event will occur. After the panel members' responses have been received, the researcher summarizes the results and determines the area of consensus on each item. The consensus area contains a majority of the responses and is usually one or two adjacent responses on the rating scale. See Appendix B.

For the 3rd round, the researcher provides the respondents with a summary of the responses from the 2nd round. Panel members are requested to consider those items on which their responses are not within the area of consensus. When a response is not in the area of consensus, the respondents have a choice of changing their responses to one that is within the consensus area or writing an argument for retaining the original response. It is important to emphasize that each panel member is making the decision in private and does not know who has made the other responses. Therefore, personalities and reputations have minimum impact. Responses on the 3rd round are mailed back to the researcher to be summarized.

If a 4th round is used, respondents again have a choice of modifying their responses to move them within consensus or to write a counter argument for the opposite response. A high level of consensus is usually achieved by the end of the 4th round. In fact, consensus is usually high after the 3rd round.

The end result of a Delphi study is a set of statements about future developments in the area studied and the panel of experts' consensus response for each statement. In addition, there will be a number of comments justifying responses that are outside of the consensus areas. These results typically provide an enhanced view of the future and a rich resource for decision making.

The authors have also used the Delphi technique effectively with other data collection techniques. For example, when a task analysis is being done in a field that is starting to experience technological change, the task survey may give a picture of what is about to be phased out, but miss certain trends. Since it usually takes one to two years to implement a new curriculum, and six months to one year to infuse changes in a program, it has been very helpful to ask what the expected emphasis for each task will be in three years. In the late 1980s, this process helped several technical program administrators in Wisconsin identify and justify the need for including word processing in their clerical and administrative assistant programs, even though the task analysis surveys indicated current use of electric typewriters. By adding Delphi items to the task analysis survey, feedback was acquired on the employers' plans to move to word processing. As a result, word processing was included in the revised curriculum.

Steps in Planning and Conducting a Delphi Study. Steps in planning and conducting a Delphi study include the following:

1. Identify the purpose of the study. The purpose needs to include the topic to be studied and a scope for the study. An example would be "The purpose of this study is to predict the technology that will be used in distance education in 2020."
2. Select the panel of experts. Identify 20 to 25 individuals who have knowledge related to the topic. This may involve experts from several fields related to the topic. In the example on instructional technology, this could include teacher educators, instructional developers, media specialists, computer specialists, and telecommunications experts.
3. Develop the questions for round 1. One or more general questions about the topic.
4. Send round 1 survey to panel members. Send the survey via mail, fax, or e-mail. If the panel members have not been contacted before about the

study, include a description of the study, its importance, and their role in the study. Also, ask if they are able to participate in all of the rounds.

5. Complete the remaining rounds. Use round 1 comments to develop the survey for round 2. Summarize round 2 ratings and identify consensus areas. Return round 2 results to the panel members along with their own round 2 surveys and ask them to change to the consensus response or write a justification for the nonconsensus responses they wish to retain. Summarize the ratings from round 3 and refine the consensus areas. Also list the arguments for the nonconsensus responses. Send the rating and comment summary back to the experts and ask them to move nonconsensus responses to consensus areas or write a counter argument for the reasons panel members have given for being out of consensus at the other end of the rating scale. Panel members receive their own surveys back in rounds 3 and 4.
6. Distribute the report to panel members and stakeholders.

DELPHI TECHNIQUE

Strengths

- The Delphi technique provides a consensus of expert opinion.
- It minimizes the impact of personalities, status, and reputation on the outcome.
- Panel members have time by themselves to consider and develop their responses.
- Results include quantitative and qualitative data.
- It provides an effective way to forecast future events.
- Panel members can be widely dispersed geographically.

Weaknesses

- The process is time-consuming to complete. Use of fax and e-mail can reduce the time involved to some degree.
- It requires more detailed planning than other techniques.
- Written comments require hand-processing.
- Panel members may drop out.

Questionnaires

Questionnaires are documents that are used to collect quantitative and qualitative data related to a topic. Individuals who have information on the topic or problem are asked to complete a questionnaire form. Questionnaires may be delivered by mail or administered in a group setting. The group setting has the advantage of generating a high response rate. Low response rates are often a problem with mail surveys. The Internet is being used more frequently to deliver surveys. It has the advantage of quick returns and relatively low cost. However, some respondents dislike only being able to see one or two questions at a time and it often is hard to determine who has responded.

Questionnaires are especially useful when a specific set of questions has been defined and quantitative results are desired. They are also the method of choice when the number of people to be surveyed is large and dispersed geographically. For instance, the authors have used questionnaires in a variety of task analyses to determine the importance of tasks and the level of competency needed. The tasks are known and are listed in the questionnaire. The people who have knowledge about the tasks are located in a variety of departments and organizations. In many instances these individuals reside in various parts of the United States.

When the participants are located in one or two organizations, the questionnaires are usually administered in a group setting. If they are located in several organizations, especially if there are only a few in each organization, the questionnaire and cover letter are sent by mail. See Appendix C.

Questionnaire Development. As with other techniques, questionnaire development starts with a review of the purpose and objectives of the study to determine the types of information needed. The next step is to identify the groups or individuals who can logically provide this information. For instance, in a task analysis, the appropriate groups would be employees who do the tasks, and their supervisors. The responses from these two groups would be processed separately so their perceptions can be compared.

Developing the questionnaire items makes use of characteristics of the people to be surveyed and the information required. The items included in the questionnaire must generate the data needed for the study. It is a good idea to cross-index the questionnaire items with the objectives and information needed to ascertain that all of the required information will be collected. Directions and questions must use terms and language the survey participants will understand. Moreover, in today's world economy, it may be necessary to reprint the survey in several languages.

Demographic items need to be included in the questionnaire. These items provide information on who has completed the survey. In the task analysis example, an item that identifies the role of the respondent needs to be included. A closed-ended question should be used to facilitate analysis. The responses should also be coded by number to facilitate processing. See Figure 2-2. The "other" response at the end makes provision for individuals who do not fit the two response choices.

FIGURE **2-2**

Which of the following best describes your job?

_______ 1. Production worker

_______ 2. Supervisor

_______ 3. Other ________________________

Coding responses by number makes processing easier.

Additional demographic items should be added to identify important characteristics of the respondents. These may include time in current position, total years of experience, and educational level. They should be closed-ended questions if possible, as handwritten comments are frequently difficult to read. Also, closed-ended questions facilitate data processing and analysis.

Directions are an important part of a questionnaire. They must be written in clear and concise language that the readers understand. Each section of the survey will need directions.

An effective cover letter is an important part of the survey package. It grabs readers' attention and motivates them to respond. It should be concise and not run much more than one page. Also, it should be printed on official letterhead, which will help increase response rates. A cover letter should do the following:

- define why it is important for the reader to respond
- identify the purpose of the study
- note how the reader can contribute to this worthwhile study
- describe how the individual participant's responses will be kept confidential
- thank the individual for responding
- include phone, fax, and e-mail addresses to contact with questions

Draft copies of the questionnaire and cover letter need to be pilot-tested with a small sample group similar to the individuals to be surveyed. The pilot test group should be debriefed after completing the questionnaire to obtain feedback on changes that need to be made. This information is used to revise the questionnaire and cover letter.

A good source of information on questionnaire design and planning a survey is Dillman, Smyth, and Christian (2014). In *Internet, Phone, Mail, and Mixed-Mode Surveys: The Tailored Design Method*, they describe the tailored design as paying attention to specific sources of survey error, comprehensive survey procedures, and building on positive social exchanges that encourage positive responses.

> Tailored design refers to customizing survey procedures for each survey situation based upon knowledge about the topic and sponsor of the survey, the types of people who will be asked to complete the survey, the resources available, and the time frame for reporting results. Tailored design is a strategy that can be applied in the development of all aspects of a survey to reduce total survey error to acceptable levels and motivate all types of sample members to respond with resources and time constraints. (p. 16)

The questionnaire package is comprised of the cover letter, the questionnaire, any additional materials needed to complete the questionnaire, a mailing envelope, and a business reply envelope. The cover letter should be printed on letterhead. Research indicates that letterhead from a reputable organization or institution increases response rates. A high-quality printing process should be used to duplicate the cover letter and questionnaire. The questionnaire should be printed on pastel-colored paper. Also, when two or more groups are involved in the study, such as supervisors and employees, color coding the two surveys will facilitate handling the returns.

At this point, a decision must be made whether to code the surveys to identify who has responded. If the contents are sensitive, the surveys should not be coded. In other words, if coding will significantly reduce the response rate, it should not be used. One way to code is to place a number on each survey, and to keep a separate roster of names with the survey number each name received. If coding is done, the participant should be informed in the cover letter and told how the code information will be used. An alternative method that researchers have used successfully is to enclose a response confirmation card with a separate business reply envelope. Respondents place their names on the card and mail it separately from the survey packet.

When materials are assembled for the mailing packet, the cover letter is placed on top and the questionnaire is next. Other materials, such as a list of definitions and a return envelope, should be placed after the questionnaire.

A formal business envelope with an organization's return address is recommended. Also, first class postage will increase the response rate. It assures better delivery and connotes that the letter is "official business." Use of second class or bulk mailing may result in the questionnaire being treated as junk mail. A business reply envelope is enclosed to encourage response. If possible, the questionnaires should be mailed so that they arrive at midweek, and should not be sent during major holidays.

Processing the Results. When the responses start to come back, they should be quickly scanned for problems and a count recorded for each day. After the return rate has decreased to a trickle, the first follow-up questionnaire is mailed if additional responses are needed. A new cover letter, noting that this is a follow-up, is developed and the questionnaire printed on a different-colored paper. If the people who have responded are known, their names are removed from the mailing list. If this information is not available, indicate in the cover letter that the questionnaire should not be completed if one has already been returned.

After the follow-up survey is mailed, returns from the first mailing and follow-up mailing will be received. These should be kept separate and processed separately. The first follow-up survey usually produces from one-third to one-half the number of responses of the original mailing.

When the returns to the second mailing become sporadic, or stop, it is time to process the results. In actual practice, responses may trickle in for a long time. The project timeline as well as the response flow rate will need to be used to determine when to start processing.

It is important to process the returns from the first mailing and follow-up survey separately. The two summaries are compared to identify any inconsistencies. Also, the demographic response summaries are compared to determine if there are any differences in the characteristics of the people who responded to each survey. If there is a separate profile of the characteristics of the population, both groups should be compared with it to determine if the respondents are representative of the total group.

If there are inconsistencies between the results from the original and follow-up mailings and/or the response rate is too low, another follow-up survey should be used. One option often used in this situation is a telephone survey of a small sample (12 to 15) of nonrespondents. If the survey is long, key items can be selected for the interview. Key items include items where the responses were inconsistent along with the most critical demographic questions.

If nonrespondents cannot be identified because the returns are anonymous, a random sample should be selected before the first mailing. This sample would not receive a questionnaire but would be interviewed.

In the report of the questionnaire results, the responses from the first mailing and follow-up can be combined when the response patterns are similar. Where the patterns are inconsistent, the results from the first mailing, follow-up, and telephone survey should be reported separately. As noted previously, group administration of the questionnaire can be used to eliminate or significantly reduce the nonrespondent problem associated with mail and e-mail questionnaires. The group process works effectively when input is needed from organizations, departments, or teams.

Steps in Designing a Questionnaire. The following steps are involved in designing and conducting a questionnaire study:

1. Review the study's purposes and objectives to identify the information needed.
2. Identify the people who have this information (population).
3. Select sample from the population. *Note:* A 100% sample, or the total population, can be used if appropriate and not too costly.
4. Write questions related to each study objective.
5. Write demographic items to identify characteristics of the respondents.
6. Write directions for the questionnaire.
7. Organize questions and place in questionnaire.
8. Develop the cover letter.
9. Pilot test cover letter and questionnaire.
10. Revise as needed based on pilot test.
11. Distribute questionnaire to the sample.
12. Follow-up with nonrespondents.
13. Process and analyze data.
14. Report results.

A lot has changed since Dillman first introduced the tailored design method. Using a combination of modes to gather data, such as mailed surveys and interviews, may produce better results than using one mode alone. Questionnaires that are laid out using publishing programs, so that they can be designed to be visually pleasing, will also increase the return rate. The Internet and technologies such as those employed by call centers add to the many methods that can be used to gather data.

QUESTIONNAIRES

Strengths

- All participants in the study respond to the same questions.
- The process takes less time and is less costly in comparison to alternatives. This is especially true when the sample is large and/or located in a wide geographic area.
- Effectively designed questionnaires facilitate data processing.
- Most people are familiar with questionnaires.
- The respondents have some flexibility in selecting the time to complete a mail survey.
- The process does not have the disruptive effect of telephone interviews.
- Special illustrations, designs, and materials can be included in the survey.

Weaknesses

- There is generally a low response rate to mail questionnaires.
- It is often difficult to obtain an accurate list of addresses for a mail survey.
- Some people have problems reading and understanding survey questions.
- It is not possible to follow up on or probe given answers.
- It is sometimes difficult to determine who responded. The people who receive the survey may pass it on to someone else to complete.

Review of Formal Research Studies

A formal research study should be designed and conducted to solve a specific problem and attain a set of objectives related to this problem. It should be designed according to sound research principles, and the research activities should be carried out within the design framework. The research report should clearly define the research problem, objectives, design, data sources, and results.

Previous research studies can be of significant value if they are relevant and timely. Their results are immediately available for a relatively low cost. These results may answer one or more of the objectives for research being proposed. In addition, these studies provide ideas for research designs, instruments, and analysis procedures. Previous research studies can also provide a baseline or reference for evaluating the results from a new study. Some research reports will also comment on pitfalls to avoid.

Modern electronic database and Internet search processes provide an efficient means to search for research studies. In many instances the complete report is stored on-line. Selection of appropriate key words that define critical concepts in the research study is important. Inappropriate key words will lead to identifying unrelated studies and missing relevant ones. A review of the studies identified in a search will reveal if the key words are appropriate. Also, check for what appears to be missing from the list. A quick review of some of the reports identified will help to refine the search. If search results appear to be deficient, select new key words and run another search. Another good resource is the reference librarian in the local community or college library.

The value of a research study to a current need or problem will be determined by the answers to the following questions:

- Is the research current? (How old is the information?)
- To what degree does the research problem match the current problem?
- How many of the study objectives are relevant to the current problem?
- Is the research design valid?
- Was the research study carried out as designed?
- Are the sources of data in the research study relevant to the current need or problem?
- Were the data analyzed appropriately?
- Does the research report provide enough information to answer these questions?
- Does the report include copies of the research instruments?

The more positive answers to these questions, the more useful the research study will be in resolving the current problem. However, even if many of the responses are negative, there may be parts of the report that are useful; for example, the instruments used to collect data may be very helpful in designing a new instrument.

The first thing to determine is when was the data collected? It is important to check the research report to determine when the data collection took place. This may be some months or even years before the report was published. If the data is old, the results of the study may not be of direct value to resolving the current problem. However, the objectives, design, instruments, and analysis procedures may be very useful. "Old" is a relative term and will depend on the nature of the problem. For a task analysis on a job that is changing rapidly, one year may be old.

Usually, the more the research study problem statement and objectives relate to the current need or problem, the more relevant and useful the study design results will be. It is important in this review step to check how the researcher has defined the core variables or concepts in the study. For instance, how has "task" been defined in a task analysis study? Does it only refer to manipulative activities, or does it apply to all job activities? This can have a major impact on the types of data collected.

The research design used must be appropriate for the research problem and objectives. It is important to determine who provided the data, how the data was collected, and response rates. The source(s) of data must be appropriate to the research problem and objectives. A task analysis of software technicians needs to have input from technicians who do this work. It would also be helpful to have responses from their supervisors.

Another consideration is where the respondents or data sources are located. Are they from one company, one city, one state, or nationwide? In reviewing task analysis studies, the authors have found that some states have regulations that vary the content of jobs. This is especially true in the allied health area. Also, terminology may vary from one section of the United States to another.

Sample size and the number of people responding also need to be checked. In general, larger sample sizes are better. They provide more opportunity to capture variations in experiences, skills, and perceptions. Response rates are also very important, as well as the strategies used to acquire a high response rate. Mail surveys often have low response rates. It is important that the researcher has done follow-up contacts with nonrespondents and has analyzed these responses separately to identify differences in response patterns. Also, the demographic characteristics of the respondents should be presented in the report. See Appendix E.

Research studies that pass these test questions should be reviewed and compared. If possible, several studies should be included in this step. Reviewing and comparing four to five studies provides much more information than looking at one study. Areas of agreement and disagreement should be listed. Also, the findings that are unique to one study should be listed.

After the comparisons have been completed, a decision on the next step needs to be made. If the studies are recent and relevant, their results could be used to solve the problem at hand. In most instances, some additional input is desired. A program advisory committee can be used to validate the results for local use. If more in-depth information is needed, a research study can be designed and carried out.

REVIEW OF FORMAL RESEARCH STUDIES

Strengths

- Information from study is available immediately.
- Some of the studies are more comprehensive than what could be done by a college or company. For example, the U.S. Census Bureau collects data from millions of people.
- Reviewing studies is inexpensive.
- Searches for relevant research studies can be done quickly using electronic databases and the Internet.
- Use of information from a well-known researcher can reinforce the outcomes of a study.
- Research designs, instruments, and analysis procedures used in other studies can be used to more effectively design a study for the problem at hand.

Weaknesses

- The purpose and objectives of the study may not match what is needed to resolve the researcher's problem.
- The research results may be out-of-date, for example, a task analysis done three years ago on a job that is rapidly changing.
- Data collection techniques and the samples used may not be appropriate or they may not be defined specifically enough to determine if they are appropriate.
- The organizations and/or geographic area in which the study is done may not be appropriate.
- It may not be possible to assess how effectively the research design was carried out and what constraints apply to the outcomes.

Steps in Using Research Studies. The following steps are used in locating and reviewing related research studies:

1. Review the current problem to identify variables to be studied and the type of information needed.

2. Use the information from step 1 to identify key words or concepts for the database search. For example, to find studies on skills needed by carpenters, try "carpenter task analysis," "carpentry task analysis," and "carpenters' skills."
3. Check the appropriate indexes and databases for relevant studies. Modify key words if searches do not find any reports.
4. Use the Internet to search for relevant studies.
5. Check with curriculum developers and educators for studies and theses that are not listed in the database or index.
6. Review studies that meet the quality criteria listed earlier.
7. Review the selected studies for relevant findings, procedures, and instruments.
8. Determine if additional information is needed.

Reports

Reports run the gamut from articles in refereed journals to personal opinions posted on the Internet. Newspaper articles, internal reports, and periodical articles are also included. With the exception of the refereed articles, much more care must be taken to ascertain the quality of a report. However, reports can provide valuable inputs for the design of a needs assessment or task analysis.

Relevant reports can be identified in the same way as noted for research studies in the previous section. Identify the key words that reflect the topic and concepts of interest and use these to select and search databases and search the Internet. Internal company and organizational reports will have to be identified by contact with the companies or organizations, or by networking with people who are familiar with them.

If a report is being used for ideas that will be utilized in designing a needs assessment or task analysis survey, the review is not as critical since there will be additional data collected. A careful review is more essential when a report is being directly used in designing a course or instructional program.

The publisher and author of the report should be identified. The mission and goals of the publisher and organization that published the report should be determined. Does the publication present only certain points of view, or is it open to a wide range of ideas? Also, be cautious of acronyms and organizational titles that refer to current problems. An organization such as the Committee for Economic Security for the Poor (CESP) may be funded to work to eliminate social security and the minimum wage. If this is the case, its publications will present data and arguments in favor of these changes.

If an author is listed, review the author's credentials related to the topic. Try to determine the author's experience, research activities, and reputation. Has the author published other documents in this area? What is the knowledge base used in developing this report? Is it personal research, on-the-job experience, interviews, and/or the work of other researchers?

The data used in a report need to be checked to determine their accuracy and scope. Specific data in the report must agree with similar data sets. For instance, if a document lists the growth rate for an occupation to be 50% over the next five years, state and national labor market reports should have similar projections. If data are omitted from the report, a judgment on the type and extent of bias created must be made. Also, the time period when the data was collected needs to be determined. Needs and job competencies change rapidly in many areas.

Another factor to consider is the degree to which the report agrees with other reports and research in the area. If it does not agree, are there logical reasons for this? Does the author have newer data or unpublished research?

The quality of writing is another characteristic to consider in evaluating a report. Report narrative should be clear and logically organized. Outcomes and conclusions must follow logically from the information given.

Reports and information on the Internet present special problems when used in a study. Often the author or publisher is not listed or, if listed, not enough information is given to make a judgment. The URL can give some idea on the source of the document. Government sources will have a ".gov" URL, educational institutions use ".edu," not-for-profit organizations use ".org," and ".com" represents commercial sites or products. Most college libraries have information and tips on how to evaluate information on the Internet on their web sites.

Steps in Using Reports. Using the following steps will facilitate locating and reviewing reports:

1. Review the current need or problem to ascertain the variables, factors, or topics involved.
2. Select key words to match these.
3. Use the key words to search the appropriate indexes, databases, and Internet for relevant reports.
4. Check with curriculum developers, educators, trainers, and associates in professional organizations for nonpublished reports.

5. Assess the relevance and quality of the reports found in the search.
6. Review the reports that pass this assessment.
7. Use information selected from the reports to design needs assessment and task analysis studies, and in curriculum development.

REPORTS

Strengths

- Information on research in progress is frequently reported in journal, periodical, and newspaper articles.
- Information in reports is relatively easy and inexpensive to access.
- Reports may provide a professional analysis of a part of a large database, such as the periodical and newspaper reports based on Census data.
- Articles based on extensive investigative reporting can be very helpful in identifying problems and needs.
- Published reports, articles, and documents can be quickly identified and located with the search engines available.

Weaknesses

- Some reports do not list an author.
- When the author and/or publisher is listed, there still may not be enough information to make a good judgment on the quality of the source.
- The writing may be biased. The Internet and many publishers do not screen out biased materials.
- A report may not provide adequate information on the sources of data on which it is based.

Records

Many companies and organizations keep records of problems, errors, accidents, and customer complaints. Often, these are regularly summarized, analyzed, and reported to managers. The information in these records and reports can be very useful in needs assessments and task analyses.

In many organizations, the quality department or group is responsible for analyzing and reporting this data. Control charts describe processes and identify when quality levels change. Frequency counts are run on problems, errors, and customer complaints. Frequency counts are relatively simple to do and quickly identify the problems that occur most often.

Pareto Charts. Pareto charts take the frequency counts one step further and provide a graphic display of the problems experienced most frequently. Pareto charts are based on the economic concepts of Vilfredo Pareto, a 19th century economist who found that a few people held most of the wealth in a country. This is often called the 80-20 principle. In its application in Pareto charts, it would suggest that 80% of the defects are caused by 20% of the problems. Thus, a Pareto chart is organized to display the five or six most common problems.

The frequencies of the problems are denoted by bars in a bar chart with the most frequent problem displayed at the left of the bar chart. The remaining problems are listed in descending frequency. See Figure 2-3. This Pareto Chart is for a telephone order company that is having problems with busy lines, bad addresses, and call orders that take a long time to complete. Note that the problems are sequenced from left to right in descending frequency. Pareto charts can also be organized on the basis of the cost of problems or errors.

FIGURE 2-3

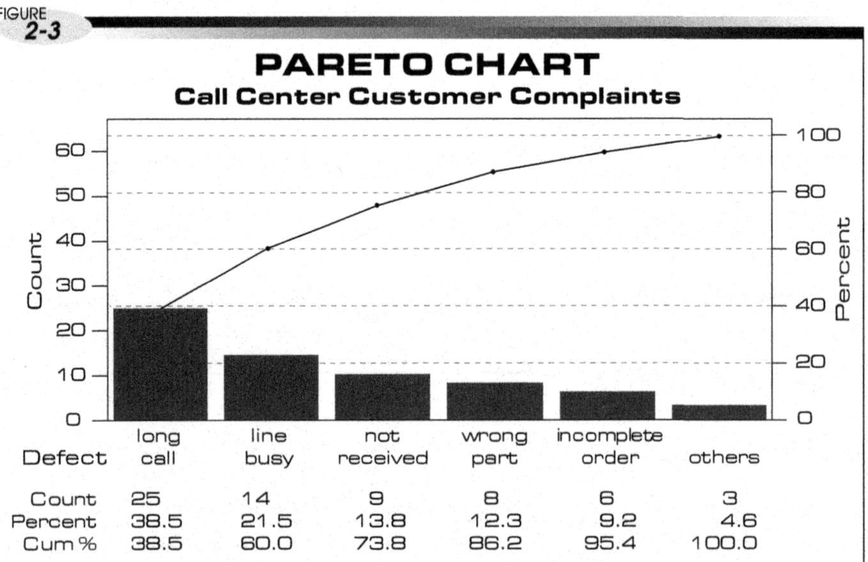

Defect	long call	line busy	not received	wrong part	incomplete order	others
Count	25	14	9	8	6	3
Percent	38.5	21.5	13.8	12.3	9.2	4.6
Cum %	38.5	60.0	73.8	86.2	95.4	100.0

Pareto charts list the frequency of problems in descending order starting at the left.

Underlying the use of Pareto charts is the concept that the problem with the largest frequency or cost is the area of greatest potential return if it is resolved. This problem is the first priority for study and remedial action. Thus, use of Pareto charts helps to effectively allocate resources.

Process Flow Charts. Pareto charts isolate major problems but they do not identify causes. Process flow charts and cause-and-effect diagrams are two tools that can be used to analyze a problem and identify potential causes. A process flow chart shows the steps in a process and how the steps are related to each other. It can be used to identify missing steps and those that are not needed. Also, the problem can be limited to a step or series of steps for more specific review. See Figure 2-4. If the chart in 2-4 is followed, the coffee drinker will have a reason to complain since the step where the filter is placed in the basket is missing.

Cause-Effect (Fishbone) Diagrams. The cause-effect diagram, or fishbone, provides a framework for analyzing a problem. The problem is listed in a box on the right-hand side of the diagram. An arrow is drawn from left to right to the problem box. Potential causes are represented by the arrow. Five or six branches are drawn on a slant and connected to the arrow as shown. See Figure 2-5. These branches identify major potential causes and usually represent personnel, machines/equipment, materials, methods, measurement, and environment. A committee or team comprised of people familiar with the problem area identify more specific causes within each of these areas (branches) and each cause is listed on a twig attached to an appropriate branch. When this chart is completed it has a semblance of a fish skeleton, hence the name fishbone chart. Also, it is sometimes called an Ishikawa diagram after its creator, Dr. Kaoru Ishikawa.

After the committee has brainstormed the possible causes and completed the fishbone diagram, it will usually prioritize the causes based on the committee members' experiences with the problem. These priorities are used in determining what areas to study first. Approaches to evaluating the causes range from trial-and-error to formal experiments.

The personnel and methods branches have direct implications for curriculum developers. The personnel branches include the skills, knowledge, and capabilities of the people completing the processes. If employees lack specific skills and/or knowledge, training will be needed. This information may also be valuable to those planning college curricula. If the methods are valid but not carried out as designed, there are implications for training and education. Also, changes in other areas, such as materials and equipment, may have ramifications for training and education.

FIGURE 2-4

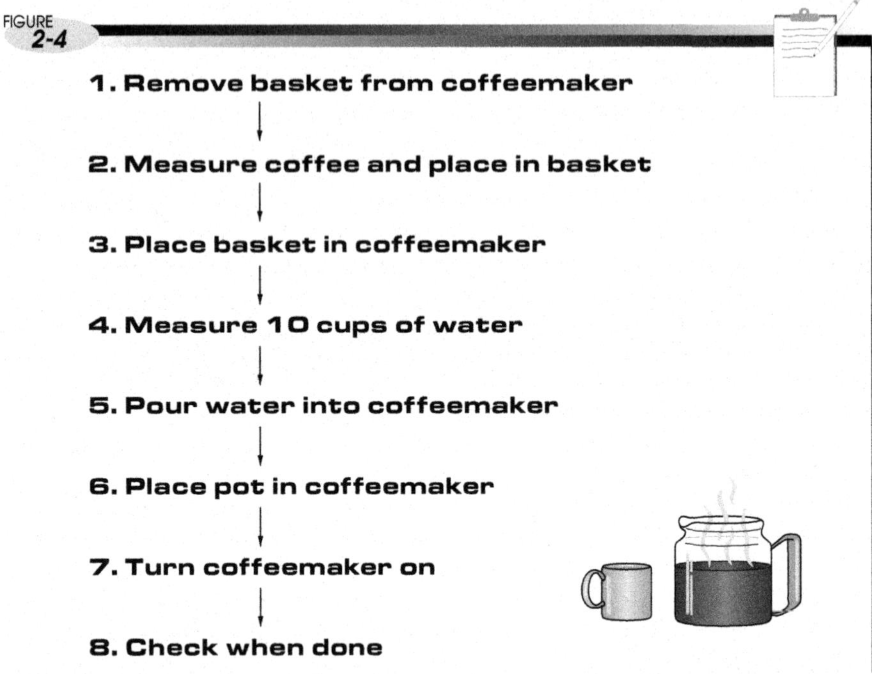

The process flow chart helps identify all the steps required in a given process. In this case, the step where the filter is placed in the basket is missing.

Reviewing the Records. Trainers should review the data, summaries, and charts available in their companies. This information can be very useful in identifying needs and competencies that have to be developed. At the least, this information is a useful starting point in planning training courses. Also, linking training to identified problems is a good selling point.

For educators planning technical programs, this information is also useful. However, it would be very helpful to have access to the summaries and charts from several companies in order to determine common threads across different settings. Also, the companies need to represent the stakeholders for the programs being planned. Many companies are willing to debrief educators on the information they collect and the problems they identify. However, they may request a sign-off on not releasing any specific data. Another way for educators to access this information is through selecting program advisory committee members who are knowledgeable about the records and reports generated in their companies.

Before using this type of information, trainers and educators need to determine how accurate and representative the data is. Was the data collected systematically? Were appropriate data collection processes used? Does the data represent current conditions? It is also important to determine the scope of activities represented by the data. Does the information reflect only a small portion of the organization's activities, or is it more broad based? Reports need to be analyzed to determine if the conclusions follow from the data.

FIGURE 2-5

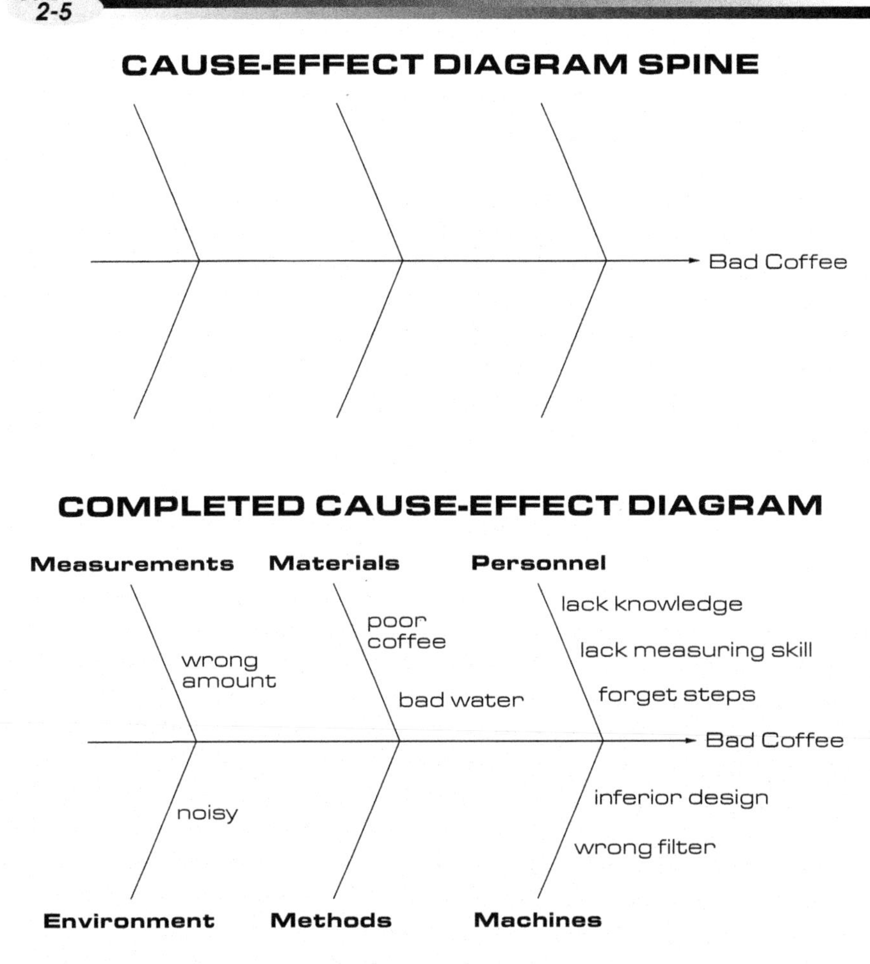

A cause-effect, or fishbone, diagram can be used to analyze potential causes of a problem.

RECORDS

Strengths

- Data are available and there is no cost.
- Data are from actual operations.
- Reports often draw on extensive experience with the processes involved.
- Data sets are frequently much more extensive than those collected by a survey.
- Data can provide a baseline for evaluating training and education programs.

Weaknesses

- Data may not have been collected in a systematic manner.
- Data may be old.
- Reports may reflect only the perceptions of the individual or unit collecting the data.
- For educators, the data and reports from one company are narrow in scope and must be supplemented by data from other organizations.

In addition, educators need to determine if the company is a logical stakeholder for their programs. Is the organization likely to employ graduates of these programs? Also, it is important to determine what level of technology the organization is using. Is the technology used cutting-edge, current, or old? Data from several organizations should be reviewed, and the mix of technology levels represented will depend on the nature of the program being planned.

Steps in Using Records. The steps to make effective use of records are as follows:

1. Trainers should regularly review the records kept in their organizations to identify needs and problems. Educators should seek opportunities to review records in stakeholders' organizations that relate to their programs.
2. Assess the quality, scope, and relevance of the data for course and program development.
3. Determine the need for training or the implications for technical course work.
4. Identify additional data needed to plan this training or course work.
5. Collect additional data.

Nominal Group Technique (NGT)

The nominal group technique (NGT) was designed to obtain ideas from an ad hoc group and develop consensus on these ideas in one session. It was designed for small groups that meet once or twice to provide input. It was not designed to develop a closely knit working group, such as a program design committee. The authors have successfully used NGT with department staff, program committees, and other working groups.

The NGT can be used to identify problems, establish goals, and develop plans. It is designed to provide all group members an equal opportunity to express their ideas and assist in developing consensus. The NGT process is relatively easy to coordinate and does not take a lot of time to complete. It is effective in generating a lot of ideas and usually concludes with strong consensus on priorities. Although the process is relatively easy to conduct, the NGT coordinator/facilitator needs to be knowledgeable of group processes and have some experience in coordinating a group.

There are three major phases in the NGT process. Participants generate ideas in a modified brainstorming format in the 1st phase. Statements listed in the 1st phase are discussed, clarified, and edited in the 2nd phase. The 3rd and last phase focuses on developing consensus.

Generating Ideas. The purpose of the 1st phase is to generate as many ideas as possible related to the topic of concern. In order to accomplish this, care should be taken in selecting group members who can provide input from different perspectives. A nominal group should have 7 to 12 members. If the group is smaller, there is a risk that some important ideas will be missed. Also, it may be difficult to develop a clear-cut consensus with a small group. Groups with more than 12 members are hard to coordinate. If more people want or need to provide input, additional nominal groups should be formed.

Since the group will be writing statements on 3 × 5 cards, the room where the NGT session is conducted needs to have tables. Also, there must be space for a flip chart, and wall space to post the completed chart pages. Supplies needed include flip chart paper, masking tape, marking pens, name tents, and 3 × 5 index cards. Extra pencils for the participants are also useful.

When the session starts, the coordinator will give an overview of the purpose and process for the meeting, emphasize the importance of each member's input, and describe how the results will be used. After the group members and coordinator have introduced themselves, the coordinator will state and post the topic or problem for the session. For example, the problem for a training department might be "How can we make our training more effective?" Participants are encouraged to provide a variety of ideas and not to evaluate them.

At this point, members of the group are given 5 to 10 minutes to write their ideas on 3 × 5 cards. This is done without interaction between group members. The next step is to record these ideas on the flip chart paper. The coordinator goes around the table and asks each group member for one statement or idea. Participants are asked not to evaluate or criticize any of the ideas given. The coordinator records each idea on the flip chart. After everyone has had an opportunity to give one idea, the process is repeated until all of the ideas on the 3 × 5 cards are listed on the flip chart. As a flip chart sheet is filled, it is posted on a wall. It helps if each comment is numbered or identified by letter as it is written on the flip chart. This makes it easy to refer to a specific statement.

Clarifying the Statements. In phase 2, the statements are reviewed, clarified, and edited as needed. This is a time when participants can ask questions for clarification and suggest possible overlaps in the ideas listed. Criticism and evaluation are not allowed in this phase. The coordinator should read each statement and ask for questions and comments. If it is apparent that a statement needs to be clarified, the coordinator should edit the statement with input and concurrence from the group. The final check is for overlaps between the statements. If two or more statements convey the same idea, they should be combined into one statement. Again, this is done with the agreement of the group members.

Prioritizing the Statements. In phase 3, the group members prioritize the statements. Participants are asked to identify the five most important or critical statements and assign five points to the most important, four points to the next most important, and continue this sequence through the fifth statement. Participants need to identify the statement number and place the priority after it. The statement number should be circled. The coordinator can collect the priorities and record them on the flip chart next to the statements or have the group members write their priorities on the chart. It is helpful to place commas between the numbers.

After the priority values have been posted, the coordinator can add up the points for each statement and record the total on the chart. At this point, the group members review the totals and identify the top priorities. The most important statement will have the highest point total. If necessary, ties can be broken by comparing the number of participants that voted for or assigned a priority value to each statement. This process will usually prioritize more than five statements since all participants will not select the same statements. Group members should identify where the priority list ends.

If it is necessary to prioritize more statements, this process should be repeated again with the statements that did not make the initial prioritized list. The statements prioritized in the 2nd round will be added at the end of the first priority list. For example, if seven statements were prioritized in the 1st round, the top priority item from round 2 will be priority number 8 on the total list.

SWOT analysis uses the NGT process. Group members are asked to identify strengths (S), weaknesses (W), opportunities (O), and threats (T) that exist for a specific product, program, or organization. These are prioritized with the process described. Each area is analyzed and strengths are compared to opportunities to ascertain potential growth areas. Weaknesses are contrasted with threats to determine major challenges.

Steps in Using the NGT Process. The following steps are included in the NGT process:

1. Identify the problem or need. Determine the type of data required.
2. Select group members who can provide valid input and ideas (7 to 12 members).
3. Identify coordinator for the session.
4. Schedule room, equipment, and supplies.
5. Prepare materials for the session.
   a. Create the agenda.
   b. Create the introductory statement or purpose and NGT process description.
   c. Develop the problem/topic statement for the session.
6. Conduct the session.
   a. Welcome the participants.
   b. Give the purpose and describe the process.
   c. Have group members introduce themselves.
   d. Have members silently generate ideas.
   e. List ideas on a flip chart.
   f. Edit ideas.
   g. Prioritize ideas.
   h. Thank participants.
7. Finish coordinator tasks.
   a. Copy prioritized list for processing; include priority point total.
   b. Note impressions and thoughts on the session.
   c. Collect flip chart sheets and retain for further reference.

NOMINAL GROUP TECHNIQUE (NGT)

Strengths

- The NGT process is an effective way for people who have not met before to work together.
- Silent generation of ideas and the round-robin process provide an opportunity for all group members to participate.
- The process generates a lot of ideas.
- The end product is a prioritized list of ideas or problems.

Weaknesses

- The group may not achieve consensus.
- The coordinator may not be competent with group processes.
- Some or several of the ideas generated may not be practical or feasible.

Case Studies

The case study technique provides in-depth information on a specific individual, group, or program. It gives a detailed and holistic look at the system being studied. All the variables and their interactions are studied and reported. A case study report provides a comprehensive description of the participants, variables, context, actions, and impacts.

Case studies are very useful in developing a comprehensive knowledge of a situation. The focus is on "why" and "how" (Yin, 2014). This can be very useful in explanatory research conducted to define variables in a situation or problem area, and in descriptive research, such as evaluation studies.

Usually, a case study provides information on a small number of participants or one organization. This leads to a concern about how representative the data are. Studying additional situations is considered to be replication and not sampling. These additional case studies help to confirm the results from the initial case study; however, they do not provide a basis for generalizing.

The usual response to this concern is that the case study technique was not designed to provide data that can be generalized to a variety of settings. Instead, it should be used where there is a need to identify the variables in a situation, determine the whys and hows related to an action, or develop an in-depth understanding of a case. If generalizable data or a comprehensive review is needed, results from a case study can be used to design a quantitative survey.

Data comes from the participants in the case situation and will reflect their views and perceptions. These will be influenced by their biases and perceptual screens. Thus, it is important to acquire data from a variety of people and sources. In addition to the people involved in a case, sources of information include documents, observation, records, and other relevant data.

The case study technique can be a useful tool in needs assessment, job analysis, and evaluation. It can provide detailed and comprehensive information on the topic studied. It may be necessary to use the results to design a test or survey for a representative sample.

Purpose. The first step in designing a case study is to state the purpose of the study. This statement needs to identify the topic to be studied, scope of the study, and expected outcomes. For example, the purpose statement for a case study to identify the problems employees have with new information-processing technology in the ABC Company would include a statement about identifying problems in using new information-processing technology. This would establish the topic for the study. The scope would be defined by the departments or units included in the study. The end product or outcome would be a list of problems.

The next step is to determine if the case study technique is appropriate for the purpose and circumstances. A case study would be an appropriate choice if one or more of the following conditions exist:

- In-depth data is needed on a situation or system that has several variables and interactions.
- Little is known about the case situation and its context.
- There is a need to identify the whys and hows involved.
- The situation involves a variety of interactions between people within a group and between the group and others.

Research Methods. After determining that the case study technique is a valid approach, the next step is to decide whether exploratory, descriptive, or explanatory research is needed. Exploratory research is used when there is little or no information available on the topic being studied. This would be an appropriate approach, for example, when the researcher is attempting to determine the skills needed by employees who are using cutting-edge technology.

Descriptive research identifies the status of selected variables. It may also look at interactions between these variables. Evaluation studies typically use descriptive methods. Explanatory research is concerned with cause-effect relationships between the variables studied. This design could be used to study the impacts of teaching activities.

An exploratory case study will have a purpose statement and a set of general questions that will generate information on the important variables and factors in the topic studied. Descriptive and exploratory case studies will have a formal set of questions based on previous research, research models, or theory. For example, program evaluation is descriptive research and an evaluation model will help define the research questions.

The research purpose statement and the type of research provide the direction for developing the research design or plan for the case study. Yin (2014) has identified five components that should be considered in developing a case study research plan:

1. the study's questions,
2. its propositions, if any,
3. its unit(s) of analysis,
4. the logic linking the data to the propositions, and
5. the criteria for interpreting the findings. (p. 29)

CASE STUDIES

Strengths

- The case study technique produces in-depth data on activities, processes, interactions, and outcomes.
- It identifies the context for the case situation.
- It is an effective method for studying and analyzing contemporary events.
- It is a good technique for identifying the whys and hows involved in a case situation.

Weaknesses

- A case study represents only one case, setting, or situation. Results cannot be generalized to a larger population.
- Not all case studies are designed and conducted in a rigorous manner.
- Case studies are time-consuming to do.
- Reports vary widely in format and amount of detail.

Study questions will be developed based on the purpose of the research and the models or theories that apply to the study. These questions will emphasize "how" and "why" in most case studies. Propositions will help to sharpen these questions. For example, most course development models for technical education and training include a job analysis step. A logical proposition for a program or curriculum evaluation study would be that valid course content is based on a current job analysis. Thus, one evaluation question would be "How does the program keep its content up-to-date?"

A research plan must also identify the unit of analysis or the "case." In case studies, the unit of analysis has ranged from an individual to a group, a team to a company, and from a course to a program of study. The purpose statement will help to define the appropriate unit of analysis. If the unit of analysis is a group, data collection will focus on group actions and interactions. If the case unit is an educational program, program design, development, and implementation activities will be studied.

Data Collection and Analysis. The data analysis and interpretation processes for case studies are less defined than those for quantitative research. Case study literature provides less direction and insight on these topics. There is more dependence on the perceptiveness and intuition of the case study researcher.

There are, however, some common suggestions and recommendations in the case study literature. There is common agreement that the purpose, study questions, and research plan need to be defined before collecting data. Also, if possible, potential data patterns should be derived from the study propositions or hypotheses so data can be collected to test them.

Another common suggestion is to collect data from a variety of people and sources. For example, in a program evaluation, data needs to be collected from students, teachers, administrators, and other stakeholders. Also, curriculum materials, follow-up reports, and other documents should be reviewed. This will allow the researcher to use triangulation to identify common perceptions of the program. In addition, the researcher needs to look at the unique perceptions that can be provided by each stakeholder group. For instance, employers are in a unique position to comment on the adequacy of the skills of the program graduates.

During interviews, participants need to be encouraged to give descriptions and explanations. This is especially important at the beginning of the interview. The interviewer will need to take notes on the comments and may want to note nonverbal behavior also. These notes will have to be detailed enough to convey the information provided by the interviewee, sequences of comments and reactions that are relevant, and any cause-effect relationships that are identified.

Information on the physical, psychological, and social environment should also be recorded. For example, in a needs assessment for a training program, the nature of the work environment needs to be recorded. The types of equipment and software used, noise levels, and interactions should be noted.

Case study researchers usually form tentative conclusions as they collect data. As these conclusions are formed, they are verified or refuted as the data collection progresses. This does have the potential to shield the researcher from other points of view; however, most case study researchers feel that acquiring input from a variety of people and sources will minimize this problem. Also, many researchers recommend that a draft copy of the report, especially the conclusions, be reviewed with a sample of the stakeholders.

Appropriate Data Analysis Techniques

Data analysis procedures need to match the types of data gathered and the data collection technique used. For example, focus groups are effective in generating comprehensive lists of problems, needs, and suggestions. If the list is going to be used to develop a survey questionnaire, duplicate statements are removed and every statement placed in the same format. For example, a series of needs statements might read, "improve computer skill" and "expand ability to interpret situations," etc. If major problem areas or themes are to be identified, the list will have to be sorted into groups by meaning, such as "same," "similar," and "unrelated." However, focus groups will not develop prioritized lists. To obtain a prioritized list, the nominal group technique (NGT) should be considered. Or, the list developed by the focus group can be used to design a questionnaire that collects quantitative data.

Focus groups and case studies will generate qualitative data. Open-ended questions in interviews and questionnaires also produce this type of data. The comments can be coded or categorized and then tallied.

The DACUM process includes a step that prioritizes the tasks within each general area of competency (GAC) and aligns them across GACs. This produces a map that displays the tasks in prioritized order. In addition, the process identifies the performance level required on each task. Since the committee used in the DACUM process is relatively small, some curriculum developers place the tasks from the map in a survey questionnaire with rating scales to identify the importance of each task and the performance level required. This survey data is used to validate the map.

Questionnaire and Delphi surveys typically include rating scales that provide interval level data. Various descriptive data analysis techniques can be used. Correlations can be run between items. The average response can be calculated, and the amount of variability in the responses can be determined. Also, responses from different groups can be compared. These surveys often collect qualitative data in the form of written comments. These can be processed and analyzed in the same way as the data collected in focus groups and case studies.

In summary, it is important to select a data analysis technique that is appropriate to the type of data collected and the decisions that will be made based on the analysis results. Also, the type of information provided needs to be considered when data collection is selected. For example, if a prioritized list of needs is required for program development, selection of the focus group technique will not be appropriate. Instead, the nominal group technique or a questionnaire should be used.

Rating Scales

Rating scales are used to collect quantitative data that can be efficiently processed. They come in a variety of formats, and some care needs to be exercised in selecting an appropriate one. (Additional information on rating scales can be found in Chapter 4.)

Three commonly used rating scales are discussed in this section. Variations of these scales as well as other scales are used in curriculum development. See Appendices A and C. When needs assessment, curriculum development, and evaluation studies are reviewed, the instruments used should be read for ideas on scale development.

To be effective a rating scale must perform the following functions:

- define a logical response continuum, usually running from low to high
- provide enough response choices to reflect gradients in the judgments and perceptions of the respondents
- have meaningful response choices or categories
- be understood by the respondents
- facilitate data processing

Numerical Rating Scales. The numerical rating scale meets the data processing requirement. It provides numbers for the respondents to select. These numbers represent the response categories or choices. The response categories must be defined adequately and be based on the purpose of the study in order to meet the other criteria. An example of this is the numerical rating scale used in a needs assessment conducted as a part of a training design project for customer service representatives (CSRs). See Figure 2-6.

FIGURE 2-6

Tasks	**Training Need ***				
	1	2	3	4	5
1. Process orders	1	2	3	4	5
2. Answer customer questions	1	2	3	4	5
3. Resolve complaints	1	2	3	4	5
. . .					

* Response Key:
1 = N = None/No Need
2 = S = Slight Need
3 = M = Moderate Need
4 = H = High Need
5 = VH = Very High Need

A numerical rating scale is used to collect quantitative data.

The list of tasks performed by the CSRs was placed in a survey questionnaire and CSRs and their supervisors were asked to identify the CSRs' needs for training on each task. A small portion of this questionnaire is given below.

One of the objectives of this study was to develop a prioritized list of training needs. Since CSRs and their supervisors responded, there was a need to process separate sets of data and compare them. The numerical rating scale provided an efficient means to do this. The categories or levels on the scale represent different levels of need. Category 1 indicates "no need" for training. At the other end of the scale, 5 reflects a "very high need." Gradients of need between the "none" and "very high" are represented in the other response choices on the scale.

The response categories sequence from low to high, and an attempt was made to make the response intervals approximately the same size. With this scale the median or mean can be used as a measure of the typical response. Some might question if this is an interval scale and whether the mean can be used. However, researchers commonly use the mean with this type of scale.

Why use a five-point scale in this application? Why not use two responses—"no need" and "high need?" The authors have found that it is valuable to have more information available. First, in almost all cases, the level of need for training on specific tasks varies. Second, usually it is not possible to develop training for all tasks where there is a need at one time. Priorities have to be established and a sequence of training courses developed. The five-point scale provides the information needed to do this.

A five-point scale is probably the shortest scale that is effective for this application. Some people have response tendencies that cause them to avoid the lowest and highest responses on a scale. Thus, it is important to provide sufficient response space. A three or four point scale would not be as effective in identifying differences in judgments and perceptions.

Bipolar Response Scale. Another scale used in needs assessment and evaluation is one that identifies the high and low responses on the scale and provides unlabelled responses between these two extremes. This is sometimes called a semantic differential scale. See Figure 2-7. In the example below, the midpoint of the scale has also been identified and the respondent also has the flexibility to respond between these levels.

This scale can also be used in evaluation instruments. See Figure 2-8. This scale could be used to collect customer feedback. Both five- and seven-point scales are given. In both cases it is best to label the middle response. Since some individuals have a tendency to avoid the end or extreme responses, the high and low choices, the seven-point scale often works better.

It is usually better to label all of the response choices on a rating scale. This helps the reader understand each response choice. Also, this simplifies the data analysis and interpretation process. However, sometimes it is not possible to develop meaningful labels for each response on a scale, so the modified bipolar scales work better.

FIGURE **2-7**

Tasks	**Training Need ***				
	N		M		VH
	1	2	3	4	5
1. Process orders	1	2	3	4	5
2. Answer customer questions	1	2	3	4	5
3. Resolve complaints	1	2	3	4	5
. . .					

* Response Key:
1 = N = None/No Need
3 = M = Moderate Need
5 = VH = Very High Need

A bipolar response scale allows the respondent choices in between two extremes.

FIGURE 2-8

Services	Evaluation *				
	VP		Ok		Ex
	1	2	3	4	5
1. Order processing	1	2	3	4	5
2. Answering questions	1	2	3	4	5
3. Resolving complaints	1	2	3	4	5
. . .					

* Response Key: 1 = VP = Very Poor
3 = Ok = Meets minimum expectations
5 = Ex = Excellent, significantly exceeded my expectations

Services	Evaluation *						
	VP			Ok			Ex
	1	2	3	4	5	6	7
1. Order processing	1	2	3	4	5	6	7
2. Answering questions	1	2	3	4	5	6	7
3. Resolving complaints	1	2	3	4	5	6	7
. . .							

* Response Key: 1 = VP = Very Poor
4 = Ok = Meets minimum expectations
7 = Ex = Excellent, significantly exceeded my expectations

Both 5-point and 7-point scales have labels on the middle and end responses.

Likert Scale. The typical Likert scale has responses that indicate the respondent's levels of agreement or disagreement with a statement. See Figure 2-9. Data on attitudes, opinions, or judgments can be collected depending on the nature of the statements used. As shown below, the response scale usually has an odd number of choices with the middle one being "undecided" or "don't know." Some researchers are concerned that the "undecided" response can become a cop-out, and they leave it out of the scale. It has been the authors' experiences that the "U" or "undecided" response is not a problem when the Likert scale is used in appropriate applications and administered with adequate directions. In addition, in many situations it important to know how many are undecided or do not know.

FIGURE 2-9

I learned a lot in this course.

	SD	D	U	A	SA		
• 5–point scale	1	2	3	4	5		
	VSD	SD	D	U	A	SA	VSA
• 7–point scale	1	2	3	4	5	6	7
	SD	D	SID	SIA	A	SA	
• 6–point scale	1	2	3	4	5	6	

Key: VSD = Very Strongly Disagree
SD = Strongly Disagree
D = Disagree
SID = Slightly Disagree
U = Undecided
SIA = Slightly Agree
A = Agree
SA = Strongly Agree
VSA = Very Strongly Agree

A Likert scale can be used to quantify attitudes and opinions.

One of the strengths of the Likert scale is that it is used frequently and respondents are familiar with it. As a result, directions can be simple and short. Also, it can be used in an instrument that contains attitude and opinion items. See Appendix D.

As noted previously, the selection of an appropriate rating scale depends on the purpose and objectives of the study. These will indicate the type of data needed, and this information can be used to select the appropriate rating scale.

The following are some suggestions for selecting and developing rating scales:

- Start the process by reviewing the purpose and objectives of the study.
- Review instruments used in other studies and note the characteristics of the rating scales used.

- Provide enough response choices on the rating scale so respondents can indicate their judgments. However, do not use too many response choices. A good rule of thumb is no more than nine.
- Number the response choices to facilitate data processing.
- Pilot test the rating scales and instrument with a small group of people similar to those who will respond to the final form.

Criteria for an Effective Instrument

There are three major criteria for the design of an effective instrument. They are validity, reliability, and efficiency. Validity is concerned with collecting the right data. Reliability is focused on minimizing the amount of error in the data collected. Efficiency is concerned with the cost and ease of collecting, processing, and analyzing the data.

Validity. Validity has several forms. Content, concurrent, and predictive will be discussed. Content validity is the first concern when an instrument is being designed. The level of content validity is dependent on the degree to which the instrument collects data related to the objectives of the study. One of the best ways to establish content validity is to construct a table. See Figure 2-10.

FIGURE 2-10

Objectives	Data Needed	Instrument Items
1. Identify job functions	1. Relevancy of functions	1. Items 1–8
2. Identify task importance	2a. Importance of listed tasks	2a. Items 9–30
	2b. Space to add tasks not listed	2b. Items 31–32
3. Determine if tasks vary by experience level	3. Experience level of employees	3. Item 33

The first two columns of the table will determine the contents of the instrument.

The first two columns in this table are the blueprint for the contents of the instrument. When a draft of the instrument is completed, the third column is completed. A review of the third column will indicate if any objectives have been missed. Also, the relative emphasis given each objective can be determined.

Content validity is relatively easy to determine and must be checked for each instrument whether it is designed by the researcher or selected from an existing set of instruments. Without content validity the instrument is not going to be worth using.

Concurrent validity is concerned with the equivalence of two measures or a measure and a criterion. For example, if performance levels of production workers are being determined by parts produced per hour, this measure needs to have concurrent validity. In other words, is "parts per hour" really a good measure of performance or do other factors need to be considered? Classroom evaluation methods also need to have concurrent validity. Test results must have concurrent validity with the knowledge and skills of the students.

Predictive validity is also a concern. It is the relationship between data collected now to performance in the future. Task analysis and DACUM data need to have predictive validity. In other words, when students can perform the important tasks identified in a task analysis, they should be successful on the job. Similarly, course grades should have predictive validity. Follow-up studies need to be conducted to assess the predictive validity of these.

Reliability. The reliability of a measurement reflects the amount of error in the data collected. An instrument that has high reliability generates data that has little error in it. Reliable measures provide consistent data over time, place, and various respondents. Cooper and Schindler (2013) describe reliability as a characteristic second only to validity in importance:

> Reliability is concerned with estimates of the degree to which a measurement is free of random or unstable error. It is not as valuable as validity determination, but it is much easier to assess. Reliable instruments can be used with confidence that transient and situational factors are not interfering. Reliable instruments are robust; they work well at different times under different conditions. This distinction of time and condition is the basis for frequently used perspectives on reliability—stability, equivalence, and internal consistency. (p. 260)

Internal consistency is frequently used as a measure of reliability in surveys and classroom tests. Determination of reliability is based on the concept that students who know more should consistently give more correct answers to items in a test. Similarly, students who have more positive opinions should consistently respond more positively on Likert items.

Software programs used to process objective test data and Likert surveys usually include an internal consistency calculator. In interviews, task analyses, and needs assessment surveys, questions are repeated or questions on the same topic are phrased differently and included in the survey to assess consistency of the responses.

Equivalence is concerned with the extent to which different forms of the same data collection process give the same results. This form of reliability is important when multiple interviewers are used in a study or when multiple judges are used to evaluate performance. Equivalence is also used in establishing parallel forms of tests.

Stability refers to an instrument's capacity to produce consistent results over time. This form of reliability is important for measures of ability and other characteristics that do not change significantly over time. Stability is not as useful for knowledge and skill tests when students are learning and changing their knowledge and skill levels.

The authors have used a stability measure in some interview surveys to assess the reliability of the data collected. For the most part, these were needs assessment and program evaluation studies where the characteristics being assessed were not likely to change between the two data collection points. In the telephone surveys, a small sample of respondents were called a second time and a set of core questions was asked again. In program evaluation, some program stakeholders were interviewed a second time during an on-site evaluation or contacted by phone after the on-site visit.

Reliability can be improved by minimizing the factors that cause error. These factors include the following:

1. The instrument is poorly designed.
   a. Directions are not clear.
   b. Items or questions are too complex for the respondents.
   c. Items or questions are poorly worded.
   d. Layout is confusing.
2. Respondents are not oriented properly.
   a. Respondents are not aware of the context from which they are to respond. For example, in a needs assessment, are they to respond based on their individual needs or their department's needs?
   b. Respondents lack motivation. This often is due to not understanding the importance of the study and how they can contribute to it.
3. The administration of the instrument is faulty.
   a. Time constraints may cause respondents to rush through the questions.
   b. Poor room conditions can detract attention from the response process (noise, temperature, cell phones, etc.).

4. There are multiple interviewers, observers, or judges.
   a. Not everyone was trained using the same process.
   b. Results were not cross-checked periodically to assess reliability.
   c. A survey instrument or rating scale was not provided to guide the data collection process.

Efficiency. Consideration must be given to the efficiency with which data can be collected, analyzed, and interpreted. A data collection process may produce valid and reliable data, but if it is extremely expensive to use or produces data that takes weeks to analyze, it is not going to be functional. Cost, ease of administration, processability of the data, and reporting requirements need to be considered.

Attempts at efficiency often result in trade-offs. The personal interview might be the preferred method based on its flexibility; however, the cost might be prohibitive, so a combination interview and mail survey process might be substituted. A researcher may prefer open-ended questions that allow respondents to more freely respond; however, the data analysis time may be too costly and time-consuming to be appropriate. In addition, this process may not provide the quantitative data needed in the report. As a result, a questionnaire with rating scales and open-ended questions might be substituted.

The Instrument Design Process

The instrument design process consists of 7 steps: (1) reviewing the purpose of the study and its objectives, (2) determining what data is needed, (3) identifying data sources, (4) selecting or developing instruments, (5) reviewing the content validity and efficiency, (6) pilot testing, and (7) revising. See Figure 2-11.

This process is used whether an existing instrument is selected or a new one developed. Both approaches need to identify the data needed and establish content validity (steps 1, 2 and 5). A careful review of the objectives in step 1 should reveal what data is needed. This process will also help to identify appropriate data sources in step 3. For example, a needs assessment to determine the training needs of production workers could use input from the workers, their supervisors, and customers who use the product.

In step 4, a decision must be made whether to use an existing instrument or develop a new one. Time can be saved if an existing instrument collects the data needed and is appropriate for the people who will provide the data. Also, use of an existing instrument may provide data from previous studies that will be helpful. Care must be taken to determine that the instrument has content validity (step 5).

FIGURE 2-11

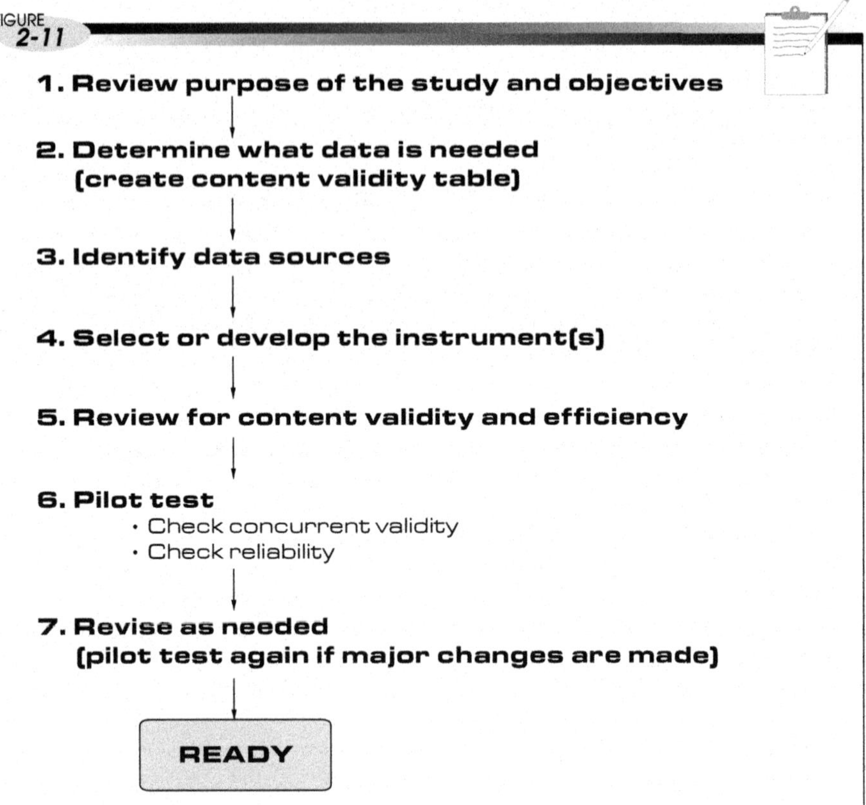

The instrument design process consists of seven steps.

In most needs assessments, task analysis studies, and program evaluations, it is difficult to find a complete instrument that has content validity for the study at hand and fits the audience to the survey. One or more instruments usually need to be designed. By this point in the process (step 4), the data needed and sources have been established. The next step is to select the technique to use. After this selection, individual questions or items can be written.

Another consideration in this step is efficiency. Quantitative data from rating scales will process faster and provide opportunities for analyses on the relationships between items. Cross tabulation can be quickly run on this type of data if appropriate demographic items are included.

Clear and concise directions must be written for the instruments. These need to inform the readers what to base their responses on, how to respond, and where to put written comments. See Appendices A and C.

If someone is going to administer the instrument, a set of directions will be needed for this individual as well. This will help to ensure that the instrument is administered appropriately and consistently if it is administered on more than one occasion.

After a draft copy of the instrument has been completed, it needs to be pilot tested with people similar to those in the population (step 6). This group can be small, 8 to 10 people. They must complete the instrument as described in the directions and then identify areas that need to be improved. Pilot test responses should be processed and the reliability checked. Also, if possible, the concurrent validity of the data should be checked. With a small group, these measures will be approximate but should catch any major problems.

The results of the pilot test are used to revise the instrument (step 7). If a number of changes are made, the instrument should be pilot tested again.

In some studies, multiple instruments are needed. The customer services representative needs assessment, for example, required two surveys. Most of the content of the two surveys was the same, but the roles of the two groups of respondents were different and the responses on the rating scales were different. In this type of situation, it is usually more efficient to develop one of the surveys first and then modify it so that it is relevant to the second group. In the CSR study, the customer service representative survey was designed first. See Appendix A.

Design Suggestions. The following are general suggestions that will help to improve the design of various types of instruments. These are based on the authors' experiences in designing and conducting a variety of needs assessment and curriculum development studies.

Use words, terms, and acronyms that are understood by individuals in the sample. Avoid long and complex sentences. Run a reading level test to ascertain the reading level of the instruments.

Some questions are sensitive. Age, earnings, and marital status are some examples. Use these only if they are necessary. In the case of age and earnings, general response categories can be provided so the respondents do not have to give exact values.

When possible, items should be sequenced from easy to difficult, and least sensitive to most sensitive. Place the most relevant and interesting questions first. The first items should be seen as directly related to the purpose of the study by the respondents. Usually, demographic items are placed at the end of the survey because they may not be perceived to be as relevant to the study.

Questions on similar content should be clustered together. However, there may be some situations in which they are separated in order to reduce the impact of the response to one item on the response to another. Typically, items with the same response format are grouped together. For example, Likert items are placed in one section. This allows the respondents to focus on the items and not have to change back and forth between response formats. It is also a good idea to use as few response formats as possible. This is less confusing and will reduce response errors.

Number items consecutively throughout the instrument. This will avoid confusion on item numbers as respondents work through the survey. This also will minimize problems when exit questions are used by allowing respondents to bypass items that do not pertain to them. Finally, this approach is helpful in the analysis and report writing stages. Item numbers on printouts will agree with item numbers on the survey. References to item numbers in reports can be made without qualifying them with part or section numbers.

Response choices also need to be labeled. See Appendices A and C. This is done primarily to facilitate data processing. It is easier to enter numbers manually, and some data processing software does not handle alpha characters. Whether numbers or letters of the alphabet are used, the labels identify specific responses for the respondents and reduce errors in processing.

A contact person, phone number, and address needs to be given at the end of the survey. This allows respondents to connect the survey to a person and communicates that the researcher is interested in their concerns and questions. If a mail survey is used, a fax number should also be included. This allows the return of the survey if the reply envelope is misplaced.

Demographic Items. Demographic items collect information on characteristics of the respondents that are relevant to the purpose, objectives, and design of the study. These items are used to run cross-tabulations on the data and determine the characteristics of the people who respond to the survey. Cross-tabulations are summaries of the responses of subsets of the respondents. For example, length of time on the job may have a significant impact on the respondents' training needs. A cross-tabulation on work experience would provide separate summaries for workers with little, some, and extensive experience in the job. The results from this item can also be used to describe the amount of work experience the respondents have.

The following is demographic information that is frequently collected:

- job title or position
- amount of work experience in present job (sometimes experience in related jobs is also requested)

- education and/or training related to current job
- age
- highest level of education completed

A demographic item was used in a needs assessment for the call service center for a national company. See Figure 2-12. The response choices are numbered to facilitate data processing. Note that "other" is listed as one of the responses and a space to list the job title is provided. This provides some flexibility in the use of the questionnaire.

Another demographic item was used in a questionnaire designed for high school educators. See Figure 2-13. Respondents were asked to select the response that reflected their primary assignment. Without this instruction, some would check two or more responses to indicate multiple assignments.

FIGURE
2-12

What is your current position?

_______ 1. CSR

_______ 2. Quality technician

_______ 3. Supervisor

_______ 4. Other ______________________________

Demographic items are collected to determine the characteristics of the individuals who respond to the survey.

FIGURE
2-13

Which of the following best describes your current position? (Check one response.)

_______ 1. Administrator

_______ 2. Counselor

_______ 3. Teacher — academic area

_______ 4. Teacher — vocational area

_______ 5. Other ______________________________

Qualification is sometimes required when writing instructions.

Since CSRs tend to have shorter job tenure than educators, the time span in their choices is less. See Figure 2-14. After three to four years, CSRs tend to move to other jobs in the call center or make career changes. Also, after three years CSRs are very experienced in their work. Education tends to have staff members who have longer tenures. Teachers have opportunities to expand their teaching responsibilities or to move into counseling or administration. Thus, the item for educators included the extra responses.

FIGURE 2-14

How long have you worked as a CSR?

_______ 1. 3 months or less

_______ 2. 4–11 months

_______ 3. 1–3 years

_______ 4. 4 years or more

How long have you worked in education?

_______ 1. Less than 1 year

_______ 2. 1–2 years

_______ 3. 3–5 years

_______ 4. 6–10 years

_______ 5. 11–20 years

_______ 6. 21 years or more

The response choices need to reflect the characteristics of the occupation.

In both items, the first response indicates someone who is new to the job and who may have unique needs. The second response choice in both items identifies individuals who are through their initial orientation to their work and are becoming familiar with all of the tasks and challenges in their jobs.

Another factor to consider in selecting the number of response choices is the expected number of respondents in each response category. A cross-tabulation with one or two people in it is usually not very useful. Also, some individuals may be reluctant to respond if they perceive they will be the only one in a response category.

A demographic item can be based on the high school to college educational sequence. See Figure 2-15. For training design, it may be more appropriate to list technical training and educational experiences more directly related to the job.

If age is an important demographic factor in a study, consideration should be given to using the U.S. Bureau of Labor, Bureau of Labor Statistics categories. These are 16–19, 20–24, 25–34, 35–44, 45–54, 55–64, and 65 years and older.

When surveying high school students, the 16- to 19-year-old category could be split into separate categories (responses) for 16-, 17-, 18-, and 19- year-olds. These can be combined and compared to the BLS statistics for 16- to 19-year-olds. Also, it would be appropriate to add a "15 and younger" response. If this is being used in a typical high school, the 25 and older categories should be left off. As long as the response categories can be joined or added together to be equivalent to the BLS age categories, the survey statistics can be compared to area, state, and national labor statistics.

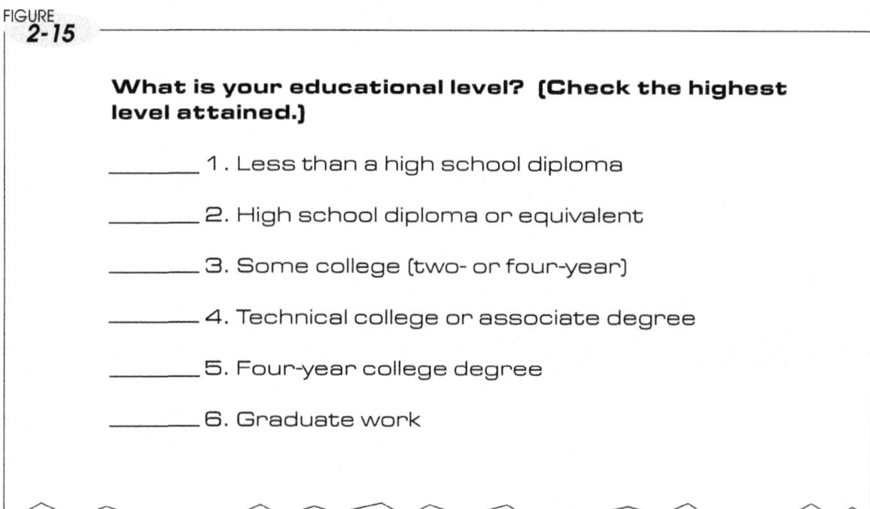

FIGURE 2-15

What is your educational level? [Check the highest level attained.]

_______ 1. Less than a high school diploma

_______ 2. High school diploma or equivalent

_______ 3. Some college (two- or four-year)

_______ 4. Technical college or associate degree

_______ 5. Four-year college degree

_______ 6. Graduate work

Choices regarding education need to fit the backgrounds of those who are using the instrument.

Cover Letters and Reminders. A cover letter is a very important part of the survey questionnaire package. It is the first document the respondents see when they open the survey envelope or e-mail. It must attract their attention and motivate them to respond. Also, the cover letter has to identify the purpose of the survey, the importance of their responses, and how the results will be used. Respondents also need to be assured that their responses will be kept confidential. This is especially important if the questionnaires are labeled or coded so nonrespondents can be contacted.

If at all possible, the cover letter should not exceed one page and should be addressed to the recipient by name. Also, there is some research evidence that indicates that the use of organizational letterhead and original signatures on the cover letter increase response rates. See Appendix C.

Dillman, Smyth, and Christian (2014) recommend that the cover letter include the following:

- Give the purpose of the study and establish its importance and usefulness in terms relevant to the respondent.
- Convince the respondents that their responses are very important to this study.
- Tell how responses will be analyzed and kept confidential.
- Summarize the purpose of the study, its importance, and how the researcher will use the results.
- Invite the respondents to call or e-mail for assistance with any questions that they might have.
- Thank the respondents for their time and consideration.
- Include the researcher's name, title, phone number, and e-mail address in the complimentary closing. If time permits, use an original signature.
- Use the sponsoring organization's stationery and a quality printer. Type or font size should be large enough to be easily read by the respondents. Usually, 10 points is the smallest that is feasible.
- Include a token incentive.

The cover letter should be reviewed as a part of the pilot test of the questionnaire. This is an opportunity to identify comments that are not clear and information that has been omitted.

Using thank-you and follow-up reminders is also helpful. A thank-you reminder is usually sent 5–7 business days after the initial questionnaire is sent. A follow-up reminder is sent to all nonrespondants 10–15 days after the initial questionnaire is sent.

REVIEW QUESTIONS

1. What factors should be considered when selecting a data collection technique?

2. What is an advantage and disadvantage of each of the following?
   a. interviews
   b. focus groups
   c. DACUM
   d. DELPHI technique
   e. questionnaires
   f. formal research studies
   g. reports
   h. records
   i. nominal group technique (NGT)
   j. case studies

3. Several community groups have been working with unemployed workers and their families. Your school has been approached to provide an education and training program for these people. What technique would you select to gather more information on their needs? Justify your selection.

4. A college is designing a technical curriculum and wants to identify technology changes that are anticipated in the next 10 to 15 years. What technique should be used to do this? Justify your response.

5. A local company wants you to design a training program for them. List two techniques that could be used when you visit the company.

6. You need input on the importance of a set of tasks in order to design a valid curriculum. Input is needed from workers and their supervisors who are located in various parts of the United States. What technique would you use? Justify your response.

7. How are the data collection techniques, such as interviews and questionnaires, related to the analysis processes used?

8. Write a sample item for a Likert, numerical, and bipolar (semantic differential) rating scale.

9. Write a brief definition or give an example for each of the following measurement characteristics.
   a. content validity
   b. predictive validity
   c. reliability
   d. efficiency

10. List the steps in developing an instrument.

11. What are the main parts of a cover letter for a survey?

12. List two reasons a questionnaire would include demographic items.

REFERENCES

Cooper, D. R., & Schindler, P. S. (2013). *Business research methods* (12th ed.). Boston: McGraw Hill.

Dillman, D. A., Smyth, J. D., & Christian, L. M. (2014). *Internet, phone, mail, and mixed-mode surveys: The tailored design method* (4th ed.). Hoboken, NJ: John Wiley and Sons.

Keeney, S., Hasson, F., & McKenna, H. (2011). *The Delphi Technique in Nursing and Health Research*. Oxford, England: Wiley-Blackwell.

Yin, R. K. (2014). *Case study research: Design and methods* (5th ed.). Thousand Oaks, CA: Sage Publications.

3 Needs Assessment

INTRODUCTION

OBJECTIVES

NEEDS ASSESSMENT

Role of Needs Assessment

Organizational Change • Program Commitment • Finding the Gap

Needs Assessment as Macro Data

Identification of Problem Areas • Extent of Problem • Other Techniques for Problem Solving

Needs Assessment and Relevant Responses

Clarification of Problem Areas • Availability of Valid Sources of Data • Sufficient Time and Resources • Availability of Resources for Relevant Response

When a Needs Assessment is Not Necessary

No Follow-Up Action Is Planned or Possible • Valid Data Cannot Be Collected

NEEDS ASSESSMENT PROCESS

Systems Analysis Concepts

Conducting the Needs Assessment

Identify the Purpose • Identify Information Needs • Identify Target Population • Collect Data • Analyze Data • Report Results • Apply/ Use Results • Evaluate Outcomes

REVIEW QUESTIONS

REFERENCES

INTRODUCTION

Needs assessment is critical in any institution or organization to determine the existence and type of performance problems and whether training is the appropriate solution. Managers of organizations or administrators in educational institutions may request a program or course without thoroughly assessing the need for it. A program or course may be offered in response to this request and then may fail because the real need was not ascertained.

Needs assessment answers the question, "Is there a need for a training course or program in business and industry or in the community and region?" Needs assessment provides the information that answers the program, curriculum, and instructional development questions.

OBJECTIVES

After completing this chapter, the reader should be able to do the following:

1. Identify the importance of needs assessment.
2. Explain the relationship between needs assessment and organizational change.
3. Explain how needs assessment can provide macro data on problems.
4. Discuss how needs assessment can develop relevant responses to problems.
5. Identify when not to use a needs assessment.
6. Define and give an example of a need.
7. Define and give an example of a system.
8. Identify the input, process, output, and environmental elements in a system.
9. Describe the eight steps in the needs assessment process.
10. Plan a single needs assessment.
11. Describe the major contents of a needs assessment report.

NEEDS ASSESSMENT

Needs assessment is a process consisting of a set of activities and procedures that identifies the merit or worth of a training or education program. Often called front-end analysis, needs assessment seeks answers to questions concerning the potential need within the workplace or community for a training or education program or course. Needs assessment is often described as seeking the difference between "what is" and "what should be," or finding the gaps between current and desired performance within an organization or a community (Altschuld & Witkin, 2000).

An organization refers to a company or a unit within a company, such as a human resource department. A community refers to a broad area, such as a town, city, or region, where an institution such as a technical college is concerned with determining the need for programs. A community may include several organizations.

Addressing people's needs, and meeting their needs, can produce amazing results. Canning, for example, was developed when Napoleon set a national goal of finding new approaches for preserving food so his army could be fed while on the march. Thomas Edison, inventor of the electric light bulb and motion pictures, had over 1000 patents. Edison used a six-step process to prioritize his work. The first step was to identify a need, and if no need was identified, no work would occur on the project.

Role of Needs Assessment

Needs assessment performs the following functions:

- gathers data on perceived needs
- identifies knowledge, skills, and behavior discrepancies
- assists trainers, human resource development (HRD) personnel, administrators, and instructors in developing relevant curriculum materials
- gathers information that brings beneficial change to an organization or community
- assesses organizational needs
- promotes buy-in by participants

Needs assessment can produce valuable data on the perceived needs of an organization, employees, or a community. Needs can be identified by asking employees about their present levels of knowledge, skills, and behaviors. Experienced employees typically know their skills and deficiencies. The difference between the skills they have and the skill levels required are the knowledge, skills, and behavior discrepancies or needs (Watkins, West-Meiers, & Visser, 2012). However, if new technology is introduced into the workplace, the identified needs will not be valid because employees who have never used the new technology cannot identify the skills they will need. If specific information on content is requested, the discrepancies can serve as the basis for curriculum development.

Another way of looking at needs assessment is through the budgetary lens. Is it truly worth the expenditure of dollars for a training or education program? Should the program or course be developed? Is there justification for it? Who will benefit from it? Will the training received be used in business and industry? How many will need the training?

Rouda and Kusy (1995) define needs assessment as a systematic exploration of the way things are and the way they should be. These "things" are usually associated with organizational and/or individual performance. Rouda and Kusy further explain why a needs assessment should be developed and performed:

> Why design and conduct a Needs Assessment? We need to consider the benefits of any Human Resource Development (HRD) intervention before we just go and do it: What learning will be accomplished? What changes in behavior and performance are expected? Will we get them? What are the expected economic costs and benefits of any projected solutions? We are often in too much of a hurry. We implement a solution, sometimes but not always the correct intervention. But we plan, very carefully and cautiously, before making most other investments in process changes and in capital and operating expenditures. We need to do the same for Human Resource Development. The largest expense for HRD programs, by far, is attributable to the time spent by the participants in training programs, career development, and/or organization development activities. In training, costs due to lost production and travel time can be as much as 90–95% of the total program costs. Direct and indirect costs for the delivery of training are about 6% of the total cost, and design and development count for only about 1–2% of the total (2) [Gilbert, 1988]. Realistically, it makes sense to invest in an assessment of needs to make sure we are making wise investments in training and other possible interventions. (para. 4)

Love (1991) writes that needs assessment provides "a systematic procedure for setting priorities and making decisions about programs and the allocation of resources" (p.64). He goes on to demonstrate that although there have been many different forms of definitions for needs and needs assessments, many say that "need assessment is a formal analytic tool for problem identification that reveals needs in terms of gaps between current results and desired outcomes, identifies unique strengths and areas of excellence, sets priorities among needs, and selects the needs to be changed" (p.64). Rossett (2009) feels that needs assessment identifies the details of exemplary performance and perspectives so they can be taught.

Organizational Change. Needs assessment can also be a significant factor in bringing about change to the organization or community. By offering training based on needs, the organization and community benefit with better trained workers. Training workers better should lead to better performance and increased productivity. Organizational needs may be determined using needs assessment strategies. Everyone in an organization has an opinion of what its problems might be. Needs assessment information can provide the big picture of what is needed at the organizational level. Needs assessment synthesizes the organization's needs and the employees' perceptions of needs. If knowledge, skill, and attitude discrepancies are identified, they can be rank-ordered, and those that are most critical can be addressed first.

Program Commitment. Addressing employees' needs also builds commitment to programs. A two-year study at Children's Hospital of Wisconsin clearly demonstrated a significantly higher level of satisfaction with training programs among participants who responded to the needs survey than those who did not respond to the survey. Needs assessment can also uncover potential barriers to success arising from knowledge or skills deficiencies such as computer math, motivation, environment support, incentives, or the lack of one or more of these (Altschuld, 2015).

When needs assessment is conducted in a methodologically sound fashion, it is responsive to the interests of participants and stakeholders. This then supplies a rational, empirically grounded base for making decisions about where to place resources to meet the greatest need. While needs assessment is a research undertaking, the process can produce credible and useful results that are not overly complex and do not require a seasoned researcher. Keeping stakeholders involved means they have a stake in the results and are thus committed to programs that are implemented.

Berkowitz and Reviere (1997) indicate that certain environmental and organizational conditions are necessary to support a successful needs assessment strategy. If employees and management are involved in the needs assessment, they are more likely to accept the results. Adequate funding to support all phases of needs assessment will ensure a more successful study and acceptance of results. Company restricting, merging, changes in technology, policy changes, etc., can affect how people respond to a needs assessment strategy. Needs assessment is a systematic and ongoing process of providing useful information about the needs of the population being surveyed. Data from the needs assessment can identify gaps in service and shape the future of service delivery. Berkowitz and Reviere show that a positive climate and adequate resources are the underpinning of sound needs assessment.

Finding the Gap. In an organization, a needs assessment should be conducted for the specific group of workers who will be affected by the training. For example, a supervisor in the shipping unit may request ISO 9001 training. The company is actively engaged in global markets. Should a training session be conducted on ISO 9001 for the shipping unit employees? Will it make good business sense? Will the training save the company dollars? Who within the unit should receive the training? How will the knowledge and skills be used on the job? How will the new knowledge and skills be reinforced? All these questions would be answered by an ISO 9001 needs assessment. People within the shipping unit should be surveyed, but others that are affected by decisions made within the shipping unit should also be surveyed. The needs assessment should determine if the training is necessary, who should be trained, how the training might be delivered, and how the new knowledge, skills, and behaviors should be implemented on the job (Leatherman, 2007).

What about needs assessment application in a postsecondary educational institution? For example, a company calls a technical college and asks that a supervisory management program be offered. Is this call from the company an isolated case? If it is, should a customized training program be developed to serve the company? Is there a broader need for such a program within the community or region? If a program is needed and developed, will graduates find employment in business and industry? To successfully implement a program will require a period of time. Will the company still be interested in graduates after that period of time? How much will it cost the institution? What is the competition for such a program? Will companies be more interested in four-year graduates? What will graduates be paid? These questions can be answered by conducting a supervisory management needs assessment.

The two examples above are typical of needs assessment. Again, needs assessment answers the question, "Is there a need for a training course or program in business and industry or in the community and region?" Needs assessment provides the information that answers the program, curriculum, and instructional development questions.

According to the instructional systems design (ISD) model, a needs assessment should be conducted whenever a manager requests training or refers a problem to HRD (Rothwell & Kazanas, 2008). A proactive approach requires HRD staff to anticipate educational needs for the next year or more, and to develop the links between the organization's strategic plan and its training plan. The assessment may need to be altered in response to conditions that change the strategic plan; nevertheless, it will serve as the basis for programming and training during a given time frame (Soriano, 2013).

Present outcomes reflect current performance level, or what is. Desired outcomes reflect desired performance level, or what should be. The environment reflects the context of the gap. The gap between the present and desired outcomes defines the level of need. In more basic terms, needs are gaps between what is and what should be. See Figure 3-1. The gap will be uncovered with the needs assessment.

For example, workers within the shipping unit in an organization do not have the skills and knowledge to compete in global markets. They may lack ISO 9001 skills and knowledge. The rationale may be that if they had the skills and knowledge of ISO 9001, then the unit would be more competitive because the product shipped would contain few or no shipping defects. The desired outcomes or desired performance levels in the company would be trained shipping unit employees who have the skills and knowledge to apply the principles of ISO 9001. Global markets would then recognize the company's products and quality.

FIGURE 3-1

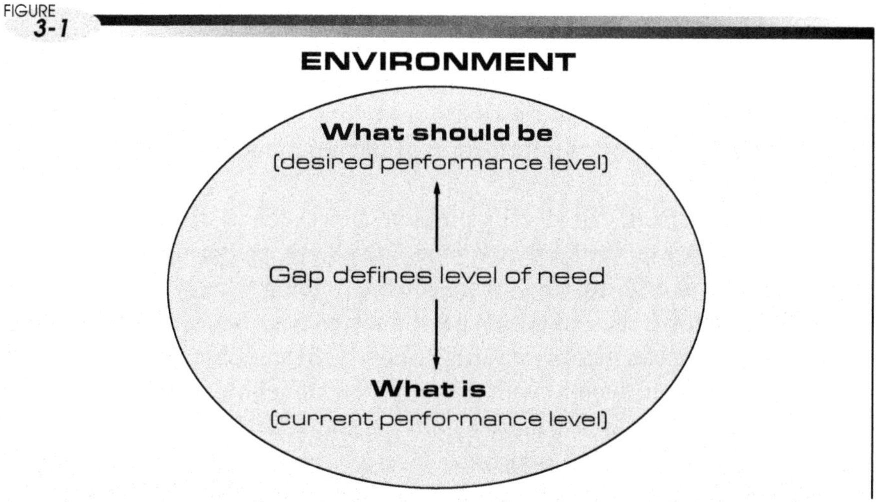

Needs assessment will determine the gap between desired and present outcomes.

Needs Assessment as Macro Data

Needs assessment provides data on problems and performance gaps. Within an organization, needs assessment builds participant commitment, generates management support, increases the HRD department's credibility, and provides data for process evaluation. Within a community, needs assessment data can support a program, provide data indicating the need for a new program, and identify the scope of the performance gap.

Needs assessment can identify problem areas, and data can provide valuable information on the magnitude of the problem. Once the problem has been identified, other techniques can be used to identify specific variables in the problem area. For example, a needs assessment identifies performance gaps, while a task or performance analysis focuses on the specific skills, knowledge, and attitudes workers are lacking.

Needs assessment can take on a variety of forms, including survey questionnaires, learner-completed inventories, interviews, reviews of training materials and employee competencies, behavior events interviews, critical incidents, and interviews of average and superior performers. Whatever the focus and format, the basic purpose remains the same, find out what is and what it should be, i.e., find the gap. (Additional information on data collection techniques can be found in Chapter 2.)

Identification of Problem Areas. Data from a needs assessment will help identify problem areas. Significant sources of potential macro training needs are management reports; quality program data; consultant reports; new plants, products, equipment, or machinery; changes in standards and trends; new policies; and company restructuring or merging. Within HRD, needs assessment can provide a valuable link between the organization's strategic plan and its training plans. It can serve as the basis for training during a given time frame. The strategic plan provides information on the required, or desired, levels for a needs assessment.

A needs assessment can identify problem areas such as training or retraining workers whose current jobs are to be phased out, preparing managers for reorganization, or offering stress management training to workers whose jobs may be restructured. A needs assessment may uncover issues before they become problems. It can identify a variety of problem areas beyond the scope of its original intention, such as with the proposed launching of a new product.

Performing a needs assessment within a community can be just as illuminating. For example, asking companies in an area about general training needs may indicate a need for personnel with management skills. A preliminary analysis of the data might demonstrate that supervisory management issues create problems. For example, the problem may have arisen because of the lack of skills in the employees appointed as managers.

But perhaps the problems the companies are having actually relate to new regulatory requirements, new technology, or procedural changes that need to be implemented because of a change in policy. Perhaps these changes are due to government-mandated regulations with which companies must comply. Little thought may have been given to the notion that problems may have resulted from regulatory changes. A needs assessment can clarify the problem.

Extent of Problem. Perhaps ISO 9001 training should not be confined to a single department. What about other departments, such as receiving, accounting, engineering, manufacturing and production, and marketing? The needs assessment may indicate that the problem is bigger than one department. Of course, the opposite could also be true. What if it were found that all of the other departments had already implemented ISO 9001, except for the shipping department?

Performing a needs assessment in a community or region to determine training needs may show that several companies have the same needs. Or it may show there are more serious problems than just supervisory management. A needs assessment is a macro-level look that identifies discrepancies and narrows in on the problem. Needs assessment can gauge satisfaction levels, usage levels, spending, interest in additional training and programs, communication, general demographic characteristics and, of course, buy-in.

Other Techniques for Problem Solving. Needs assessment identifies the problem or gap, but other techniques may be needed to identify the variables. These techniques may include using competency-based models, self-reports, third-party reports, focus groups, in-depth interviews, participant observations, case studies, exit surveys, interviews, or alumni surveys. Assessment activities should also take into account the cultural, ethnic, religious, and linguistic diversity of the participants. Rather than relying on a single indicator to demonstrate success, companies and educational institutions should value the use of different strategies to provide essential needs assessment data.

Needs Assessment and Relevant Responses

Presenting relevant responses to problems should be the primary focus of needs assessment. Needs assessment information can be used in a number of ways to solve problems.

The needs assessment process can be used when there is concern about the impact and contribution an organization is making to society and its clients.

Needs assessment is also useful in determining what an organization is delivering to internal and external clients. It can look at internal operations and delivery efficiency if there are concerns about resources or about results, impacts, consequences, and accomplishments of the service or training. However, these problems and concerns need to be clarified before relevant responses can be presented (Leatherman, 2007).

Clarification of Problem Areas. Needs assessment areas need to be defined. Various indicators may suggest that a problem exists; however, the analyst may not be sure what the problem is. For example, customer complaints are up, sales are in decline, warrantee claims are increasing, or enrollments are declining. These indicators suggest there is a problem, but they do not identify the specific problem.

Needs assessment can help narrow the broad range of possible problems to one problem that is focused and precise. Since the purpose of needs assessment is to identify the differences between actual and ideal performance and determine the cause of the discrepancies, clarifying the problem seems especially critical. Without a clearly defined problem, resources, time and effort will be misdirected, and the design of effective learning experiences will be off the mark. Not involving job incumbents in a survey to determine problems on an assembly line will produce results that may be unreliable and untrustworthy. It may be helpful to ask a series of question to help clarify the problem. Consider the following questions:

- Is the problem noted important enough to devote time and effort to? Why?
- Is the problem connected to a group or an individual?
- Does the problem involve knowledge, skills, or attitudes?
- Can the problem be investigated with the present resources?
- Are there sufficient resources available to address the problem?
- Can fixes be applied?
- Is desired performance rewarding?
- Is desired performance punishing?

Answers to questions such as these should help narrow the scope and determine if undertaking the project is worthwhile. But more important, clarifying the problem will provide focus for possible solutions.

Availability of Valid Sources of Data. Sources of data include quality or accident reports, customer feedback, management incidents, policy changes, research, and other data that a company normally collects. Valid sources of data must be available and must relate to the problem. Sometimes organizations will not permit access to relevant data. An example might be accessibility of data within cigarette companies and any research on lung disease. In an attempt to solicit needs concerning supervisor/employee problems, an analyst may find that data is confidential and not readily accessible.

Data might be accessible but in a form that cannot be utilized. For example, a company has problems with shipping, but shipping data is on several different databases and cannot be consolidated. Or perhaps asking open-ended questions of supervisors on training issues results in comments that cannot be used directly in a training session for employees.

Sometimes there is not sufficient time to gather information. Administrators must spend money discovered at the end of the fiscal year with no time to survey needs, or a training session is planned at the last minute by a supervisor without input from employees.

In most cases, valid sources of data should not be a problem if the needs assessment is planned appropriately. It is, however, essential that valid sources of data be checked and considered as each needs assessment is planned.

Sufficient Time and Resources. A proper needs assessment takes time to clarify, develop, pilot, administer, analyze, and report. If there is not sufficient time to do it correctly, it should not be done. If adequate time to devote to the needs assessment is not available, then it should be put off until sufficient time is available. It may be possible to hire someone to assist with clerical and administrative tasks to free the researcher to pursue the needs assessment. It may also be possible to hire someone to do much of the needs assessment under the researcher's guidance. In either case, the situation should be discussed with supervisors or managers and a reasonable timeline for conducting the needs assessment should be developed.

The selection of data-gathering techniques is often related to budget considerations. Low-cost techniques usually involve searching records and management requests. Records may exist and are easy to interpret. Management makes a request and it is fulfilled. It does not require a lot of people to collect and analyze the data.

Questionnaires and surveys that a trained person can develop and administer are medium-cost techniques. Focus groups and interviews are high-cost techniques. Not only do interviews and focus groups require trained facilitators, which has budget implications, but pulling workers away from their jobs (and sometimes scheduling replacement workers) and involving them in the process of collecting, analyzing, and interpreting needs assessment data is costly.

Resources needed for needs assessment usually include time; available personnel to assist with the needs assessment; an appropriate budget to cover expenses of duplication, mailing, and analysis; funds to cover consultants; and travel expenses (if necessary) to conduct interviews and focus groups. It is helpful to develop a budget to determine the costs of carrying out the needs assessment and identify the resources needed to conduct it.

Availability of Resources for Relevant Response. Before starting a needs assessment, it is important to ascertain the resources available for analyzing and using the data. Resources need to be available for implementing the results. If a training program is needed but no resources are available for instruction or worker release time, the needs only become greater. If it is known that resources will not be available to deal with the results, the assessment should not be conducted.

Also, following the schedule for the needs assessment should be a priority. The data must be available when the decision makers need it.

When a Needs Assessment is Not Necessary

Under certain conditions, a needs assessment should not be conducted. For example, a manager requests a needs assessment, but past practices indicate that the data and analysis will be ignored. The same is true if the data sources are not dependable or if access to personnel cannot be secured.

No Follow-Up Action Is Planned or Possible. If there are reservations about the needs assessment because of political interests, and the results of the needs assessment are unlikely to be used for decisions that need to be made, then performing the assessment should be reconsidered. Politics could, for example, cause the needs assessment report to be ignored or the results to be misinterpreted because it did not support someone's point of view. The responses to a situation where no follow-up is planned will vary with the experience of the individual performing the needs assessment, the support, and with each individual case.

Valid Data Cannot Be Collected. There may be situations where valid data cannot be collected. For example, constraints may be placed on data collection that make accurate determination of needs impossible. The sponsor could restrict the selection of sites for data collection, regulate the use of certain types of techniques, withhold information, or deny people time to complete the instrument. Also, data sources frequently change rapidly in business and industry.

NEEDS ASSESSMENT PROCESS

The previous section defined the concept of need and discussed the various roles of needs assessment. It also presented several factors that are critical to performing an effective needs assessment. The last portion of this chapter will detail the steps in the needs assessment process and illustrate them with an example. The role of systems analysis and systems design concepts in needs assessment will also be explained. Since systems analysis concepts were used in designing the needs assessment process, these concepts will be discussed first.

Systems Analysis Concepts

A system is a set of elements that interact to produce an outcome. Also, a system typically operates in an environment that influences the outcomes. Elements in a system can be people, hardware, software, information, and/or equipment. The environment may contain the same elements. Environmental elements either facilitate or inhibit the processes used to create the outputs. For example, a comfortable, well-equipped classroom can facilitate the learning process. Application of systems analysis concepts in planning and conducting a needs assessment is essential to ensuring that the design of the assessment is relevant and its outcomes valid.

A system can also be thought of as a set of interrelated parts that are brought together for a specific purpose. See Figure 3-2. Kozar (1989) uses the example of the various systems found on a car, such as the engine, power train, electrical system, and suspension system, that work together to move the vehicle. Every system has inputs and processes them into outputs. The inputs in a car are the fuel, driving skill, and oil that process into transportation.

FIGURE 3-2

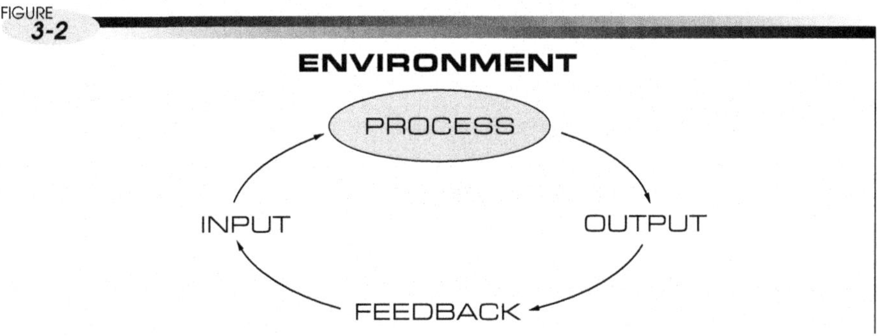

A system is comprised of elements that interact to produce an outcome. A system typically operates in an environment that influences the outcomes.

The following are basic principles of a systems approach:

- Every system has a purpose.
- Inputs are changed into outputs. Thus, the characteristics of the inputs must be identified.
- Processes change inputs to outputs. Thus, characteristics of processes and desired outputs must be identified.
- Elements in a system interact. Thus, the interactions of the elements in a needs assessment need to be studied.
- The most effective systems are created when the appropriate balance of resources is applied to the elements. Thus, this balance needs to be identified.
- Most systems are a part of a larger system or systems. Thus, larger systems that influence the system under study need to be identified and their impacts need to be considered.
- A self-correcting system has a feedback loop.

To illustrate a systems approach to needs assessment, consider the situation that occurs when an organization decides that its instructors will use computers in their classrooms. First, the purpose or goal for adding computers will need to be identified. Is the purpose to facilitate accessing and projecting visual aids, or is it to make more significant changes in their instructional methods and content? Elements in this system include the instructors, their students, the types of computer hardware and software to be used, and the classroom/lab equipment. The types of applications the instructors are expected to use with these computer systems must also be considered.

Since it is likely that these instructors will need to link their computers to other computerized information systems inside and outside of their organization, these larger systems must also be studied. If this project is to be effective, there must be an appropriate balance of elements in the system. The computer hardware and software selected must be functional in the classroom and communicate with existing computer systems, and adequate resources must be available for in-service training of instructors.

To create an effective computer-based instructional system, the needs assessment is used to determine the best combination of the following elements:

- purpose
- instructor training and technical assistance
- computer hardware
- computer software
- classroom/lab equipment
- communication interfaces with other computer systems

Conducting the Needs Assessment

A needs assessment process is depicted in Figure 3-3. The authors have used this process in a variety of projects and found it to be very effective. Consistently using this systematic approach will do the following:

- simplify the needs assessment process
- ensure that the same process is used by every one conducting needs assessments
- direct needs assessment planners to consider all the steps
- provide documentation of the process

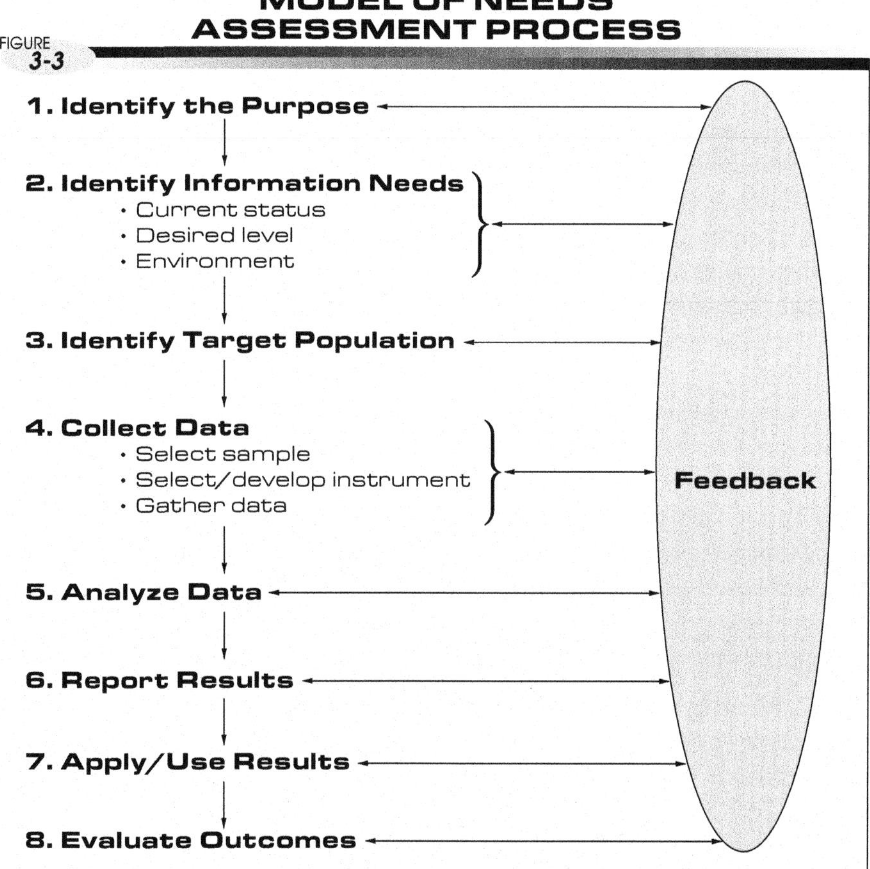

Consistent use of a systematic approach will result in an effective needs assessment.

The arrows between the steps are important. They indicate the flow of the needs assessment process. Usually it is best to complete the steps in the sequence given. However, it may be necessary to go back a step or two at times to clarify the work done in those steps.

Step 1. Identify the Purpose. The purpose statement provides specific direction for planning and conducting the needs assessment. It must identify the following:

- topic or subject of the study
- end products or information needed at the end of the study
- scope or limits of the study

Start by identifying the topic to be studied. This is the area of need that will be the focus of the study. After the topic has been identified, the end products, or information required at the end of the study can be determined. Finally, the scope of the study needs to be specified. The scope will establish the limits of the study. Limiting the study makes it manageable and functional. Care must be taken to avoid making the study too narrow or too broad. The scope needs to be compatible with the topic and end product.

To illustrate this process, let's continue with the "instructional use of computers" example. The decision has been made to use computers in instructional activities in classrooms and labs. A study has been completed and appropriate computer hardware and software have been selected. The next step is to perform a needs assessment to determine what in-service training the instructors will need.

In order to identify the training needs, the current level of competency the instructors have with the selected computer hardware and software, and the level of competency needed to make effective use of it must be determined. Since this technology will be new to the instructors, they will not be able to define the competencies needed to use it in their classrooms. Other sources of data will have to be used to determine the needed competencies. Instructors and their supervisors will be able to identify the instructors' current levels of proficiency once the competency areas have been identified. See Figure 3-4.

Step 2. Identify Information Needs. The previous step should provide ideas for the types of information required. In Step 2, the information needed will be identified in sufficient enough detail to direct the rest of the needs assessment project.

One way to identify the specific data or information required is to develop a model of the situation being studied. This model will identify component parts and their interactions. Systems analysis is a useful tool in developing this model. See Figure 3-5. However, other tools such as flow charts, cause-effect diagrams, and affinity charts can also be used to define the elements in the model.

FIGURE 3-4

PURPOSE OF NEEDS ASSESSMENT

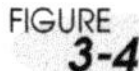

Topic
Competencies instructors need to develop in order to effectively use computers in delivering instruction.

End Products
- List of competencies needed
- Instructors' current performance status in these competency areas
- Gaps—competency areas where there are significant differences between instructors' current competencies and the required competency levels

Scope
- Instructors at ABC Technical College
- Competencies needed to use the computer system selected in conducting classroom instruction

Combining the topic, end products, and scope statements will generate the following purpose statement for this study.

PURPOSE
The purpose of this needs assessment is to identify the competencies that instructors at ABC Technical College need to develop in order to effectively use computers to deliver instruction in their classrooms and labs.

In Step 1 of the needs assessment process, the purpose of the assessment is identified.

Continuing with the example, a systems analysis for the instructor in-service training might produce the diagram given in Figure 3-5. The word "might" is used because systems analysis and diagramming are not exact sciences. Another analyst, trainer, or researcher analyzing this situation may develop a different diagram. However, any diagram will be effective for designing the study as long as it is developed in a logical manner.

When building the model, input from other individuals is helpful. This can be accomplished through a committee, a focus group, or peer reviews. Recent reports of similar needs assessment studies should be reviewed if they are available.

FIGURE 3-5

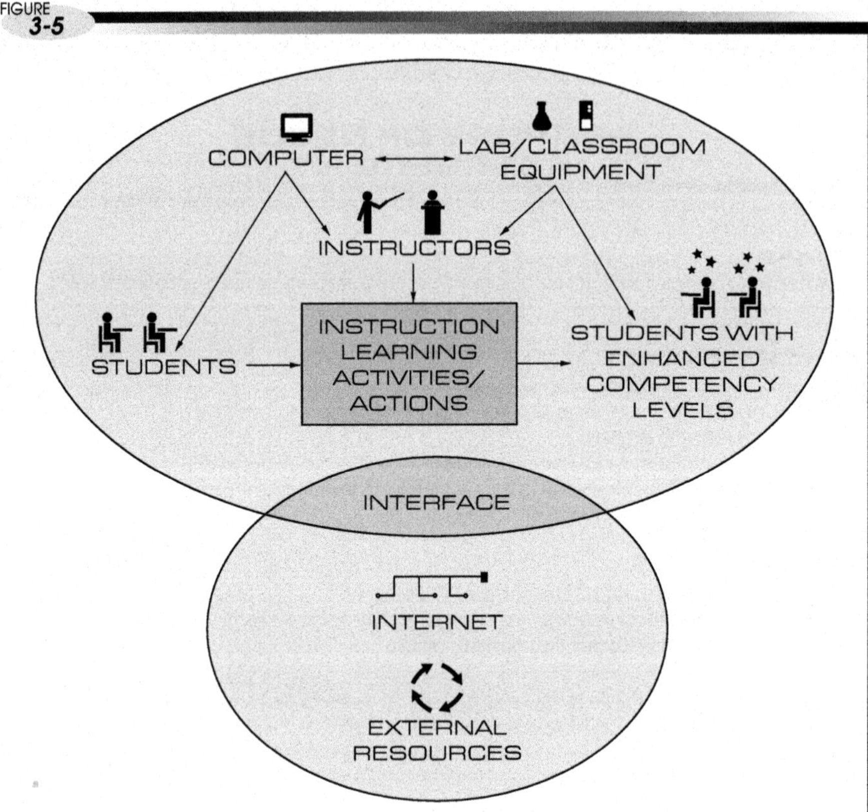

A systems analysis for the instructor in-service training might produce this diagram.

The diagram in Figure 3-5 shows that instructors will be using and interacting with computer hardware and software, lab and classroom equipment, and the Internet in order to provide instruction to their students. Since the reason for providing computers to instructors is to give students more realistic and effective learning experiences and expose them to modern information technology, there will be a need to collect data on the instructors' competencies in the following areas:

- computer hardware
- computer software
- instructional design
- instructional techniques
- instructional media design

The next step is to more specifically define the data needed in each of these areas by identifying the activities and applications for each area. Activities performed by instructors in order to deliver instruction will have to be identified. For example, in terms of the computer hardware, these actions will likely include keyboarding, loading and running programs, storing data, and using peripheral devices. Also, there are several different data storage systems and peripheral devices. A list of those available to the instructors should be compiled.

At this point, the process has generated specific information on the types of competencies needed to use the computer hardware. The same process should be used for the other areas identified. The information may not be complete, but this is not problematic because more information will be gathered to further refine the competencies. The information on competencies developed to this point will be very useful when interview questions are developed in Step 4.

The last activity in this part of the process is to write objectives for the remaining portion of the assessment. These objectives will identify the information that needs to be available at the end of the study. See Figure 3-6. An objective should be written for each of the identified competency areas: computer hardware, computer software, instructional design, instructional techniques, and instructional media design.

FIGURE 3-6

WRITTEN OBJECTIVES FOR COMPETENCY AREAS

The objectives of this study are as follows:

1. Identify the computer hardware competencies instructors will need to develop.
2. Determine the software competencies instructors will need to develop.
3. Identify the instructional design competencies instructors will need to acquire.
4. Identify the instructional techniques instructors will need to develop.
5. Determine the instructional media design skills instructors will need to acquire.

In Step 2 of the needs assessment process, objectives are written for each competency area.

The systems analysis process used in this step identified instructional design, teaching techniques, and instructional media as important competency areas. Without the systems analysis process, it would be easy to focus on the hardware and software involved and leave the other areas out. Also, the concept of balance in systems needs to be kept in mind as the needs assessment progresses. An effective instructional system will have an appropriate balance between its component elements.

Step 3. Identify Target Population. The competency areas and information needed were identified in the previous step. In Step 3, the best sources of information on the current and desired levels of performance must be determined. In the computers in instruction example, it would be appropriate to obtain input from instructors and their supervisors on the instructors' current competency levels and areas that need to be improved. See Appendix E.

However, instructors and their supervisors at ABC Technical College may not be able to provide all of the data needed on desired performance levels because they have not worked with the new system. Sources of data on the desired levels of performance should include reports from projects and interviews with instructors who use similar computer systems. If the application is cutting edge and no one has any data on its implementation, a pilot study with three or four instructors should be conducted to determine the competencies that need to be developed.

In this example, there are three target populations from which data are needed in order to define not only the current competency levels of instructors at ABC Technical College, but also what competency levels will be required:

- instructors at ABC Technical College
- supervisors at ABC Technical College
- current users of computer systems similar to the one selected for use at ABC Technical College

Step 4. Collect Data. In Step 3, the sources of the data needed in the study were identified. Step 4 involves three major activities: (1) planning the data collection, (2) selecting or developing the data collection instruments, and (3) collecting the data. Also, an efficient process for collecting valid and reliable data from these sources must be designed.

Planning involves making decisions on data collection techniques, samples, procedures, and data collection schedules. These decisions are interdependent. For example, if an interview technique is used to gather data, a sample group of people will need to be contacted, and a survey instrument will need to be designed for the interview process.

A logical way to start on the planning process is to review the nature of the data sources and contrast these with potential data collection techniques. In the example, the need to collect data from instructors who will use the computer systems and from their supervisors was identified. Acquiring data from other organizations that had implemented these systems is also determined to be of importance in identifying the competencies needed.

Instructors and supervisors can provide information on the instructors' current competency levels in relation to using the computer system in their classroom instruction. Also, it would be helpful to have some simple statistic that describes the instructors' current performance level on each competency. This suggests that a paper and pencil survey should be used with both the instructors and the supervisors.

There is one obvious problem with developing this survey: the lack of a complete competency list. However, the early adopters in other organizations were included in the study to help identify these competencies. For this source of data, a data collection technique that is flexible and helps respondents recall and analyze their experiences is needed. The interview technique is appropriate for this situation. The main drawback would be travel costs and time. If it is not feasible to use the interview technique, a modified Delphi technique could be used. Since the survey to be used with the instructors and supervisors is dependent on the results of the interviews, the interviews must be done first.

The next decision to be made is to determine whether to sample or collect data from everyone. A sample is a representative subset of members from a larger group that is usually referred to as a population. Sampling is used to save time and costs. When compared with sampling the entire population, sampling that combines surveys and interviews can provide more useful data in some situations. To illustrate this, consider a situation in which response rates to e-mail or mail surveys are very low. There is also concern about whether the responses are representative of the total population. In this situation, a sample in combination with interviews would produce more valid data.

Another consideration is the impact sampling will have on the stakeholders of the study. Stakeholders are the people concerned with and/or affected by the study. In the example of the computers in instruction project, instructors comprise one of the key stakeholder groups. If a sample of instructors is selected for a needs assessment, there is a risk of having those who were not included criticize the study for not representing their needs. Therefore, in this situation, all of the instructors should be surveyed. All of their supervisors should be surveyed for the same reason.

For input from other organizations that have implemented similar systems, a sample should be selected to acquire information on competencies that need to be developed. Organizations should be selected that have completed, or are nearing completion, of implementing computers in instruction. If possible, more than one organization and those with different approaches should be selected. Within each organization, a sample of stakeholders should be interviewed and/or surveyed. These stakeholders, or the people involved, would include instructors, their supervisors, students, curriculum specialists, media specialists, and administrators.

At this point the plan for the needs assessment data collection and analysis can be formalized. It should consist of eight major activities, each with a time schedule. See Figure 3-7.

FIGURE 3-7

DATA COLLECTION AND ANALYSIS SCHEDULE

Activities	Schedule
1. Select interview sites and schedule interviews	Weeks 1 & 2
2. Develop interview questions	Weeks 1 & 2
3. Conduct interviews	Weeks 3 & 4
4. Analyze interview data	Weeks 4 & 5
5. Develop survey for instructors and supervisors	Week 5
6. Survey instructors and supervisors	Week 6 thru 8
7. Process and analyze data	Week 9
8. Report results *	Weeks 10 & 11

* Note: Step 8 must be completed by the date that results are needed for program planning.

The process of collecting, analyzing, and reporting needs assessment data is time sensitive.

The interviews with previous adopters are scheduled first and the results are used to develop the survey for the instructors and supervisors at ABC Technical College. The timeline for the activities would be established by identifying when the data is needed and working back from that point.

In the second activity, the data collection instruments are selected or designed. A valid instrument from previous studies can be used, but usually, new instruments must be developed since needs assessments are generally designed for specific situations. However, it is helpful to review other studies to acquire information on the procedures and instruments used.

It is important to select a type of instrument that fits the setting in which it will be used and the nature of the data. In the computers in instruction example, the researchers decided that information on the competencies required to operate the system was needed from people who had experience with similar systems. Since the researchers had little specific information about the nature of these competencies, the decision was made to use the interview technique. The technique provided the flexibility needed to identify the competencies and examine the applications that had been made.

An effective interview requires planning and preparation. Interview questions need to be prepared. For the computers in instruction example, questions are designed to identify competencies within the five major competency areas of the model developed for the project. Also, in a project like this, it is helpful to identify what problems the adopters encountered and how they were resolved. One of the goals of the computers in instruction project is to enrich instruction; therefore, it would be appropriate to ask the adopters to comment on how the use of computers has influenced their instruction. Finally, the interviews should elicit information on the relative importance of the competencies in order to determine the balance needed.

After the interviews have been completed, the next step is to analyze the interview data and identify the competencies needed. The competency list will be used to design the survey instrument for instructors and supervisors. Since the researchers want to have statistical data on the skill levels of their instructors, a rating scale instrument should be used. Each competency identified in the interviews will be listed in the rating scale and instructors will identify their competency levels by circling a number on the scale.

Supervisors should complete two forms of this survey. First, supervisors need to identify their competency levels. Second, they need to identify the competency levels of their instructors. The supervisor competency levels can be identified with the same survey used by the instructors. The surveys will need to be color coded or identifiable for separate analysis. The instructors survey can be modified to allow the supervisors to rate their instructor's competencies.

After the surveys are ready, they can be distributed to the instructors and supervisors. A concentrated effort needs to be made to achieve a good response rate. One way to accomplish this would be to have the surveys completed during a department meeting. If they are sent out by mail, there will be a need to follow-up with those who do not respond. Whatever the delivery system, the instructors need to know how the survey's results will affect them.

Step 5. Analyze Data. Data analysis processes will be selected based on the types of data collected and how the results will be used. Also, the analysis process must be compatible with the collection process. See Appendix K.

In the computers in instruction example, the interview data must be analyzed to identify the competencies needed to implement the system. The competency statements should identify what instructors and support staff must be able to do in order to make this system work in the classroom. The interview notes are reviewed to identify the required skills and knowledge. One way to do this is to record the competencies on 3 × 5 cards. Each card will have one competency or activity that instructors should be able to do. After all of the interview notes have been reviewed, the cards can be sorted into piles, with each pile representing a competency.

The next step is to analyze the implementation problems identified in the interviews to determine the competencies needed to prevent and/or resolve them. The interviews should produce the set of competencies required to successfully implement the computers in instruction program. Also, a review of available reports on similar projects can be used to validate this list. These competencies should be compared with those identified in the interviews, and those that are unique should be added to the competency list. The final competency list will be used to design the survey for the next phase of the assessment.

The instructors' and supervisors' surveys will need to be processed separately since they provide two different perspectives. A review of the decisions to be made in the next step will help to identify the types of statistics to run. Also, the target performance levels for each of the competencies needs to be identified at this time. In other words, what is the "desired/required" performance level for each competency? This level may vary across competencies depending on the resources and support staff available.

Usually, it is helpful to have a statistical summary that provides the number and percentage of respondents at each competency level and the median and average level for each competency statement. Measures of variability such as the range and standard deviation are also useful. See Appendix K.

It is typically more efficient to use a computer to run these analyses. The survey responses can be stored on disk and a variety of analyses can be run. It is a good idea to leave a draft copy of the survey with the computer or data processing staff to determine if any changes are needed before the survey is conducted. After the data has been processed, the results should be compared with the target competency levels to determine needs. The average response for the current level of competency (what is) is compared to the desired/required level of competency (what should be) to identify the gaps.

In the computers in instruction example, this gap analysis is done separately on the instructors' and the supervisors' data. Next, the gaps identified by each group are compared, and areas of agreement and disagreement are noted. The areas of disagreement are reviewed again, and any other data available are used to gain a better understanding of the discrepancies. For example, the interview data may be useful in clarifying the differences.

Another data analysis activity that can be done in the computers in instruction example is running summaries for subgroups of instructors. For example, the needs of instructors who teach technical courses may differ from those who teach English and communication skills. In order to run these separate summaries, there needs to be a way to identify the surveys from each group. This could be done by including an item on the survey that asks the respondents to identify their departments or subject matter areas.

Step 6. Report Results. Several types of reports should be considered. Usually it is appropriate to develop written and oral reports. An oral report will ensure that decision makers receive the results. However, the needs assessment written report is an important document. It will be one of the major communication channels used to inform stakeholders of the results of the study. Also, it will be a permanent record of both the processes used in the study and the results. (Additional information on writing reports can be found in Chapter 5.)

The report should be designed in a format that is comprehensible to the decision makers. Some decision makers find tables and charts very useful; others will need a narrative to comprehend the results. Also, the statistical results should be organized to facilitate interpretation. For example, need areas can be listed by extent of need or size of gap, with the largest need given first.

A needs assessment report should include a concise description of the processes used to collect the data and should present the results. Any instruments used should be included in an appendix.

Step 7. Apply/Use Results. For a needs assessment to have an impact, the results must be used in a timely and logical manner. Needs can change quickly and needs assessment data can loose some of its validity. Decision makers involved in the application process must understand the needs assessment results and use the results in their decision making.

Where the individuals doing the needs assessment are also part of the decision-making group, this is usually a smooth transition. Where needs assessment study results are given to individuals who were not involved in the study, problems can arise. The decision makers may not understand the needs assessment process and the data generated by it. In this situation, it is important to involve the decision makers in the needs assessment from the beginning. After the needs assessment study has been completed, the program, curriculum, and/or staff development decision makers should be briefed on the results.

Step 8. Evaluate Outcomes. There are two types of evaluations. A formative, or process, evaluation results in useful data on all of the needs assessment activities and provides information that is useful in managing the needs assessment and interpreting the results. This is an ongoing activity throughout the assessment. (Additional information on evaluation can be found in Chapter 9.)

A summative, or product, evaluation at the end of the needs assessment process will determine if the needs assessment attained its objectives. If possible, the summative evaluation should be done after the needs assessment results have been implemented in program or course development. A summative evaluation will provide an opportunity to determine if the needs assessment produced valid and sufficient data.

Applications of formative and summative evaluations in the computers in instruction example will illustrate the role of evaluation in needs assessment. Formative evaluation activities are used to manage the project and determine if the needs assessment is being carried out as planned. If changes are made, they should be documented. Also, the level of agreement between the needs identified and the contents of the instructors' in-service programs should be assessed. In addition, there should be a check to determine if the training program is being carried out as planned. Finally, instructors in the project should provide feedback on the factors that facilitate and inhibit their use of computers in instruction.

Summative evaluation would be focused on three areas: (1) sufficient data for planning, (2) valid data for developing the program, and (3) impact of the use of computers in instruction. The sufficiency of the data will be tested as decision makers plan the training program in Step 7. Adequate scope and depth of the data will provide the information they need to plan and implement the program. Validity of the needs assessment data can be evaluated when the instructors use computers to enhance their instruction. If the data and the in-service training program are valid, instructors will be able to use computers to enhance their instruction. The last element in the summative evaluation is the impact computers have on improving and enhancing instruction. Data should be collected from instructors, students, and supervisors to determine if instruction has changed and improved.

REVIEW QUESTIONS

1. Why is needs assessment important?
2. Explain how needs assessment can affect organizational change in your setting.
3. How can macro data be supported by needs assessment?
4. Describe how needs assessment data can be used to develop relevant responses to five problems.
5. Identify the reasons why needs assessment should not be performed.
6. What is a need? Give an example of a need you experienced recently.
7. What is a system? Give an example of a common system.
8. What are the inputs, processes, and outputs in the system you identified above? What are the environmental factors influencing this system? What is the feedback loop in this system?
9. Describe the eight steps in the needs assessment process.
10. What are the three parts of the purpose statement for a needs assessment project?
11. What are the sources of needs assessment data?
12. In what ways are the reports of previous needs assessment studies useful?
13. How is the schedule of activities for a needs assessment study developed?
14. Describe the contents of a needs assessment report.
15. What steps can be taken to facilitate the use of needs assessment results?
16. Develop a plan for a simple needs assessment study.

REFERENCES

Altschuld, J. W. (2015). *Bridging the gap between asset/capacity building and needs assessment: Concepts and practical applications.* Thousand Oaks, CA: Sage Publications.

Altschuld, J. W., & Witkin, B. R. (2000). *From needs assessment to action: Transforming needs into solutions strategies.* Thousand Oaks, CA: Sage Publications.

Berkowitz, S., & Reviere, R. (1997). The need for needs assessment. *PA Times, 20*(6), 12.

Kozar, K. A. (1989). *Humanized information systems analysis and design: People building systems for people.* New York: McGraw-Hill.

Leatherman, D. (2007). *The training trilogy: Conducting needs assessments, designing programs, training skills* (3rd ed.). Amherst, MA: HRD Press.

Love, A. (1991). *Internal evaluation: Building organizations from within.* London: Sage Publications.

Rouda, R. H., & Kusy, M. E., Jr. (1995). *Needs assessment the first step.* Retrieved September 10, 2014, from http://alumnus.caltech.edu/~rouda/T2_NA.html

Rossett, A. (2009). *First things fast: A handbook for performance analysis* (2nd ed.). San Francisco: Pfeiffer.

Rothwell, W, J., & Kazanas, H. C. (2008). *Mastering the instructional design process: A systematic approach* (4th ed.). San Francisco: Pfieffer.

Soriano, F. I. (2013). *Conducting needs assessments: A multidiscipline approach* (2nd ed.). Thousand Oaks, CA: Sage Publications.

Watkins, R., West-Meiers, M., & Visser, Y. L. (2012). *A guide to assessing needs: Essential tools for collecting information, making decisions, and achieving development results.* Washington, DC: World Bank.

Performance and Task Analysis

INTRODUCTION

OBJECTIVES

ANALYSIS

Performance Analysis

Knowledge and Skills • Capacity • Standards • Feedback • Measurement • Conditions • Incentives

Occupational Analysis

Task Analysis

DIRECT OBSERVATION

Select the Behaviors to Be Observed

Choose Observational Method

Develop Guide

Observe Task Performers

Consolidate Data

SMALL GROUP METHOD

Interviewing

Focus Groups

DACUM Process

CRITICAL INCIDENT

Identify General Aims

Develop Plans and Specifications

Collect the Data

Analyze the Data

Interpret and Report the Data

Modifications

RESEARCH

Define Occupation or Job

Geography • Outside Influences • Incorrect Assumptions • Scope of Analysis • New and Emerging Trends • Distribution of Employment Opportunities

Review Sources of Occupation or Job Analyses

Draft Duty and Task Statements

Duty • Task • Step

Review Initial List of Duty and Task Statements

Review the Inventory • Edit and Regroup • Pilot Test the Items

Develop Instrument

Select Rating Scale • Develop Instructions • Determine Background Information • Write Cover Letter • Write Follow-Up Letter

Identify Job Incumbent Sources

Develop Sampling Plan and Analysis Design

Sampling • Sample Size • Analysis Design

Administer Instrument

Analyze Data

Record Task Inventory

Write Report

REVIEW QUESTIONS

REFERENCES

INTRODUCTION

As curriculum is developed into a coherent program, the processes of performance and task analysis must be undertaken to determine the specific content. One of the most critical skills needed to determine content is analysis. Analysis is reducing or breaking apart a whole into organized parts while relating the parts to each other or to the whole. Analysis means to dissect, break down or divide a complex whole or unit into its component parts or constituent elements. In the same manner, the training or education curriculum has to be divided or broken down to determine what is to be taught.

OBJECTIVES

After completing this chapter, the reader should be able to do the following:

1. Describe the benefits of a task analysis.
2. Explain how a task inventory is developed.
3. Explain under which conditions the observation, small group, critical incident, and research methods might be used.
4. Discuss the steps in conducting a research task analysis.
5. Identify the characteristics of a task statement.
6. Appraise different types of rating scales.
7. Design cover letters for a given questionnaire.
8. Explain the difference between the four types of samples.

ANALYSIS

Seaman (2011) discusses Benjamin Bloom's taxonomy for categorizing levels of cognition that commonly occur in educational or training settings. The taxonomy consists of seven levels, with the fourth level being analysis:

- evaluation (level 6)
- synthesis (level 5)
- analysis (level 4)
- application (level 3)
- comprehension (level 2)
- knowledge (level 1)

Hunter (1982) felt that all creative thinking and problem solving begins with analytic thinking, or mentally taking something apart to better understand the relationship of the parts to each other and to the whole. This is what performance and task analysis accomplishes, it breaks down a job or occupation into its constituent parts.

Performance Analysis

Performance analysis is a very broad term used in the training industry to mean working with clients and customers to help define and execute their goals. The process involves maintaining contacts with clients and customers to identify problems and barriers that affect performance. Suggesting solutions based on the diagnosis, and not what has been done in the past, is essential (Rossett, 2009). Performance analysis can also be defined as the process of aligning business results, performance processes and products, and performance support (Langdon, Whiteside, & McKenna, 1999).

By looking at the factors that affect performance, an instructional developer can determine if there really is a performance problem. In some cases, training may not be the appropriate solution. In an industrial and technical education setting, dealing with performance is critical.

Performance problems and solutions may be classified into seven categories: (1) knowledge and skills, (2) capacity, (3) standards, (4) feedback, (5) measurement (6) conditions, and (7) incentives. (Langevin Learning Services, 2014). See Figure 4-1.

Knowledge and Skills. Knowledge and skills deal with what employees know and can do. This category also deals with an employee's ability to meet performance standards in the work setting. It is not unusual for new people being hired or for those being transferred to lack the knowledge and skills for a particular job. If employees are unable to apply knowledge and skills to meet the requirement of the job, then training is required.

It is interesting to note that one-half of the people who are referred for training in business and industry already have the knowledge and skills to do the job. In other words, they were sent to the training for the wrong reason. Following are knowledge and skills checklist questions to consider asking if knowledge and skills are suspected as the cause of a performance problem:

- Did the employee ever perform the task properly?
- Is the task performed often enough to ensure retention?
- Do they know that the task is still expected of them?
- Was training previously provided?
- Was the training effective?
- Was there sufficient practice during the training?
- Could they perform properly after training?
- Was the training reinforced back on the job?
- Are job aids available?
- Are job aids effective?
- Does performance fail to improve with experience?
- Is the task procedure stable?
- Could they perform the task if their lives depended on it?

Capacity. Capacity refers to the employee's ability to do the job. Does the employee have the mental or physical capacity to perform the job or to obtain the skills and knowledge needed? This is the only potential performance cause that looks at the existing employee or position.

FIGURE 4-1

PERFORMANCE ANALYSIS

Problems	Solutions
Knowledge and Skills	• Improve current training or provide training, refresher training, practice, simulation, job aids, coaching.
Capacity	• Fitting the person to the job—provide job training and vocational guidance and improve the selection process. • Fitting the job to the person—develop work techniques and use different equipment, improve work conditions and make other local improvements on the job, provide rewards. • Change personnel.
Standards	• Develop standards to use on the job. • Publicize the standards. • Certify the standards.
Feedback	• Provide feedback (must be immediate and specific). • Improve use of feedback.
Measurement	• Develop measurements for performance. • Update existing measurements. • Publish and disseminate measurement tools.
Conditions	• Reorganize workplace. • Upgrade tools and equipment. • Redesign job.
Incentives	• Recognize what incentives work with which worker. • Provide and strengthen positive incentives. • Remove and weaken negative incentives. • Remove and weaken positive consequences for poor performance.

Potential performance causes generally fall into seven categories.

If it is desirable to fit the person to the job, then job training, vocational guidance, and selection criteria for the job should be considered. If it is desirable to fit the job to the person, then developing work techniques, making local improvements in the job, changing the working conditions, and giving rewards should be considered. If the answers to all of the following capacity checklist questions are no, then it may be best to simply move the employee to another job:

- Do they have the mental capacity?
- Do they have the physical capacity?
- Do they have the prerequisites for training?

Standards. Standards refer to detailed descriptions of how the employee is to perform a job in terms of quality, time, or cost. Standards tend to be job and company specific. Instructors use standards in the curriculum, and supervisors use them for evaluation. It is critical that employees be familiar with the applicable standards to determine whether their performances can meet them.

Standards are where task analysis and performance objectives are used. The task analysis breaks down the job, duty, or task into meaningful steps. Employees can use these steps to ensure they are performing up to the standards. Performance objectives provide criteria against which to measure the work being done. Employees may make the mistake of measuring what they are as opposed to what they should be. Checklist questions to consider when dealing with standards as potential performance criteria include the following:

- Do employees know what to do?
- Do they know when to do it?
- Do supervisors agree on what and when something should be done?
- Are there written standards?
- Do employees know how they are being evaluated?
- Are there clearly defined standards?
- Are standards clearly communicated?

Feedback. Feedback is about supervisors providing verbal or written information to employees on how they are performing in relationship to the standards. Feedback to employees should be part of the operating procedure of any supervisor. If feedback is not provided, then employees do not know if they are doing a good job. Feedback should be immediate, frequent, understandable, specific, and accurate so that employees know exactly what they are getting feedback for. It is also important that the feedback be given by someone who matters and provided in a way that it will be accepted. If an employee had training, it is essential that feedback on the job be integrated with the post-training evaluation. Feedback checklist questions include the following:

- Are employees informed about how they are performing?
- Is feedback provided soon enough?
- Is feedback understandable?
- Is feedback tied to performance within the employee's control?
- Is feedback specific?
- Is feedback accurate?
- Is feedback given by someone who matters?
- Is feedback given in a way the employees can accept?

Measurement. Measurement deals with objective benchmarks based on established standards and is the norm for determining job performance. Any standard for a job should consist of specific criteria and objective measures to determine performance. The measurement used by the supervisor or peer might involve a checklist, rating scale, critical incident report, etc. Measurement checklist questions include the following:

- Is performance measured?
- Are measurements based on task performance?
- Are measurements based on results rather than activities?
- Are the purposes of the tasks measured?
- Are the measurements objective?
- Are the designers of the measurements qualified?

Conditions. Conditions within the job setting may affect whether the task or job is completed. Many times, obstructions within the work environment affect work standards. Also, interference with a job process may affect its outcomes. Resources needed to complete a task or job such as tools, equipment, materials, time, and information fall under this category.

For example, errors in a software application constantly cause a computer to reboot. There is constant noise and chatter in the work environment and employees are not able to concentrate. There are physical barriers on the plant floor that affect movement of essential parts for production. The supervisor in marketing came from finance and does not understand the marketing expectations. These are examples of obstructions and the types of interference that can cause performance problems. Conditions checklist questions include the following:

- Are task procedures clear and workable?
- Is the workplace physically organized?
- Is enough time available to complete the task?
- Are tools and equipment available?
- Are tools and equipment operative?
- Is necessary information available?
- Is information accurate?
- Are distractions and interruptions minimized?
- Are policies and procedures flexible enough?
- Do employees have enough authority?
- Can the job be done by one person?
- Is support available for peak periods?

Incentives. Incentives refer to what happens to employees when they do something correctly, and what happens to them if they do something incorrectly. In many organizations, if something is done incorrectly, it is simply done that way again.

There may be times when an employee does something correctly and then feels punished. For example, an employee completes a table-cleaning assignment quickly and efficiently, so the supervisor assigns the employee the undesirable task of cleaning out the grease traps in the kitchen. There may also be times when an employee does a job incorrectly and something good happens. For example, a portion of the job may be assigned to someone else, thereby reducing the original employee's burden.

It has been said that 50% of the performance problems fall within the incentive category. Therefore, there may not be a match between success on the job and incentives. Incentive checklist questions include the following:

- Is the task deemed worthwhile?
- Do employees believe they can perform the task?
- Is there an incentive for performing well?
- Do the incentives really matter to them?
- Is the incentive contingent upon good performance?
- Do they know the link between incentives and performance?
- Are incentives scheduled to prevent discouragement?
- Are all available incentives being used?
- Do they find work interesting?
- Is there inner satisfaction for good performance?
- If incentives are mixed, is the balance positive?
- Is punishment for good performance prevented?
- Is reward for poor performance prevented?
- Is there peer pressure for good performance?
- Is task unpleasantness or stress within acceptable levels?
- Does poor performance draw attention?

The performance analysis step is critical, because even though training may be the solution, Langevin Learning Services (1998) have indicated that training is effective in only 40% of the cases where training was proposed as the solution. This means that training is not a solution in 60% of cases where training is suggested to solve the problem identified in the need. Stated another way, training was not the appropriate solution to the problem.

Occupational Analysis

Occupational analysis (sometimes termed job analysis) is the systematic method of gathering information on occupations and industries, their jobs, tasks, and positions. It focuses on occupations, requirements, and environments by identifying the knowledge, skills, and attitudes needed for performance.

Everything possible about that occupation is looked at. Different industries are surveyed to determine the number of people working in the occupation and the number of positions needed in the near future due to turnover, retirements, and changes in the occupation. Will there be outside forces affecting that occupation that will require different performance requirements in the future? Are there significant technological advances on the horizon that will affect the occupation? Needs assessment and task analysis are part of an occupational analysis.

Task Analysis

Task analysis is the identification of the activities and responsibilities carried out by an individual within an occupation. It is the process of collecting and organizing the elements of a job for the purpose of generating a training or occupational curriculum.

A task analysis will produce a list of selected and appropriately stated tasks—manipulative, cognitive, and attitudinal—grouped into categories called major duties. These duties are normally performed by individuals in a specified occupation. The occupations may be teacher, chef, auto mechanic, LPN, draftsperson, aircraft mechanic, etc. Task analysis can be applied to any occupation, job, duty, or task. Task analysis may be applied to content for a training program or to develop a comprehensive curriculum. Task analysis can also be used to identify management skills and the soft skills used in business and industry.

Too often task analysis is viewed only in the context of developing programs of instruction. The benefits, however, go far beyond this use. Task analysis can be used to do the following:

- identify what job incumbents are required to do based on their present jobs and associated tasks
- build a foundation for the development of job descriptions and specifications
- select applicants for jobs or training
- determine training that can be reduced or eliminated
- identify the objectives for training
- identify the context for training and education programs
- build the foundation for performance aids, including checklists, procedures, decision tables, and performance appraisals
- write or amend operating manuals and technical publications

Sometimes, a task analysis goes beyond just a single occupation. A task analysis may be required to analyze a cluster of occupations to save time or when seeking efficient program or training implementation. An occupational cluster is the grouping of related jobs into a family of occupations or a homogeneous grouping of jobs. In technical college settings programs may be offered that share content because the task analysis demonstrates that some of the content in the occupations is similar. See Figure 4-2.

Students enrolled in the secretary cluster may have several courses in common based on similar knowledge and skills needed in all of the occupations. Analyzing occupations as clusters is especially useful in a technical college setting or in companies that have numerous technical and soft-skill training programs.

FIGURE 4-2

Family of Occupations	Occupations with Similar Content
Electronics Cluster	Secretary Cluster
• Radio technician • Biomechanical electronic technician • TV technician • Microprocessor repair technician	• Account clerk • Administrative assistant—secretarial • Clerk—general office • Clerk—typist • Clerk—typist, medical • Data entry • Insurance clerk • Legal secretary • Medical secretary

A cluster analysis will help group jobs into a family or into a group with similar content.

It is not necessary to do a cluster analysis if only a single job or part of job needs to be analyzed for a training program. This analysis will produce a series of duties and tasks for use in the training or education curriculum that cover the content of the occupation.

Another related term is task inventory. A task inventory is a list of selected and appropriately stated tasks grouped into categories called duties or divisions that are normally performed by individuals in a specified job. It is basically a list of the instructional content developed when performing a job/occupation or task analysis. See Figure 4-3. This task inventory is the result of a task analysis process and can be used to implement the curriculum for training or a course of study.

There are many methods for performing a task analysis. Some of the methods include detailed planning and analysis, while others can be performed quickly with minimum analysis. Besides the obvious application to training and technical education, these processes can also be used for general education courses and curriculum. Most task analysis methods can be divided into four distinct groups:

- direct observation
- small group
- critical incident
- research

FIGURE 4-3

Task Inventory for Industrial Engineering Technician

1. Selcting process equipment.
   - Evaluate process equipment.
   - Make recommendations on process equipment.
   - Perform cost-benefit analysis of equipment.
   - Conceptualize future equipment needs.
   - Maintain database for future reference.
   - Serve as a communication bridge between management and supplier.

2. Analyzing equipment for appropriate design layout.
   - Create preliminary design of equipment layouts.
   - Plan the work flow associated with equipment installation.
   - Examine the impact of safety and quality.
   - Define start-up plans for equipment.
   - Determine auxiliary needs.
   - Assist in equipment installation.
   - Write technical reports and written descriptions of equipment.

3. Testing performance and efficiency of people, processes, and sytems.
   - Perform line studies including downtime analysis.
   - Conduct annual capacity studies.
   - Conduct time and motion studies to utilize available resources.
   - Inspect and evaluate the quality of products.
   - Develop measurement tools for production use.
   - Establish worker measurement programs.

4. Optimizing efficiency of people and materials.
   - Examine production costs for areas of improvement.
   - Examine production schedules for areas of improvement.
   - Evaluate existing systems/materials for process improvement.
   - Diagnose equipment problems.
   - Develop standards for production efficiency.
   - Initiate use of robotics and/or automation.
   - Make recommendations for handling materials and/or improving standards.
   - Interact with production line workers.
   - Determine adequate spare part inventory.

5. Analyzing equipment for product implementation.
   - Evaluate equipment for adaptability.
   - Evaluate scheduling for available capacity.
   - Determine resources needed for production.
   - Create preliminary graphical layout using CAD.

6. Coordinating technical support training.
   - Make recommendations for training programs.
   - Develop training manuals.
   - Provide troubleshooting guidelines to support daily production problems.
   - Accurately communicate technical instructions.

The task inventory consists of a list of tasks subdivided into duties.

Direct observation involves observing workers in the work setting. The small group method involves asking workers what they do, either one-on-one or in a control group setting. Critical incidents look at existing data and utilize interviewing techniques. The research method requires surveying job incumbents. All four methods are effective and produce desirable results. They also all have disadvantages.

DIRECT OBSERVATION

Observing workers in their actual work setting to determine how tasks are normally performed is an effective strategy. Michalak and Yager (2001) indicated that direct observation of workers performing tasks was the most valid method of collecting task analysis data. The assumption is that competent workers are being observed and that the observer is trained and able to capture what the worker is doing. Training of the observer is critical, especially in the area of interviewing skills. Once the observation takes place and is recorded, other incumbent workers are needed to validate the task analysis.

The two types of observation methods are obtrusive and unobtrusive. Obtrusive methods seek details about tasks that have mental decisions or complex operations. A few selected workers are observed for an extended period of time with follow-up observations and questions. Unobtrusive methods imply observation not affecting performance. Several workers performing the same job are observed, with limited, focused behavior being the object.

Reasons for using the direct observation method include lack of existing resources on the occupation in question; the qualities of the resources are suspect; new and emerging technologies are affecting the occupation; special detail is needed; and/or site-specific training needs to be developed. Observation should be accurate in detailing a worker's performance. It is also extremely helpful to make a record of the most up-to-date equipment in operation.

Weaknesses of the observation method are that the whole job needs to be observed over a period of time, jobs may tend to be site specific, and workers tend to perform the job differently when under observation. See Figure 4-4.

There are several steps to follow when using observational techniques for task analysis. They include (1) selecting the behaviors to be observed, (2) choosing the observational method, (3) developing an observation guide, (4) observing the performers, and (5) consolidating the data.

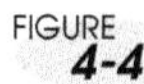

FIGURE 4-4

OBSERVATION

Advantages

- Realistic data source—capture the whole event while it occurs.
- Collect original data at the time it occurs.
- Minimizes interruption of routine work flow (unobtrusive).
- Inexpensive—possible to be unobtrusive.
- Flexible—can be used in conjunction with other data sources (obtrusive).
- Subjects may accept observation better than questioning; may be less demanding and biasing.

Disadvantages

- Requires a highly skilled observer.
- Difficult to identify mental operations—observers must make inferences from surface indicators.
- Potential for affecting the operation being observed.
- May be intimidating and exhausting to the employee, unless adequately explained.
- May cause employee anxiety or resentment.
- May provide biased information if just one or two people are observed due to time and expense.
- Observer must be at the scene of the event when it occurs.
- May be slow and expensive because of human observations and expensive surveillance equipment used.

The direct observation method has a fair amount of both advantages and disadvantages. (Jonassen, Tessmer, & Hannum, 1999, pp. 245)

Step 1. Select the Behaviors to Be Observed

Any starting point in the process should involve careful selection of the behaviors to be observed (Zemke & Kramlinger, 1982). This selection might include the specific duties or tasks to be observed as the focus of the study. Confirmation about the selection should take place with the supervisor or individual who wanted the task analysis done.

Step 2. Choose the Observational Method

Will the obtrusive or unobtrusive observation method be used? There are many factors to consider based on the kind of duty and task being observed, environmental factors (noise, space, hazards, climate, etc.), and who is being observed.

Step 3. Develop an Observation Guide

After selecting the behaviors to be observed and the observational method, the next step is to consider using a guide sheet for the observation. This can be a simple form for recording actions and results. The specific observed actions are listed and numbered. See Figure 4-5. Any result or product associated with the action is noted. Mental processing that is not observed, but implied, should also be noted.

FIGURE 4-5

Duty or Task	Observed Action	Result	Cognition
1. Perform startup procedure.	Follow manufacturer checklist.	All steps followed.	Made adjustment.
2. Read job order.	Review list of materials for job.	All appropriate materials assembled.	Consider manufacturer process.
3. Use safety equipment.	Put on safety glasses, apron and hearing protection.	Operator is prepared to start machine.	Safety equipment is adjusted.

When using direct observation, a guide sheet is helpful for recording information.

Step 4. Observe Task Performers in Actual Settings

To provide the most useful data, it is important to observe workers in their normal environment. While it is always desirable to ask questions when observing, be careful to not distract the worker, especially when safety concerns are encountered. When using unobtrusive observation methods, keep the following in mind:

- The worker should be observed without any intrusion or interaction on the part of the observer.
- All action of the worker should be recorded on the observation guide.
- A videotape can be used if the tasks are performed at a rapid rate.
- The worker and observer can review the tape later to clarify actions and mental processing for the task.

Two observers observing the same worker simultaneously, or at a separate time, are desirable if funding permits. Funding may limit the length of the observation. An adequate sample of workers and time is necessary for useful data.

Step 5. Consolidate the Data

When sufficient data has been collected, the findings can be summarized. Make sure the summary is comprehensive and includes all the duties and tasks observed, including steps to complete each step (Jonassen, Tessmer, & Hannum, 1999).

SMALL GROUP METHOD

Another method of performing a task analysis involves using small groups to gather information. Interviewing, focus group techniques, and DACUM fall into this category. (Additional information on interviewing, focus groups, and DACUM, is given in Chapter 2.) The small group method is especially effective for new and emerging tasks, task analysis that needs to be accomplished quickly, or when it is determined that a group of job incumbents and workers from business and industry can be assembled for a day. Some advantages of this method are the direct involvement of job incumbents and supervisors from whom a variety of expertise can be drawn and, generally, state-of-the-art information is provided.

One of the challenges of this method is the difficulty of getting an adequate cross section of incumbent workers and business and industry supervisors involved. Also, excellent facilitation skills are required, or one person in the group can end up dominating the discussion.

Interviewing

The purpose of the interview is to solicit information on duties and tasks. To do this, several decisions need to be made concerning the degree of structure desired during the interview, the level of information sharing that is necessary, and the method of note taking that will be used.

The structure of the interview can be any of the following:

- highly structured—face-to-face filling out of questionnaire (e.g., census takers)
- moderately structured—specific questions asked, but in a conversational manner

- unstructured—no specific questions, but a topic; the flow depends on where the interviewee leads the conversation

An example might help illustrate the line of questioning to use when conducting an interview. See Figure 4-6. This highly structured questionnaire was developed to respond to needs of used car dealers in a specific geographic location. The used car dealers wanted to find out their customers' experiences with purchasing used cars. After meeting with a group of dealers, interview questions were developed. In this example, everyone was asked the same seven questions.

FIGURE 4-6

Purchase of Used Car Questionnaire

1. Where did you purchase your used car? Dealer, used car lot, friend, private party?

2. What was the type of vehicle you desired and the purpose it would serve?

3. What is the range of price your were willing to pay?

4. How was service and repair a factor in your decision?

5. How did you feel about the purchase experience?

6. Did you feel you received a good deal?

7. Anything else?

Using a highly structured questionnaire is one method of gathering information during an interview.

A decision also needs to be made about the level of information sharing:

- confidentiality—"This will be kept between the two of us."
- anonymity—"Your data will be made public, but you will not be quoted directly."
- full disclosure—"Your data will be made available to other people."

Note taking or tape recording can be a major disruption to the flow of the conversation. Consider using only key words during the interview and then expand the notes immediately after the interview.

Focus Groups

Another effective technique when using the small group method for task analysis is to use a focus group. Focus groups are fast and inexpensive. They can uncover information on how the job is performed because they allow in-depth probing. The data, however, tend to be more difficult to analyze, and because it is a group of job incumbents that are being interviewed, a trained facilitator is required.

Focus groups are especially useful for task analysis because participants have the opportunity to share their perceptions and knowledge about the job. Participants can share their feelings, and workers are often surprised to find they have much in common. Focus groups are effective in confirming how tasks are performed within the work setting.

For example, electronics enrollments were at an all-time low, and certain technical education entities wanted to find out what problems the instructors were having. See Figure 4-7. Focus groups were employed at three separate locations across the state, with four questions asked at each location to a group of 5 to 10.

DACUM Process

Developing a curriculum (DACUM) is a small group technique used almost exclusively for task analysis. DACUM is an occupational analysis process that taps the expertise of a small group of skilled workers to determine what knowledge, skills, standards, tools, and attitudes are required to perform a specific job. Through a highly structured process, participants brainstorm, question, and discuss content of the specific occupation in which they work. Sufficient detail is captured by this small group process to permit training, organized restructuring, employee recruitment, and career planning models to be developed and used, then updated as changes occur. It is an effective task analysis method used by both education and training organizations.

FIGURE 4-7

Electronics Instructor
Focus Group Questionnaire

1. Is there a need for specific training in curriculum design, teaching methodology, or technical skill to help students successfully complete your course? What training would be the most beneficial?

2. What kinds of collaboration and cooperative efforts are needed at your technical college to improve program offerings?

3. What training needs do you have for working with special populations:
   A. Differing ages?
   B. Gender?
   C. Race?

4. Should there be more cooperative efforts by the state system to assist you? What are your suggestions?

Focus groups allow in-depth probing.

CRITICAL INCIDENT

The critical incident method is basically a combination of direct observation and interviewing. It identifies the critical components of a job, duty, task, or performance behavior that influence job performance. Subject matter experts and/or supervisors classify the information collected. Critical incident data may be reports, observations, anecdotes, stories, logs, interviews, or focus group information.

An incident is a complete situation common to someone in a position, job, or role. It becomes critical because success spells the difference between adequate and inadequate performance.

The critical incident method was first developed during World War II to reduce pilot error. John C. Flanagan was a military psychologist faced with the problem of improving military flight training. Too many trainees were crashing planes, and it was suggested that the training was not emphasizing the critical things. Flanagan asked surviving pilot trainees what they had done incorrectly. He also interviewed successful first-time pilots. This examination resulted in "... identifying critical job requirements ... those behaviors which are critical in making the difference between doing a job effectively and doing it ineffectively" (FitzGerald, Seale, Kerins, & McElvaney, 2008).

A critical incident is an event that is judged to be important and may be an accident, problem, or successful action. It usually requires the participant to respond by explaining what is being described or recommending an action to be taken. A critical incident might read, "The machine stops, but all dials indicate normal." The analyst then identifies the possible causes of the machine stoppage based on what has been learned earlier.

Another example might be, "You are the new training director in a large organization. You are told that your predecessor was fired for spending all of her time in an ivory tower. What do you think you should do?" The critical incident technique has both advantages and disadvantages. See Figure 4-8.

Critical incident is very flexible and has many uses. It may be used to measure typical work performance, to determine levels of proficiency at the end of a training program, or to determine which duties and tasks are considered critical to a job. It can also be used to redesign existing jobs and remove barriers, to analyze the successes and failures of processes, especially for safety, and to modify or redesign equipment. The technique has been used to analyze specific actions dealing with leadership and attitudes and to improve counseling techniques with patients.

Despite its simplicity, this is a very helpful method. The major advantage of the critical incident process is that it is relatively simple and does not require sophisticated skills or complex statistical procedures. Since it is based on lessons learned the hard way, by experienced supervisors or employees, it appears to them to be more powerful. The major disadvantage is that it is past- or present-oriented; results are based on conditions existing at the time lessons were learned, not on future and perhaps different conditions likely to be faced by job incumbents. However, it is possible to simulate future job or group conditions and then prepare critical incidents based on those simulated experiences.

The critical incident technique is extremely useful for task analysis and has been employed in many areas, including health care and safety, as well as to gauge customer perceptions. Modifications can easily be made to the five-step process. It is very useful when working with subject matter experts (SMEs) to determine a task analysis for a specific field.

The five main steps of the critical incident process as developed by Flanagan are (1) identifying the general aims, (2) developing the plans and specifications, (3) collecting the data, (4) analyzing the data, (4) and interpreting and reporting the data.

FIGURE 4-8

CRITICAL INCIDENT

Advantages

- Critical incident identifies reliable, relevant, and valid task events.
- Criteria are based on objective evidence. Incidents point out job behaviors that can be used to develop criteria for training programs.
- Incidents reflect what people do on their jobs. Critical incident is handy for the development of performance appraisal instruments that are based on actual behaviors observed.
- Method is highly objective. Qualified observers' can identify behaviors and the effects of those behaviors.
- Observation documents the variety and complexity of performance by classifying incidents as the job is performed.
- Information gathered by this technique is very comprehensive.

Disadvantages

- It is critical to have qualified and trained observers and data collectors.
- Duties and tasks are essentially subjective and may be difficult to organize.
- Technique is time-consuming.
- Objectivity will always be questioned by the manner or style of training provided to data collectors.
- Routine or overgeneralization may produce trivial events that are not important.
- Critical incident has limited application to primary job analysis.
- Respondents' memory may have biases/preferences, and some events recorded may be subject to error.

The critical incident method has certain advantages and certain disadvantages. (Jonassen, Tessmer, & Hannum, 1999, pp. 189–190)

Step 1. Identify General Aims

This involves developing an introductory statement to guide the direction of the process. The goal of the process is a functional description of the activity that specifies precisely what is necessary to do and not do if participation in the activity is to be judged successful or effective. For example, an introductory statement may read, "We are doing a study of wet and dry packaging operators. We believe you are especially well-qualified to tell us about what you do as a packaging operator and what makes you effective and/or ineffective."

Step 2. Develop Plans and Specifications

Plans and specifications consist of instructions given to observers to focus their attention on those aspects of behavior that are crucial in formulating a functional description of the activity. This step answers the who, when, what, and how of the incident. The situations observed might include places, persons, conditions, and activities. Specifications may refer to the following:

- persons to make observations (knowledge concerning the activity, relations to those observed, training requirements)
- groups to be observed (general description, location, persons, times, conditions)
- behaviors to be observed (general type of activity, specific behaviors, criteria of relevance to general aim, criteria of importance to general aim)

Step 3. Collect the Data

Interviews, focus groups, and questionnaires are all good methods for collecting data. As data is collected, the behaviors or results should be evaluated, classified, and recorded while the facts are still fresh (within 24 hours).

Step 4. Analyze the Data

The purpose of this step is to summarize and describe the data so that it can be used effectively for practical purposes. A frame of reference must be used, usually in relation to selection, training, measurement of proficiency, or the development of procedures for evaluating on-the-job effectiveness. Categories must be formulated and the data divided into basic tasks. Finally, general behaviors need to be stated in terms of duties.

Step 5. Interpret and Report the Data

In this step, a report is presented with specific interpretation. The report can be used for the following:

- checklist for evaluation of performance
- at the end of training programs to determine levels of proficiency
- to identify task and duty, which are critical to the occupation of job
- as an assessment instrument for selection and classification purposes
- to analyze factual data on successes and failures to improve the effectiveness and efficiency of operations

Modifications

Since this process first appeared there have been modifications to it, as reported by Meister (1985). The following steps are an example:

1. Gather two groups of subject matter experts (SMEs).
2. Have the SMEs describe, in writing, specific job incidents and the results produced.
3. Have the SMEs sort the incidents into factors and then name the factors.

4. Have the SMEs sort the incidents as "good" and "bad" along a 7-point scale.
5. Have the SMEs fill any gaps in the scales with additional incidents.
6. After both groups have finished their tasks, bring the two groups together and let them look at each other's work and reconcile the differences.

Critical Incident Technique Tips

1. A good orientation for all people involved is essential. Providing a strong rationale for the study, reasons everyone can buy into, is important.
2. Anonymity must be assured of all job incumbents.
3. Give examples of critical incidents to illustrate that they are specific observed behaviors that lead to successful or unsuccessful outcomes.
4. Specify precise definitions for the observer's report. What kinds of incidents should an observer relay? An example may be to include an incident in which the job incumbent performed poorly because of inadequate training.
5. Establish the necessary criteria for conducting the critical incident study. For example: All observations must be direct or firsthand; incidents should focus on behavior rather than individuals; incidents should have occurred during the past couple of weeks.
6. Establish time limits and define the job or situation being observed.
7. Inform observers when, where, and how incidents should be collected.
8. Check to be sure that critical incidents are precise accounts rather than generalized stories or impressions.
9. Identify incidents that are causally related to consequences. For example, 50% of employees move to different floor to make room for another unit. Staff members on the new floor must travel back to the mailroom to pick up letters, messages and packages. Productivity drops and turnaround time for correspondence increases sharply. To remedy the situation, the supervisor of the mailroom implemented a plan whereby the mail is delivered and picked up twice a day on the new floor. Within one week productivity and correspondence rates returned to normal and are expected to exceed the norm. The supervisor's plan (behavior) led to increased efficiency (consequence).

10. Use individuals who know the job or occupation, such as peer workers and supervisors.
11. Observers should use good judgment. They should report whether or not a job is being performed according to standards; where, if at all, the discrepancies occurred; and if the end product is the same or better or worse than it should be. Observers should make recommendations or suggestions.
12. Consider using independent raters when forming categories for incidents. The results may be more objective and, therefore, more reliable.
13. Employees can also file critical incidents based on problems they encounter and the training department can review these on a continuous basis to determine training needs (Callanhan, 1992).

RESEARCH

The research method of doing a task analysis typically uses a mailed survey to gather data to identify what tasks are performed on the job. This method works well if there is a lot of lead time, adequate resources are available, there is an established occupation to analyze, and job incumbents are willing to participate.

A handy method of considering training curriculum or content development is asking the questions of what, why and how, process and product. A task analysis may be requested, but is it really needed? The questions asked depend on the approach to the occupation. See Figure 4-9. Products will be different depending on the question and process.

If one is asking why content is to be learned, actual content will not be uncovered. Policy decisions and training aims will be the products. If the question is what is the content to be learned, then specific content and intended learning will be the product. If the question being asked is how will the content be learned, then the products are instructional lesson plans. The actual teaching of the lesson is covered in the last question. A series of decisions starting with why, then moving to what, then how, provide for a progression of decisions resulting in students leaving the learning setting with new skills and knowledge.

FIGURE 4-9

Questions	Processes	Products
A. **Why** content is to be learned?	Policy setting	Policy decisions, training aims, mission
B. **What** is the content to be learned?	Training curriculum planning and outcomes	Curriculum content, intended learning outcomes
C. **How** is content to be learned?	Instructional planning and design of learning experiences	Instructional lesson plans
D. **How** are curriculum and instruction guides implemented with learners?	Instruction or teaching methods	Learning experiences

When considering content for a course, asking certain types of questions leads to enacting certain processes, which leads to specific products.

When planning an analysis of a complete job or occupation, a task analysis model is very helpful. See Figure 4-10. Each step in the model ensures outcomes that can be used to develop instruction that reflects the occupation or job. This model is especially useful for a training or education curriculum.

This is a very detailed process, consisting of 11 steps, but portions of it may be used to analyze a specific task or duty rather than a whole occupation. The main purpose of this task analysis is to uncover the existing duties and tasks in an occupation or job. The authors have used this process many times in varying situations, and it has produced excellent results.

Step 1. Define Occupation or Job

The first step in preparing for a task analysis is to narrow down the area to be analyzed. Will it be for part of a job, one specific job, or a cluster of jobs that have common content? This decision must be made as early as possible in the process to ensure proper focus.

If the job is defined narrowly and very specifically, the transferability to other jobs is limited. Jobs defined very broadly or in clusters of related jobs will usually result in a large number of duty and task statements and tend to be cumbersome. The needs assessment will help focus on the reasonable attributes of the job. Environmental factors, capabilities of staff, level of potential students, budget constraints, and available equipment, materials, and supplies will likely be factors in the definition of the scope of the occupation or job.

FIGURE 4-10

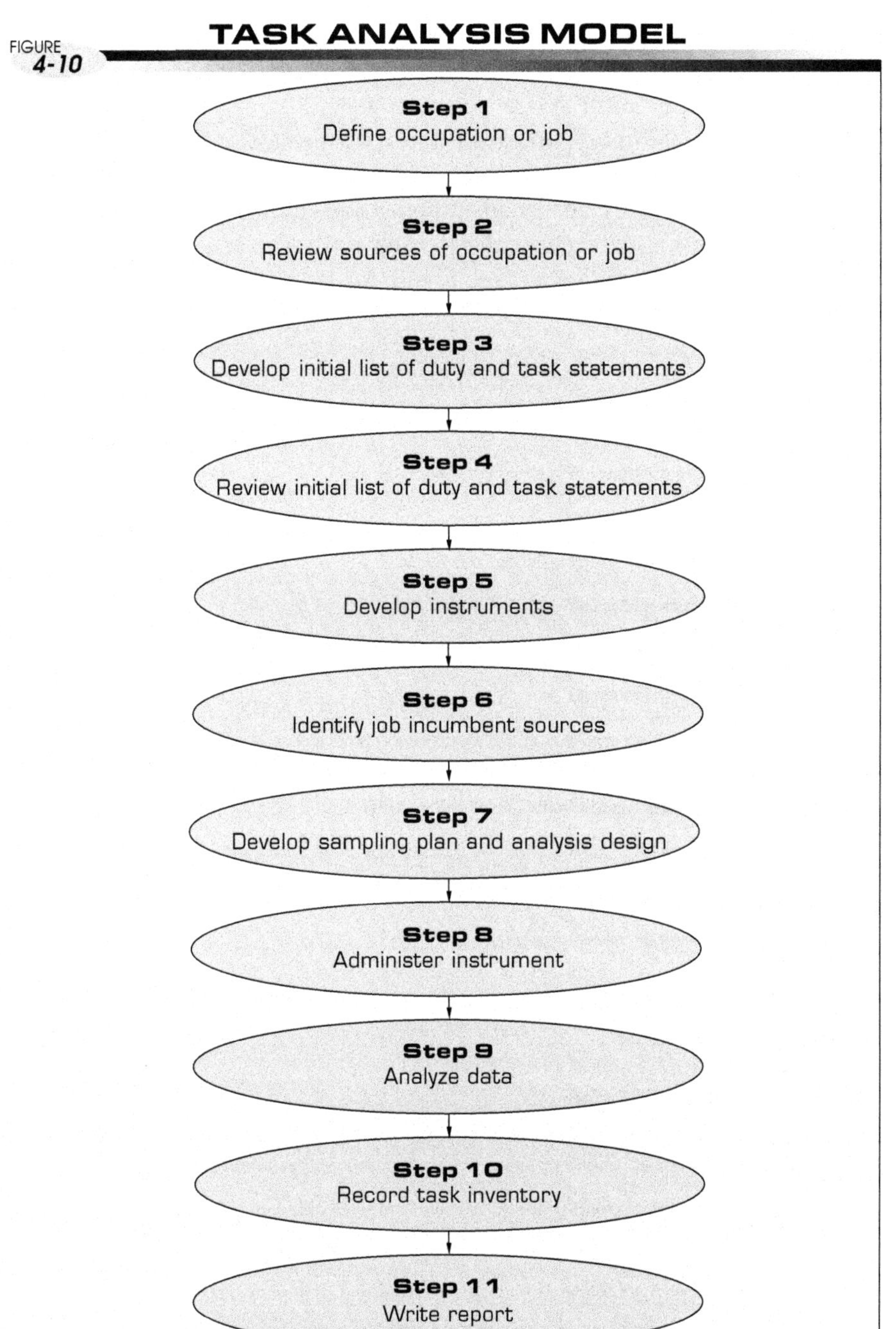

Following a model is helpful when planning a task analysis.

A large consideration for defining the occupation is the existing job description for the job or task being investigated. A job description is simply a narrative description of the occupation in general terms. It lists the duties, how these duties are to be performed, the skills needed to do the work, and why the job is necessary. In some cases, responsibilities, special aptitudes, and educational prerequisites are also identified. A job description is a summary of the important facts about a particular job and assists the analyst in narrowing down the job being investigated. See Figure 4-11.

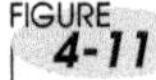
FIGURE 4-11

Job Description

Working Title: Packaging Machine Operator

Operation: General Operations

Pay Range Classification: Paraprofessional

Range of Possible Scheduled Hours: 1st, 2nd, or 3rd shift

Average Time Commitment: 40 hours per week, plus overtime if necessary

Minimum Qualifications:

A high school diploma is required, and a summer job or previous experience working as a packaging operator or any other positions along the production line is preferred.

Preferred Knowledge, Skills, and Abilities:

The person would have to be mechanically inclined and have good judgment and initiative. The person has to be ready to identify a problem and fix it. The person needs to be flexible, dependable, and able to concentrate on the task at hand.

Skills Developed in This Position:

Judgment
Flexibility
Dependability
Responsibility

General Responsibilities:

The Packaging Operator would tend the machines that perform one or more packaging functions. The Packaging Operator spends a majority of his/her time monitoring the production line. The person needs to be constantly looking for problems, such as pileups, jams, or glue that isn't sticking properly. Quality Control is also a huge aspect of the packaging operator job. Some packaging operators will be trained to maintain the equipment, control panels equipped with indicators, and flag any unforeseen changes.

A job description can provide the analysts with a good source of information about a job or occupation.

A description may provide not only a list of duties and tasks, but also the approximate time the worker spends on the task. These details can be helpful to the analyst in defining and narrowing down the occupation for the task analysis, which is critical. Research may be required, but in some cases, if there is an existing job description, the analysis is very straightforward. See Figure 4-12. Before starting the occupational analysis process, consider the following:

Geography. Will the approach be different for rural or urban populations? You might obtain different results for the same job depending on rural or urban settings. What about coastal/inland regions? Change generally occurs faster on either coast before being implemented in the Midwest. Are there any climate, north vs. south, or hot vs. cold conditions that may affect the analysis outcomes? What about cultural differences? Will any of these affect the results of the analysis? What will have to be overcome to address these possible concerns?

Outside Influences. Social, political, civic, agency, or department interaction may affect the analysis. At times there may be unusual contingency situations that need to be considered. One company asked for an occupational analysis because they felt machinists were making too many errors. It was found before the occupational analysis was started that machinists were working from incomplete designs. The problem was with the engineering department, not the machinists.

Incorrect Assumptions. As with any analysis in business and industry, the assumption is that there is a problem. In some cases this may not be true. Problems encountered on the job could be due to malfunctioning of equipment. Frequent equipment breakdown or using the wrong equipment, tools, or materials may be the problem. There may be severe time constraints, and unless the job incumbent is provided with more time to complete the task, it will not be correct. In an education setting, the focus is on determining the appropriate content to teach. Developing an educational program based on a visit to a single company may result in a program that is not serving the total needs of business and industry.

Scope of Analysis. Consider the scope of the task analysis. Is there interest in only one occupation, such as automotive mechanic or medical secretaries? Is it just part of an occupation or job, such as purchasing tasks or supervisory tasks? In a technical college setting, the analysis might include a cluster of related occupations, such as secretarial science or building construction. Is the interest in just entry preparation or the advanced development of experienced workers? The type of work may include an occupational cluster or may be a single duty across several related occupations. Perhaps the interest is in worker retraining or career advancement preparation. Should the analysis include a range of possible employment settings or be restricted to a particular location, industry, or employing agency?

FIGURE 4-12

Job Description			
Manager to Complete		**Human Resources to Complete**	
Position Title: Industrial Engineering Technican		**Range of Schedule Hours:** Primarily 1st shift. All other shifts as needed.	
Operation: General Factory	**Dept:** Production/Engineering	**FSLA Status:** Exempt	**Avg. Time Commitment:** 40 plus hours
Reports to: John Smith		**Pay Range Classification:** Professional/Technical Pay Band	
Title: Typically Production Manager or Engineer Manager		**Date Approved:** 4/08/15	**By:** HR Dept/Ritter & Geissler

POSITION SUMMARY:
Industrial Engineering Technicians assist Industrial Engineers with problems dealing with the efficient use of workers, materials, machines, equipment, and information in producing goods and providing services. They will provide support for improvement of overall production capabilities at the facility. Direct efforts to continuously improve yields, efficiencies and schedule attainment. Assist in setting standards and actively communicating the achieved results to all levels of the factory.

PRIMARY RESPONSIBILTIES:	% OF TIME
Selecting process equipment. • Evaluate process equipment. • Make recommendations on process information. • Conceptualize future equipment needs. • Maintain database for reference. • Serve as a communication bridge between management and supplier.	5%
Analyzing new equipment for appropriate design layout. • Create preliminary design of equipment layouts. • Plan the workflow associated with equipment installation. • Examine the impact of safety and quality. • Define start-up plans for equipment. • Determine auxiliary needs. • Assist in equipment installation. • Write technical reports and written descriptions of equipment.	10%
Testing performance and efficiency of people, processes, and systems • Perform line studies including downtime and analysis. • Conduct annual capacity studies. • Conduct time and motion studies to utilize available resources. • Inspect and evaluate the quality of products. • Develop measurement tools for production use. • Establish worker measurement programs.	25%
Optimizing efficiency of people and materials • Examine production costs for areas of improvement. • Examine production schedules for areas of improvement.	45% continued...

PRIMARY RESPONSIBILITIES:	% OF TIME
Optimizing efficiency of people and materials (continued). • Evaluate existing systems/materials for process improvement. • Diagnose equipment problems. • Develop standards for production efficiency. • Initiate use of robotics and/or automation. • Make recommendations for better ways of handling materials and/or improving standards. • Interact with production line workers. • Determine adequate spare part inventory.	45%
Analyzing equipment for new product implementation. • Evaluate process equipment for adaptation. • Evaluate scheduling for available capacity. • Determine resources needed for production. • Create preliminary graphical layout using CAD.	10%
Coordinating technical support training. • Make recommendations for training programs. • Develop training materials. • Provide troubleshooting guidelines to support daily production problems. • Accurately communicate technical instructions.	5%
Job descriptions are not intended to be exhaustive lists of all responsibilities, skills, or efforts. They are intended to be accurate summaries of what the position involves and what is required to perform it.	

Some job descriptions can be very detailed.

New and Emerging Trends. For any analysis, each occupation represented and new and emerging factors affecting the occupation need to be described. The geographic location, which affects the occupation, will also need to be described.

Distribution of Employment Opportunities. One final factor in determining the occupation to be analyzed concerns the distribution of employment opportunities. Is the particular occupation being analyzed nationwide, or just within the geographic region? Perhaps there is immediate employment within a company, which will limit the analysis, but serve the company. For training, the concern may be only within the plant or company.

Step 2. Review Sources of Occupation or Job Analyses

Once the scope of the task analysis has been determined, the second step in completing an analysis is to research other analyses for the selected occupation.

This involves searching research centers, Internet sources, catalogs, indexes, and other available references. The main questions asked are "Are there other analyses that have already been done in this occupation? If so, are these existing analyses useful for the task analysis being considered?" The purpose of this step is to find out what already exists and to decide if it can be used to jump-start the task analysis. See Appendix H.

Step 3. Draft Duty and Task Statements

In Step 1, the job or occupation was narrowed down. In step 2, a literature review should have provided a list of tasks and duties from the occupation. Step 3 in the task analysis process involves drafting relevant task and duty statements for the selected occupation or job. This draft of duty and task statements will eventually be sent out to job incumbents and supervisors who will rate the statements for importance and frequency of use. An understanding of the differences between a duty and a task might be helpful at this point.

Duty. A duty is a large segment of an occupation that contains a number of related tasks. It is a functional division of a job that represents a relatively large segment of work performed. Duties are usually divided into categories of related tasks for descriptive purposes. A duty statement is a label reflecting the types of tasks grouped under a particular job/occupation. In a lot of ways, a duty is an arbitrary segment of an occupation because there is no significant method for identifying a duty.

In general, there should be a minimum of two tasks to support each duty. There are generally 7 to 16 duties per job or occupation. Other common names for a duty are functions, categories, general areas of competency, and responsibilities. A duty is usually identified prior to the identification of the task, but the opposite might be true depending on the available information, the nature of the content, and the expertise of the analyzer.

When correctly stated, a duty contains an action word ending in "ing" to reflect a general area of responsibility or function, such as organizing, planning, implementing, training, inspecting, installing, etc. The relationship among tasks within a single duty is typically based upon a commonality of the following:

- types of action
- systems or subsystems of objects acted upon
- areas of responsibility
- location of time of performance
- work goals
- types of technical knowledge or subject matter that is of practical use in performing tasks

A duty statement is a single action word and a system acted upon. See Figure 4-13. Three duties typically performed by a teacher are developing curriculum, developing instructional materials and evaluating students' progress. Three of the duties performed in the occupation of photography technician are determining lighting requirements, exposing and developing film, and interpreting assignments and selecting appropriate procedure. The criteria for stating duties are as follows:

- The duty is based on job performance requirements.
- The duty is large enough and important enough to warrant instructional time.
- The segment of learning in the duty is somewhat independent of other segments.
- Tasks included are related in content, complexity, or level.

FIGURE 4-13

Job — Teacher

Duties:

1. Developing curriculum.
2. Developing instructional materials.
3. Evaluating student progress.

Job — Photography Technician

Duties:

1. Determining lighting requirements.
2. Exposing and developing films.
3. Interpreting assignment and selecting appropriate procedure.

A duty statement consists of an "ing" action word and the thing that is acted upon.

Duties as a major training segment for job preparation can be classified into either supervisory or work-related activities. Supervisory duties might include managing, supervising, organizing, planning, directing, training, inspecting, evaluating, etc. Work duties might include fabricating, maintaining, repairing, troubleshooting, removing, replacing, adjusting, installing, etc. There are many elements to each duty; this is where task statements come into play.

Task. A task is a meaningful unit of work activity performed on the job by a worker within a limited period of time. It involves exerted mental and/or physical effort toward the accomplishment of a predetermined goal. Tasks may be manipulative (psychomotor), informational (cognitive), or attitudinal (affective). Tasks are reflected by an action sequence designed to state what the learner is to do, to know, or to feel. Tasks are discrete learning items having a definite starting and stopping point and can be performed and/or learned within a relatively short period of time.

Task statements begin with an action verb and include a very brief and specific description of what is to be done or known. They may also include a qualifying phrase. See Figure 4-14. Tasks contain two or more steps (elements), and are essential for the completion of a job or work activity. Tasks are also the backbone of the content to be learned. They are measurable and observable and lead to a product, service, or decision.

FIGURE 4-14

Action	Object	Qualifier
Compute	product moment correlation	on desk calculator
Counsel	staff personnel	on career advancement
Replace	brake pads	
Submit	receiving reports	for new library books
Type	legal affidavits	

A task statement consists of an action verb, and object, and sometimes a qualifying phrase.

Each task statement contains an action verb, some object related to the verb, and a qualifier if needed. At times, different jobs within an occupation may use the same action verb for task statements to reflect different tasks. For example, "type legal leases" and "type medical records of patients." The same task statement may also be used in different occupations. For example, meteorology and art may have the same task statement of "interpret photographs." When writing task statements, avoid using ambiguous or vague verbs such as assist, assure, establish, manage, plan, or supervise.

Verbs that can be used on rating scales should be chosen. Where the object of an action is a paperwork form, the type of form should be indicated. For example, "job application form," or "stock inventory form." Multiple action verbs should not be used unless several actions are invariably performed together; for example, "clean, gap, and test spark plugs" not "inspect and remove spark plugs." Multiple objects should not be used unless they are acted upon together; for example, "replace ball joints and lubricate front suspension" not "adjust carburetor, brakes, and headlights."

Each task statement must be capable of standing alone. Technical terminology that is consistent with current usage should be chosen. Abbreviations should be used cautiously. The task statement should be grammatically correct.

Task statements of job-oriented tasks (what gets done) rather than worker-oriented statements (what the worker does) should be used. Statements that are too specific, such as "dial operator," "start machine," and "stop machine," should not be used.

Each task should meet the following criteria:

- be either manipulative, informational, or attitudinal
- have a definite starting point and ending point
- be self-contained and independent of others
- contain learning content that is beyond merely a step in the procedure in performing a skill or obtaining knowledge
- occupy a significant place in the career ladder development process
- be ratable
- be identified as a task by job incumbents
- include two or more steps to complete the task

In the job or occupation of a teacher who has the duty of evaluating students' progress, three task statements fall under the duty. See Figure 4-15. Each task begins with an action verb and would take several steps to complete. There are more task statements under this particular duty that are not noted. When all of the tasks are completed, a person would be competent in that duty. Other examples of a task include "attach stock with specified fasteners," "file incoming letters," "list safety regulations," and "identify kinds of finishes."

FIGURE **4-15**

Job — Teacher

Duty — Evaluating Students' Progress

Task — 1. Write multiple-choice test items.

2. Grade students' work.

3. Assign grades.

A duty is generally made up of several task statements.

Use the following checklist against any written task statement:

1. Avoid task statements that are too general or too specific.
2. Avoid obvious trivial tasks; for example, "count students."
3. Avoid task statements that are actually steps of tasks.
4. Use short words instead of long words or expressions.
5. Avoid vague or ambiguous words, such as "check," "work with," or "handle."
6. Avoid task statements that cannot be rated in terms of time spent on them. Example: "skills and knowledge" items that begin with words such as:
    a. "Have responsibility for"
    b. "Know how to"
    c. "Understand"
    d. "Have knowledge of"
7. Avoid redundant qualifying phrases, such as "in accordance with," "as required," "as necessary," "when appropriate," or "as appropriate."
8. When qualifying the task, use "such as" followed by two or three examples. Avoid "and/or" and "etc."
9. Tasks should be independent and distinct.
10. Avoid compound objects if possible.
11. Avoid the use of colons or semicolons. This suggests the statement is probably too long or represents a combination of tasks.
12. Use practitioner/field terminology so that the task will have the same meaning to all administrators.
13. Keep statements brief.
14. Avoid overlap between tasks within or between duties. A task may appear only once in a task list.
15. Look for parallel tasks across duties, for example:
    a. Equipment that is purchased is probably inventoried.
    b. Equipment that is inspected is probably repaired.
16. Whenever possible, avoid multiple verbs in a task statement, unless the actions are always performed together.
17. Spell out all abbreviations, at least the first time they are used, followed by the abbreviation in parenthesis.
18. Each statement should stand alone as a sentence (the pronoun "I" is understood; the sentence begins with the verb).

Many guidelines indicate that task inventories for a job should contain 150 to 400 task statements. Most job incumbents are not willing to spend more than an hour responding to an instrument. Borcher and Melching (1973), indicate that respondents with higher aptitudes were more likely to return the questionnaire. Their Ohio State University experience shows that secretaries are more likely to fill out and return a longer questionnaire than auto mechanics. Questionnaires containing fewer than 150 task statements may yield limited information about a job, and 400 statements probably indicate unnecessary details.

The number of task statements in an inventory is largely dependent on the scope of the task analysis noted in step 1. If the occupation or job was defined very broadly, many duty and task statements will be developed. On the other hand, if it was defined very narrowly, or as part of a job, there will be few tasks developed. The size and scope of the job also affects the number of tasks. A roofing job will have fewer tasks than a carpentry job.

Step. A step is a listing of very small specific performances or knowledge items. It does not stand alone but is put together with other steps in the correct sequence to form a task. Task steps describe exactly what the learner is to do, or know, and are the smallest units into which a task can be divided. See Figure 4-16. Examples of steps include "remove the left pin," "avoid touching hot element," "record temperature data," and "return to start."

FIGURE **4-16**

Job — Teacher

Duty — Evaluating Students' Progress

Task — 1. Write multiple-choice test items.

Steps:
1. Review objectives
2. Write a stem that presents a definite problem.
3. State the problem. Be specific, clear and as brief as possible.
4. Use illustrations to demonstrate the problem.
5. Write four, or preferably, five choices.
6. Place all choices at the end of the stem.
7. Write all choices so they are grammatically consistent with the stem.
8. List each choice on a separate line.
9. Disperse the correct response.

A task is made up of steps.

Step 4. Review Initial List of Duty and Task Statements

Once lists of duty and task statements are drafted they need to be reviewed to ensure consistency. The purpose of this step is to review the inventory, edit and regroup, and pilot test the statements.

Review the Inventory. This step is useful in adding missing task statements or deleting irrelevant tasks. This is the opportunity to improve vague wording or lengthy task statements and to clarify them. It might be helpful to use reviewers, such as advisory committee members or consultants who have job knowledge or practical experience within the area. It is also wise to include a job incumbent and supervisor. The number of people used for this review will vary with the list of duty and task statements. Generally, five to eight individuals should be sufficient, but more is better. This review might best be handled as an interview.

Consider the following when conducting the review:

- Is the task statement clear? Will everyone understand what this means?
- Is this task covered by a previous task statement?
- Does the task fit better under another duty?
- Are there any other tasks that should be under this duty?
- Is the task performed in your business?
- Do any workers in the occupational area perform the task?

Edit and Regroup. Once all the reviewers have returned the duty and task statements and they have been tabulated and/or summarized, comments can be incorporated into the draft. Sometimes, additional technical consultation is needed. Each statement is checked for consistency. At the very minimum, each task statement should have a single action verb and something acted upon. It may be necessary to regroup the statements and arrange them in some logical order. They might be sequenced in terms of when they are learned, in terms of interest, chronologically, or by what is natural to the job incumbent.

Pilot Test the Items. Once the task statements have been reviewed, edited, and regrouped, they can be pilot tested to obtain some firsthand feedback from incumbents about the communicability of the statements. Job incumbents who represent the occupation should be used. In this phase, each statement should be read to determine if it is clear enough for the pilot test. Also, any obvious missing tasks should be added.

With the completion of this step, the duty and task statements are now ready to be placed into some kind of questionnaire so that a larger sample of job incumbents can respond.

Step 5. Develop Instrument

Step 5 consists of selecting a rating scale, developing the instrument instructions, determining background information items, and writing cover and follow-up letters. All of these stages are important, related, and must be accomplished to ensure a good return. (Additional information on rating scales can be found in Chapter 2.)

Survey Design Tips

1. Make sure you use random selection when deciding whom to survey.
2. Use a small sample size and try to get them all returned.
3. Avoid the temptation to ask too much. This should be a pinpoint investigation, not a fishing expedition.
4. Leave white space for respondents to insert comments.
5. Number each page.
6. Use the simplest wording possible.
7. Begin with simple, non-threatening words.
8. Emphasize key words with bold type, underlining or italics.
9. Don't put key items at the end.
10. Don't hint at the desired answer.
11. Avoid items that are worded negatively. If you must use them, bold the word "not."
12. Avoid words that are too open to interpretation (e.g. occasionally, sometimes, seldom, etc.).
13. Always have an open-ended session for write-in responses.
14. Avoid biased scales (e.g., 5 choices: excellent, very good, good, acceptable, unacceptable—4 choices are positive and only one is negative).

Select Rating Scale. The purpose of a rating scale is to permit job incumbents to make judgments about a particular task statement. Do they agree that the task statement represents what they do? How important is the task statement in terms of their present job? With what frequency do they perform the task? Rating scales allow respondents to express themselves using a rating that can be easily tabulated and used to determine the importance of teaching one task over another. See Appendix A. There are advantages and disadvantages with using a rating scale. See Figure 4-17.

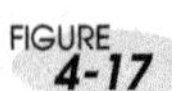

FIGURE 4-17

RATING SCALES

Advantages

- Rating scales may be administered to people or job incumbents at the same time. A mailed or web survey can be adjusted to arrive on the same day for each participant, regardless of their location.
- Participants are given time to think about their answers with rating scales. Because most surveys are either mailed or administered on the Internet, job incumbents can take as long as they wish to thoughtfully consider each response.
- Rating scales provide greater uniformity across measurement. The responses are confined to established criteria. If the scale is numbered 1–5, then each number has a meaning attached to it.
- Data is easily analyzed when using rating scales. Rating scales permit a numerical value to be assigned to each response, thus facilitating the analysis. The numerical value for each response may be tabulated manually or scanned for easy central tendency calculations.
- Rating scales may be mailed or administered to large groups of people. A large number of job incumbents can be sampled simultaneously reducing survey results contamination. Job incumbents in different locations can be surveyed.
- Anonymity is assured when using rating scales. Respondents need not identify themselves, and this usually increases the return rate.

Disadvantages

- Rating scales are not as flexible as interviews. There is no opportunity for respondents to ask questions or to probe responses.
- Many people can express themselves better orally, in person, or on the telephone. With a rating scale, respondents never really have the opportunity to express their concern about each item.

Using rating scales has both advantages and disadvantages.

For example, when rating scales are received through the mail or via Internet, respondents can take time with their responses. However, rating scales are not as flexible as one-on-one interviews.

Rating scales may take different forms (Falletta, 2008). A five-point rating scale is typically used to spread responses. Figure 4-18 gives responses typically used in a five-point Likert or agreement rating scale.

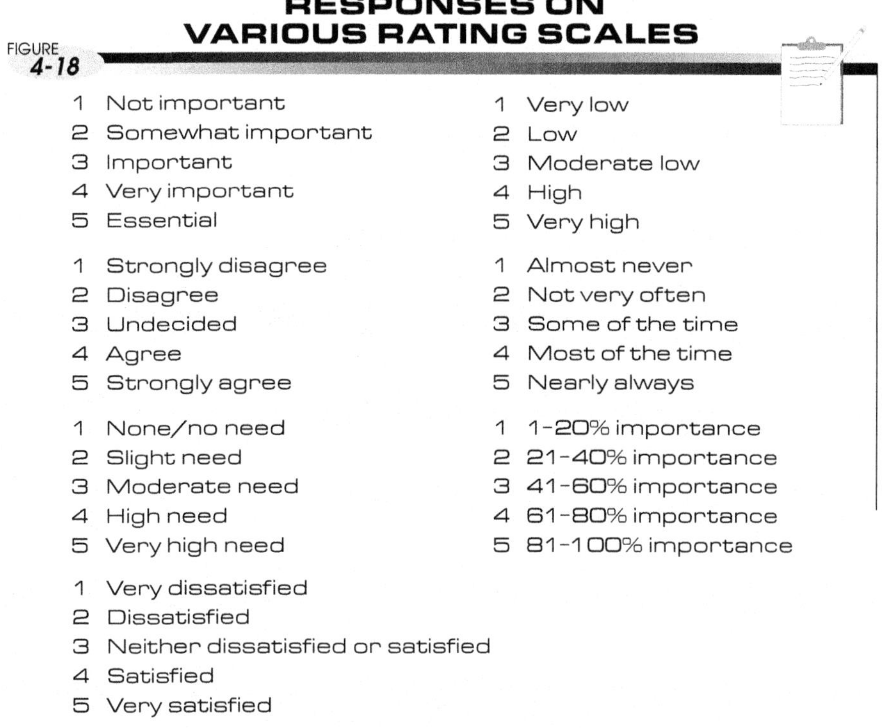
FIGURE 4-18

RESPONSES ON VARIOUS RATING SCALES

1 Not important
2 Somewhat important
3 Important
4 Very important
5 Essential

1 Very low
2 Low
3 Moderate low
4 High
5 Very high

1 Strongly disagree
2 Disagree
3 Undecided
4 Agree
5 Strongly agree

1 Almost never
2 Not very often
3 Some of the time
4 Most of the time
5 Nearly always

1 None/no need
2 Slight need
3 Moderate need
4 High need
5 Very high need

1 1-20% importance
2 21-40% importance
3 41-60% importance
4 61-80% importance
5 81-100% importance

1 Very dissatisfied
2 Dissatisfied
3 Neither dissatisfied or satisfied
4 Satisfied
5 Very satisfied

Five-point scales are often used for a spread of responses.

While only one of these rating scales would be used in a single survey, these options allow a survey to be customized to a specific audience. It is important that audience members understand what is being asked of them as they use the rating scale to indicate their level of agreement about the task.

When using rating scales with task statements, consider the following information:

- how often each task is performed by a job incumbent
- how often each task should be performed

- proportion of job incumbents concerned with each task
- importance of each task to effective (business) operation
- existence of a discrepancy between what is done and what job incumbents should do
- how soon task competence is expected after assignment
- tasks for which all essential learning can be, and is being, adequately acquired on the job in the time available
- tasks for which all essential learning has occurred prior to school attendance
- tasks on which job incumbents are having difficulty in acquiring competence on the job
- tasks for which training difficulties are being experienced
- tasks for which procedures could be improved through school training efforts

While there are numerous possibilities, not every question identified above should be asked. Serious consideration should be made to narrowing down what is desired based on the scope of the study, and selecting a rating scale that represents what the survey is attempting to measure. It is a good idea to keep the response burden low by not putting more than two or three rating scales on a single questionnaire.

If it has been determined that it is desirable to know if the task is important and the frequency of performance, the performance scale might read 1 = not applicable, 2 = not important, 3 = slight importance, 4 = some importance, 5 = high importance, 6 = critical, and the frequency of use scale might read 1= never, 2 = seldom (1 – 2 times per year), 3 = monthly, 4 = weekly, 5 = daily.

It may be important to involve supervisors as well as job incumbents. The questions might be as follows:

1. actual task occurrence (worker rating)
2. desired task occurrence (supervisor rating)
3. extent to which task is part of position (worker rating)
4. extent to which task is part of job (supervisor rating)
5. frequency of performance (worker rating)
6. frequency of performance (supervisor rating)
7. task importance to job (worker rating)
8. task importance to job (supervisor rating)

These questions imply that there would be two surveys, one for job incumbents and one for supervisors. The task statements would be identical, but the rating scales would be different. Utilizing this method, discrepancy between supervisors and job incumbents can be uncovered. The assumption is that supervisors have work experience and/or are keenly aware of what workers are supposed to be doing. See Appendix A.

Another consideration in the selection of the rating scale is tabulation and analysis. If tabulation is done manually, then a simple rating scale should be considered. If it is done with a scan sheet, then more sophisticated rating scales can be employed. A typical survey consisting of task statements along with the rating scale can now be developed. See Figure 4-19.

FIGURE 4-19

B. Assisting with changes in occupancy

Please rate each task according to its importance and frequency. Place an X in the column that best describes the task.

Check if performed by beginning worker	Task	Importance 1: Of no importance	2: Of limited importance	3: Of some importance	4: Of considerable importance	5: Of extreme importance	Frequency 1: Rarely performed	2: Performed monthly	3: Performed weekly	4: Performed daily	5: Performed continuously
	1. Assist with admissions procedures										
	2. Assist with transporting resident										
	3. Assist with discharge procedures										

This typical survey consists of a duty, task statements, and a rating scale.

In Figure 4-19, the duty is stated first (assisting with changes in occupancy), with some tasks listed below and to the left. The rating scales, consisting of importance and frequency, are noted to the right. Each rating scale has five possible choices. Note also that an extra box to the left of each task is provided to determine if beginning workers perform the particular task. This will be of valuable assistance when establishing the training or education program. (Additional information on rating scales can be found in Chapter 2.)

Develop Instructions. Once the rating scale has been selected, the next step is to write instructions for the survey. The instructions inform the readers how they are to proceed and let them know when they are done. The instructions should also explain the rating scale. See Figure 4-20. The instructions direct the job incumbent to circle the appropriate response in relationship to the task.

FIGURE 4-20

Instructions:

Please read and answer the questions below by circling the appropriate number. If a task is relevant to your position, you will be rating how often you perform the task and how important that task is to your job. If the question is not relevant to you or your position, please circle *unimportant.* There are empty blanks provided at the end of this survey for you to add other duties or tasks that you feel are relevant that have not been covered.

Importance of the Task	Frequency of Performance
1. U - Unimportant	1. N - Never
2. MI - Moderately Important	2. S - Seldom
3. I - Important	3. M - Monthly
4. VI - Very Important	4. W - Weekly
5. EI - Extremely Important	5. D - Daily

Instructions inform the reader of what steps to take and explain how the rating scale works.

The instructions that accompany the nursing assistant duties and task statements and the rating scale previously shown is another example. These instructions let the readers know what they are supposed to do to complete the survey. See Figure 4-21.

In the last example, the directions are to the left, with importance and frequency again used. Note that frequency has only a three-point scale. See Figure 4-22.

Determine Background Information. Many surveys provide a section to solicit background information of respondents. The main purpose of this section of the survey is to collect data that describes the characteristics of respondents. It also serves to permit comparative analysis within groups. For example, is there a difference in how incumbents respond based on education, years of experience, or age? Is this of interest? It is easy enough to describe the different levels of education of those who responded to the survey, such as 40% are high school graduates, 50% are technical school graduates, and 10% have more than a two-year degree.

FIGURE
4-21

Nursing Assistant Task Survey
Western College, La Crosse, Wisconsin

Directions: The following survey is intended to identify those nursing assistant skills essential for an entry-level industry worker. Your careful completion of the document will help assist the State Nurses Registry in setting nursing assistant certification requirements and help Western College develop effective training programs.

The survey is divided into 11 duties. Below each duty are corresponding tasks. First, check the box on the far left if an entry-level employee typically performs that task. Second, place an X in the box that indicates (1) the importance of the task, and (2) the frequency with which it is performed. You may add any duties and tasks you believe have been omitted on the bottom of the page.

These instructions let the readers know what they are supposed to do to complete the survey.

FIGURE
4-22

Please read the following task statements. Place an X in the box that best describes each task statement. For each statement, you will have one check for the level of importance and one check for the frequency used. *Optional:* List and rate any additional task statements on the last page.

Level of Importance	**Frequency Used**
1 = Of no value	1 = Monthly
2 = Of slight use	2 = Weekly
3 = Moderately useful	3 = Daily
4 = Quite useful	
5 = Extremely useful	

Instructions can be written and formatted in a variety of ways.

A more interesting question might be, "Is there any difference in responses based on educational level?" If it was found that more high school graduates responded to the task statements than technical school graduates, then perhaps the hiring practices need to be changed. If the background information was not noted, then this analysis is not possible. Typical background information collected is as follows:

- present job title
- type of business where employed.
- years of experience or years at present job
- where training was received
- female/male
- size of company
- location within company

These items can be placed within the survey to solicit background information for the nursing assistant program. See Figure 4-23. Specific questions may request information determined to be useful for analyzing the data in terms of the number of years ago they received their training and where they received their training.

In another example, information on incumbents' present job title, the type of business in which they work, years of experience, and where they received their training is determined to be useful for the analysis. See Figure 4-24. Analyzing the data in terms of the number of years ago they received their training and where they received training can, thus, be segmented by these categories that would be factors in the analysis

Write Cover Letter. The cover letter is a very important document that introduces the whole survey to the reader. This is the item that hooks the job incumbent into the questionnaire and gives the incumbent a reason for completing the questionnaire and returning it on time. It is always best to use official letterhead stationary when printing a cover letter. This is especially true if incumbents can identify with the company and/or educational entity on the letterhead. The seven essentials that should be in any cover letter are (1) the heading, (2) the purpose of the questionnaire, (3) a request for assistance, (4) the deadline, (5) a guarantee of anonymity, (6) information on obtaining the results, and (7) a closing. See Appendix C.

Heading—Every effort should be made to customize the letter to respondents with a salutation. Proving their name, title, and address will personalize the letter and should elicit cooperation. It is also important that a date is noted. Keep in mind that it sometimes takes time to get the cover letter and correspondence put together, so the date should reflect as closely as possible the mailing time frame.

Purpose of the Questionnaire—Why is data being collected? How will the data be used? This needs to be explained in the cover letter. This portion of the correspondence will establish a link between the profession and the job incumbent. Making a solid connection to the profession will get the attention of the respondent.

FIGURE
4-23

Nursing Assistant Task Survey

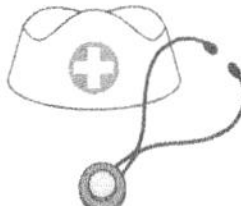

Sponsored by
Western College
and
State Nurses Registry

Thank you for participating in this study.

You may use either pen or pencil to complete the entire document. The survey focuses on skills performed by nursing assistants in Wisconsin. All information provided by you will be used for data collection purposes only and will be kept strictly confidential.

Before proceeding, please provide the following background information. Place an X in the box that most closely describes you.

1. At what age did you receive your nursing assistant training?

☐ 15 to 19 years old ☐ 26 to 31 years old
☐ 20 to 25 years old ☐ 32 years and older

2. Where did you receive your nursing assistant training?

☐ Vocational-technical college
☐ In high school
☐ In a nursing home facility
☐ Other (please describe)

3. How many years have you been a certified nursing assistant?

☐ 0 to 5 years
☐ 6 to 10 years
☐ 11 to 15 years
☐ 16 years and over

4. Are you currently employed as a nursing assistant?

☐ Yes (proceed to question #5) ☐ No (turn to next page to continue)

5. How many beds are in the nursing facility where you are currently employed?

☐ 1 to 60 beds ☐ 141 to 200 beds
☐ 61 to 140 beds ☐ Over 200 beds

Background information in a survey permits comparative analysis with groups.

FIGURE 4-24

Background Information

Check your present job title:

- ☐ Automotive mechanic apprentice
- ☐ Job specialist
- ☐ Automotive mechanic
- ☐ Service manager
- ☐ Service advisor or writer
- ☐ Garage owner

Other (specify) ______________________________

Check the type of business in which you presently work:

- ☐ New car dealer
- ☐ Service station
- ☐ Independent garage

Other (specify) ________

How many years have you worked as an automotive mechanic?

________Years

Where did you receive your training in automotive mechanics? (Check all that apply)

- ☐ On-the-job
- ☐ Apprenticeship program
- ☐ Military training school
- ☐ High school program
- ☐ Private automotive mechanic school
- ☐ Post-high school program
- ☐ Company training program
- ☐ Adult education program

Questions can be categorized and segmented for ease of analysis.

Request for Assistance—In this portion of the cover letter, the exact assistance is spelled out: "We would appreciate if you would take a few minutes to complete and mail back the attached survey." In some cases the survey may not be in the hands of the appropriate person; for example, the job incumbent may have been promoted. A request that the survey find its way to an expert in the field is helpful.

Deadline—Providing a due date for the return of the questionnaire is important. This lets the respondent know when the survey needs to be completed and in the mail. This is usually one or two weeks after receiving the questionnaire. The receipt of the questionnaire by the respondents and the deadline need to be coordinated.

Anonymity—Cover letters need to offer assurances that the information will be handled in a confidential manner. Respondents might not complete the questionnaire about their job if they feel the information could be traced back to them or their supervisor. Surveys are sometimes numbered to keep track of when questionnaires are returned or for follow-up purposes. This needs to be explained in the cover letter.

Results—Many respondents want information about how they can access survey results. Will the results be mailed or posted on the web? Sometimes a results request return card can be enclosed with the survey. The completion and return of the card indicates that respondents are requesting that the results of the survey be mailed to them.

Closing—This section of the letter includes a sentence thanking the respondents for their cooperation and participation in the survey and a salutation that includes a name, title, contact information, and a signature (Dillman, Smyth, & Christian, 2014). See Figure 4-25.

Write Follow-Up Letter. A process for a follow-up before the cover letter and questionnaire have been mailed should be part of any mailed survey process. The purpose of the follow-up is to increase the return rate of mailed or web surveys by providing another exposure to the questionnaire. It has been the authors' experience that a follow-up approximately two weeks after the initial mailing usually produces additional returned questionnaires. In the follow-up letter, it is important to review items from the original cover letter with emphasis on the participant's input. The letter should be shorter with a new deadline. See Figure 4-26.

Whether to attach another questionnaire or not is often a budgetary decision. If it can be afforded, another survey can be attached. This will save time if the original has been lost or misplaced. The survey can be run on a different-colored paper so responses from the first and second mailing can be kept separate and analyzed separately to identify differences in response patterns. If the questionnaire is not attached, some specific ways to obtain the survey should be noted in the follow-up letter. Sometimes a postcard or reminder note will suffice. See Figure 4-27. Points to remember are as follows:

- The follow-up letter should be sent two or three weeks after the original mailing.
- It should summarize items from the original cover letter, with emphasis on the participant's input. It should be kept shorter than the original letter.
- A new deadline of one week should be given.
- A new questionnaire or a note letting the respondent know how to obtain a questionnaire should be included.

FIGURE 4-25

WESTERN COLLEGE

304 South Street
P.O. Box 888
Five Rivers, Wisconsin 54602
(631) 555-9172

September 8, 20__

<Respondent Name>
<Institution>
<Address>
<City, State, Zip>

Dear <Respondent Name:>

Western College and the State Nurses Registry are conducting a joint study to identify the skills and competencies required to be an effective nursing assistant. As a Certified Nursing Assistant registered in the state of Wisconsin, your name was randomly selected as one of the 384 participants in this project, and we value your comments. This important project will shape the training program for nursing assistants and define skills necessary for certification. Your expertise is critical and will assist us in curriculum development by:

- Identifying critical skills necessary for a certified nursing assistant;
- Identifying skills no longer necessary for a certified nursing assistant;
- Ranking job tasks in order of their importance and difficulty; and
- Identifying skills that are critical for entry-level nursing assistants.

Enclosed is a seven-page questionnaire. Responding to the survey should take approximately one hour. We are asking that you complete and return the survey to us by September 23. A stamped, self-addressed mailer is enclosed for your convenience. Your responses will be kept confidential and will be used only for data collection.

The data gained from this project will provide a broad, statewide perspective of the certified nursing assistant occupation. As a participant, you are entitled to a complimentary survey summary. If you would like to obtain a summary or have any questions about completing this survey, please call project coordinator, Karen Jones, at (631) 555-9172.

Thank you for your commitment to the health care profession. Your experience and knowledge is valuable to us.

Sincerely,

Karen Jones, Project Coordinator
Western College
888 South Street
Five Rivers, Wisconsin 54602

Richard Smith. Certification Officer
State Nurses Registry
555 North Street
Madison, Wisconsin 53705

Cover letters explain information on the questionnaire and the manner and time in which it should be completed.

FIGURE
4-26

304 South Street
P.O. Box 888
La Crosse, Wisconsin 54602
(631) 555-9172

September 15, 20__

<Respondent Name>
<Institution>
<Address>
<City, State, Zip>

Dear <Respondent Name:>

Thank you for your interest in the Nursing Assistant Survey that you received last week. We would like to encourage you to complete the survey and return it to us by September 23. The information gathered from the survey will be critical in guiding the Certified Nursing Assistant Program at Western College.

Rest assured that the information you provide will be held in strictest confidence. If you have misplaced the survey or the response envelope, please contact Karen Jones at (631) 555-9172, and the materials will be forward to you. Your input is essential to the success of this project.

Thank you.

Sincerely,

Karen Jones, Project Coordinator
Western College
304 South Street
Five Rivers, Wisconsin 54602

A follow-up letter should be developed as part of the survey process.

FIGURE 4-27

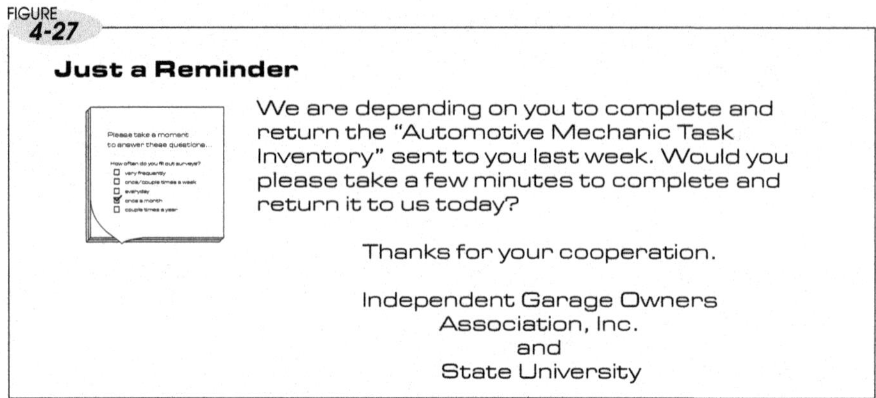

Just a Reminder

We are depending on you to complete and return the "Automotive Mechanic Task Inventory" sent to you last week. Would you please take a few minutes to complete and return it to us today?

Thanks for your cooperation.

Independent Garage Owners
Association, Inc.
and
State University

A reminder note may help in increasing the number of returned surveys.

Step 6. Identify Job Incumbent Sources

In most cases, the survey will need to be distributed and collected. The questionnaires could be distributed in person, mailed, or made available on the web. In person can be very effective, especially if a large number of job incumbents are meeting together. For example, job incumbents may be attending an association meeting whereby the surveys could be distributed in person. However, receiving them back as they leave the event is sometimes a problem, especially if time and writing instruments are not provided. Contacting job incumbents to complete a survey might work well if it were mailed to them, but a decision must be made whether to send the survey to their homes or places of work. Sending job incumbents an e-mail and having them hit a link, which brings them to the web survey, would work well, especially if all job incumbents have access to the Internet.

It may be desirable to contact employee organizations, employer organizations, professional organizations, or employers and employees directly to solicit participation. These entities may provide a mailing or an e-mail list of members or suggestions as to where the survey could be administered in person. Securing endorsements from various organizations is always desirable and usually leads to high participation rates.

Besides providing names, these organizations could also cooperate in a sampling of the total membership and suggestions as to whether mailing directly to the worker at work or at home might be more desirable. Sometimes reminder cards (before and after the survey is received) are used. Also, an article written in the organization's newsletter can be an effective communication tool.

Step 7. Develop Sampling Plan and Analysis Design

Developing a sampling plan and analysis design is very important for reliability of any survey. Sampling and deciding the kinds of analysis that will be undertaken once the surveys are returned needs to be decided before the surveys are mailed out.

Sampling. Very few surveys take in the total population, so sampling becomes an important tool for the researcher. It might be helpful to understand some important concepts in sampling by looking at some definitions. Population is all of the people in the study to which generalizations will be applied. A sample is a representative group of individuals or elements from the total population.

The sample selection process occurs prior to the construction and validation of the data-gathering instrument. The sample selection and instrument development are interrelated. Since samples are used to draw inferences about a population, the population must be clearly defined. Using procedures that are not representative of the population bring into question the confidence in their response and the survey. Sampling can be divided into four types: (1) the simple random sample, (2) the systematic sample, (3) the cluster sample, and (4) the stratified sample.

Simple Random Sample—In this type of sample, every person in the population has an equal chance of being selected. Being selected as a member of a random sample is based purely on chance. This method is not used often, because, in most cases, it is not efficient. Let's say that your total population is 100 people and you want to select 25 as a random sample. You need to give each person a number, 1 – 100, and then use a table of random numbers to select your sample.

Computer programs are available to generate a random sample for a given population. If the names or identification labels for the members of the population are stored in a computer data bank, it is relatively easy to obtain or write a program that will randomly select members from the population and print a list of names, addresses, and/or other data on the members of the sample. The names and addresses may be printed directly on mailing labels to facilitate a mail survey. This procedure gives everyone in the population an equal chance of being selected for the sample and that is the basic requirement of a simple random sample.

Systematic Sample—This is a version of the simple random sample, but only one out of every 3, 5, 6, 10, etc., is selected. This is a more common procedure. In this procedure, you would take every Kth person from the list when K = N/n, where N is the total population and n is the sample size. For example, in the same 100 people, the sample size is 25. What is the Kth person? The answer is 4 because 100 ÷ 25 = 4.

This brings up a sampling frame. A sampling frame is the actual list used to select the sample. A sampling frame may be the business office printout listing all drill press operators by an identification number. That list becomes the sampling frame. The sampling frame could be a phone directory.

Cluster Sample—This type of sample takes advantage of the existence of natural classes or groups in the population. People are clustered in houses, offices, factories, dorms, grades, ages, etc. The cluster is selected depending on the data being collected. Once the cluster has been defined, a sample of that cluster is taken. In a cluster sample, only a certain population is looked at.

Stratified Sample—This sampling ensures that certain groups are adequately represented in the sample. In this method, the population is divided into strata, or groups of concern to your study. To stratify, as used in sampling, means to break up the people or things to be sampled into groups that have common characteristics distinguishing them from other groups. Let's say all drill press operators are being surveyed within two companies. One company has 100 and the other has 20 drill press operators. Stratified sampling implies that you take a portion of the 100 and a portion of the 20 to include in the sample.

Sample Size. Sample size should be selected based on the level of accuracy needed for the study. Sample size is really concerned with two basic items: level of precision and level of confidentiality.

Level of precision deals with error levels and how much can be tolerated. An error rate of ±5% is acceptable in most instances. To decrease the error rate, the sample size should be increased. Level of confidence deals with the generalizability of the results. In other words, if the sampling is repeated, will the same results occur? See Appendix E.

Dealing with Nonrespondents—After surveys are returned, the researcher needs to contact nonrespondents, either through the mail or by phone. This will usually produce another 12% to 15% of returns. Nonrespondents may complete the questionnaire by mail or over the phone. The nonrespondents may be asked a sample of the questions or all of the questions. This information is then summarized and the findings compared to the findings of the other returned surveys. Usually the results will be the same, and if not, the researcher will have to adjust and discuss the difference in findings.

Sample Design—The following are steps in the sample design process:

- Decide on the population. Consider the cost implications of your population definition for various sample sizes.
- Select or set up a sampling frame, that is, a list of all the units in the population from which a random selection can be made.
- Decide on how much "error" can be tolerated.
- Consider the various sampling designs and select a design.

Analysis Design. Analysis design deals with how the data will be analyzed and how to decide whether to use the task in the curriculum. Since a rating scale is being used, basic descriptive statistics would be useful to calculate. Computer spreadsheet programs or specialized programs can be used to provide summary data. These resources should be prepared as the instrument is being developed so any questions about the design can be added. Likewise, it is wise to discuss the analysis of data and how it might be presented before the questionnaire is mailed.

A key decision that needs to be made before the survey is sent out is the selection criteria of the task once the data is tabulated. A decision table is a handy tool to assist the researcher in formulating the decision. The decision may be to accept the task for training, reject the task for training, or to question the task. A decision table provides specific criteria to aid in making one of the three decisions.

For example, suppose that a task analysis survey instrument was developed using a 5-point rating scale of "importance of a task." The importance scale consisted of 1 = not applicable, 2 = not important, 3 = important, 4 = very important, and 5 = highly important. The survey was sent out and summary data of the mean and standard deviation of each item was noted. The job of the researcher is to now decide which tasks will be retained for the curriculum, which will be questioned, and which will not be used in the curriculum. See Figure 4-28.

FIGURE 4-28

DECISION TABLE

Mean ($\bar{X}$)	SD	Rating	Decision
3.5 – 5.00	<1.0	High	Include
3.5 – 5.00	>1.1	Medium	Question
1.0 – 3.4	><1.1	Low	Omit/Exclude

A decision table assists the researcher in formulating a decision about which tasks to include in a course.

In this example, if the task had a mean of 3.5 or higher, with a standard deviation of less than 1, the task would be included in the curriculum. A mean of 3.5 or higher would indicate that most job incumbents responded between 3, "important" and 4, "highly important." Standard deviation (SD) is the spread or variability of the scores by respondents. A low standard deviation indicates a high level of consensus. A large SD would indicate disagreement and suggest that cross tabs be used on background items of respondents to ascertain if variability can be reduced.

For example, cross tabs might show that there was a difference in response based on length of time on the job. Those with over six months experience responded more positively to the task than those with less than 6 months of experience. In this example, if the mean was between 3.5 – 5.0 but the SD was greater than 1.1, indicating low consensus, then the decision is to question the item. This may imply performing a cross tab for further analysis or possible review by a panel of incumbents. A final decision would be made to include the task or omit it. In this example a mean ratings between 1.0 – 3.4 of a task, regardless of the SD, would automatically be rejected and not used in the curriculum. Keep in mind that this is just one example of the decision table. A middle range of $\overline{X}$ = 2.5 – 3.5 could also be included depending on the description of the rating scale.

An application to the decision table can easily be made. See Figure 4-29. A few tasks (A1 – A7) with their mean scores and standard deviations are included in Figure 4-29. Task A1 has a mean of 3.7 but an SD of 1.2. According to the decision table, this task should be questioned. Task A2 has a mean of 4.5, but an SD of .56, and the decision should be to accept this task. Each decision table is different, depending on the rating scale selected. A decision table that has more segmented mean ratings and a lower or higher SD can easily affect the decision on task statements. The researcher will decide based on experience and consultation where to establish appropriate decision table cutoffs.

FIGURE 4-29

Decision Table

$\overline{X}$	SD	Rating	Decision
3.5 – 5	<1.0	High	Accept
3.5 – 5	>1.0	Med	Question
1 – 3.49	><1.0	Low	Reject

Data Analysis

Task	$\overline{X}$	SD	Rating Decision
A1	3.7	1.2	Question
A2	4.5	0.56	Accept
A3	3.6	0.39	
A4	2.59	1.09	
A5	4.6	0.98	
A6	2.5	1.0	
A7	3.8	0.89	

Each decision table is different, depending on the rating scale used.

Decision tables may be two-tiered and include both importance and frequency ratings scales. See Figure 4-30. A process must be established to deal with questionable items. Further analysis might need to be done using cross tabs or the item may have to be reviewed by an advisory committee.

In Figure 4-30, Task A1 has an importance mean of 3.7, with an SD of 1.2, and a frequency mean of 3.5, with a SD of .91. The means of both importance and frequency are high enough, but note that the SD of importance is 1.2. The decision of this task is questioned. Task A2 meets the criteria of the decision table and the decision is to accept. Task A3 has interesting data, but must be rejected because it does not meet the SD criteria for frequency. Task A4 is also interesting and does meet the level of importance criteria, but does meet the frequency criteria and the decision is to question.

FIGURE **4-30**

	Importance		**Frequency**		
Task	$\bar{X}$	**SD**	$\bar{X}$	**SD**	**Rating Decision**
A1	3.7	1.2	3.5	0.91	Question
A2	4.5	0.56	3.6	0.87	Accept
A3	3.6	0.39	2.5	1.52	Reject
A4	3.59	1.09	3.2	0.87	Question
A5	4.6	0.98	3.6	0.77	Accept
A6	2.5	1.0	3.6	0.81	Accept
A7	3.8	0.89	3.4	0.69	Accept

A decision table may include both importance and frequency rates scales.

Another strategy is to use the median and interquartile range. The interquartile range (IQR) statistics can be used to compare levels of agreement on rating scale data. IQR encompasses the middle 50% by subtracting the difference between Quartile 3 and Quartile 1 (Q3–Q1). The median is located within this range. The range for the IQR for a rating scale ranging from 1–5 could run from a high of 0.50 to a low of 4.0. See Figure 4-31. A higher median does not necessarily ensure a small IQR, nor does a low median rating ensure a larger interquartile range. Figure 4-31 shows the median value and how it might be matched against the frequency of performance, level of proficiency, or level of agreement.

FIGURE 4-31

Median Value	Frequency of Performance
0.00 to 1.50	Never
1.51 to 2.50	Yearly
2.51 to 3.50	Monthly
3.51 to 4.50	Weekly
4.51 to 5.50	Daily

Median Value	Level of Proficiency
0.00 to 1.50	No proficiency
1.51 to 2.50	Slight proficiency
2.51 to 3.50	Moderate proficiency[1]
3.51 to 4.50	Considerable proficiency
4.51 to 5.50	Complete proficiency

IQR Value	Level of Agreement
0.50 to 1.66	High level of agreement
1.67 to 2.83	Moderate level of agreement
2.84 to 4.00	Low level of agreement

[1] Sub-tasks that received a median of 2.50 or less for Level of Proficiency were considered as rejected counselor responsibilities. Those rated at 2.51 or higher were considered as valid counselor responsibilities.

A decision table can use the median and interquartile range to facilitate the selection of tasks.

Regardless if the mean and standard deviation or the median and interquartile range are used, the decision table provides rules to facilitate selection on which tasks should be used in the curriculum and should be developed before the survey is mailed. See Appendix K for a complete explanation of data analysis.

Step 8. Administer Instrument

In this step the survey is administered. The introductory letter and endorsement of appropriate organizations and the follow-up letter are written, copied, and signed. Instructions for self-administration of the instrument along with the background information and list of duty and task statements have been pilot tested, revised, and printed. Self-addressed, stamped envelopes are prepared. An incentive for completing and returning the instrument has been produced. A follow-up procedure is developed, documented, and readied. Instructions for self-administration of the questionnaire have been piloted tested and revised. If a service is being used, bulk-mailing rates have been investigated. Letters and questionnaires are assembled and mailed on the same day, increasing the probability that all participants will receive the task analysis survey on the same day. See Figure 4-32.

FIGURE 4-32

MAIL SURVEY RETURNS

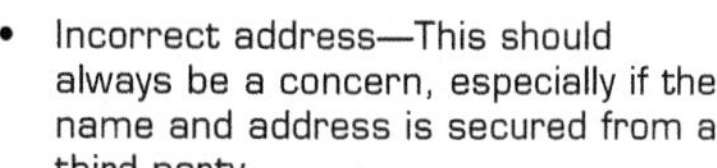

High Return Rate

- Preliminary notification—A pre-notice either by a postcard or through the job incumbents' professional organization, follow-up, or phone call will help.
- Concurrent techniques—This implies that mail, Internet, and phone interviews should increase participation.
- Questionnaire length—Shorter length questionnaire decreases the response burden and increases the return rate.
- Survey sponsorship—Surveys that are jointly sponsored, especially by a professional organization known by the job incumbent, will increase the return rate.
- Return envelope and postage—Don't expect respondents to return questionnaire if a self-addressed stamped envelope is not enclosed.
- Personalization—Salutation with their name and address personalizes the communications and increases the probability of a return.
- Cover letter—Explaining expectations is a must.
- Anonymity—Every effort must be made to assure confidentiality or the return rate will decrease.
- Size, reproduction, and color—Don't get carried away with the size of the page. Consider what respondents are used to. Reproductions must be crisp and clear. Stick with pastel colors and avoid colors that may offend.
- Incentives—Any incentives, such as a token or reward might increase the response rate.
- Deadline dates—Absolutely essential.

Low Return Rate

- Incorrect address—This should always be a concern, especially if the name and address is secured from a third party.
- Letter looks like junk mail—It is desirable to have the respondent open the mail and at least read the cover letter. If it looks like commercial mail, many respondents simply recycle it.
- No convincing explanation of importance—Without this, the respondent will not complete the survey.
- Lack of proper instruction—If the directions have not been piloted or are not clear, respondents will probably throw the survey away.
- Complicated rating scale(s)—Nothing increases response burden more than a confusing rating scale. Pilot testing and review by several people should help clarify the rating scale.
- Return address lost—Avoid enclosing only a self-adhesive address label that tends to get lost. If you want the survey returned, enclose a self-addressed stamped envelope.

Return rates can vary depending on how well the researcher has done the necessary work.

If the survey is administered on the Internet, then appropriate procedures and measures need to be in place to ensure anonymity and a secure site. If working with or within a company, appropriate lines of communications have been established.

One of the best ways to increase the return rate is by making multiple contacts with respondents. Another effective strategy is to provide some kind of token incentive, such as a gift or financial reward (Dillman, Smyth, & Christian, 2014).

Step 9. Analyze Data

In this step, the data from the questionnaire are analyzed. The analysis method should have been decided when the questionnaire was developed and a decision table developed. In this step, a record of places and persons the inventory was sent to is reviewed. A database of which inventories were returned and when they were mailed may be handy for future studies. Each returned questionnaire is checked for completeness or incompleteness.

The data from the returned questionnaire needs to be entered into the computer to compute the general statistics and use the decision table. The data can also be tabulated manually if computer software is not available, and could be entered manually by recording each score, or optical scanning can be used.

Computing the general summary statistics using software can save tremendous time and effort. More time can, thus, b e devoted to analysis of the data.

Based on the background data developed and used, the kinds of sorts can also be calculated. There may be additional ways the data would need to be analyzed, depending on who the clients are.

Step 10. Record Task Inventory

The preliminary task inventory of those task statements accepted is recorded. A list of tasks that were questioned, along with those that were rejected based on the decision table, are all listed. An advisory committee or some similar process is used to review the preliminary list, along with the questionable and rejected tasks. The committee will indicate if they approve of the list and determine if any of the questionable tasks should be included. They will also review any tasks that were written and determine if they should be included in the final inventory.

Step 11. Write Report

The last step in this process is to write the report, covering processes used in the previous ten steps. When writing the report, it is best to develop an outline very early in the process and to follow it during the writing process. In this manner the report can be done in stages, as each step is completed. Another useful method is to have folders for each section. By placing information in each, future writing will be easier. An outline for the report is essential. See Figure 4-33. (Additional information about report writing can be found in Chapter 5.)

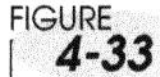

FIGURE 4-33

Report Outline

Executive summary or abstract

1. Introduction
    A. Purpose and rationale of the study
    B. Definition of the occupational area
    C. Description of specific jobs within the occupational area
    D. Job overlaps (similarity) and difference
2. Methodology
    A. Literature review
    B. Construction of the task questionnaire
    C. Validation of the questionnaire
    D. Pilot study
    E. Decision table
    F. Selection of job incumbents
    G. Data collection procedures
    H. Correspondence
3. Data Analysis
    A. Presentation of data
    B. Follow-up procedure—questionable tasks
4. Summary and Conclusions
    A. Final task inventory
    B. Recommendation
5. Appendix
    A. Group summary
    B. Background information
    C. Questionnaire and correspondence

An outline provides the framework for the report.

REVIEW QUESTIONS

1. How does performance analysis differ from task analysis? How are they similar?

2. Identify advantages of the task analysis process from your own setting.

3. Explain in your own words what a task inventory is and how a task inventory is obtained.

4. Of the four task analysis methods, which would be the easiest to accomplish and which would be the most difficult?

5. What would be the major barriers to the observation method in your own setting? Why might workers like the observation method?

6. Compare and contrast the major advantages and disadvantages of the critical incident technique.

7. Under what conditions would you consider using the critical incident technique in your own setting?

8. What might be the result if the occupation is defined too narrowly in the task analysis research procedure?

9. What are the advantages of having position descriptions?

10. What are the main differences between a duty and a task? What do they have in common?

11. What are the advantages of conducting a pilot study for the developed duty and task statements?

12. Why are rating scales important to use in a survey questionnaire?

13. What are the basic requirements of any cover letter?

14. What basic rule(s) should be followed when selecting sample size?

15. Explain the usefulness of a decision table. When should it not be used?

REFERENCES

Borcher, S. D., & Melching, W. H. (1973). *Procedures for constructing and using task inventories.* Columbus, OH: Ohio State University, The Center for Vocational and Technical Education.

Callanhan, M. R. (Ed.). (1992). Be a better task analyst. *Infoline No. 8503.* Alexandria, VA: American Society for Training and Development.

Dillman, D. A., Smyth, J. D., & Christian, L. M. (2014). *Internet, phone, mail, and mixed-mode surveys: The tailored design method* (4th ed.). Hoboken, NJ: John Wiley and Sons.

Falletta, S. V. (2008). Organizational intelligence surveys. *Training + Development, 26*(6), 52–58.

FitzGerald, K., Seale, N. S., Kerins, C. A., & McElvaney, R. (2008). The critical incident technique: A useful tool for conducting qualitative research. *Journal of Dental Education, 72*(3), 299–304.

Hunter, M. (1982). *Mastery teaching.* El Segundo, CA: TIP Publications.

Jonassen, D., Tessmer, M., & Hannum, W. (1999). *Task analysis methods for instructional design.* Mahwah, NJ: Lawrence Erlbaum Associates.

Langdon, D. G., Whiteside, K. S., & McKenna, M. M. (Eds.). (1999). *Intervention resources guide: 50 performance improvement tools.* San Francisco, CA: Pfeiffer.

Langevin Learning Services. (1998). *Training needs analysis.* Workshop held in Chicago, IL: Author.

Langevin Learning Services (2014). *Performance analysis checklist.* Ottawa, ON: Author.

Meister, D. (1985). *Behavior analysis and measurement methods.* New York: Wiley & Sons.

Michalak, D., & Yager, E. (2001). *Making the training process work.* Carlsbad, CA: Writers Club Press.

Rossett, A. (2009). *First things first: A handbook for performance analysis* (2nd ed.). San Francisco: Pfieffer.

Seaman, M. (2011). Bloom's taxonomy: Its evolution, revision, and use in the field of education. *Curriculum & Teaching Dialogue, 13*(1–2), 29–43.

Zemke, R., & Kramlinger, T. (1982). *Figuring things out: A trainer's guide to needs and task analysis.* Reading, MA: Addison-Wesley.

Developing Reports, Presentations, and Proposals 5

INTRODUCTION

Reports, presentations, and proposals play a very important role in course, curriculum, and program development for education and training. Typically, this developmental work must be approved by at least one or two decision makers. In the case of program development, several levels of decision makers must approve, and this often includes an external board. Therefore, it is essential that instructional developers be skilled in writing reports and presenting information to decision makers.

In addition to the approval process, report writing and presentation skills are important in specifying the content for new courses and programs. Usually this developmental work involves a team of individuals, and good communication within the team is essential to effectively completing the project. If the developmental work is funded by a grant, a final report will be required. Finally, documentation of curriculum and program development projects provides an important historical record and a basis for improving the development process.

A number of online templates are available to help write reports, presentations, and proposals. Some are available for free and some for a small fee. Anything from project management report templates to student report templates can be found online.

Presentation software is also available online that can be used to develop graphs and plan presentations. Also, agencies that solicit requests for proposals (RFPs) will often have a standardized template online. This ensures that the proposal fits within the page layout and makes it easier for the funding agency to review.

The instructor must judge the appropriateness of these online templates. Often, they are simple and may need extensive modifications to fit the needs of both the writer and the audience.

OBJECTIVES

After completing this chapter, the reader should be able to do the following:

1. Analyze the audience when writing a report.
2. Explain the general considerations of report writing.
3. Describe the different parts of a report.
4. Explain the importance of developing an outline and use the different types of outlines.

5. Identify the advantages of using graphics, illustrations, and photography in a report.
6. Define the role of objectives in developing effective reports, presentations, and proposals.
7. Define RFP, RFA, and RFC and their role in proposal writing.
8. Discuss the different sections of a proposal and develop a proposal addressing all the sections.

REPORT WRITING

Many writers say that the most difficult part of report writing is composing the first two or three paragraphs. The information given in this chapter should significantly reduce this problem. The purpose, objectives, and type of activity or project to be reported will guide the selection of the content for the report and provide ideas for organizing it. The formats for brief and detailed reports will provide a framework for selecting and organizing information in preparation for writing. Consideration of the audience will help to establish an appropriate approach to presenting the content. Using the outlining process described will help to identify the main points and the best sequence in which to present them. Usually, the outlining process also facilitates the transition into writing the report narrative.

The Message and the Audience

An important first step in developing good reports is to determine what information to present. Two factors enter into this decision:

- nature of the information to be presented
- information needs of the audience

Many organizations have their own report formats and requirements. Professional journals specify the format and style required for their publications. Funding agencies typically specify reporting requirements for the projects they support. The appropriate reporting requirements should be reviewed before starting to write the report.

The audience must also be considered as the content and format are selected. The audience for a report may be comprised of several diverse groups. A variety of stakeholders may need to be informed of the need for a new course or program and convinced to give their support to the project. Managers and administrators will need to give their approval to proceed. External agencies may need to review the project and give their approval.

A common mistake is to treat each group in the same manner and provide only one report. Usually each group has different interests, priorities, and needs related to the project reported. Those closest to the project and the most involved will be the most interested. For example, the instructional developer and staff members working on the project will be more involved and interested. They will be most interested in the results and will not need much detail on the design of the project. An administrator who is being informed for the first time will need a more comprehensive report that includes the project purpose, design, and results.

Before work on developing a report is begun, an analysis of the audience needs to be done to determine the following:

- What information do members of the audience need?
- What type of information do they process best?
- What communication modes attract their attention most effectively?

Most decision makers have an oversupply of information available to them. However, in many instances, the information does not apply to the decision at hand or is in a format that makes it hard to apply to the decision-making task. An instructional developer can facilitate decision making at higher administrative levels by determining what information and criteria these decision makers use. This can be done by asking them what information they need and use. Also, observing how these decision makers come to a decision and their rationales for decisions will help to identify the factors and criteria used.

Decision-making factors and criteria will vary by management level. For example, a department head will use different factors than a higher-level administrator. See Figure 5-1.

A report to a department head should clearly identify the need and how it relates to the work and goals of the department. Attention also needs to be given to the staff, resources, and costs associated with the solution. If the purpose of the report is to identify the need for a new course or program, the focus will be on clearly defining the need and its relevance to the department. In addition, there should be some information on the extent to which the department has the staff and resources required to respond to this need. It may also be appropriate to suggest potential next steps in exploring the feasibility of the new program. A final feasibility report should contain specific information on staff and resource needs and how these relate to department resources. In addition, a cost estimate for developing and implementing the program must be provided.

Upper-level administrators will be more concerned with the extent to which a solution to the need should be a priority and how it fits the organization's mission. They will want to review how the solution or new program fits with the rest of the organization's programs. Also, they will want an assessment of how the new program positions the organization for future growth and development.

DECISION-MAKING FACTORS

Department Head	Higher-Level Manager
• Is there a need?	• Is the need a high priority?
• Does the need relate to my department?	• Does the need fit our organizational mission?
• Does our department have staff and resources that relate to this need?	• Does the need fit our programs?
• What is the cost to develop a new/revised program?	• Can this be funded without hurting other programs?
• What is the cost to implement it?	• How will ongoing costs be covered?
• What are the future implications for our department?	• Will the new program position our organization for the future?

Decision-making factors can be broken down into factors to be considered by a department head and factors to be considered by a higher-level manager.

In addition to presenting the appropriate information, it is important to present it in an effective format. Some individuals process information in a graphic format better than written narrative. Others want a lot of data in table format. And some prefer to receive information in an auditory format.

Care should be taken to prepare the report in a structure that matches the managers' thinking styles. Do they like to see the big picture first and then the details, or do they prefer the details first? Are they logical thinkers who want to have information presented in logical steps, or do they prefer a less structured presentation that allows them to more actively participate in defining the solution?

A number of thinking styles assessment instruments are available. These instruments and associated manuals can also be useful in identifying thinking styles and their characteristic behaviors. This information will help to identify and understand managers' thinking styles as they react to requests, reports, and proposals.

Another consideration when communicating with decision makers is the communication channel or mode that attracts their attention. A brilliantly written report will not be effective if it is not read. An e-mail with narrative, tables, and attractive graphics will not have an impact if the decision maker wants a paper copy.

Again, it is important to find out what communicates most effectively with decision makers in the organization and use this mode. A written report or proposal is usually required. It provides a reference document and an approval record. However, if one or more decision makers or managers tend not to read or respond to written documents, an oral presentation should be made to review the main points of the report with them.

Some decision makers may be willing to approve the report and further actions associated with it at this meeting. Others may want some more time to consider the decisions and another meeting may be needed. Knowledge of the habits of your decision makers will identify the best course of action.

It is important to monitor feedback if response to a report or communication is needed. Feedback might include requests for more information, project approval, changed policies, or new practices. If adequate and timely feedback is not received, follow-up will be necessary.

In summary, it is important to identify the information that needs to be communicated and the thinking styles of the administrators and managers who will receive it. This knowledge can then be used to develop documents and presentations that will efficiently and effectively convey the information to appropriate decision makers. In some instances it may be necessary to use more than one type of report to communicate with all the audience members or stakeholders.

General Considerations

Correct grammar and spelling are basic essentials in reporting. These are discussed in many sources and will not be repeated here except to reinforce their importance. Correct spelling is facilitated by the spell-check function in wordprocessing programs. However, spell-check is not infallible. When *t* is left off "the," "he" is still a valid word to spell-check. Often the word created when a letter is left off can produce strange meanings or raise questions about the writer's vocabulary. For example, if a *w* is left off the word "whole," the result is a "hole" in the sentence. The moral of this situation is that proofreading is essential to quality written reports. Writers need to proofread their reports and, if possible, a second person should proofread each report.

Accurate presentation of information is essential. The first concern in this area is content. The content of the report must reflect all of the information available and be unbiased. The second concern is the selection of terms and vocabulary that accurately communicate with the audience. Good reports accurately depict the knowledge gathered and convey the information in words that members of the audience can readily understand. Acronyms must be defined and used judiciously. Sufficient context and background information has to be provided to allow correct interpretation.

Before preparing a report, the author needs to select the style and format to be used. These decisions affect many aspects of a report and can take considerable time to change if they are made after the draft copy is completed.

Decisions need to be made on whether to write in the first or third person, how to avoid gender-biased terms, and ways to select nonoffensive labels for people and groups. Also, the format for quotations, references, and text should be selected.

An accepted style manual should be used when preparing reports. The *Publication Manual of the American Psychological Association* (hereafter "APA Manual") is commonly used and widely accepted. There are several other style manuals, with the style required by the funding organization taking precedent. If none is specified, use a style manual that is familiar. It is important to be consistent. Styles should not be mixed in a report.

The APA Manual has the advantage of being designed to facilitate communicating research results and publishing reports. Study guides for the APA Manual are available on the Internet. Entering "APA manual study guide" or "APA style crib sheet" into a search engine will generate a list of several sources of information on using the APA Manual. Since the APA updates the manual frequently, any study guide used should be checked for its publication or revision date.

Written material should be double-spaced and the margins need to be at least 1″ wide. The type font used needs to be 10 point or larger and easy to read. Care should be taken in using italics. Italics can be hard to read and may not copy clearly on a copier. Use bold type instead. Headings will assist the reader in finding information.

Outlining is a very effective tool for preparing good reports. The process stimulates thinking, and the outline facilitates organizing the information in a logical flow. Moreover, outlining helps to improve clarity, reduce gaps in information, and remove redundancy. In addition, an outline is often used to guide a presentation.

An outline may be prepared in different ways. Some can be easily done on a notepad or computer screen. For more complex reports, it may work better to place major topics and associated subpoints on 3 × 5 cards. This provides the flexibility to change the sequence of topics and lay out the complete outline on a table. A visually oriented person will probably prefer the note cards over scrolling through several computer screens.

Several types of outline formats can be used. These range from the traditional format to informal outlines that use graphic symbols to identify topics and subpoints. If an outline is used only by the person preparing the report, it can be informal and brief. See Figure 5-2. A topic outline uses one or two words to identify points. Complete sentences are used in the sentence outline. In the traditional format, Roman numerals, uppercase and lowercase letters, and numbers are used to identify main topics and subpoints.

FIGURE 5-2

OUTLINES

Topic Outline

I. Objectives
    A. Problems
    B. Training needed
    C. Number
        1. Retrainees
        2. New
II. Design

Sentence Outline

I. Objectives of the needs assessment study
    A. Identify the problem areas in XYZ department
    B. Determine if training is needed
    C. Identify the number of people to be trained
        1. Number of current workers
        2. Number of new employees
II. Design of the needs assessment study

Numerical Outline

1. Objectives
    1.1 Problems
    1.2 Training needed
    1.3 Number
        1.3.1 Retrainees
        1.3.2 New

Informal Outline

• Objectives
    ➢ Problems
    ➢ Training needed
    ➢ Number
        - Retrainees
        - New

The types of outlines are topic, sentence, numerical, and informal outlines.

A numerical outlining system uses numbers to differentiate levels and topics. One advantage of this system is that all subpoints are always identified with their main topic. In a number of situations, a more informal format can be used. Graphic symbols can be utilized to identify major points and subpoints.

Whatever outline format is used, the outlining process is worthwhile. The time spent on outlining will be saved several times over during the preparation of the report. In addition, the report will be of much higher quality.

Developing the Report

As noted previously, the first step is to review the audience for the report and determine what information the audience members need. Writing for the key decision maker first is appropriate. After this draft has been completed, it can be revised and supplemented for the other members of the audience if different information is needed.

The next step is to decide on the amount of detail and scope of information to place in the report. The nature of the decision maker, size of the project reported, cost and impact of the decisions to be made, and reporting requirements have an impact on this decision. A brief report will probably be sufficient for a small needs assessment study conducted in a department. A more detailed report will be needed for a large-scale curriculum project that has a sizable budget.

The detailed report format is used for larger projects and when the audience expects and/or needs more detail. This longer format is appropriate for upper-level management, conference presentations, and project archives. With brief reports, two brief report formats are used. The formal version would be used when more information needs to be conveyed for larger projects or the audience wants to have additional information on the project design. The informal version may be appropriate for department-level reports and when used with presentations. See Figure 5-3.

Detailed Report Contents. Contents of detailed reports follow a specific hierarchy. All parts are essential for the report to be effective.

Cover Page—The cover page for the detailed report will contain the same information as the one used on brief reports: title, author, date, and sponsoring organization. When cover stock is used for front and back covers, the cover may contain only the title of the report and the author's name. In this case, the cover page is followed by a title page that repeats the title and author and lists the date of publication, sponsoring organization, and any disclaimers.

Abstract (Executive Summary)—A good abstract is a very important part of an effective report. It may determine whether the reader goes on to read the rest of the report. Also, it can be used in other documents and media to describe the project. An abstract should be one page or less. It should describe the need, purpose, objectives, design, and outcomes of the project. It is usually easier to write the abstract after the rest of the report has been completed.

Table of Contents—A table of contents is used in a detailed report. The table of contents helps the reader quickly locate information within the report. It identifies the sections in the report and their page location. These sections are identified by center and side heads.

List of Tables and Figures—A list of tables and figures follows the table of contents. Tables and figures that are identified by number in the report are listed in sequence by table or figure number and their location in the report is given by page number. The full title of each one is also given.

FIGURE 5-3

REPORTS

Detailed Report Sections

Cover page
Abstract (Executive summary)
Table of contents
List of tables and figures
Project purpose and significance
Project objectives
Review of related information/literature
Project design
- Approach
- Participants
- Procedures and activities
- Evaluation
- Budget

Results
Summary
Conculsions
Recommendations
References
Appendices

Brief Report Sections

Formal

Cover page
Abstract (brief)
Project purpose
Project objectives
Project description
Results/outcomes
Recommendations
Appendices

Informal

Project title
Purpose and objectives
Overview project activities
Results/outcomes
Recommendations
Appendices
Project design

The sections of a report vary according to whether the report is a detailed or brief report. Brief report sections vary according to whether the report is formal or informal.

Purpose and Significance—The purpose and significance of the study are presented in the next section of the report. The purpose statement will identify the topic, scope, and end products of the project. The topic is the need, course, program, or content area on which the project is focused. Scope sets the boundaries within which the project is operated. End products are the outcomes of the project. These might be a list of competencies, course designs, and/or instructional materials.

Comments on the significance of the study answer the question, "Why was this study done?" It is important to relate this statement to the nature of the decisions to be made and the goals of the organization. Significance of a training project can be defined in terms of improved quality, enhanced safety, increased productivity, and/or keeping up with competition. In an educational setting, significance can be established in terms of relevant course work, up-to-date programs, and/or more competent graduates.

Project Objectives—Project objectives define specific outcomes. They relate to specific aspects of the project's purpose. For example, an instructional development project could involve identification of competencies through a task analysis, developing a curriculum plan, writing course outlines, and designing an evaluation. This example contains four major phases, and one or more objectives would be associated with each phase. Since objectives are critical elements in a successful project, they should be highlighted by listing each one separately and numbering each one.

Review of Related Information—A review of related information should be a synthesis of the major pieces of information relevant to the project. This information may exist in published reports, books, journal articles, internal reports, and other documents. The curriculum project noted in the previous paragraph has four major segments. Information related to each of these should be presented.

In the task analysis area, information on task analysis techniques and data on competencies related to the topic area should be reported. The curriculum planning area would include a review of relevant curriculum planning techniques and a summary of curriculum plans developed for similar topic areas. Similar types of information would be presented for the course planning and evaluation areas.

Project Design—The project design portion of the report will typically include information on the approach used, participants involved, procedures and activities, evaluation processes, and budget for the project. Enough detail must be given in the description of the project approach, procedures, and activities that another educator could replicate the project

Characteristics of the participants are important to the interpretation of the results. In a task analysis, the participants will be the people surveyed to determine what tasks are required in the job and the competency levels needed. In the implementation and evaluation of a course or program, the participants are the students and instructors involved.

The section on evaluation needs to describe the evaluation system, data collection methods and schedule, and data analysis procedures used. Each objective needs to be evaluated and the outcomes of the evaluations should be reported in the results section.

Information on the budget will be determined by the audience for the report. For some, the total cost will be sufficient. For others, a breakout by cost area will be needed.

Results—Outcomes of the project are defined in the results section. The discussion should cover negative as well as positive outcomes. One way to organize this section is to report the results by objective. This establishes a logical organization and provides a direct check on the extent to which each objective has been attained. Frequently, outcomes are achieved that do not directly relate to one of the objectives. These can be reported as "additional outcomes."

Narrative for the results section needs to be clear and concise. Also, it must move at a pace that allows the reader to acquire and interpret the information presented. Major outcomes should be highlighted with bullets. Supporting information can be placed in the appendix.

Summary—The summary provides a brief statement of the project's purpose, design, and activities. Most of the summary should be devoted to identifying the major outcomes of the project.

Conclusions—Conclusions are decisions or judgments about the outcomes related to each objective. In a task analysis project, conclusions can include the following:

- The tasks identified are valid. (A page reference to the task list would be helpful.)
- Workers and supervisors place the same priority on the tasks.
- The task analysis process used was efficient and valid.

Conclusions follow from the discussion of results. They must be supported by the information presented in the results section. Conclusions should be stated for each objective. Listing each conclusion in a subparagraph and numbering them facilitates presenting and discussing them in other presentations.

Recommendations—Recommendations are based on the outcomes of the project and identify future actions. For instance, if the conclusions for the task analysis project just mentioned include one to the effect that the tasks are valid, the recommendation would be to proceed with curriculum planning and development work. If the conclusions raised some questions about the validity of the tasks, the recommendation would be to redo a part or all of the task analysis.

Recommendations typically deal with three areas: content of the project, processes used, and ideas for additional projects. Content recommendations indicate whether one or more of the outcomes or products should be used. Process recommendations are concerned with modifying and improving the processes used. Ideas for additional projects often occur as a project is progressing. These ideas need to be noted and passed on.

References—All sources cited in the report need to have a complete reference listed in the reference section. Also, other sources that had an impact on the report but are not cited in the text should be listed. Each reference needs to have enough information to identify the source and retrieve it. The APA Manual is commonly used for reports and would be a good reference source if the writer and sponsoring organizations do not have a preferred style manual.

Appendices—Appendices provide a place for materials that are not essential in the text but need to be available to the reader. Also, some detailed materials, such as statistical formulas and tests, may provide too much detail for the text and distract readers. Some examples of material that can be placed in appendices are survey instruments, cover letters, complete task lists, meeting agendas, committee member lists, and compliance forms. A report on a curriculum project might include some sample curriculum materials in an appendix.

Brief Report Contents. The cover page on a formal brief report should include a title that clearly describes the nature of the project. If the report is for a needs assessment, note this in the title along with the area or topic studied. If it is a curriculum development project, list this in the title together with the content area involved. In addition, the title page needs to include the author's name, organization, and date of publication. On the informal report, the report title, author, and date should be listed at the top of the first page.

A brief abstract should be included in the formal version of the brief report. This needs to include the purpose of the project, a summary of project activities, and a description of the major outcomes. It may also be helpful to include a brief description of the project objectives. This abstract should be limited to one or two paragraphs.

The project purpose needs to identify the scope, topic, and end products of the project. For an instructional development project, the purpose statement would include the content area involved (topic), competency levels included (scope), and the materials to be developed (end products).

Each objective will list specific outcomes or products to be completed in relation to the purpose. These can be listed individually or discussed in summary form. The latter approach would be used in the informal format.

The project description in the brief report formal format should include information on the project design, major activities, schedule, and evaluation. Usually one paragraph on each of these is adequate. For the instructional development project example used previously, the design paragraph will describe the curriculum development model used and discuss how this was applied to the project. Major activities carried out in the project would be identified next. This is the place to note any problems that occurred as these activities were completed. If the project is relatively small, the schedule on which these activities were completed can be included in the activities section. The evaluation section will describe how the processes and products of the project were evaluated.

Project results are presented in the next section. One way to organize this section of the report is to present the results by objective. The results need to be discussed in enough detail to communicate effectively with members of the audience for the report.

Recommendations relevant to the project are placed in the next section. Recommendations may relate to applying or implementing results of the study, conducting additional studies, or changing procedures in future projects.

In the instructional development project example, one recommendation could be a recommendation to implement the new curriculum, and a second could focus on how to implement it. Experiences with the curriculum development model or process used may also lead to a recommendation to change the process in future projects. In addition, instructional development activities and experiences often generate ideas for new programs and courses that should be developed. These should be identified in one or more recommendations. The recommendations section will have more impact on the reader if the recommendations are listed separately and numbered.

Supporting materials for the report are placed in the appendices. These would include surveys, advisory committee member lists, and other relevant documents.

The informal brief report will include the report title, author, and date at the top of the first page. A brief introduction can be used in place of an abstract. Each of the sections should be concise and focus on major project activities and outcomes.

Selecting Content

Three factors will help guide the selection of the report format (detailed or brief). First, the purpose and objectives of the project will define the focus and scope of the content. Second, the amount of detail the audience needs and prefers will influence the content included. Third, there must be enough information in the report to support the conclusions and recommendations made.

Organization

An effectively organized report is easy to read and understand. The report formats discussed in this chapter provide a framework for organizing reports.

It is also important to consider the nature of the audience for a report. Some individuals prefer to receive an overview or framework first and then move on to details. Others prefer to start with the details. In the report formats given, the narrative flows from the purpose to objectives, design, results, conclusions, and recommendations. It is imperative that all of these sections are relevant to each other and connected. The objectives must deal with variables that are relevant to the purpose. Similarly, the design, results, conclusions, and recommendations must relate to the objectives. The one exception to this would be the recommendations for additional projects. Some of these may be outside of the scope of the original project.

Transitions between paragraphs, sections, and ideas facilitate continuity and comprehension. Transitional words are described in the APA Manual (American Psychological Association [APA], 2010) as words that aid the flow of ideas:

> Another way to achieve continuity is through the use of transitional words. These words help maintain the flow of thought, especially when the material is complex or abstract. A pronoun that refers to a noun in the preceding sentence not only serves as a transition but also avoids repetition. Be sure the referent is obvious. Other transition devices are time links (*then, next, after, while, since*), cause-effect links (*therefore, consequently, as a result*), addition links (*in addition, moreover, furthermore, similarly*), and contrast links (*but, conversely, nevertheless, however, although, whereas*). (p. 65)

Sometimes redundancy is useful in maintaining a consistent and clear flow of ideas. For instance, if a paragraph contrasts the response patterns of workers and their supervisors, use of the pronoun "they" later in the paragraph or in the next paragraph will not clearly identify which group is being discussed. Also, project objectives are key elements in a project and will need to be repeated in various parts of a report.

Words and Graphics

Clear and concise writing is critical to an effective report. It is important to use words and technical terms that are understood by the audience. When technical terms have to be used, they should be defined in the report. Acronyms also need to be defined the first time they are used. Actually, it is helpful to define them again in later sections of the report that might be read separately. For example, the recommendations may be reviewed at various times without checking other parts of the report. A list of definitions should be included in an appendix of the report when several terms need to be defined.

Sentence length has a significant impact on readability. Adding two to three words per sentence increases the reading level by one grade level. Using multisyllabic words, especially those with three or more syllables, also increases the reading level of reports. Sentences do not have to be long and contain complex words to have an impact. Lincoln's Gettysburg Address has 275 words and 196 have one syllable.

Several readability formulas are available, and most are available on the Internet with a search for "readability formulas." These formulas include FOG, SMOG, and RAIN. Also, most wordprocessing programs include a readability check. Most of these formulas use a combination of two or more of the following factors: sentence length, number of multisyllabic words, known words, and word length. These factors should be kept in mind when writing a report.

There are several pros and cons related to reading formulas. There is general agreement that readability tests have increased awareness of the need to write at an appropriate reading level. There is also agreement that these tests are not precise measures of readability. These formulas are, however, useful in determining if the reading level of a report is appropriate for a given audience.

Some suggestions to improve the readability of materials include the following:

- Review the audience members and determine their vocabulary and knowledge in the topic area.
- Organize the material in a logical flow.
- Use an appropriate pace for introducing new ideas and information.
- Write short sentences when possible.
- Define, explain, and illustrate technical terms that may not be understood by the audience.

Graphics can significantly enhance a report. Graphs, charts, and photos can be used to emphasize specific ideas. Illustrations and other graphics are especially effective with visual learners.

Graphics must be integrated with the text and related to the purpose of the report. Graphs, illustrations, and photos follow their introduction in the text. The amount of written discussion will vary according to the complexity and type of figure used. A bar graph that depicts the amount of work experience of respondents in a task analysis will need less commentary than a flow chart that describes an instructional development process.

The report narrative has to present enough information to allow the reader to interpret the contents of the graphic. Since some readers do not process graphic materials effectively and others will overlook them, the report narrative needs to identify the major facts and ideas in each figure. This discussion needs to include the figure number. To avoid confusion, graphics are numbered consecutively throughout a report. Figure titles should be concise and identify the topic covered in the figure.

Graphics are designed to present the main facts and ideas in a set of data. Extraneous data and details make them more difficult to read and interpret. Tables can be used to present specific data, statistical values, and details associated with the figures. There are several types of figures. Graphs, illustrations, and photographs are the most common figures.

Graphs. Graphs present comparisons, trends, and the current status of factors in a set of data. The independent variable is usually presented on the horizontal, or x-axis. The vertical, or y-axis represents the dependent variable or outcome. These will be explained in more detail as the bar, line, pie, and scatter graphs are discussed. The values on the axes may be the original response values or scores, percents, or standard scores.

Graphs are relatively easy to generate with computer software. However, care must be taken to determine that the charts have the correct x- and y-axes, scaling on the two axes is appropriate, and enough information is given to identify the contents of the graph. The latter concern entails the figure name, labels for the axes, and a legend. Also, care must be taken to avoid placing too much information in a graph.

If it is anticipated that others may copy the report, the graphs should be designed to copy effectively. Color should be avoided if color copiers will not be used. Symbols and shading used must copy clearly.

Many times the graphs from a report will be used in a presentation. If there is some likelihood that this will happen, the graphs should be projected ahead of time with the projection equipment that will be used to determine if they can be read by the audience. Since the lighting is not always optimal for a presentation, the graphs should be viewed under different light conditions.

Bar Graphs—This graph is used when the independent variable is categorical. For example, in a comparison of supervisors' and workers' evaluations of a training program, supervisors and workers are members of two separate groups. Each group is a category and would be identified on the x-axis. See Figure 5-4. Evaluation ratings in this example are the dependent variable and are plotted on the y-axis.

Bar graphs are also used when the independent variable is continuous. A continuous measure is one that can have a range of values, including fractional values. Temperature, weight, and time are described with continuous measures. Distributions of responses and scores are often displayed as bar graphs. This type of bar graph is also called a histogram. See Figure 5-5. A histogram shows the high and low scores, typical scores (highest bars), and the shape of the distribution. Figure 5-5 presents a histogram for the workers' evaluation responses summarized in Figure 5-4.

FIGURE 5-4

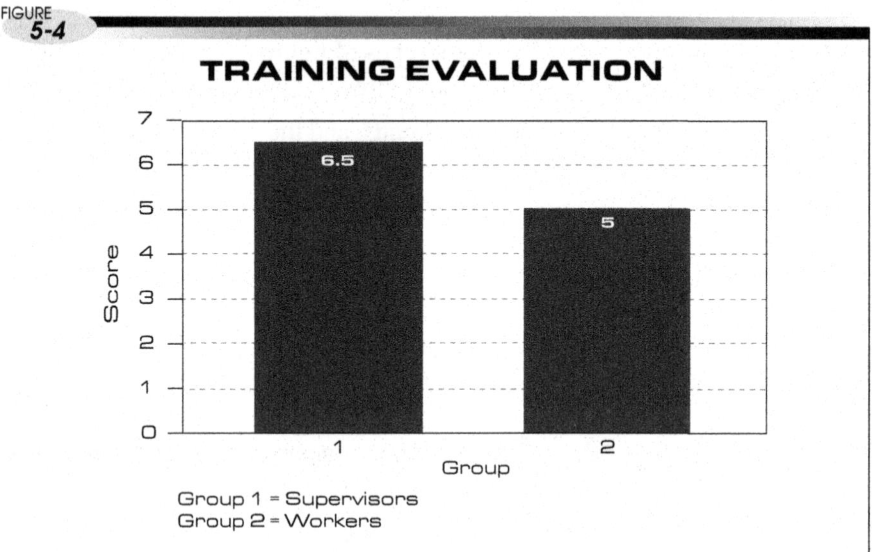

A bar graph can be used to show a comparison of supervisors' and workers' evaluations of a training program.

Additional comparisons could be placed in Figure 5-5. Results could be plotted by experience levels in each group. See Figure 5-6. In Figure 5-6 the evaluation results are presented by experience levels within the supervisor and worker groups. In this example, the new supervisors and workers gave more favorable evaluation ratings. Some caution must be exercised when displaying subgroup data to avoid making the graph too complex.

Line Graphs—Both the x- and y-axes on a line graph depict continuous or quantitative variables. As in bar graphs, the dependent variable is plotted on the y-axis. See Figure 5-7. Figure 5-7 presents the average math performance of high school seniors in Home Town High School for the years 2009–2014. Time is the independent variable and is plotted on the x-axis. Time is not the cause of any changes in performance; it represents the math programs in place during each school year.

FIGURE 5-5

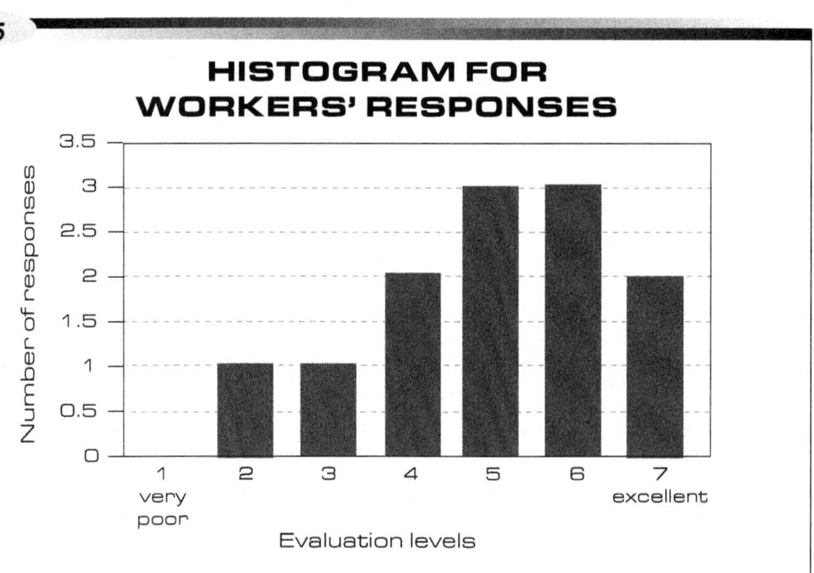

A histogram presenting workers' evaluation responses shows the high and low scores, typical scores (highest bars), and the shape of the distribution.

FIGURE 5-6

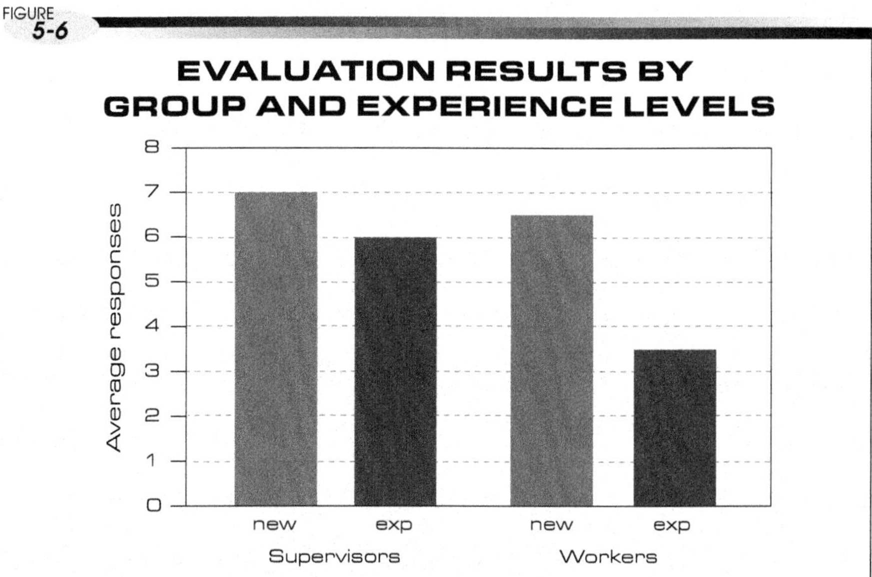

By using shading or color, a histogram can show additional detail such as breakdown of the two groups (supervisors and workers) by experience.

FIGURE 5-7

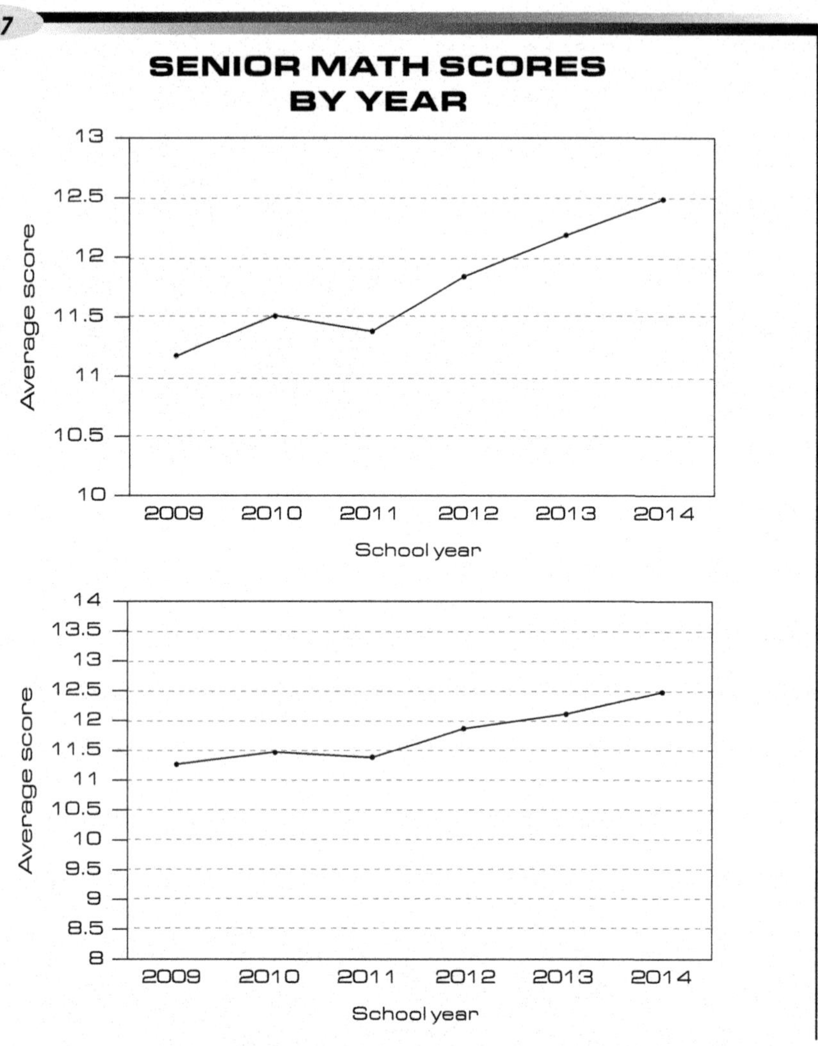

The scale used on the y-axis for presenting senior math scores can have a significant impact on the visual appearance of the trend line.

Average performance is plotted on the y-axis. Grade level is used as the metric or unit of measure in the example. This has the advantage of immediately informing the reader of the group's performance in relation to typical seniors. In the example, the classes of 2010, 2011, and 2012 perform slightly below grade level. In 2013 and 2014 the classes improve and end up above grade level (12th) in 2014. In addition, the trend line is up or positive for the last two years. As additional years are tested and the results added to the graph, this trend should be monitored.

Selecting the scale or units of measurement for the x- and y-axes is more art than science. The units must be selected to give a fair and unbiased depiction of the data. Note the effect of changing the y-axis scale in Figure 5-7. Changing the scale has made a significant impact on the visual appearance of the trend line. Which scale is valid? The writer must decide which graph most honestly represents the changes in performance and performance levels.

Pie Graphs—Pie graphs are an effective way to display proportions and percentages. Each subgroup or category is represented by a slice of the pie or circle. See Figure 5-8. The example in Figure 5-8 presents the levels of work experience of respondents in a task analysis study. It is readily apparent that two to three years is the most common level of experience.

FIGURE 5-8

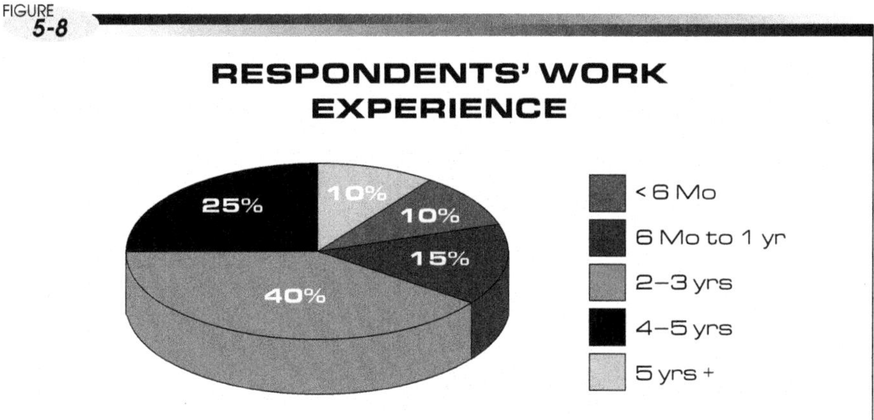

A pie graph can be used to present the levels of work experience of respondents in a task analysis study.

Pie graphs are used frequently in newspapers and magazines; thus, most readers are familiar with them. However, care must be taken in constructing a pie graph to avoid creating too many slices and using shading that makes the graph hard to interpret. When too many slices are created, several become small and hard to read. No more than five or six slices should be used. Smaller slices can be combined and relabeled. Also, care must be used in selecting the shading or colors to use for the slices. Some shading and colors are hard to distinguish from each other, especially if the graph is small or the printing process is not high quality.

Scatter Graphs—Scatter graphs or diagrams are used to graphically describe the relationship between two variables. See Figure 5-9. Many relationships or correlations are of interest to educators, such as grade point average and performance on the job, entrance test scores and grade point average, performance test results and performance on the job, and retest scores and posttest scores.

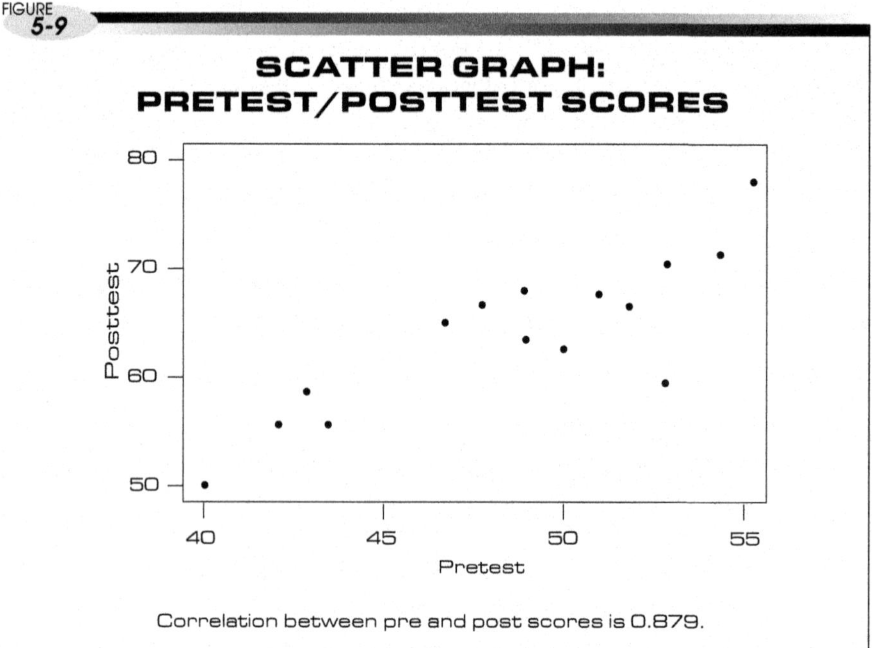

In a simple scatter graph showing performance on the pre- and posttest, the pattern of the dots shows a strong relationship between pre- and posttest results, indicating that students who score high on the pretest also tend to score high on the posttest.

Figure 5-9 shows a sample scatter graph. The points or data in the graph represent performance on the pre- and posttest. For example, the first dot on the left indicates that the person had a pretest score of 40 and a posttest score of 50. The pattern of the data indicates a strong relationship between pre- and posttest results. In other words, students who score high on the pretest also tend to score high on the posttest.

Dots in Figure 5-9 cluster around a straight line that runs diagonally from the lower left corner to the upper right corner. This slope indicates a positive correlation between the two sets of data. The closer the data are to this line, the higher the correlation. When the data fall in a straight line, the correlation is 1. When there is a negative correlation, the line runs from upper left to lower right.

Illustrations. Illustrations graphically describe the relationship between elements in a system. Flow charts, system diagrams, organizational charts, and drawings are examples. Boxes, circles, or triangles are used to depict elements. Lines and arrows are used to identify the flow of activities, information, or authority. Sequencing from left to right or top to bottom is also used to reflect the flow of information, activities, or time.

Illustrations are very useful. They provide a global view of a process, system, or organization. However, they do require adequate narrative to explain the components and how they relate to each other. Also, the narrative must provide information on how to conduct each step.

Photographs. Photographs can make a report more attractive and interesting. Digital cameras and computer software make it relatively easy and quick to add photographs to reports. It is important that photographs are relevant and of good quality. Photographs need to be clear and have good contrast. Image size must be large enough to convey the intended message. Photographs should be cropped to eliminate extraneous materials.

The title for a photograph should list who is included and what they are doing. Individuals do not have to be named but can be identified as members of a class or work group. The nature of the situation in the photograph and its use in the report will determine whether individual or group names are used. Also, if the report is published, it may be necessary to obtain a release from the individuals in the photographs.

PRESENTATIONS

One-on-one and small group presentations are the most effective way to convey information to key decision makers. Written reports and proposals are important documents, but there is no assurance that they will be read or understood. Most decision makers are very busy and some have an aversion to reading reports. A presentation ensures that decision makers hear the information and their comments and questions will identify areas that have to be clarified.

This section is concerned with the role of presentations in proposal and instructional development. Thus, the content will focus on planning, preparing, and managing a presentation. Specific techniques and skills, though important, are not stressed. A number of reference sources on presentation skills and techniques are available, and thus this information will not be emphasized here.

Planning a Presentation

Most decision makers are busy and have full schedules. Thus, a presentation must be focused, concise, and clear. Before scheduling a presentation, determine the amount of time usually available in the decision makers' schedules. Is 10 minutes available on a meeting agenda? Does the key decision maker usually schedule 15 minutes for this type of presentation? Request a meeting with these time limits in mind.

After the meeting has been scheduled, the presentation can be planned to fit within the time allocated. The presentation will have to be focused on one or two objectives. All of the information presented will need to be germane to these objectives. Also, in most instances time should be allowed for questions.

The first step in planning is to analyze the audience. Determine how much they know about the topic. For example, if a proposal for a project to develop a new course is to be presented, is the audience already aware of the need for this course? If they are, the need for the course can be established quickly without going into detailed data, and the majority of the time can be spent on the course development process and the budget for these activities.

Another factor to consider is how members of the audience receive and process information most effectively. Some individuals are more visually oriented and others process verbal information more effectively. For some, statistics and other quantitative data are critical; others will not easily relate to this type of information. An initial big picture is preferred by some decision makers, while others prefer step-by-step detail that leads to the big picture. A review of experiences and interactions with members of the audience should identify the best approach.

After the approach has been selected, the next step is to prepare an outline of the presentation. This should include four major sections: introduction, body, recommendations, and questions/answers. The introduction must gain the attention of the audience, identify the importance of the topic, and inform them of the structure of the presentation. Their attention can often be gained by noting the magnitude of the need related to the project report or proposal being presented. In addition, the impacts of the project can be identified.

The body of the presentation contains the information needed to make the decisions requested at the end. Thus, it is helpful to draft the conclusions and decisions that will be made at the end of the presentation and analyze them to determine the information needed. In addition, the presenter should review the members of the audience and estimate the types of questions they will ask. This estimate needs to include friendly and hostile questions. For instance, Joe may always be interested in the amount of staff time required in a project, while Sally is concerned about the process to be used.

A valid set of recommendations should be presented after the main content or body of the presentation has been completed. These recommendations must follow from the information presented. Some decision makers may prefer to have some options given in the recommendations. If this is the case, logical options should be prepared. However, avoid presenting an option that is not appropriate. For example, if a needs assessment has shown that it is critical to add new competencies to a program, do not provide the recommendation "make no changes."

Also, it is helpful to identify the impacts and ramifications of each recommendation before making the presentation. If questions have eroded the support for some recommendations, it may be best to defer the decisions on these until additional information can be provided.

It is important to plan the closing. Identify what needs to be accomplished before completing the presentation and develop one or two ways to make a transition from the body of the presentation or questions into the closing comments. These closing comments should briefly summarize the main points in the presentation and identify the decisions that need to be made. Also, any follow-up actions need to be noted.

Most presenters need notes or a script to guide their presentations. Reading from a report is usually not effective. A report contains more information than will be presented and typically is not structured appropriately. Note cards are effective for many presenters. A combination of note cards and visuals is another option. The visuals present the main points and guide the flow of the presentation. Detailed data, quotes, and reminders to the presenter should be included on the note cards.

At this point visual aids and handouts can be planned and prepared. Since presentation time is limited, these will be confined to those that are essential. If slides or projected visuals are to be used, care must be taken in designing them. Three common problems with projected visuals are that the type size is too small to read, there is too much information included in each slide, and the type color and/or background color makes the slide hard to read.

Computer software makes it easy to construct slides. However, care should be taken not to overload the slides with too many graphics or animation simply because they are available. Each slide should be limited to two or three points and a total of 15 to 20 words. Type size should be 20 pt or larger and the font must be easy to read. Colors for type and background must not detract or make the visual difficult to read. Many visuals look attractive on the computer monitor but do not project effectively.

Detailed schematics, flow charts, and designs probably will not be readable when projected. A handout with the detail will be more effective. In some cases, a handout plus a visual with the major components of the projected diagram will be effective.

Visuals should be previewed ahead of the presentation to determine if they can be read from various points in the audience. The presenter should also determine if a complete trial run of the presentation is needed. A practice is a good time to gain a feel for the presentation, improve the flow, and work out any problems. Also, the length of the presentation can be checked.

It is a good idea to have a backup for any visuals used. Audiovisual hardware and software can fail to operate. One-half-size or one-third-size copies of the visuals should be made for members of the audience. These are also useful for note taking during the presentation.

Effective planning and preparation allow the presenter to relax and communicate more effectively with the audience. Also, this allows more efficient use of the time available for the presentation.

Presenting

It is important to gain the audience's attention during the introduction. This can be done by relating the presentation to their needs and defining the impacts of the project to be discussed. Moreover, it is important that the speaker show a high level of interest in the project. The introduction should also give an overview of the major parts of the presentation. Members of the audience should be informed whether the presenter would like to take questions as they arise or prefers to wait until the end of the presentation.

During the body or main portion of the presentation, the presenter needs to maintain eye contact with members of the audience. Use of note cards and visuals will facilitate this and help to maintain a logical flow of information. Also, it is important that the presenter stand in a location that allows the audience to see the visuals. A mechanical or laser pointer will allow points on the visuals to be identified without blocking the screen. Pacing and other extraneous movements should be avoided. Gestures must be meaningful.

Although the presentation may have significant time constraints, the presenter must speak slowly enough for the audience to follow what is said. Also, it is important to speak loud enough for everyone to hear. Emphasis can be added by changing pitch and volume.

Good preplanning will allow the presenter to handle most questions. All questions should be accepted in a positive manner. If there is a chance that some members of the audience did not hear a question, repeat the question so everyone can hear it. This also gives the presenter a bit more time to reflect on the question. Give simple, direct answers to questions. Relate the answers to one or more points in the presentation. Give honest answers. If information is not available to respond to a question, indicate this and decide how this question will be handled. If it is critical to the decisions to be made, arrangements will have to be made to provide the answers.

Try to involve as many members of the audience as possible. Shift eye contact to different people to encourage them to ask a question. Do not lock in eye contact on one person. This is especially important if the person is negative or trying to block a project.

When presenting to a new group, it is usually better to err on the side of being more formally dressed than the members of the group.

PROPOSALS

In many situations, course and instructional development projects will require a formal proposal. This is especially true if the project is large or external funding is sought. Proposal writing uses most of the concepts and skills discussed in the first part of this chapter. However, there are several unique aspects that will be covered in this section.

Proposal Contents

The amount of detail in a proposal will vary with the size of the project. Projects that require extensive resources will require more detail. Also, those that may have a significant impact on courses, programs, or procedures will need more detail. It is always a good idea to check on the proposal format and level of detail required before starting to write. Many organizations will have a format for internal requests.

When seeking funding from an external organization, ask for a copy of the format it requires for proposals. Often these will be published in requests for proposals (RFPs), requests for assistance (RFAs), or requests for contracts (RFCs). Some organizations post these on their web sites. If no format is provided, use the outline that follows. It is based on the formats found in many RFPs and RFAs.

Most proposals include the following sections.

I. Cover Page
II. Submission Forms
III. Abstract
IV. Table of Contents
V. Purpose
VI. Objectives
VII. Need
VIII. Project Plan
IX. Dissemination Plan
X. Evaluation Plan
XI. Qualifications
XII. Budget
XIII. Appendices

The suggestions on report writing given earlier in this chapter should be applied to the proposal to create clear, concise, and interesting narrative. Also, correct grammar and punctuation are very important in creating a positive impression.

Section Contents

Each of the following sections used in a proposal should be identified with a side head. This makes it easier to access information in the proposal. This is especially important when the proposal is being reviewed during the approval process.

I. Cover Page. The cover page provides the title of the project, author, and date prepared. It also identifies the unit and organization submitting the proposal. If not included in other parts of the proposal, the author's phone number and e-mail address should be given.

II. Submission Forms. In many cases, specific forms must be submitted with a proposal. These may be required by the organization submitting the proposal and/or by the organization receiving the proposal. These forms usually ask for the project title, project director, cost of the project, and the organization submitting the proposal. Signatures of the project director and authorizing administrator for the organization are also requested. Some ask for a one-paragraph abstract for the project. Usually these forms can be found on the funding agency's web site.

III. Abstract. This presents a concise summary of the project's purpose, design, and outcomes. It should be limited to one page or less and include a concise description of the need or problem to which the project is directed, the purpose, objectives, activities, and cost. The project's purpose and outcomes should be linked to your organization's goals and to those of the funding agency. In some settings and organizations this is called an executive summary.

A good abstract is a very important part of the proposal package. It is one of the first items the reviewers see. If it attracts their attention and interest, they are likely to read the rest of the proposal. This is especially critical because the reviewers have a major impact on the decision to approve or disapprove the project.

IV. Table of Contents. Unless the proposal is very short, a table of contents should be included. It will list all of the proposal's sections identified by headings and give the page on which each starts. The table of contents helps the reader quickly access specific information in a proposal. Thus, the table of contents is important and consideration needs to be given to providing appropriate headings when writing the proposal. Any block of information that a reader will want to directly access should have a heading.

V. Purpose. The purpose statement is one of the most important parts of an effective proposal. If readers cannot understand the purpose for the project, they usually will have problems with the rest of the proposal as well. The purpose statement must identify the topic or problem to be addressed by the project and the intended outcomes. In addition, it needs to define the scope of the project. The scope limits the project to a defined area. For example, a task analysis study is typically limited to a specific job or set of related jobs. The outcomes or end products would be the list of tasks and the priorities identified for them.

Since it is a critical part of the proposal, the purpose statement needs to be placed at the beginning of the proposal and identified with a header. One sentence within this section must give the topic, end products, and scope. The writer may prefer to place this at the beginning of the purpose section; however, it could be placed at the end also.

Other information might be placed in the purpose section to accomplish the following:

- relate purpose to the goals of the funding source
- establish a strong link to the mission, objectives, and needs of the unit proposing the project
- provide a transition to the proposal objectives

The relevance of the project in relation to the proposing unit and the funding source has to be established somewhere in the proposal. The advantage of placing it in this section is that reviewers will be able to see the purpose and relevance at the same time.

Some proposal formats place the need section ahead of the purpose statement. There is logic in doing this. The project's purpose and objectives are developed to meet the need defined in the need section. However, the need section is frequently several pages long and keeps the reader from quickly finding what the purpose of the project is.

The transition to the proposal's objectives can be done in a one-paragraph overview of the project design. For example, in an instructional development project, this paragraph can identify the instructional development model to be used and its major steps.

VI. Objectives. Objectives deal with specific outcomes related to the purpose of the project. They must be clearly stated, and the outcomes must be measurable. There should be at least one objective for each aspect or factor in the purpose. An instructional development project, for example, would include the following objectives:

- determine the overall goals of the program
- identify courses
- determine course sequences
- develop course objectives and outlines

Additional objectives would be included if the project also will develop instructional materials and assessment instruments.

Each project must also include an evaluation objective. This is usually the last objective listed and states that the outcomes of the project will be compared to those specified in the objectives to determine the success and impact of the project.

Each objective should be stated separately in a subparagraph and identified by number. This format makes it easier to discern what the proposal's objectives are. Numbering the objectives will assist in identifying the objectives in later sections of the proposal.

VII. Need. This section must clearly identify the need, problem, or opportunity to which the project is directed. A need is the difference between "what is" and "what should be." A problem is similar to a need but is often used in a more generic way to identify any situation or system that is not working properly. An opportunity is a chance to improve or develop something new while current programs and services are working well. For example, computer technology has created a number of opportunities to expand and enhance programs and services. Many opportunities become needs if a department or company waits too long to take advantage of them. (Additional information on needs assessment can be found in Chapter 3.)

The need statement has to clearly define the current status of programs and services. It must also describe the people served. Next, the need statement has to define what should be. For example, a program may have a 50% completion rate and the desired level is 90%. The "should be" in this situation is 90% and the gap or difference between that and "what is" is 40%.

Specific data on the situation is presented to identify and justify the need. Results of local studies and data collected from the students involved will help define the need and identify specific factors involved. Usually some of this data can be found in organizational records. Special studies may need to be completed to provide all of the information required. For instance, a follow-up study of completers and dropouts would provide useful data for the example given above. (Additional information on data collection techniques can be found in Chapter 2.)

Data and results from studies conducted at other schools and organizations can also be presented. This information is especially appropriate when funding is being requested from an external agency. This will show that the need is not a local one but exists in a number of places. Also, this demonstrates more extensive effort to study and define the need or problem.

Toward the end of the need section there should be a paragraph identifying the importance of the need to the unit preparing the proposal and the organization. In addition, this statement must demonstrate how the need and the project relate to the mission of the funding agency when external funds are being requested.

The need statement should end in a concise paragraph that focuses the definition of the need and identifies the solution to it. Details on the solution will be given in the project plan. At this point, the comments on the solution are kept brief. They identify the approach that will be used to solve the need and give two or three major thrusts in the approach.

VIII. Project Plan. A good plan is essential. It will help to sell the project to decision makers. After the project is approved, it becomes the basis for conducting the project. Typical contents of the plan section include the following:

- overview
- review of related literature
- approach or strategy
- activities and time schedule
- data collection and analysis

The overview links this section with the project's purpose and objectives. This can be done by providing a summary statement of the purpose and major objectives. Another role of the overview or introduction is to provide a brief description of the contents of this section and how they fit together.

Some proposals may not require a review of related literature. The requirements of the organization funding the project will be the major factor in determining if this needs to be included. The review should present a synthesis of the approaches used and results from projects that have been conducted to meet the same or similar needs. Strengths and weaknesses of each approach should be identified. The final portion of the review should identify and justify the best approach to use in the project. The scope and depth of the review depends on the size of the project, the amount of information needed to plan the project, and the requirements of the funding source.

Although it may not be required, it may be useful to include a brief review in proposals that are funded within a department or organization. This review could include information on past projects that were done in the department. In addition, information on relevant developments could be included.

The approach or strategy will have been broadly identified in the review of literature section. In the approach section it needs to be described in more detail to justify the activities that will be listed in the next section of the proposal. A schematic or flow chart may be helpful in describing the approach. As the approach is defined, it also needs to be justified. Some of this information is presented in the review of literature section. However, the justification needs to be given in more detail as each component of the approach is presented.

The approach section also needs to describe the characteristics of the populations and samples involved in the proposed project. If the project involves a task analysis, the characteristics of the populations to be surveyed need to be described. If samples are to be selected, the sampling process must be defined and justified. In an instructional development project, the nature of the students for which the curriculum will be designed needs to be described in at least general terms. The project purpose and objectives provide direction for selecting valid populations and samples.

The strategy and population descriptions should lead naturally into the activities and time schedule section. The activities needed to attain the project objectives are listed in chronological order in a table. Breaking a project into activities and naming them is part science and part art. Various analysis techniques, such as flow charting and task analysis, can be used to identify the activities. Each activity needs to be specific enough to guide the work of project staff and to permit a reviewer to understand what is being done. On the other hand, the activities should not be so specific that the list is endless.

After the activities have been listed, the next step is to identify a schedule for their completion. If the project is complex, it may be helpful to place each activity on a 3 × 5 card. These cards can be laid out in sequence on a table, and the relationship between activities can be reviewed and changed as necessary. Some projects involve streams of activities that intersect periodically. These streams and intersections can also be identified in this process. If the 3 × 5 cards are laid out on a long sheet of kraft paper and taped in place, the cards can be connected to form a network. This is a helpful visual tool that is useful in planning and conducting the project.

The time schedule for each activity should have a starting and completion time. These will be estimates; however, they need to be logical estimates. If the overall time frame for the project is known, actual calendar dates can be used. If this time frame is not known, the starting and ending times can be identified with "week 1," "week 2," etc.

Listing the objective or objectives associated with each activity helps the reader understand how each objective will be attained. The process of listing the activities by objective helps the project planner develop a set of activities that will meet all of the project objectives. In larger projects that have several staff members, it is also helpful to identify the staff who will work on each activity.

The narrative in this section should give an overview of how the project will be conducted and justify the approach. It is not necessary to mention each of the activities in the narrative.

IX. Dissemination Plan. Usually a project funded by an external organization, such as a government agency or foundation, will require a dissemination plan. Projects funded internally may not require one; however, a dissemination plan would be appropriate for most of these also.

A dissemination plan identifies the target audiences and the methods that will be used to inform them. The proposal should justify the selection of members of the target audiences and the dissemination methods. Decision makers interested in the project and other stakeholders need to be informed. Also, consideration needs to be given to scheduling periodic interim reports for key decision makers during the project. As these communications are developed, the funding organization should be asked how it wants to be identified in them. Government agencies and foundations will usually provide a statement that can be inserted.

Dissemination activities should be included in the project plan and scheduled with other activities. Funds for these activities must be included in the project budget.

X. Evaluation Plan. An evaluation plan needs to include a description of how processes and products will be evaluated. Product evaluation activities focus on the project objectives. This portion of the evaluation is concerned with defining the degree to which project objectives have been attained. Evaluation data and judgments must be provided for each objective.

Process evaluation is concerned with the impacts of critical processes and activities used in the project. The project developer will have to decide which processes should be monitored. The relationship of the processes to project objectives and input from stakeholders will help the developer decide.

To illustrate process and product evaluation, consider the instructional development example used earlier. A valid need for a new course has been identified and a project is proposed to develop this course. One of the key sets of processes in this project is those used to develop the course design and outline. These are determined by the instructional development system selected. Thus, one aspect of the process evaluation needs to monitor the course development activities and determine how effective they are and what problems were encountered as they were deployed. This information can be used to make changes as the course is being developed and to improve the course development process for future use.

The product evaluation in this example will determine how effective and efficient the course is. Measures for this would include student learning and performance. Also, it would be useful to include feedback from students and instructors. For example, instructors may find that some information is missing and they had to speculate on what the intent was. (Additional information on evaluation can be found in Chapter 9.)

XI. Qualifications. This section needs to answer the question, "Why are you and your organization qualified to do this project?" One of the key elements in the response to this question is the quality of project staff. It is very important to have staff members who have the credentials, ability, and experience to conduct the project activities. This is especially important for large and complex projects. The competencies and accomplishments of key staff members need to be presented. Also, these have to be linked to the project purpose and objectives. Vitae for these staff members should be placed in the appendix.

An organizational chart can be included to show lines of authority and decision making. Some funding organizations may request a separate section for the staffing and management plan. The organization's proposal guidelines will specify what is desired.

Reputations of the project director and the organization are important. If both the project director and staff have a reputation for successful projects, it is easier to gain approval. This also emphasizes the importance of identifying as many project staff members as possible in a proposal. The reputation of the department or organization that developed the proposal is also important. Their previous work in the area and success with projects will be a factor in receiving funding, especially with large projects.

In some projects, facilities are critical. When specialized lab facilities and equipment related to the project are available, project activities can be initiated faster and at less cost. In addition, the presence of these facilities demonstrates an interest and commitment to the area. This point needs to be made in the proposal and the facilities' importance to the project noted.

Any existing computer systems that can be used in the project should be noted. Specialized hardware and software that can be used in the project should be identified in the proposal.

In most instances, the organizations that fund projects are interested in what will happen after the project is completed and project funding has ceased. A proposal should contain a statement about what will be done with the products developed. It should describe how the products will be used and what dissemination will take place.

XII. Budget. Budget formats, categories, and line items vary by funding organization. Also, some funding sources will not cover the cost of some resources; for example, equipment may not be an allowable expense. It is important to check with the organization that will fund the project to determine what budget information is required and what expenses are allowable.

The budget needs enough detail to communicate the nature and scope of the resources that will be used in the project. Large projects need more detail. In contrast, an internal proposal for a small project in a familiar area would not need as much detail.

The budget section usually contains a line-item budget and a budget narrative. The line-item budget identifies specific cost areas and lists the amount for each. See Figure 5-10. Additional detail is given in the budget narrative. The narrative relates the budget items to the project activities and justifies the costs associated with them. It will tell how salaries, fringe benefit rates, and travel reimbursement rates were determined. It is usually a good idea to use current salaries and rates in the proposal. Salaries for new positions should be comparable to salaries for similar positions in your organization unless there is a good justification for going above them. Adjustments for raises and inflation need to be identified and justified.

The amount of personnel time should be justified in relation to the work to be done. FTE or full-time equivalent is usually given for each salaried position. Also, a one- or two-sentence description of what each person does will give the readers a better understanding of each person's relationship to the project activities.

Each organization has a fringe benefit rate. These costs are substantial and need to be included in the budget. These rates vary by type of employee and are usually expressed in percentages.

Travel costs are determined by the travel activities in the project and the proposing organization's reimbursement rates and travel policies. A brief description and justification of the travel activities should be given in the narrative. In addition, the travel policies and rates that apply should be identified.

The budget narrative for supplies and services should identify the content of each line item, relate it to the project activities, and note its cost basis. Consultants are included as a service since they are not regular employees and do not receive fringe benefits. Their daily rate and the number of consulting days need to be listed. Some funding organizations limit the daily rate of consultants. Thus, it is important to check their policies before entering an amount in the budget.

Some organizations will not fund equipment or place a significant limit on the amount that can be spent on equipment. Any equipment included in the budget needs to have a solid justification in relation to the project's objectives and activities. Also, it must be an allowable expense.

When the cost of all these items has been determined, all of the line items are added together to obtain total direct expenses. Indirect expenses are a percentage of total direct expenses or of selected categories of expenses within the budget. The funding organization will indicate how indirect expenses should be calculated. In some instances, organizations will place a limit on the amount of indirect expenses they will pay. Indirect or overhead expenses include costs that are difficult to place in line items. Some of these costs are heat, electricity, office space, business office expense, and upper level management's time in relation to the project.

Some funding organizations require the proposing organization to cover part of the budget costs. This is called matching, and the amount of resources provided is the match. Care must be taken in identifying the match to ensure that it is relevant to the project and does not create budget problems for the proposing organization. Both the match and the funds provided by the funding organization are auditable. Thus, the match must be comprised of resources that will be used in the project.

FIGURE 5-10

Sample Budget Format

	Funds Requested
A. Personnel	
1. Project director (FTE, salary)	
2. Content specialist (FTE, salary)	
3. Media specialist (FTE, salary)	
4. Clerical (rate/hour, number of hours)	
5. Total Personnel	
B. Fringe Benefits	
1. Staff (%)	
2. Clerical (%)	
3. Total Fringe Benefits	
C. Travel	
1. Lodging	
2. Meals	
3. Mileage	
4. Commercial carrier	
5. Total Travel	
D. Supplies and Services	
1. Office supplies	
2. Telephone	
3. Copying	
4. Postage	
5. Data and information processing	
6. Resource books and materials	
7. Consultants	
8. Total Supplies and Services	
E. Equipment	
Total Equipment	
F. Total Direct Costs (A + B + C + D + E)	
G. Indirect Costs (% of direct costs)	
H. Total Project Cost (F + G)	

A line item budget identifies specific cost areas and lists the amount for each.

XIII. Appendices. Supporting materials are placed in the appendices. These are materials that are too detailed or are not required in the body of the proposal. For example, vitae, support letters, sample evaluation instruments, and in-depth information on the proposing organization are placed in the appendices. Appendices provide the grant writer some flexibility in keeping within the page limits established for the proposal narrative.

Proposal Constraints

Most funding organizations place some constraints on the length and format of proposals. These requirements should be checked before the proposal is drafted. Page limits vary by organization and grant programs. Other common requirements are as follows:

- font size—12 pt or larger
- line spacing—double
- page size—8.5″ × 11″
- page margins—minimum of 1″
- binding—check requirements

Check the RFP or with the funding organization to determine its proposal format and length requirements. Proposals can be quickly rejected if they do not meet these requirements.

Review Questions

1. List two reasons for writing a project report.
2. When would a short written report be used?
3. What information is usually placed in a report abstract?
4. What materials are placed in the appendices of reports and proposals?
5. What information is included in the long report format that is not found in the short report?
6. When should the long written report be used?
7. When would an oral presentation be appropriate?

8. What information is sought from an audience analysis?
9. What precautions need to be taken when designing visual aids to use in presentations?
10. What are the three components of the purpose statement in a proposal?
11. What is the role of objectives in a proposal?
12. How does the project plan relate to the objectives?
13. Give examples of two process measures and two product measures that might be used to evaluate an instructional development project.
14. How is the budget for a project developed?
15. Contrast the contents of the line item budget and budget narrative.

REFERENCES

American Psychological Association (APA). (2010). *Publication Manual of the American Psychological Association* (6th ed.). Washington, DC: Author.

American Psychological Association (APA). (2012). *APA Style Guide to Electronic References* (6th ed.). Washington, DC: Author.

Instructional Design

INTRODUCTION

Instructional design is the process of using coherent instructional theory in a systematic fashion to achieve desired training or educational outcomes. The process incorporates systematic content analysis, development of performance objectives and appropriate delivery strategies, implementation of the instruction, and evaluation and feedback.

As the content experts, instructors must take their expertise, and that of the other instructors with whom they work, into consideration as the instruction is designed. The needs of the students are also critical. The environment in which the training or education program is offered affects what is developed and delivered. Taking the setting into consideration is critical, as the approach would differ in a technical college, university, or in business and industry. The type of content analysis may also differ in an education or training setting. Available media specialists will have to be consulted to develop audiovisual resources, which takes considerable time. The resources available to assist as the programs or courses are being developed and the kinds of learning technologies available will affect the organization and delivery of the course or training.

OBJECTIVES

After completing this chapter, the reader should be able to do the following:

1. Explain the importance of a systems approach to instructional design.
2. Place an education or training setting into a system.
3. Differentiate between the behavioral and cognitive psychology approach.

4. Describe an instructional design model used in a school or training setting.
5. Identify characteristics of a task analysis.
6. Describe how an instructor or teacher might implement the ADDIE model.
7. Explain the six basic categories of performance problems.
8. Review a task inventory to determine the sequencing of tasks.
9. Explain the advantages and disadvantages of using LMS software.

Principles of Instructional Design

In *Principles of Instructional Design*, Gagne, Briggs, and Wager indicated that all models of instructional design have three commonalities: (1) identifying the outcomes of instruction, (2) developing the instruction, and (3) evaluating the effectiveness of the instruction. They also stressed that instructional systems design is the systematic process of planning instruction. If an instructional systems design is followed, then the instruction will lead to learning and desired outcomes (Moore & Lockee, 2009).

Diamond (2008) indicates several conditions that must be in place for instructional improvement to occur:

- Faculty must have ownership of content and curricula.
- Administration must support curricula and teaching.
- Priorities must be established and resources allocated accordingly.
- Student performance and assessment is integral.
- Instructional resources must be available as needed.
- Procedures must be in place to ensure success.

Working from a model that everyone understands and with which everyone agrees, will also facilitate success with instructional design. If there are core instructional issues such as standards, content that must be integrated within all courses or training, or effective utilization of task inventories, airing them on the front end or during the design stage will also assist in successful implementation.

When considering instructional design, two basic principles are necessary to guide the development process: (1) Instructional design should always follow a systems approach, and (2) instructional design should be based on learning theory. While the principles presented here are not all-inclusive, they offer a framework within which to consider instructional design.

SYSTEMS APPROACH TO INSTRUCTIONAL DESIGN

Much of what happens in education and training is tied to various systems that contribute to its effectiveness. There are systems that determine prerequisites before students enter a class. In a technical college, students have gone through a series of classes (or a system) before entering the technical college. The system determined what kinds of preparation they had in English, social studies, math, etc. In an industrial setting, trainees may have also gone through a similar system before taking a training course, such as knowledge assessment, interviews, and job-specific training.

Systems Fundamentals

A system is an organized way of doing something. It is a structure that consists of elements that influence one another to achieve a goal. The elements that form the system may be interrelated, interacting, or interdependent.

A system is like a room heating system. In a heating system, a thermostat, furnace, and controls, along with the room, the building, and the external environment, are the components of the system. See Figure 6-1. A thermostat detects a difference between the actual temperature and the desired temperature. It signals the controls to operate a furnace. Once actual and desired temperature are equal, the thermostat once again signals the controls, this time to turn off the furnace.

FIGURE 6-1

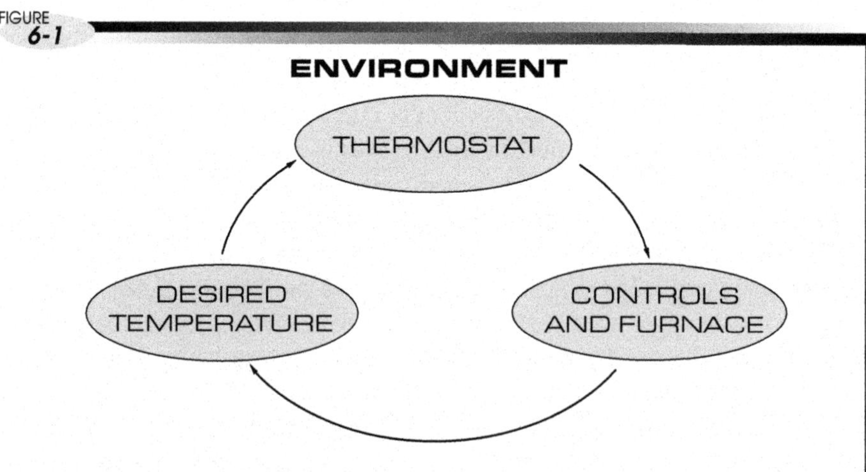

A room heating system consists of environment, thermostat, controls and furnace, and desired temperature working as interdependent elements.

There are a number of factors that may affect this system. If a door or window near the thermostat is left open and cold air enters the room, the furnace will operate even if other rooms in the building are at the set temperature. Other factors within the building would be the number of people in the room, the number of doors they came through to get to the room, etc. The environment surrounds the system and would include the outside temperature, condition of the building, and other external and internal factors that may affect the heating system. The system operates within the environment and the environment affects how the system operates.

The assumption with instructional design is that needs are established, goals and objectives are developed, content is analyzed, sequencing is considered, evaluation is made integral, and fine-tuning and adjustments are made in all phases based on feedback. There is input, process, and output within a given environment. The cycle must be complete, with decisions based on data along the way. Instructional development will remain a complex process because changes in one or more of the elements in the system will automatically result in changes to all others.

Educational and Training Systems

In a technical college system or in business and industry, learners entering the program function as an input, the technical college course or program or the training course is the transformation, and the program graduates represent the output. Assessment of course or program graduates (e.g., contributions to society, job satisfaction, competence gained, skills acquired) serves as feedback for adjustments to the system. Lack of a graduate's competence in certain areas may necessitate revisions in the curriculum or transformation. See Figure 6-2. The environment (school, community, business, industry, government, etc.) within which a technical or training system operates can influence the input, transformation, and output.

Input includes information, people, energies, and materials that enter into the system from the environment. It is also the process by which such entry occurs. Inputs into the system are students. They enter the course or training session with prior experience. In some cases they have been screened for their knowledge and skills, but for the most part, they enter the training or course at various levels of skills and knowledge. Any curriculum design must deal with the prerequisite knowledge and skills. If the systems model for the development of curriculum is used, then input would be the results of the needs assessment, content analysis, and selection.

Transformation is the process by which the input is changed. This is where instruction, reinforcement, and practice occur. In this stage the content is presented using the various resources, approaches, methods, and techniques, and is learned by the student. The student has thus been transformed.

Output is whatever the system produces and sends back to its environment. These would be the graduates of the course or training session, graduates who have knowledge and skills they did not have before. In an education setting, graduates may leave before graduating because they acquired sufficient skills to be recruited and hired. In business and industry, the competencies a trained individual brings to the job are critical, and outputs must be consistent with needs. Evaluation is a product of the output piece. Output also has a feedback route that leads to the transformation and input stages of the system.

FIGURE 6-2

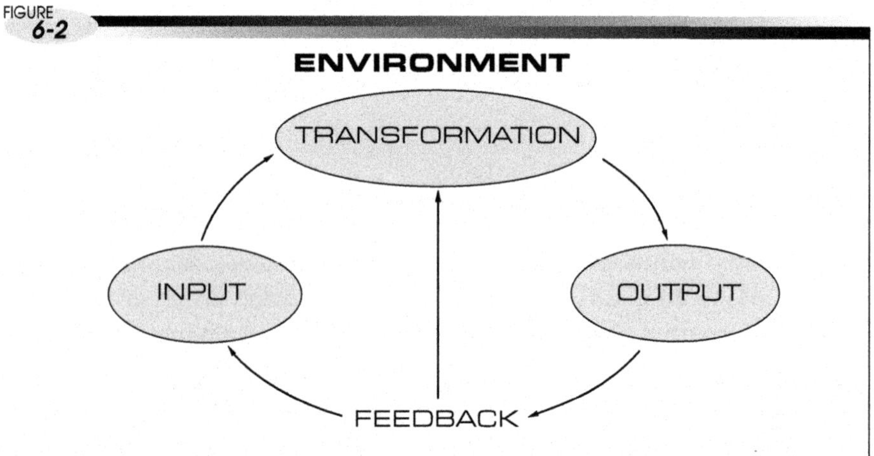

Key system components are environment, input, transformation, output, and feedback.

Environment is the context within which a system exists. It is composed of all the things that surround the system and includes everything that may affect the system and that may be affected by the system. In the case of business and industry, the environment is the company and the factors that influence it (competition, country, markets, etc.). In a technical college, the environment is the institution and the community it serves, but it is also the department, program, and people with which all of these interact. Economic, political, and cultural forces are all part of the environment.

Feedback is the process by which information concerning the state of the output and the operation of the system is introduced to the system. Follow-up studies, feedback from supervisors, data reports, instructor evaluations, performance reviews, etc., that would impact curriculum and instruction would be considered feedback in business and industry. Technical college feedback would be advisory committee reports, follow-up studies, standards, certification exams, and instructor evaluations.

System concepts apply most readily to instructional efforts. Instructional design systems provide a framework for deciding what ought to be taught (Beauchamp, 1975). Beauchamp also indicated that a curriculum system has three primary functions: "(1) to produce curriculum, (2) to implement the curriculum, and (3) to appraise the effectiveness of the curriculum and the curriculum system" (p. 71).

Input for an instructional design system comes from sources such as social and cultural values, community characteristics, and the personalities of those involved. The same applies to training in business and industry. Input into the instructional system would be from supervisors or managers, changes in technology, or altered or amended procedures. In the transformation phase, the process includes content selection, objective/competence writing, lesson plans, the delivery of instruction or implementation of training, and appraisal procedures. The output phase includes the graduates placed in the job and feedback from them and their employers. In business and industry, changes within the environment of a company may result in a need for training. These changes may include new hires or promotions, new plants or products, or new policies.

A systems model and approach for instructional design ensures relevance of needs, identification of content, and methodologies that match the learning theory approach. It increases the probability that the instruction and evaluation will fit with the goals and objectives, and that a feedback loop will produce changes that constantly improve the whole system. All the components within the system interact with one another, and when one thing changes, then all components in the system are affected. The systematic model approach means that the instructor will follow a systematic process and produce effective output results.

Learning Theory

The second principle of instructional design is the relationship of sound learning theory to instruction. Learning is commonly defined as a change in learner behavior or the process that happens when learning takes place. Learning takes into account many factors, such as a learner's knowledge, psychological state, affect, environment, and how information is presented to the learner. What happens during the learning process or the conditions under which learning takes place is what learning theory attempts to explain.

Thus, instructional design must reflect these conditions in order to ensure learning. All efforts made in the instructional design process should reinforce learning and assist learners. Sound instructional design not only reflects what the instructor or trainer knows, but how the students learn and apply that knowledge.

Understanding learning approaches is crucial to understanding the instructional strategies and techniques used with instructional design. These approaches link the design of instruction with instructional components that match content and learners. While there may be many learning theories, those most frequently discussed in the literature are behavioral, cognitive, and constructivist.

Behavioral Approach

The behavioral approach has its roots with many famous psychologists such as Pavlov, Watson, Thorndike, and Skinner (Kantar, 2013). Behaviorists believe that the brain responds to behavior, which is displayed overtly and can be observed by others. Observable behaviors are indicators of learning. The salivating dog that Pavlov observed is the result of an unconditioned response. Thorndike extended this thinking with the "law of effect," "law of exercise," and "law of readiness." By establishing general laws, Thorndike was able to extend the stimulus and response model. If the response is positive and reinforced, then natural bonds are formed into patterns of behavior (Saettler, 1990) and learning takes place.

Watson extended Pavlov's and Thordike's concepts and refined the theory of conditioning to certain stimuli in the development of emotional responses. Skinner was also a strong believer in the stimulus-response pattern and its effect on behavior. Skinner also explored behavior shaping and the importance of reinforcement scheduling.

Many of the early training and education models drew on the behavioral approach and the development of behavior objectives. Behavior objectives usually consist of three parts: the behavior or task, the condition under which the student will be tested, and the criteria, or how the students will evaluate. In 1956, Benjamin Bloom, an American educator, developed a taxonomy of cognitive learning consisting of six levels that has been used extensively to develop behavior objectives with the behavior approach, the educator or trainer is the knowledge expert, and the student absorbs the knowledge.

Closely related to behavior objectives and following them were mastery learning, programmed instruction, self-instructional packages, and computer-assisted instruction. All of these strategies were based on the behavioral psychology approach (Saettler, 1990).

Cognitive Approach

As learning was explored for deeper understanding, it was found that behaviorist theory could not explain everything. Even rats in a maze seem to recall routes that would lead nowhere and thus took longer routes to get at the food. Researchers found that children and adults could model behaviors weeks later that were never intended. It seemed as though rats and people alike were processing information they had not previously learned and that was not reinforced. Bandura and Walters, and later Piaget, developed significant aspects of cognitivism that include schema, processing models, meaning, practice, transfer, interference, and organizational effects. Context learning and mnemonic and advanced organizers were also significant parts of the cognitive approach.

The cognitive approach emphasizes mental processing. It focuses on how to store and retrieve information. Learning is attained through rehearsal and consistent use of the information. Retention strategies, such as breaking down information and comparing it to information already in long-term storage, are emphasized.

Doing task and learner analysis and checking information to assist students with a schema are parts of this approach. The use of mnemonic devices, metaphors, and advanced organizers are also significant tools for helping students learn and recall information. The educator or trainer organizes experiences that are meaningful, and the student reorganizes the experiences into new understanding and insights. The development of computer languages that incorporate information processing, receiving, storing, and retrieving and that parallel how humans process information is based on the cognitive approach.

Constructivism

Constructivism is based on the premise that learners construct their own reality with perceptions of experience and knowledge that are used to make interpretations of things and activities. This means that acquired learning is directly connected to the physical and social occurrence of the learning and based on previous experience. The new learning is locked in time with the experience (Brandon & All, 2010). In this approach, learning is a personal interpretation and has meaning based on the experience. Thus, knowledge is constructed from the experience and is individual. Learning should be realistic, and testing is integrated with the experience (Kantar, 2013).

Constructivism is an individual learner approach whereby a more open-ended learning environment is fostered and learning is also more difficult to measure. Since learning is not predictable, instruction should facilitate learning and not attempt to control it or its outcomes. The implications are that learning is based on internal and social negotiation, by exploration of actual environments, using mental models, collaboration, intellectual toolkits, problem solving, and one's own understanding or learning (Richey, Klein, & Tracey, 2011).

The constructivist approach is frequently applied in K-12 school settings and in colleges and universities as more and more problem-based learning is employed. The educator or trainer acts as a facilitator who encourages students to explore within a given framework. Students may collaborate with others to organize their ideas and learn from each other to construct their own knowledge.

Learning Theory Approach and Instructional Design

In the behavioral approach, learners are focused on a clear goal. Where to start instruction is based on learner assessment, or what instructors feel students know. Task analysis is required and learning objectives are developed. Evaluation looks at the outcomes of the objectives.

In the cognitive approach, an assessment of learners is done to determine their feelings or attitudes about the task. Strategies to aid in retention, such as the development of a schema, guided practice, connecting present learning to prior learning, etc., are stressed. Again, behavior objectives are developed with the goal of performing the task consistently.

Learning style is not a consideration with the behavioral approach; it is somewhat more so with the cognitive approach. It is integral with the constructive approach. The constructive learner deals extensively with problem solving and transfer is more likely to occur to new situations.

Ertmer and Newby (1993) summarized the three approaches in the following manner: A behavioral approach can effectively facilitate mastery of the content of a profession (knowing what). Cognitive approaches are useful in teaching problem solving tactics where defined facts and rules are applied in unfamiliar situations (knowing how). The constructive approach favors a more open learning experience where the methods and results of learning are not as easily measured for each student. Because learning outcomes are not always predictable, instruction should foster and not control learning.

In terms of instructional design, the cognitive approach seems to be the most frequent approach (Ertmer & Newby, 1993). Instructional design in business and industry and technical education takes into account what is important for students to learn. With task analysis, performance objectives and evaluation consistent with the objectives are delivered. Many of the approaches do overlap, but the assumption of technical training is that learners must be able to know and do something that is usually very specific when the training or technical education experience is completed.

MODELS

A model is a standard used for comparison or imitation. It is a roadmap, a strategic approach, a representation of a particular product used to show the construction or appearance of something and the relationship of its elements to each other. It is an organization or structure that represents something. Using models is important for educators and trainers as it helps them visualize the instructional analysis process.

The interest for education and training is in instructional design modeling, which may be viewed as a broadly based activity that deals quite extensively with content identification, organization, and steps and generally includes instructional development and evaluation. A model helps us look at the presence or absence of something. Models help visualize a complex process and see how its component parts fit together.

A model is a simplified yet communicable representation of a real-world setting or situation. Models communicate systematically, procedurally, and conceptually. Some models communicate by systems, in a linear fashion, or by an arrangement of concepts. A good model shows a logical relationship between all its elements.

With any model that tends to be generic, it is important that the implementation of the model be based in the context of the setting. Keep in mind that when models are used, they should always be adapted to the setting and never adopted. The process of instructional development will vary according to the interests, skills, and concerns of the parties involved. The backgrounds, philosophies, knowledge, and interests of group members all contribute to the selection of one or more curriculum-development processes over others. Thus, the output of a model will vary, even if the same content and process was addressed.

Curriculum Planning Models

Gay (1980) identified four different models used to conceptualize the curriculum-planning process: the academic model, the experimental model, the pragmatic model, and the technical model.

Academic Model. This model utilizes scholarly logic as the basis for curriculum decision making. Emphasis is focused on utilizing the inherent structure of a discipline or disciplines to help shape the content selection. The academic curriculum model is viewed as having distinctive features found in a specific school setting. English, social studies, math, and science courses tend to use this particular model when developing curriculum.

Experimental Model. In this model, the focus is on the learner and activities. The person, and the process-oriented objectives that assist the learner as an individual and member of a social order, are emphasized. Alternative schools and those using modular flexible scheduling tend to use this model when developing curriculum.

Pragmatic Model. This model looks at the context of decisions and ensures that planning is done at the local level. Social and political factors dictate that the planning be a localized process rather than one imposed from outside the school setting. Schools and programs that have strong locus of control will use a portion of this model.

Technical Model. In this model, learning itself is perceived as a "system." The system can be divided into its constituent parts. Instruction occurs in specific systematic and predictable ways and its efficiency and effectiveness can be improved through control or management. Incorporated into this model are needs assessment, content selection, and objectives development consistent with content and the establishment of concrete evaluative measures.

INSTRUCTIONAL DESIGN MODELS

Instructional design is a systematic method of analysis, planning, developing, delivering, and evaluating training or technical education. It also includes managing the students in the instructional process. The design process is both systematic and specific (Kemp, Morrison, & Ross, 1998). "Systematic" implies a logical or orderly method of identifying, analyzing, developing, delivering, and evaluating a set of strategies aimed at attaining a specific instructional goal. "Specific" implies that each element of the design is applied with precision. Designing effective instruction can be accomplished by applying systematic procedures with precision. The following models deal with instructional design. While these models have wide application, they are also very relevant to business and industry training and in technical education settings.

Three-Stage Systems Model

Bartel (1976) and others (e.g., Mager and Pipe, 1997) use the three-stage system as an instructional design model. Each of the three stages consists of specific tasks that are performed for the selection and development of content. See Figure 6-3.

In this model the preparation and description stage deals with the background information necessary before beginning the actual training or delivery of the program. Learning theory and its implications for content identification for training or education are considered at this stage.

In the next stage, identification and selection, the content identification, validation, scope, and sequence are specified for the education or training program. A task inventory serves as a specific guide for performance objectives.

In the final stage, development and application, the specified content is matched with resources and learning strategies specific to learners' needs. Units of instruction, lesson plans, information sheets, and other teaching aids are identified based on the learning theory application. Evaluation procedures are also developed at this stage.

Bartel (1976) further breaks down the three stages into 10 distinct steps. See Figure 6-4. All of the steps are critical to systematic instructional design.

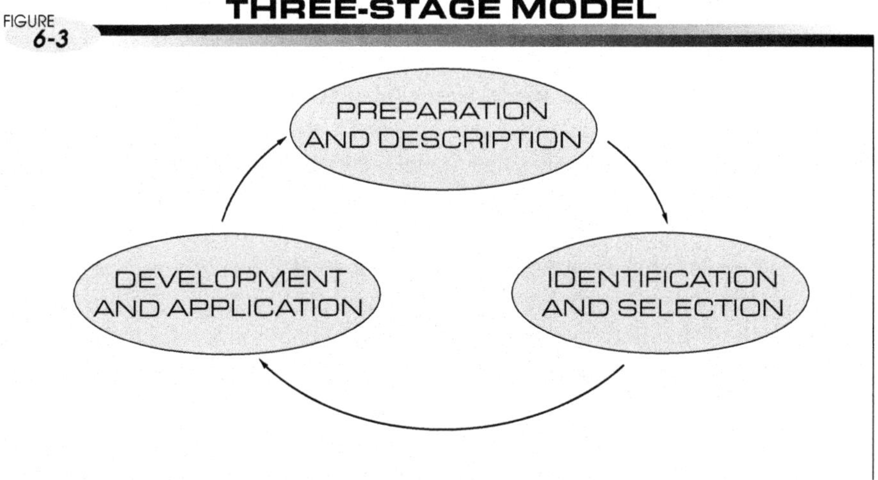

The three-stage model consists of preparation and description, identification and selection, and development and application.

FIGURE 6-4

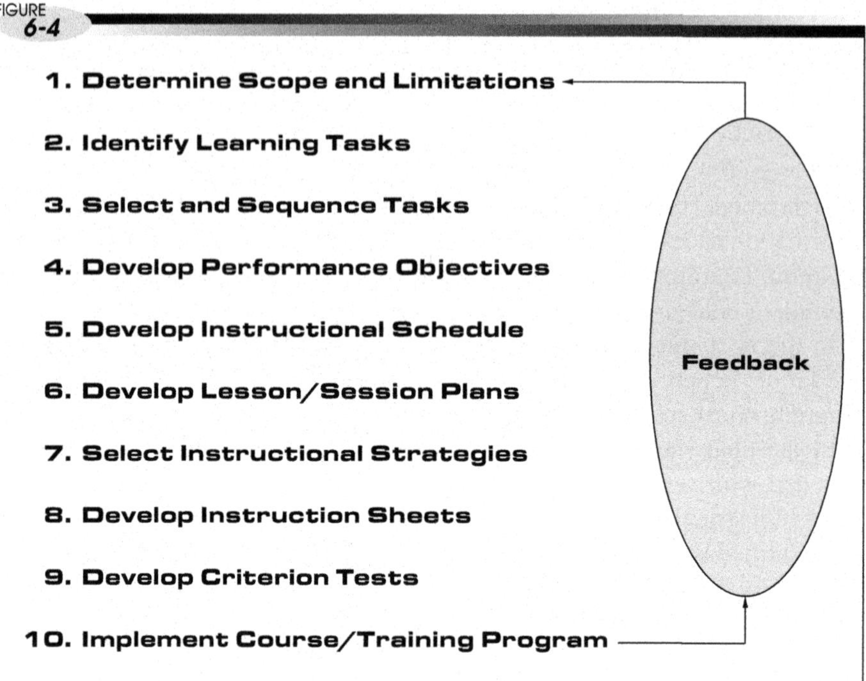

Bartel further breaks down the three-stage model into 10 steps. (Adapted from Bartel, 1979, p. 9)

Dick and Carey Model

The Dick and Carey model has gained prominence in the training industry, and with adaptations, in education. The model is significant to instructional design because it fosters a systems view of instruction as opposed to the view that instruction is the combination of its separate parts. The model views instruction as a whole system by concentrating on the interrelationship between setting, content, learning, and instruction. This popular systems approach for designing instruction is similar to the ten-component step approach of the previous model. See Figure 6-5.

The model mirrors a software engineering approach to designing instruction. The strength of the model seems to be in the replicable procedural process of designing, producing, transmitting, and revising instruction in a systematic fashion according to the context of K-12 education, higher education, business training, and/or government training. According to Dick, Carey, and Carey (2014),"the instructor, learners, materials, instructional activities, delivery system, and learning and performance environments interact and work with each other to bring about desired student learning outcomes" (p. 1).

FIGURE 6-5 **DICK AND CAREY MODEL**

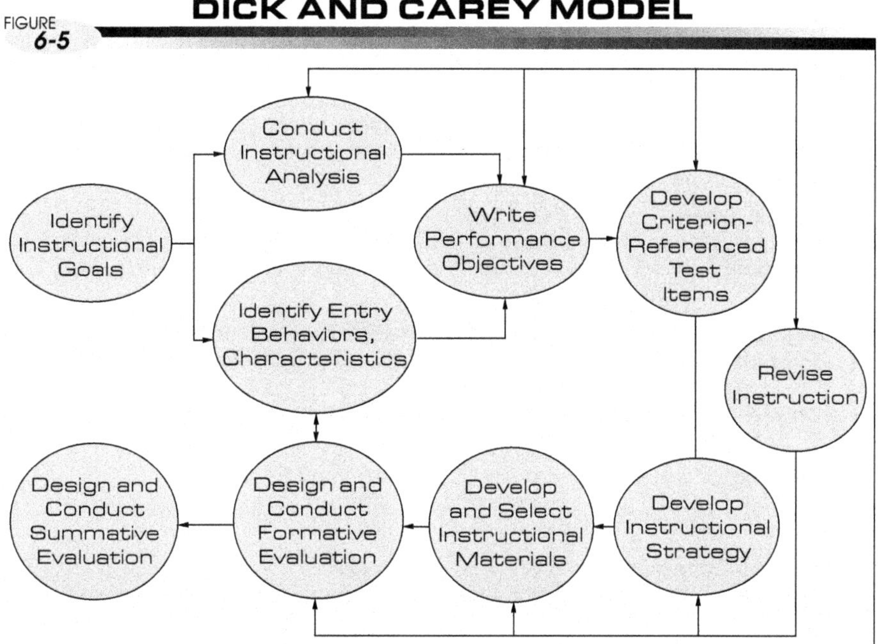

The Dick and Carey model used for instructional design consists of 10 distinct steps. (Adapted from Dick, Carey, & Carey, 2015).

The model consists of nine stages, starting with the identification of instructional goals and ending with summative evaluation. See Figure 6-6. All nine stages consist of a purpose and a function.

Instructional System Design Model

The instructional system design (ISD) model employs a very popular, systematic instructional development process for use in postsecondary educational institutions and technical training. The ISD model is not new (U.S. Army Institute for the Behavioral and Social Sciences, 1979) and has been used by the Army, Navy, and Air Force with slight variations since the early 1960s. Many of the present-day models are adaptations of this basic model.

The model consists of five stages: analysis, design, development, implementation, and evaluation (ADDIE). See Figure 6-7. The "ADDIE" model was popularized by the United States armed forces, and then adopted by business and industry. The five elements of the model basically remain unchanged, but modifications to the five elements have occurred over the years.

FIGURE 6-6

Stage 1. Instructional Goals
Purpose: Identify instructional goals for the course or training session.
Function: Complete a needs analysis that looks at the discrepancy between an instructional goal and the present state of affairs or a personal perception of needs.

Stage 2. Instructional Analyses
Purpose: Determine skills involved in reaching the goal.
Function: Perform task analysis, information processing analysis, and learning task analysis.

Stage 3. Entry Behaviors and Learner Characteristics
Purpose: Determine which required enabling skills learners bring to the task.
Function: Identify the intellectual skills, abilities, and personality traits.

Stage 4. Performance Objectives
Purpose: Translate needs and goals into specific objectives.
Function: Determine if instruction is related to goals, focusing lesson plan on condition, performance, and criteria.

Stage 5. Criterion-Referenced Test Items
Purpose: Develop psychomotor, cognitive, and affective test items based on performance objectives.
Function: Diagnose prerequisite learning skills, monitor student learning,document attainment, evaluate instruction, and identify performance measures prior to lesson plans and instructional materials.

Stage 6. Instructional Strategy
Purpose: Identify instructional activities that relate to the objectives.
Function: Lesson design reflects objectives, criterion-referenced test items, knowledge of learners, tasks, and effective teaching strategies.

Stage 7. Instructional Materials
Purpose: Select appropriate resources and/or develop materials.
Function: Use existing materials and develop new materials based on objectives, tests, and instructional delivery strategies.

Stage 8. Formative Evaluation
Purpose: Assess throughout the system.
Function: Collecting and sharing information for program improvement which includes evaluating the instruction development process, students, assignments, and exams and connecting with appropriate stage for improvements/changes.

Stage 9. Summative Evaluation
Purpose: Determine the total impact of the course or program.
Function: Assessing if the course or program should be continued, expanded, dropped, recommended to other audiences, etc.

The nine stages associated with the Dick and Carey model each consist of a purpose and a function.

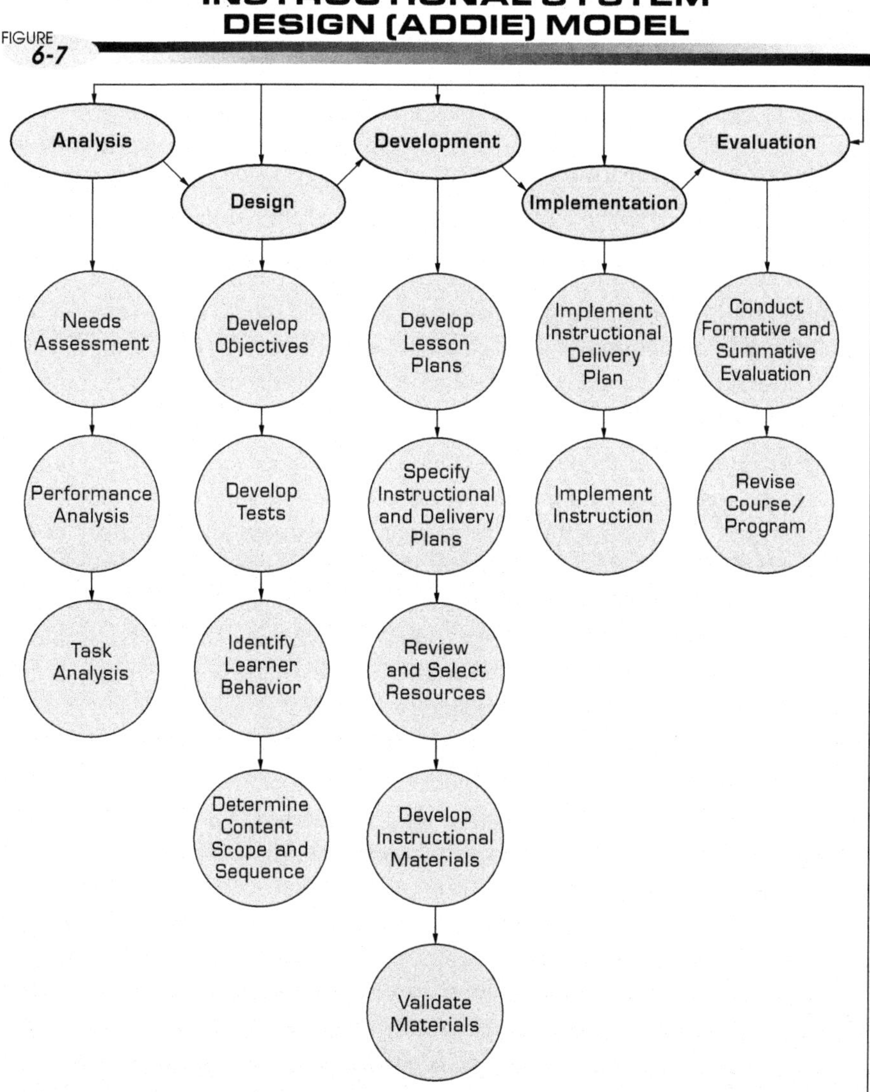

The instructional system design model consists of the following categories: analysis, design, development, implementation, and evaluation. Each main category also has a number of subcategories.

This model also utilizes features from both the behavioral and cognitive approaches. Behavior objectives are a significant part of the model, as well as instructional delivery that addresses multiple learning styles and strategies to increase learning.

The ADDIE model is a systematic approach to the instructional design process. This generic framework ensures that the appropriate content is included and that the instructional products are effective and address the needs of the students. Careful scrutiny of the relationship among the five stages ensures that the needs, content, instructional strategy, and outcomes are accompanied by focused assessment instruments that measure performance objectives.

As shown, the five stages do not end once the training or technical education program is implemented. As a system, the five stages interact with each other in the flow diagram. What happens in one stage affects the other stages.

The ADDIE instructional design model is a basic model that works for any type of learning, including web-based learning (Piskurich, Beckschi, & Hall, 2000). The ADDIE model is simple and includes all the components found in other instructional design models.

Analysis. Analysis is about finding and defining the problem. Is there breakdown in the manufacturing lines? Is the product not getting out the door? Are the graduates not meeting the expectations of business and industry? Is the human resource department indicating that there are too many accidents in the warehouse area? Is it a training or education problem? The problem may not be easy to isolate. It is necessary to find out what is causing the problem. Once it has been determined that it is a training problem, what content should be taught? How is the content validated?

The analysis stage consists of three distinct phases: identification of the problem (which is the needs assessment), needs or performance analysis, and task analysis or content identification. See Figure 6-8. The analysis stage is sometimes called front-end analysis and must be completed before any of the other stages can be developed. If training has been identified by the needs assessment as the solution, appropriate content has been identified, and assessment of learners has been accomplished, then the rest of the stages should be on track for an excellent systematic training effort and result. If there are problems with the analysis stage, problems will arise in the other four stages.

The major function of analysis is to determine the instructional content for the technical education, development, or training program. The underpinning of analysis is to identify, relate, separate, and limit the specific work behavior to the job, duty, and/or task under investigation. The first step in this process is the needs assessment.

Needs Assessment—Needs assessment is determining the gap between "what is" and "what should be." The needs assessment will generate data that can assist in determining the root cause of the problem. A goal of this step might be to analyze training needs and produce a needs assessment document.

FIGURE 6-8

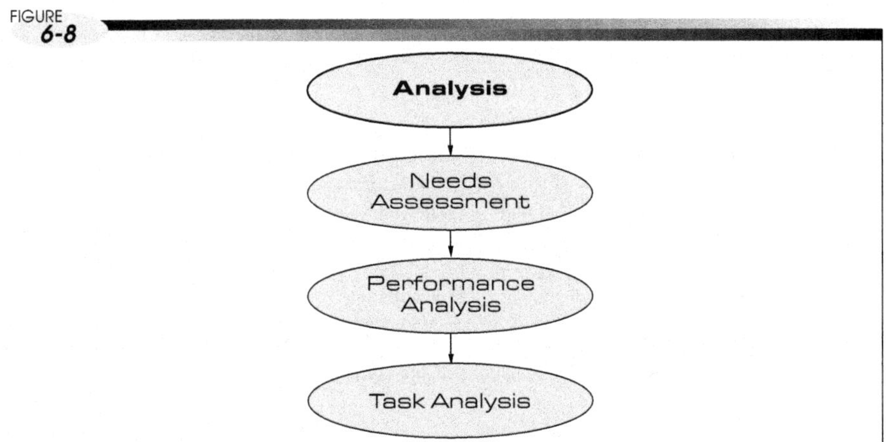

The analysis stage consists of needs assessment, performance analysis, and task analysis.

An employee needs assessment is used to identify the problem that is being experienced on the job and its causes. A cause may be recently purchased technology equipment, reorganization of a manufacturing line, or changes in company procedures. More specifically, it is important to identify whether it is a performance discrepancy or a skill deficiency.

A performance discrepancy identifies the difference between what the employee should be doing and what the employee is presently doing. Skill deficiency implies that the skill—which can be cognitive, psychomotor, or affective — was never learned or was lost because of lack of practice. Lost skills can be addressed with in-service training that incorporates guided practice. If the skill was never learned, a training session will need to be developed. Once the needs assessment has been accomplished, performance analysis is the next step.

Performance Analysis—Performance analysis determines solutions to the problem. See Figure 6-9. The needs assessment identifies the problem, and performance analysis identifies where the problem is and how it can be solved. Needs assessment always comes first, and performance analysis follows. Needs assessment looks at the gaps, while performance analysis seeks reasons for the gaps. Needs assessment determines the significance of the need, while performance analysis looks at the relationship of the needs to other factors such as process, procedures, and the environment. Lastly, needs assessment focuses on the most important need, and performance analysis attempts to find the cause and solutions to the most important need. (Additional information on performance analysis can be found in Chapter 4.)

FIGURE 6-9

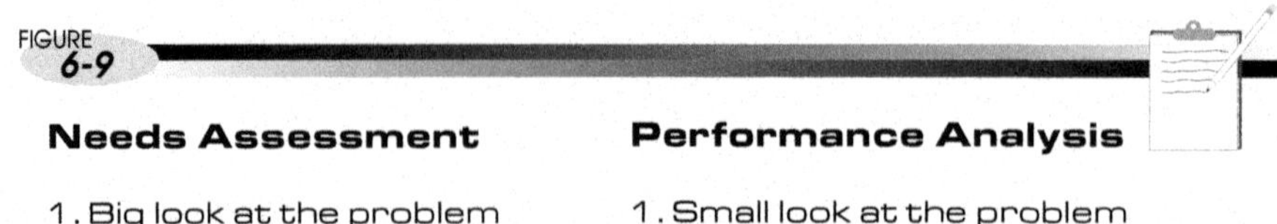

Needs Assessment	Performance Analysis
1. Big look at the problem	1. Small look at the problem
2. Occurs first	2. Occurs second
3. Identifies gaps	3. Identifies the reasons for the gaps
4. Problem identification stage	4. Problem resolution stage
5. Determines the significance of the need	5. Determines the relationship of the need
6. Focus on the most important need	6. Focus on causes of and solutions of the most important need

There are six principal differences between needs assessment and performance analysis. (Adapted from Benjamin, 1989)

If the problem really is training, then a training solution can be implemented. Once this is determined, a task analysis can be undertaken.

Task Analysis—Task analysis is the identification and validation of the content for the training session or technical course. There are many ways to analyze the content for training. Subject matter analysis, troubleshooting process analysis, and job analysis are the three basic types of task analysis.

Subject-matter (or content) analysis is used in fields that are heavily dependent on learning cognitive information. Learning new concepts would fall in this area. The subject matter is broken down into learning the pieces that will most likely result in understanding the whole.

Troubleshooting analysis (also called process) is used to identify the skills and knowledge used to monitor or troubleshoot an operation or machine. This process is very similar to job and task analysis, except it includes possible cue sections and error patterns of decision-making logic that an operator would be expected to perform.

Job and task analysis is used to identify the steps and procedures required to execute a basic task. It may also include the decision used to carry out the task. Critical knowledge and skills are identified and broken down. Sometimes the job and task analysis will look at activities or general areas of responsibility, the level of performance acceptable, and conditions for performing the job. Methods for sequencing tasks are covered later in this chapter.

The fundamental purpose of the task analysis step is to determine the content for the training session or technical course. The underpinning here is a comprehensive analysis to identify the duties and task or content. In this step the question, "What are the knowledge, skills, and attitudes that need to be addressed?" is answered.

Design. The design stage consists of four steps that lay the foundation for systematic design. See Figure 6-10. The steps in the design stage are to develop objectives, develop tests, identify the entry behavior of participants, and determine the scope and sequence of the content. By following these steps, a complete blueprint is developed for how the completed lesson might look.

FIGURE 6-10

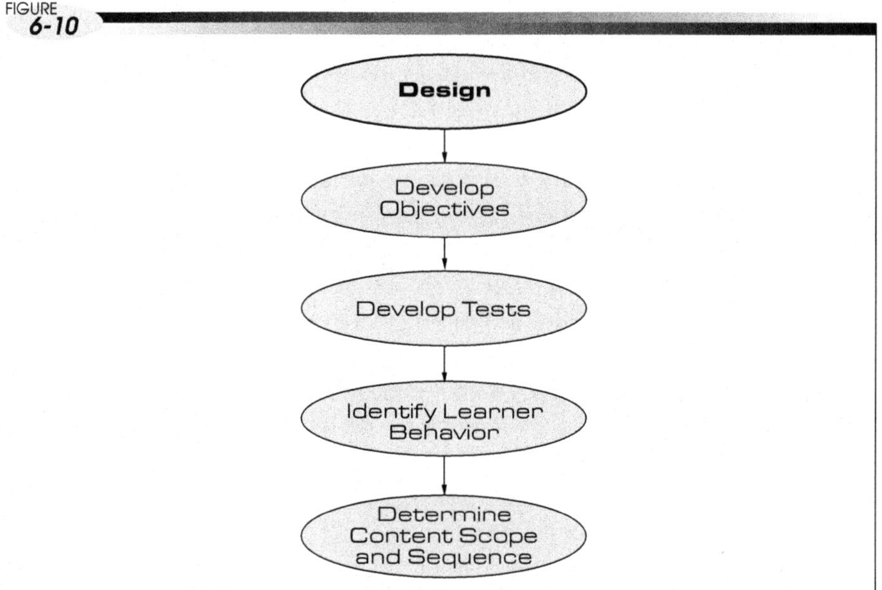

The design stage consists of the following processes: develop objectives, develop tests, identify learner behavior, and determine content scope and sequence.

Develop Objectives—The first step in the design stage is the development of performance objectives based on the task analysis. The objectives may include cognitive, psychomotor, or affective skills, and may be written so that the performance, conditions, and criteria are explicit. The purpose of the objectives is to provide direction for the rest of the design stage. If the performance, conditions, and criteria for exit behavior are known, then the rest of the design steps can be performed.

Develop Tests—Once the performance objective is stated, test questions and performance measures can be written. Depending on the method of testing, objective and subjective test questions may be used. Objective questions, such as true-false, multiple choice, matching, and completion questions, may be used. Subjective questions include essay and problem-solving questions. An answer key should also be developed. Validation of the exam questions using face and content validity should be done prior to use. Performance tests, such as a product and process checklist consistent with the performance objectives, should also be developed. Case studies and simulations should also be considered for testing the knowledge and skills of participants.

Identify Learner Behavior—Learner analysis identifies the audience for which the training or technical course is intended and the needs of that audience. The analysis includes identification of the learners, their learning characteristics, what they need or want to learn, why they need it, and the environment and conditions under which they will be applying the knowledge and skills learned. This may take the form of a preassessment of possible participants or assessment by the supervisor of possible enrollees. This information can be used to customize learning activities and to fit the delivery to the participants. Appropriate resources based on their knowledge and skill levels can also be employed. This kind of assessment is especially helpful in ensuring that examples that the audience can relate to are used in the delivery of the content.

Malcolm Knowles' andragogy (adult education) theory assumes that adult learners become self-directed. This affects the need for demonstrating relevance, intrinsic learner readiness, and the benefit of life experiences. Adragogy contrasts with pedagogy (instructor-focused) science of educating children. Pedagogy requires the instructor directing the learning

Instructors that understand the learners' characteristics can use instruction and psychological approaches that match the students' needs. In some cases, a test may be administered to determine the entry-level skills of participants. It may also be desirable to develop a pretest that measures the trainees' current knowledge so that instructional units already mastered may be bypassed. All of these strategies are used in the "identify learner behavior" step in order to better address the needs of the students enrolled in the technical course or training session.

In this step, provision is also made for informing supervisors and possible participants about the training session. Thus, dates may need to be established or classrooms arranged, or the instructional technology department may need to confirm or prepare any impending two-way interactive training or Internet delivery.

Determine Scope and Sequence—The general scope of the content is usually based on the needs assessment. If the needs assessment is correctly done, then the scope of the content should be well outlined. But how much time is really needed for instruction? It would be best to set the scope of the content to be covered in terms of time required, number of lessons, and topic areas. However, the delivery of the content may vary, depending on other factors over which the instructor or trainer may not have control. Management may decide that only three days will be devoted to the training; thus the trainer must pare back the content. Even with hard data from a needs assessment and performance analysis, management may decide to limit the content based on political factors, thereby affecting the delivery of content.

Determining content sequence may be based on student characteristics, content being delivered, activities, equipment availability, and physical location. There are five basic ways that content can be sequenced: general to specific, frequency, skill, logical, and interest sequencing.

Development. The third stage is development, which consists of lesson plan development, specifying instructional and delivery plans, reviewing and selecting resources, developing instructional materials, and validating materials. See Figure 6-11. Specific learning events and activities, such as developing video scripts and other media, producing resources, and utilizing programmers, graphic artists, SMEs, etc., to assist development, all happen at this stage.

Develop Lesson Plans—In this stage, a lesson plan consisting of required information, performance objective, references, instructional aids, materials and supplies, along with a content outline, is documented. The lesson plan can be divided into day or session, units of instruction, or tasks. At this step, the instructional developer must determine the presentation form. Will it be stand-up lecture, interactive TV, computer-aided instruction, booklet modules or other print materials, videos, simulations, case studies, or web-based instruction? The lesson plan is just that, a plan to determine the direction the lesson will take. The content covered, time, resources, budget limitations, and the expertise of the instructor/developer will help determine if the materials are to be developed in-house or sent out for development.

Specify Instructional and Delivery Plans—It is at this stage that the decision is frequently made about who will be delivering the instruction and where it will take place. Frequently, companies may decide to outsource the required training. The training may have to be delivered by a technical college or outside consultant. The program or training may also be offered on-site or off-site. In the case of a technical college, the training could be conducted in business and industry, especially if there are specialized pieces of equipment required for training.

FIGURE 6-11

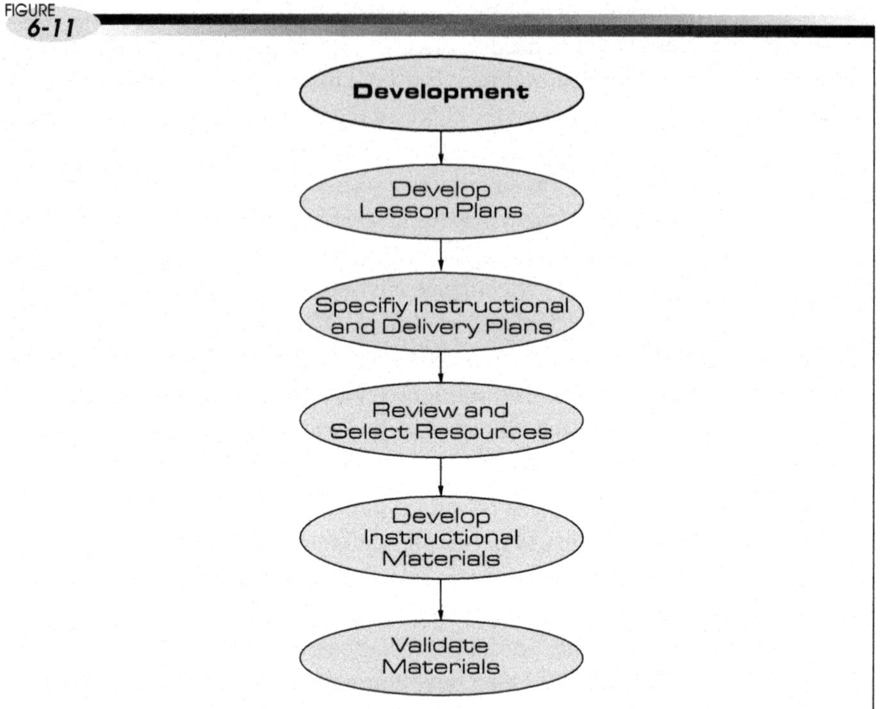

The development stage consists of the following processes: develop lesson plans, specify instructional and delivery plans, review and select resources, develop instructional materials, and validate materials.

The delivery plan may include selecting a web-enhanced approach or stand-alone web-delivery method, depending on what was selected in the lesson plan. Delivery plans may be based on media requirements or delivery requirements, along with cost-effectiveness of various delivery systems. If two-way interactive video is being considered, then the instructional technology department needs to become involved.

Some training departments have established some kind of quality control procedure designed to evaluate instructional objectives, tests, and materials in preparation for delivery. The timelines for implementation are firmed up, facilities and procedures for training are scheduled, and learners are enrolled. All of the tools for implementation are reviewed.

Review and Select Resources—In this step, the wide range of resources are reviewed and selected. The developer may have to obtain and/or create the required media and plan activities that permit learning groups to be supportive of the social environment (Simonson, 2000) if part of the plan. Media selection is based on learning objectives, course content, student characteristics, and teaching methods.

Develop Instructional Materials—The purpose of this step is to prepare materials, including materials for performance objectives that are not covered by existing resources. The plan should include what, who, where, when, and how; and a timeline, evaluation, and deadlines. During this stage or phase all audio, visual, and text material are reviewed, collected, and developed. The tools and processes used to develop instructional materials are addressed. Multimedia, storyboards, instruction, procedural sheets and other handouts, web-enhanced courses, and full-web courses are examples. Blended learning, which utilizes the learning activities from a variety of sources, is developed.

This stage builds on the analysis stage and design stage to meet the objectives. The real focus of this stage should be a detailed plan that identifies step-by-step procedures for implementing the instruction. Media selection should be based on the type of information to be learned: intellectual skill, cognitive strategy, verbal information, motor skill, or attitude.

Validate Materials—In this step, resources selected or developed are validated for face and content validity. This validation can occur through review by other development or instructional staff, supervisors, and managers or through outsourcing. In addition, a pilot study could be implemented using prospective students to determine how the materials work. The materials can then be revised based on feedback sources. A record of what was changed should be kept for future reference. The reviewed materials can then be matched against the original lesson plan and performance objectives to ensure they have not drifted from the original intent.

This validation is really a part of formative evaluation. With the completion of this step, the development stage is finished and the implementation stage begins.

Implementation. In the implementation stage, the instruction is delivered following the instructional delivery plan in the appropriate setting. This stage consists of two steps: implement the instructional delivery plan and implement instruction. See Figure 6-12.

Implement Instructional Delivery Plan—Execution of the instructional delivery plan before instruction is accomplished during this step. If the delivery plan calls for direct instruction, then the instructor prepares all lesson plans and gathers all resource materials for presentation. Any handouts are copied and packaged in preparation of the instruction. Guest speakers are confirmed. Facilities are also confirmed and checked for proper arrangements. Information on the training session is sent out and participant lists are established and confirmed. Materials for class or training are duplicated and distributed beforehand. This may be accomplished through the web using appropriate software or the instructor's web page. It is wise to consider posting materials as PDF files to permit easy downloading.

Implementation may involve sending participants information on text materials, session outlines, or how to make the best use of interactive learning materials. Dates are set and the instructor completes all preparation for delivery.

Implement Instruction—In this stage, the instruction is implemented using the setting, methods, and media specified by the instructional delivery plan. This may involve presenting classroom instruction or facilitating and managing a distance learning program.

FIGURE 6-12

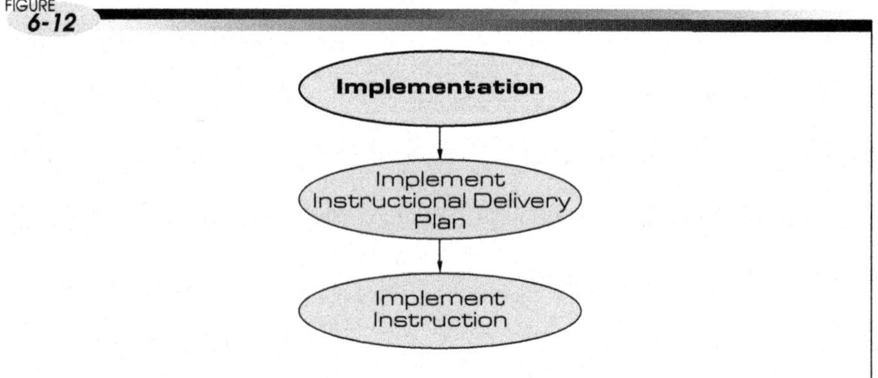

The implementation stage is made up of two steps: implement instructional delivery plan and implement instruction.

Evaluation. Evaluation is the final stage in the ADDIE model. Evaluation answers the questions, "Did participants learn?" and "Did they learn what the objectives said they were going to learn?" This involves a thorough collection of data from students, instructors, and supervisors and an analysis of the data. While it is the last stage, the process of formative evaluation should be integral to each stage. See Figure 6-13. In this stage, all aspects of student learning are examined. A feedback sheet after each session will produce valuable data for the next session. Feedback data from each unit will facilitate success in future units.

An important aspect of this stage is the revision that must take place for continuous improvements in instructional design. In-class evaluation of instructors and materials and out-of-class evaluation of graduates on the job are essential in order to revise instruction and make educated judgments about revising the system. The relationship between entry behavior and terminal performance behavior should be documented. The whole ADDIE model is evaluated. Data is collected in all phases of the program, with discrepancies noted and planned and actual outcomes documented. Documentation of what was revised is an essential part of this stage. Evaluation consists of two steps: formative and summative evaluations and program revisions.

FIGURE 6-13

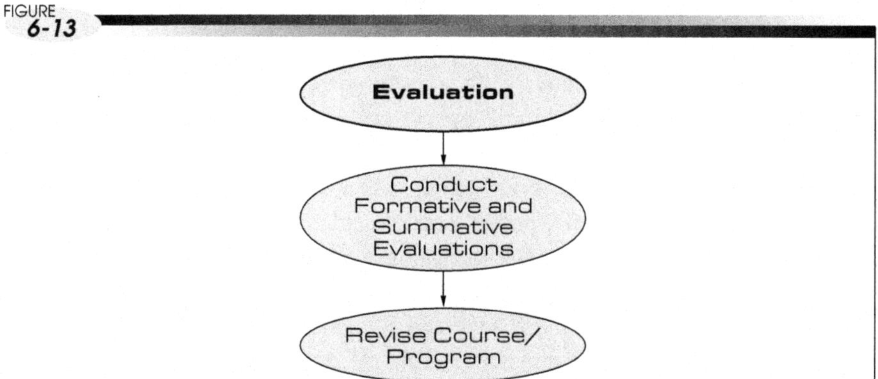

The evaluation stage consists of two steps: conduct formative and summative evaluation and revise course/program.

Formative Evaluation—Formative evaluation is part of each processing stage of the ADDIE model and determines the effectiveness of each phase. It is also used in the implementation of instruction and takes on the form of constant feedback from participants and instructors alike. The six phases of formative evaluation are as follows:

1. Specify goals for each phase of the model. Established goals can easily be measured.
2. Arrange the necessary personnel and measurement instruments, tests and quizzes, checklists, etc., for each stage of the model.
3. Collect data and elicit feedback from target audience and experts. It may be necessary to hire and train data collectors, involve the quality control department, or hire a third-party evaluator.
4. Tabulate statistical data. Decide on the kinds of analysis that will be used: mean, standard deviation, median, interquartile rank, t-test, or other test of significance.

5. Modify the product to improve effectiveness and efficiency based on data collected about the stakeholder goals.
6. Move to summative evaluation and dissemination after removing weaknesses.

Summative Evaluation—Summative evaluation consists of feedback from the participants to assess learner outcomes. Summative evaluation is the process of collecting data following implementation of the course in order to determine its effectiveness in meeting the instructional objectives. Summative evaluation may also measure learners' outcomes, attitudes, and knowledge and skill learned, along with transfer of learning.

Long-term effects of the training should also be evaluated to ensure that the training in fact made a difference. In a training facility, a follow-up is always conducted with the participants and supervisors a week after the training and six months after the training. This is to ascertain whether the participants learned and are applying the training in the work setting. Supervisors are also surveyed a week after the training to determine whether they noticed a difference in performance of the individual, and six months after the training to see if there was really a return on the investment.

As information comes in and is analyzed, a decision has to be made to modify the course materials, training and educational methods, or delivery settings. Tests for instructional standards (assuming that they were identified in the analysis stage and developed during the design and development stages) require scrutiny.

A systematic process that determines the quality and effectiveness of the instructional design and delivery is part of evaluation. Evaluation is thought to be an ongoing activity conducted at each stage of the developmental model, but a follow-up with documented changes is essential. If a test was determined not to measure what it was supposed to, was the test revised, validated, piloted, and shared with others in a systematic fashion? The cycle has to be completed.

Revise Course/Program—Whether to modify the process and initiate another training session must be determined from data and consultation with supervisors and those in charge. The development of a process to improve the process must be established and in place for all portions of the system to work. (Additional information on evaluation can be found in Chapter 9.)

SEQUENCING TASKS

There are several ways to sequence tasks in a task inventory. The sequencing determines which task will be taught first, second, third, etc., under each duty. This sequencing for tasks also applies to duties.

General to Specific

Tasks may be listed and taught from general to specific, or from specific to general, depending on the occupation. If how to operate a vacuum-forming machine is taught before teaching how to maintain it, that would be general to specific. If identification of the vacuum forming machine's parts is taught before teaching the theory of operation, that would be specific to general.

Frequency

Tasks that are taught first are most frequently performed on the job. In the automotive field, engine tune-up is taught before teaching valve adjustments or transmission rebuilding because engine tune-up would occur more frequently on the job.

Skill

Sequencing of tasks is based on the skills needed to perform other tasks or jobs. The skills needed to be a helper are different from the skills needed to be a journeyman. A student may need skills in basic hand tools before the worker is expected to do shingles and framing. Students need skills in reading tire wear before they can do alignments.

Logical

One task may naturally be taught before another. Many programs start with terminology before they go into something else. Perhaps students can learn the parts of the machine as they learn the function and operation. Is it essential to know the basic terms relating to a wordprocessing program before learning how to use the program? Should they be learned together? What is logical in learning a wordprocessing program? Is it logical to know letter styles before actually composing a letter?

Interest

This is teaching tasks that interest students first, or tasks at which you know they will be successful and that have implications for other tasks. This is done to motivate students. Teaching tasks that get students involved with their hands right away, rather than cognitive learning tasks, tends to keep students more interested. Teaching programming by starting students on a computer game and then dealing with the specific intricacies of the program may be done to keep students interested and motivated.

PERFORMANCE-BASED CURRICULUM

Performance-based curriculum implies that only performance objectives are being used and that the conditions, performance, and criteria for testing are developed first. Specific performance measures are developed and used throughout the instruction and are shared with students before the beginning of instruction. Other names for performance-based curriculum are individualized instruction, learning for mastery, programmed instruction, self-paced instruction, and competency-based instruction (CBI).

Early CBI programs articulated competencies developed by either a panel of experts or instructors, and with support personnel, individual learning materials were developed to address each competency. Students who enrolled in these programs could move at their own pace and graduate earlier or later. Upon graduation, students would have a competency profile chart to show employees what they had learned and the level of mastery they had acquired for each competency. Criticism of CBI was the loss of values, insights, and judgment and lack of training in affective, social, cultural, aesthetic, and ethical skills.

Each of the steps used to develop a CBI program requires a tremendous amount of time and training on the part of the instructor, SME, instructor-developer, and many support personnel. The steps include the following:

1. Competencies are identified, sequenced, printed in a task listing, and made public.
2. Each competency is developed into a terminal performance objective that includes conditions and criteria for evaluation.
3. Supporting materials for each competency, such as information and procedure sheets, activities, written and performance tests, CD-ROMS, and references, are developed.
4. All of the materials are compiled into a module, or learning activity packet (LAP).
5. The learning packet is field-tested and revised as needed.

DISTANCE EDUCATION DESIGN

Distance education, or e-learning, has exploded in the education and training sector recently. Over 7.1 million students enrolled in distance educated courses in 2013 (Allen & Seaman, 2014). And while delivery methods may change, quality standards are still needed, various instructional design elements are still required, and the presentation, management, and evaluation are still the responsibility of the instructor. The instructor must ensure that the various design elements, such as course materials, audiovisuals, graphic design, and equipment, are present and part of the sound instructional design.

In some cases it would be helpful to meet with the entity's distance-education web-design team to see if best practices, as identified in *Best Practices for Electronically Offered Degree and Certificate Programs* published by the Higher Learning Commission in 2007, have been incorporated into the course. New courses should also be tested with a peer, or the distance-education web-design team, to ensure efficient and effective use of the management software (Bersin, Howard, O'Leonard & Mallon, 2009). In many cases, if the course is offered by an educational entity, then the distance-education course must meet the same standards as an on-campus course.

Not every course should be offered online. Course content and face-to-face experiences, such as hands-on training, may not lend themselves to distance education delivery. However, almost all the same procedures used for face-to-face courses need to be followed when implementing distance courses. An instructor or trainer still needs to follow the principles of good instructional design, determine the overall course methods and strategies, analyze the students, write the student learning objectives, develop appropriate instructional materials, and become familiar with the technical resources that are needed and available for the course.

In terms of distance education, deciding the manner in which students will access the learning materials and how the students will be supported during the course is essential. Also, if a time frame for interaction between the instructor and students is not developed and followed, everyone will be frustrated. Student writing skills are even more critical in distance learning courses. In addition, if instructors are not supported when teaching distance education courses, the courses will not be successful.

Most instructors will agree that online courses require far more development time. Everything from syllabi, assignments, resources, chat-room assessments, evaluations, etc., should be set up in advance. If course material is not organized, instructors can expect a high volume of emails from students about the assignments. A learning management system (LMS) is a software application used mainly for the delivery of online distance education courses. Many educational institutions use LMSs to manage their online courses or with blended or hybrid strategies to support face-to-face instruction. Corporate training also makes extensive use of LMSs to deliver online training. LMS software provides a rich array of opportunities for the delivery of instruction, learning, and keeping track of student involvement and progress.

Most LMSs are web-based systems that the instructional developer, educator, or trainer can use to lay out the content and develop teaching strategies such as collaborative learning, discussion threads, etc. LMS software keeps detailed records of student engagement and learning. Many LMSs also offer registration, course administration, and reporting. Common LMSs include, but are not limited to, Blackboard®, Desire2Learn®, and Moodle®.

Generally included in LMS software are tools for organizing course content and building various presentations, chat rooms that permit student-to-student and student-to-instructor communication, and a place where students can do collaborative work with instructor monitoring. LMSs also include evaluation tools. Quizzes and tests can be taken online with immediate feedback given. Students can monitor their progress in the course with a grading tool, and the instructor can get reports on student progress and monitor student involvement in discussions, chat rooms, and collaborative work.

The implementation of an LMS requires an institute- or company-wide deployment that integrates with processes across the entity to provide best practices for teaching and learning while supporting important business practices. An LMS implemented in this manner results in improved management of e-learning, reduced costs through greater efficiency, and better service to instructors, staff, and students. Thus, LMSs have the following advantages:

- reduction in material tasks
- reduced training costs
- increased student/employee competency
- manageable learning facilities in conjunction with human resources goals
- flexibility for instructors, students, and employees
- incorporation of sophisticated multimedia

Along with advantages are the following challenges:

- selection of a single LMS can be time consuming
- integration of LMSs with other services involves several people and departments
- lining up IT support may be costly
- training instructors and support staff takes time

All LMSs are capable of using systematic instructional design, such as analyzing learners' needs. Instruction can be designed using measurable learning objectives. An LMS can also help an instructor determine the effectiveness of instruction through formative and summative evaluations and enable any needed revisions of the evaluations.

Companies and nonprofit organizations may engage in online or distance education on a smaller scale, making the purchase of an LMS too expensive.

Given this situation, open source content management systems (CMSs), which permit the user to see and make changes to the source code, may be more beneficial.

Content management is the process of planning, creating, managing, storing, and distributing content. Content may include graphics, documents, media, etc. In a CMS, content is stored in a database that can then be used based on rules established in advance. In an open-source CMS, this content can be formatted by a template and displayed in a variety of ways. Thus an open-source CMS, such as WordPress®, Joomla!®, or Drupal®, can be used to develop just-in-time training for small companies or nonprofit organizations.

Blended Learning

Educators and trainers who use face-to-face instruction may also teach distance education courses via the Internet. When these two delivery methods are combined and integrated, it is usually termed blended learning. Other names used to describe the use of synchronous and asynchronous instruction in a single course include hybrid or web-enhanced instruction. The advantage of a blended learning course is that it provides numerous ways to access content and engage students through collaboration, assessments, and feedback throughout the course (Driscoll & Carliner, 2005).

Blended learning requires the use of an LMS to provide students with access to lectures, chat rooms, discussion threads, and support materials and to allow collaborative learning to take place. The instructor is required to utilize new modes of delivery for learning materials and develop self-directed guided information, resources, and tutorials. There are many blended learning strategies to choose from (Bower, Dalgarno, Kennedy, Lee, & Kenney 2014). Blended learning uses the strengths of both face-to-face instruction and distance education.

REVIEW QUESTIONS

1. Define instructional design.

2. What are the two main principles of instructional design?

3. Explain why a systems approach to instructional design is needed.

4. Identify the environmental factors found in your own setting.

5. Explain why feedback is critical within a system.

6 What are the three basic psychological approaches to learning?

7. List the psychological approach for each learning level noted below:
   a. elementary school
   b. high school
   c. technical education
   d. college or university
   e. training in business and industry

8. Gay identified four basic models to conceptualize curriculum (instruction). Which one would be used for technical education? Which one would be used for training in business and industry? Indicate why.

9. What is the advantage of each of the following instructional design models?
   a. three-stage system model
   b. Dick and Carey model
   c. instructional system development model

10. The ADDIE model can be adapted to any education or training setting. Explain why this is true.

11. Explain the difference between needs assessment and performance analysis.

12. What is the main difference between formative and summative evaluation?

13. In what ways do training and technical education curricula differ?

14. Explain performance-based curriculum.

15. Explain the five ways to sequence tasks.

16. Performance analysis explores potential performance causes and solutions. What are the most common performance problems and how can they be addressed?

REFERENCES

Allen, I. E., & Seaman, J. (2014). *Grade change: Tracking online education in the United States.* Retrieved November 3, 2014, from: http://onlinelearningconsortium.org/survey_report/2013-survey-online-learning-report/

Bartel, C. R. (1976). *Instructional analysis and materials development.* Homewood, IL: American Technical Publishers.

Beauchamp, G. A. (1975). *Comparative analysis of curriculum systems* (2nd ed.). Wilmette, IL: Kagg Press.

Bersin, J., Howard, C., O'Leonard, K., & Mallon, D. (2009). *Learning management systems 2009: Facts, practical analysis, trends and provider profiles.* Oakland, CA: Bersin & Associates.

Bower, M., Dalgarno, B., Kennedy, G., Lee, M. J. W., & Kenney, J. (2014). *Blended synchronous learning: A handbook for educators.* Retrieved October 15, 2014, from: http://blendsync.org/handbook

Brandon, A. F., & All, A. C. (2010). Constructivism theory analysis and application to curricula. *Nursing Education Perspectives, 31*(2), 89–92.

Dick. W., Carey, L., & Carey, J. (2015). *The systematic design of instruction* (8th ed.). Upper Saddle River, NJ: Pearson.

Diamond, R. M. (2008). *Designing and assessing courses and curricula: A practical guide.* (3rd ed.). San Francisco: Jossey-Bass.

Driscoll, M., & Carliner, S. (2005). *Advanced web-based training strategies: Unlocking instructionally sound online learning.* San Francisco: Pfeiffer.

Ertmer, P. A., & Newby, T. J. (1993). Behaviorism, cognitivism, constructivism: Comparing critical features from an instructional design perspective. *Performance Improvement Quarterly, 6*(4), 50–70.

Gay, G. (1980). Conceptual models of the curriculum-planning process. In *Considered action in curriculum improvement, ASCD 1980 yearbook* (pp. 120–143). Alexandria, VA: American Society for Curriculum Development.

Kantar, Lina D. (2013). Demystifying instructional innovation: The case of teaching with case studies. *Journal of the Scholarship of Teaching & Learning, 13*(2), 101–115.

Kemp, J. E., Morrison, G. R., & Ross, S. M. (1998). *Designing effective instruction*. New York: Merrill.

Mager, R. F. & Pipe, P. (1997) *Analyzing performance problems: Or you really oughta wanna*. Atlanta, GA: The Center for Effective Performance.

Moore, D. R., & Lockee, B. B. (2009). Re-visiting the instructional strategy diagnostic profile: A comparative analysis. *International Journal of Instructional Media, 36*(2), 187–194.

Piskurich, G. M., Beckschi, P., & Hall, B. (Eds.). (2000). *ASTD handbook of training design and delivery: A comprehensive guide to creating and delivering training programs, instructor-led, computer-based, or self-directed.* New York: McGraw-Hill.

Richey, R. C., Klein, J. D., & Tracey, M. W. (2011). *The instructional design knowledge base: Theory, research, and practice*. New York: Routledge.

Saettler, P. (1990). *The evolution of American educational technology*. Englewood, CO: Libraries Unlimited.

Simonson, M. (2000). Making decisions about the extent of the use of electronic technology in on-line classrooms. In R. Weiss, D. Knowlton, and B. Speck (Eds.), *Principles of effective teaching in the online classroom.* San Francisco: Jossey-Bass.

U. S. Army Institute for the Behavioral and Social Sciences (1979). *An annotated bibliography for instructional development.* Alexandria, VA: Author.

Course Development 7

INTRODUCTION

Course development includes finalizing the content for the course, narrowing the scope and sequence, developing course and syllabus, and developing performance objectives. This is the background work that encompasses course development that must be completed to ensure professional delivery and implementation. Courses that have been developed as part of a sequence are incorporated into the overall curriculum.

Many education and training institutions offer both face-to-face and online distance courses and programs. There has also recently been an increase in the use of online elements to supplement course design and delivery. Thus a basic consideration during course development is when and how to offer interactive learning as opposed to traditional lectures.

OBJECTIVES

After completing this chapter, the reader should be able to do the following:

1. Explain how an instructor can select course content.
2. Describe the importance of learning to learn.
3. Develop a course syllabus utilizing a course goal, course description, course objectives, content outline, and evaluation.
4. Develop a unit of instruction that includes unit objectives, resources, visuals, and evaluation.
5. Write performance objectives with performance, condition, and criteria components.

Program and Course Identification

In occupational and training programs, the expectation is that workers are being trained to perform their work well. If a needs assessment and occupational analysis have been completed, then content should have been identified. The scope and sequence of the content may have to be sharpened. If the needs identified go beyond the breadth of a single course, then a question must be asked: Should a program be offered as opposed to a single course?

Identifying whether to deliver a course or program may be determined by the delivery setting. In a business or industry training setting, a course is the usual format in which to deliver the content. In some cases however, there may be a series of courses all related to a specific area.

For example, a set of competencies for certification may imply a program made up of courses. A company may want to have certain employees in their organization who have had ISO 14,000 training. The content may be too long for a single course and thus a series of five two-hour courses may be developed to address the ISO 14,000 training. If an employee completes all courses, the employee would become certified and, in some cases, this may result in a pay upgrade. The content for the training may have been determined by supervisors, through a needs assessment, from standards from the ISO 14,000 manuals, or from other sources.

Technical colleges usually develop their own programs. The program may consist of a series of courses, all related to each other, or all related to the mission and goals of the program, that build on each other. General education content such as English, communications, math, science, and the arts, which relate to the program, are usually required, although some of the general education courses may have little direct relationship to some of the technical courses. Dental hygiene programs offered by technical or community colleges, for example, use job occupational experience instructors to teach specific dental hygiene content. Usually, a needs assessment has already been performed and a task listing of competencies is available. Chunking the tasks into manageable courses may require consulting all content instructors.

The instructional faculty, the advisory committee, and the accrediting group usually determine the specific general education courses needed by the dental hygienist. In some cases, content faculty may also teach some of the general education courses. Content faculty may teach technical math and communications for health professionals. In other cases, an instructor with a math background, or one with a communications background and/or degree, would teach the math and speech courses. These faculty members are often on the advisory committee, so they are aware of the content issues and the strong need for specific occupation examples in the content area.

The Dental Hygienist Program in most places is a two-year associate degree program broken down into four semesters and two summer sessions. See Figure 7-1. Most of the courses are very specific to the content area, such as Dental Radiography, Dental Materials, and Nutrition and Dental Health, to name a few. Anatomy and Physiology, Introduction to Psychology, and Written Communications are some examples of general education courses that are required in the program. Technical and general education courses make up this particular program.

FIGURE 7-1

Mountain Technical College

Program Requirements

START DATE(S): August	EFFECTIVE: August 20__

Dental Hygienist
Associate Degree

Course Number	Course Title	Hrs./Week	Credits	Prerequisite(s)/Comments
	Summer Semester (8 weeks)			
806-177	General Anatomy and Physiology (T, L)	10	4	
	Total Semester Hrs./Week and Total Credits	**10 hrs.**	**4 cr.**	
508-101	Dental Health Safety (L) (August, 32 hours) **Internet and on-campus lab**		1	Program student, must be completed prior to program start (See tip sheet)
	First Semester			
508-102	Oral Anatomy, Embryology, Histology (T, L), (T)	6	4	Program student, 806-177
508-103	Dental Radiography (T, C), (C) and (T)	4	2	Program student, 508-101 and 508-102 or concurrent
508-105	Dental Hygiene Process I (C) and (T)	7	3	Program student, 508-101 and 508-102 or concurrent
806-186	Introduction to Biochemistry (T, L)	4	3	Fall only
806-197	Microbiology (T, L)	5	4	806-177
	Total Semester Hrs./Week and Total Credits	**26**	**16 cr.**	
	Second Semester			
508-106	Dental Hygiene Process II, (T, C)	10	4	508-102, 508-103, 508-105
508-108	Peridontology, (T) and (L)	4	3	508-102, 508-103, 806-186, 806-197, (508-106, 508-111 or concurrent)
508-109	Cariology, (T)	1	1	806-186, 806-197, (508-106 or concurrent)
508-110	Nutrition and Dental Health, (T)	2	2	806-186 or concurrent
508-111	General and Oral Pathology, (T)	3	3	508-102, 508-103
801-195	Written Communications	3	3	
	Total Semester Hrs./Week and Total Credits	**23**	**16 cr.**	
	Third Semester			
508-112	Dental Hygiene Process III, (T, C)	13	5	508-106, 508-108, 508-109, 508-110
508-113	Dental Materials (T, L), (T)	3	2	
508-114	Dental Pharmacology, (T)	2	2	806-186, 806-197, 508-106, (508-112 or concurrent)
508-115	Community Dental Health	2	2	508-112 or concurrent
809-196	Introduction to Sociology	3	3	
809-198	Introduction to Psychology	3	3	
	Total Semester Hrs./Week and Total Credits	**26**	**17 cr.**	
	Fourth Semester			
508-107	Dental Hygiene Ethics and Professionalism	1	1	Program student

The Dental Hygienist program is a two-year associate degree program broken down into four semesters and two summer sessions.

Content Selection

General content is usually identified with the needs assessment. Specific content is further refined with a task analysis that results in a task inventory. The task inventory is a complete listing of all the tasks that make up the program. How the tasks are grouped into courses depends on the number of tasks, kind of program, and the instructor or people providing input. From the task inventory, a course developer can decide how to chunk the information into courses and assign how much time it will take to complete each course. In the case of training in business or industry, this may result in a single day or a one-week course. At times it becomes necessary to break up the course into smaller chunks based on the schedule.

In business or industry only a limited number of tasks are used for the training program. The needs assessment may have only focused on safety issues and encompassed only a few tasks or a single duty that had a few tasks under it. This serves as the content for the training session. If there are a lot of issues on safety, it may be decided that the training should take several days. Based on interaction with supervisors, it may be decided to break up the training and let it occur over several months using four half days. In this example, the supervisors felt they could not free employees for more than this amount of time. In another company, the decision may be to have two full days of training.

Another way of looking at content is to consider the potential course content adjusted for the content constraints. This should result in usable content (Finch & Crunkilton, 1999). Constraints may be students' knowledge and preparation, instructor's knowledge and background, availability of support staff, time available to teach the course, amount of content, and the availability of equipment, supplies, and facilities. All of these affect what students learn in the course and how the instructor spends time in preparation and delivery. These constraints are always present and it is how they are managed that makes the difference in what students learn in a training or course situation.

How the instructor finalizes the content selection is determined by many factors. A task analysis will very clearly indicate the content to teach. The task analysis will produce a task inventory that lists all the duties and tasks that would be appropriate for a technical college program or a training course or program. Task inventories tend to be shorter in business or industry because they generally address only a specific need/problem area, or one or two courses, and not a whole program. Final content selection may be based on criteria such as the following:

- Frequency of performance and use—More frequently performed tasks should be included in the final content.
- Importance and need—An important task is critical in the work environment and must be performed. A task that is needed might be a health and safety task. It may not be performed with great frequency, but it is very important.

- Basic and required—Prerequisite tasks needed for future learning will have to be selected. Tasks common to other related tasks should also be considered.
- Complexity and difficulty—Frequently, complex and difficult tasks are delayed for more advanced courses. If it is still critical to the job, then it should be included in the content.
- Appropriateness for setting—Because of specialized equipment and materials, or the training setting, some tasks are not appropriate. They may be best learned in the work setting.
- Duplication—While some duplication may be desired, tasks that are covered in a previous course or training program should be avoided (Bartel, 1976).

While there may be other reasons to include tasks in the course content, the above criteria establish a framework within which to make the decision. There may be additional circumstances and considerations to assist in the decision, depending on the setting. Additional resources, such as textbooks, audiovisual materials, other programs or course outlines, and web resources may all be used to finalize the content. Whatever method is used, it is important to remember that the task is the backbone of the content and must be selected based on the needs of the students.

Sequencing Content

Sequencing is the ordering of content into a structure that will help the student learn in an effective and efficient manner. Sequencing ensures that prerequisite knowledge and skills are taught before higher knowledge and skills are taught. Once the content has been selected, appropriately sequencing it within the program and course is the important next step. Sequencing content is especially critical for learning and may be approached in a number of ways. General to specific, topical, chronological, concrete to abstract, separate to whole or vice versa are just a few of the possibilities. (See Rothwell & Kazanas, 2008, for many different ways to sequence content).

In a technical education or training situation, task-expertise sequencing tends to be the predominant method. This means that elementary tasks are taught first, with more complex tasks taught later. Prerequisite knowledge and skills are needed for intermediate and advanced knowledge and skills. In general, it makes sense that sequencing should build towards greater complexity. The task analysis may ask for sequencing of duties and tasks, and result in a sequenced task listing. The course developer would then follow the sequence noted in the task inventory.

Some technical education programs and training courses may deal with duties or general areas of responsibilities. Supervisors who perform these duties, instructors/trainers, or advisory committee members may do the sequencing. The sequencing is usually based on what may be first encountered in the job, frequency of performance, importance to the job, or other factors.

The activities under each task are also sequenced in a similar manner. In a training program, one can identify the tasks the workers must do and perform a backward analysis to determine the prerequisite tasks. In general, duties should be sequenced first, then tasks under each duty. A short training course may deal only with tasks when division of the job or duties has not been documented. In these cases, it would be appropriate to sequence all of the tasks.

Criteria could also be developed and used to sequence duties and tasks; and, in many cases, the criteria might be similar to that used for selecting tasks for content. The relationship of a duty and task also needs to be considered when using selection criteria. For example, there may be a prerequisite duty or task that must be performed before the next duty or task. Specific knowledge and skills are needed to address more complex knowledge and skills. The following criteria should be considered when sequencing duties and tasks.

- Prerequisite—Those duties and tasks that are considered fundamental to perform another duty or task should be taught first.
- Frequency of use—Duties and tasks that are performed often, in a real-world setting, should be introduced early in the training course or program.
- Essential—There may be duties and tasks that are considered essential but not used frequently. For example, a safety lockdown procedure is really essential, but not used often.
- Learning difficulty—Duties and tasks that are difficult or complex to learn affect the sequencing of content in the course. There may be some complicated piece of equipment that requires the integration of several tasks, which may require prior student experience.
- Whole to the part—This implies covering a "big picture" duty before focusing on the tasks that deal with the function of each part. For example, learning about the capabilities of a milling machine and observing it in action may be necessary before learning the basic parts of the machine.

Course Development

One of the primary focuses when engaging in course development should be on the student and the learning. Focusing on how students learn by providing training and classroom activities that reinforce learning is essential for course development. Regardless of whether the student is from business or industry or in a technical college setting, learning should remain the main focus. It is assumed that after a training situation trainees will return to the job setting. If trainees have not learned the material that was presented in the training setting, then a lot of money will have been wasted. If the returning trainees know the content but cannot apply what has been learned, this is also a waste.

Learning to Learn

With the rapid changes in technology and the short half-life of information, it becomes essential to teach trainees and students how to learn. Students' value to business or industry will be significantly greater if they can manage their own learning. Knowing how to find and use resources, and how to analyze and critically evaluate information to make it useful, becomes more important than just knowing selected bits of information.

Much has been written on learning to learn. Every course developer should be concerned with learning to learn strategies and students' abilities to apply them to solve problems they have not experienced before. There seems to be evidence that breadth of preparation of instructional development leads to lifelong learning (Mentkowski, 2000). In other words, what course developers do in planning courses and programs could have a lasting effect on the student's ability to learn and apply information in new situations.

In a U.S. Department of Labor and American Society for Training and Development (ASTD) study, learning how to learn was considered the most fundamental skill identified in a survey of over 6000 companies. "Learning to learn . . . knowing how to learn—is the most basic of skills because it is the key that unlocks future success. Equipped with this skill, an individual can achieve competency in all other basic workplace skills" (Carnevale, Gainer, & Meltzer, 1990, pp. 8–9).

Another focus related to learning is encouraging students to take greater responsibility for their own learning. Students in a training session, or in a technical college course, need to be more responsible and demonstrate initiative for course and training materials. If students are provided materials to learn before the course begins, what is the process used to learn the information? Of course, it is recognized that much of this increased responsibility for students rests with the instructor and how instruction is provided so students can buy into the content and activities. Grunert O'Brien, Mills, and Cohen (2008) suggest that students should be involved in the following:

- clarifying their own goals for the course
- participating in and planning tasks to meet their individual learning goals
- monitoring and evaluating their own progress
- developing their own criteria for judging their own performance

Instructors must place more responsibility on students to learn for their own good. If students can learn to learn, they can be much more productive. Research by Heiman and Slomianko (1998) found that successful students use four major thinking strategies:

- Ask questions or get materials presented in lectures or books—thinking about which questions the materials answer, and which they do not.
- Break up large tasks and complex ideas into smaller parts.
- Are goal-directed; direct their study to meet their instructional objectives.
- Take feedback, testing themselves informally to see how much they're learning. (p. 7)

As part of course development, instructors should plan for and provide strategies to assist students in accomplishing the above items. Strategies found to be effective and affect a student's achievement include identifying similarities and differences; summarizing and note taking; reinforcing effort and providing recognition; assignments and practice; nonlinguistic representations; cooperative learning; setting objectives and providing feedback; assigning homework and providing practice; generating and testing hypotheses and questions; cues; and advanced organizers (Dean, Hubbell, Pitler, & Stone, 2012).

Lifelong learning is another critical issue for all students enrolled in training or an educational program. It was noted in *Continuing Education and Lifelong Learning Trends* (2009) that building a quality workforce will require more education than ever before. More states are mandating continuing education for some professionals, higher skill levels are required for increased productivity, technology is constantly changing, and competition is increasing within a global economy. All these have implications for lifelong learning. The instructor can capitalize on many trends and gear instruction to lifelong learning so that the course in which students are presently enrolled is not an isolated education and training opportunity, but is a part of the total longitudinal development of the person.

Course development cannot be conducted in isolation. Research cited by Thomas Sherman in Weimer's (1993) *Improve Your Classroom Teaching* suggests that there are five components of effective instruction. The five components are knowledge of content, preparation and organization, ability to stimulate a student's thought and interest, clarity, and enthusiasm. Content selection and sequence must fit within the context of effective instruction.

As in any course geared to business or industry, or in a technical education setting, critical thinking should always be encouraged. Critical thinking would involve assignments that build upon a sound theory base and tend to pose an issue, problem, or question related to actual occurrence in the industry. Advanced planning on the part of the instructor is critical to formulating the parameters of the problem and to considering evaluation criteria. Kurfiss (1988) identified eight guiding principles for consideration when infusing and designing critical learning into courses:

1. Critical thinking is a teachable and learnable skill. A number of resources are available to support critical thinking.
2. Issues, problems, or questions serve as a point of entry for the students. This usually provides a source of motivation.
3. Successful courses blend content with the task of thinking critically, with appropriate support based on students' needs.
4. Critical thinking assignments utilize goals, research, interactions, and evaluation of specific content.
5. Formulating ideas in writing is an expectation in formalizing the solution. Sharing the solutions is also important.
6. Collaboration to stretch thinking and interaction is considered essential to the process.
7. Metacognitive abilities (thinking about your thinking as you think) are strengthened through critical thinking.
8. Specific evaluation criteria are developed and shared with students as the problem is shared.

Integrating critical thinking in any training or technical education course will assist students to solve problems on the job. Active learning, collaborative activities, and critical and creative thinking all contribute to academic success and intellectual development of students (Pascarella & Terenzini, 2005). The next significant development in course development is the course syllabus that reflects the content, sequence, and learning conditions.

COURSE SYLLABUS

The course syllabus is a document developed by the instructor or course developer that identifies students' responsibilities, instructor's role, objectives, evaluation, how the course will function, communication, and resources. The syllabus consists of many pieces that, when put together, form a whole that welds all parts of the course together. Grunert O'Brien, Millis, and Cohen indicate that the syllabus has a number of functions that engage learners. Some of the functions of a syllabus are as follows:

- Establishes an early point of contact and connection between students and instructor. Essential information about the instructor and the course is outlined.
- Helps set the tone for the course. The syllabus is a significant communication tool that lets the student know how you plan to conduct the course.
- Describes your beliefs about educational purposes. The syllabus outlines expectations for students and the relationship of course goals and objectives to activities.

- Acquaints students with the logistics of the course. A well-written syllabus will outline how students need to prepare for each class meeting.
- Contains collected handouts. A syllabus sometimes contains important information sheets, references, and resources that are essential for the completion of the course.
- Defines students' responsibilities for successful course work. A good syllabus answers the who, where, when, what, and how questions for students.
- Describes active learning. A complete syllabus will provide assignment sheets so students can clearly see how they will be actively involved in their learning.
- Helps students assess their readiness for your course. Many syllabuses indicate the prerequisites for the course. Some have detailed course descriptions, goals, and course objectives which students can read to evaluate their readiness to tackle the content and activities of the course.
- Sets the course in a broader context for learning by letting students know that instructors are engaged in research within their discipline.
- Provides a conceptual framework by placing the information about the course in the context of current events so students can see the relevance in their everyday lives.
- Describes available resources. Resource needs in the course, such as references, software, media, lab equipment, and email protocols, are usually listed in the syllabus.
- Communicates the role of technology in the course by explaining how students will be expected to access and use the required resources.
- Can include materials that support learning outside the classroom. Outside speakers that students can contact or resources they can use beyond their classroom assignments may be listed.
- May improve the effectiveness of student note-taking by requiring journals and written communications. (pp. 25–34).

Weimer (1993) feels that the syllabus identifies a set "of necessary decisions to be made about course objectives and content, learning activities, and classroom policies and procedures" (p. 29). The syllabus establishes for the student that the instructor has taken the time to consider all facets of the course.

The syllabus is an important tool for setting the tone, letting students know what is expected, and providing necessary information and resources to help students succeed. A well-thought-out and well-designed syllabus helps the instructor prepare and deliver the content and design activities that also help students learn.

There are many parts of a complete syllabus, depending on the level of specificity. Is the syllabus only going to cover the general aspects of the course, or will it also cover the units of instruction? Some requirements of any course syllabus are a course goal statement, course description, course text if used, course prerequisites if applicable, course objectives, course content outline, references, and any special considerations. A more thorough syllabus would also include units of instruction, unit objectives, unit content outline, student activities, resources, questions, evaluation, class policies, class etiquette, grading policies, the cheating and plagiarism policies of the institution or department, and any ancillary information, such as websites, CD-ROMS, or unit study guides. In addition, some syllabuses also contain a tentative schedule that outlines the topics, times and dates, and assignments.

Course Goal

A course goal is a general statement about the purpose of the course. It lets the reader know the intent of a course and establishes the parameters of the content. It assists the course developer with course development and planning and provides a general focus for the course. The course goal also serves as a means of communication between professionals and nonprofessionals.

A course goal is a general statement that describes the intent of the training or course, is not measurable, and generally does not convey meaning in a behavioral sense. By reading the course goal, the general intent of the course should be clear. Only one goal needs to be written for each course. The following are examples of course goals:

- develop attitudes of cooperation and consideration with fellow workers
- gain an understanding of the injection molding processes used in the company
- become proficient in employee-employer relationships
- understand ISO standards used in the company
- become knowledgeable in laboratory safety procedures
- develop competencies in financial transactions

The next step in the development of a syllabus is the course description.

Course Description

A course description describes the content of the training or technical education course. The course description lets the public know what the course covers. It is written in a manner such that people familiar with the content can recognize it, and people not familiar with it will have a basic understanding of the content. Course descriptions are frequently used in announcement bulletins, flyers, and other materials that managers use to share information of an upcoming training event.

Technical training colleges may use the course descriptions in catalogs and newspapers to advertise a course. In the case of a technical college, the course description also serves as an official document. A course description differs from the course goal in that the description may include the major units of instruction and describe the content more thoroughly. See Figure 7-2. Following are some suggestions for writing course descriptions from the UW-Stout 2014 Curriculum Handbook:

- Catalog descriptions are published in bulletins; therefore, they should be written in a consistent style.
- Descriptions should be written in noun phrases, rather than in complete sentences.
- Unnecessary words should be avoided as much as possible.
- Repetition should also be avoided.
- Phrases to avoid include "introduction to," "study of," "elementary," and "intermediate."
- Focus should be on the content and not activities.

A frequent mistake when writing course descriptions is to spend time on the activities in which students will engage as they participate in the course. These tend to fall into methodologies, are subject to change, and vary from instructor to instructor. The content, however, once decided upon, should be more stable. Course descriptions tend to be short and to the point, written in noun phrases, with a focus on the content.

There are many ways to write the course description. It would be best to check with the institution or company regarding their policy for course descriptions before writing the description. See Figure 7-3.

Course Objectives

Course objectives are more focused general statements that begin with a verb indicating either the knowledge skills, or attitude the student will be able to display upon the completion of the technical course or training session. Course objectives provide more specifics about general outcomes as a result of taking and completing the course, and make the course goal and description more specific. Course objectives tend to be statements that may not result in specific measureable behavior, but are an indicator of what students will be able to know, do, or express in attitude upon completion of the course.

FIGURE 7-2

Course Descriptions

The Role of Management in Hospitality Industry: Definition and analysis of work, people, change, and education and their interrelationships within the hospitality industry.

Engineered Tailoring: Industrial production methods applied to construction of tailored garments.

Introduction to Early Childhood Program: History, types of programs, and staff requirements in early childhood professions.

Principles of Technology I: Contemporary applications of the principles governing force, work, rate, resistance, energy, power, and force transformers in mechanical, electrical, fluid, and thermal systems. Technical content especially appropriate for educational applications.

Course descriptions should be short and to the point.

FIGURE 7-3

Training Course Descriptions

Workplace Violence Awareness: Potential for violence, people types, environmental triggers, handling potential situations, and case studies.

Group Leader Development Program: Skills needed to be an effective group leader, applying basic principles to interpersonal interactions, using the Personal Profile System, and application of action tools when dealing with emotional behavior.

Training course descriptions should conform to any policies of the institution or company.

A course may be subdivided into units. Unit objectives are geared to a smaller group, or chunk, of content, indicating the level of performance with specific criteria to meet for demonstration of mastery of that content. Unit objectives will also need to be developed and are covered later in this chapter. Consider the following when stating course objectives:

- Broad objectives let the reader know, in more specific terms, the content of the course.
- Course objectives should be consistent with the catalog description and with the course outline.
- Course objectives may be in the form of competencies, behavioral objectives, or other student outcomes.
- Course objectives that the student is to achieve by taking the course should be listed.

- Generally six to eight course objectives should be sufficient.
- Course objectives should provide more detail than a course description because basic outcomes of the course will be stated.

Course objectives are written statements of what the student will be able to do as a result of learning. Consider the following examples of course objectives:

- Describe the anthropological approach to the analysis of contemporary issues facing the world community.
- Design a package in which the form of the product is integral to the package.
- Apply the basic principles of differential equations to practical problems.
- Evaluate the effectiveness of training and development programs within an organization.
- Explain the metabolism, functions, digestion, absorption, and transport of each of the macronutrients.

The course objectives above begin with an action verb and describe for the reader the course content. Each objective is also only a sample from a listing of course objectives from different content areas. Course objectives for a training or education course should attempt to cover the main content areas. See Figure 7-4. Thus, there would be a number of course objectives, the number depending on the amount of content.

Courses and seminars can run for different lengths of time. A list of course objectives for a four-hour training session will look different than a list of objectives for a course that lasts a semester. See Figure 7-5.

While course objectives are made by the instructor or course developer to guide the delivery of content, they are also intended for the student. A student returning to the training session a few years after taking a course should be able to recall certain types of information. This should be information related to the course objectives. Once the objectives are established, the course developer can move on to the course content outline.

Course Content Outline

A course content outline provides the main content headings for what will be covered. The task or duty statements may be subheadings in the content outline. Most content outlines use first-, second-, and third-order outline formats. A course content outline should do the following:

- consist of topic headings of content, usually using one or two words to capture the content essence
- be concise yet complete enough so that students and other instructors of the course will have a reasonable knowledge of the content the course will cover
- be consistent with the catalog description
- match the course objectives and the evaluation of student achievement

FIGURE 7-4

CTE-534 Performance Analysis Course Objectives

1. Identify and use resource materials related to analysis.
2. Define and apply basic terminology common to education and training analysis.
3. Compare and critique several curriculum-based models and techniques that could be used in development of a curriculum base, and develop or refine own model.
4. Analyze the relationships of society, the world of work, industry, and individuals as they fit into a task-based model for developing and/or revising curriculum or a training program.
5. Identify a needs assessment area and develop a rationale for assessment.
6. Develop a procedure and instruments for analyzing present and future education or training needs.
7. Distinguish between methods of collecting needs assessment data.
8. Develop procedures and instruments necessary to complete a task analysis.
9. Perform an observation/question analysis.
10. Describe other uses of task.

Course objectives for a training or education course should attempt to cover the main content areas.

FIGURE 7-5

Group Leader Development Program

1. Identify the skills needed to be an effective group leader.
2. Apply basic principles to interpersonal interactions.
3. Use the Personal Profile System (PPS) to more effectively relate to and work with others.
4. Apply key actions as tools for workplace communication and for dealing with emotional behavior.

A list of course objectives for a short training session will look different from a list of objectives for a course that lasts a semester.

The purpose of the content outline is to provide content topics in the order and depth in which they will appear in the course. This not only helps the student in determining direction for the training or education course, but also requires the instructor to think about what needs to be covered in the course based on the course objectives. Content not consistent with the course description and course objectives should be noted in the content outline.

Figure 7-6 shows a partial completion of a course outline. Again, the purpose of the course outline is to provide the main content topics that will be discussed in the training or technical education course. The outline is especially useful for instructors as a clear picture of what will be covered is provided.

The course outline facilitates the development of units of instruction and also performance objectives. It is especially advantageous when developing the midterm and final exams. Once the content is laid out, the exam questions can be developed following the outline. The content outline is the road map to the content that will be covered. Instructional planning and class time should not be spent on content not in the content outline.

Special Considerations

A course syllabus may have a section that deals with special considerations, such as a time schedule or special materials that must be supplied by the student. Special course fees, purchasing of a manual, testing equipment, field-trip dates, selected websites, and CD-ROMs may also be covered in this section of the syllabus. If using this section, consider the following:

- Use this section to provide any additional statements about the course that should become part of its permanent record.
- If the course type is other than lecture, laboratory, discussion, or seminar, describe the intended arrangements, including the student's required time commitment.
- Special equipment, materials, software, and supplies that are required for the course should be noted.
- Selected reference materials that students need to access in the library or learning center may be also be noted in this section.
- Time schedule or calendar of when classes meet, including when assignments are due, may fall into this section.
- Class policies dealing with attendance and excuses, class participation, and how assignments should be turned in should be covered.
- A syllabus must also include the instructor's name and title, email address, work phone, office location, office hours, and the method in which the instructor prefers to receive queries (e.g., email, phone, after class).

- Class etiquette or procedures for asking questions or responding to other students either in class or by email should be covered. This is especially important for students working in groups or for students participating in discussions or chat rooms online.
- Plagiarism and cheating policies and academic misconduct that are either department or institutional policies should be noted.
- Explain any other special considerations in this section.

An item frequently outlined under special considerations is a schedule of what will occur when. A schedule indicates topics or activities planned by class session, reading assignments, other assignments, due dates, and special meeting plans and times for the course.

When developing a schedule, constraints on class time should be considered. How often the class meets should be taken into account, as well as any holidays, special events, or interruptions that may take away from class time. Assignments should be spread out so that students can manage the workload. In Figure 7-7, the dates are noted along with the day the meetings are to occur, the assignment for that session, and any reading assignments or general assignments due.

In this schedule, "HA" stands for homework assignments and "CD" stands for class discussion. Note, also, that the midterm and final exams are indicated. This is for a semester course that might occur in a technical education setting. A training session might not have as much detail, but might include a day-by-day schedule. Some schedules include the week in the beginning column.

In a short training session, the amount of detail will vary by course developer. See Figure 7-8. The kind of schedule developed will vary based on what it is felt students need and how useful the document is in planning.

Course Evaluation

Every syllabus should include a section on evaluation. The evaluation section provides information on how students will be evaluated, how grades are earned if used, and how students will know when they have completed all the requirements. Clear assessment criteria and standards should always be available to participants. If a grade will not be earned, then how will participants know they have mastered the content of the training session? See Figure 7-9. At the end of training sessions conducted in business and industry, participants may be required to report what they have learned and how it will affect their job performance to their supervisor and peers.

FIGURE
7-6

Sample Content Outline

1. Introduction to Curriculum
   A. Philosophy of education
      1) Types
      2) Characteristics
      3) Implications for curriculum and teaching
   B. CTE philosophy and mission
      1) History of philosophy
      2) Changes over the years
      3) Present philosophy
   C. Philosophy and mission of technical college
      1) Early mission
      2) Changes affecting mission
2. Curriculum Models
   A. Selecting model and rationale for model
      1) Evaluation criteria
      2) Developing a rationale
   B. Curriculum model setting
      1) Considerations
      2) Other factors
   C. Developing a visual model
      1) Purpose of a visual model
      2) Steps in constructing a visual model
      3) Requirements of a visual model
   D. Components of a model
3. Context for Curriculum
   A. Program area
      1) Identification criteria
      2) Arriving at consensus
   B. Course
      1) Rationale
      2) Criteria for writing
      3) Getting reaction
      4) Position within the curriculum
      5) Course fit
      6) Prerequisite requirements
   C. Follow-on courses
      1) Prerequisite knowledge of students
      2) Students' needs
   D. Special accommodations
   E. Determining requirements
      1) Consider learning style
      2) Consider instruction
      3) Assess students
      4) Assess materials
4. Curriculum Content Identification
   A. Occupational analysis
      1) Purpose
      2) Advantages and disadvantages
      3) Steps
   B. Task analysis
      1) Purpose
      2) Advantages and disadvantages
      3) Steps
   C. Locating and collecting data
      1) Where to find data
      2) Advantages and disadvantages

A content outline provides content topics in the order and depth in which they will appear in the course.

FIGURE 7-7

Performance Analysis CTE – 334/534

Tentative Schedule

Fall Semester 20__
Mondays 4:40–7:40 p.m.

Session & Date	Topic	Assignment for Session
Session #1 September 12	• Introduction/Overview	
Session #2 September 19	• Learning Resource Center • Terms and Definitions	Unit I HA #1 & CD #1
Session #3 September 26	• Models and Systems	Unit II Assignment #1 HA #2 & CD #2
Session #4 October 3	• Needs Assessment	Unit III Assignment #2 HA #3 & CD #3
Session #5 October 10	• Sampling • Needs Analysis	
Session #6 October 17	• Interviewing • Focus Groups	Unit IV Assignment #3
Session #7 October 24	Δ Midterm Exam	
Session #8 October 31	• Task Analysis • Task and Duty Statements	Unit V HA #4 & CD #4
Session #9 November 7	• Rating Scales and Instructions • Correspondence	
Session #10 November 14	• Analysis of Data • Converting Task to Objectives	Unit VI HA #5 & CD #5
Session #11 November 21	• Observation and Question Analysis	Unit VII Assignment #4
Session #12 November 28	• DACUM • Using a Different Approach	Assignment #5
Session #13 December 5	• Delphi Technique • Matching Technique with Problem • Consultation with Instructor	
Session #14 December 12	• Group Reports	Assignment #6
Session #15 December 19	Δ Final Exam 4–5:50 p.m. Rm. 221 AA	

A schedule indicates topics or activities planned by class session and due dates, along with the day the meetings are to occur, the assignment that session, and any reading assignments or general assignments due.

FIGURE 7-8

Group Leader Development Program
Module 1—The Basic Principles of Leadership—
On-Shift Emergencies
June 4, 20__
7:00 AM – 11:30 AM

Agenda

7:00 AM
- Welcome
- Learning Objectives
- What Is the Group Leader Development Program?
- Transition to the Leadership Role
- Qualities of an Effective Leader – What Does That Mean?
  - My Development Plan – What Do I Need to Be an Effective Leader?

8:00 AM
- Leadership and Work Atmosphere
  - The Basic Principles of Leadership
  - Company Harassment Policy
  - Review Policy – Matching Quiz
- Leadership Role

9:30 AM
- Handling On-Shift Emergencies
  - Review Drug and Alcohol Policy – Pop Quiz
  - Emergencies: Evacuation, Seek Shelter, Injury, and Illness/Impairment
  - Case Studies: Emergency Situations
  - Plan for Dealing with On-Shift Emergencies

The schedule for a short training session will vary in the amount of detail and according to what students need.

In Figure 7-9, points have been assigned to all assignments and exams. Exams count toward 29% of the student's points, with the midterm and final worth 14.5% each. Assignments count toward 71% of the student's points, with homework assignments worth 16% and outside assignments worth 55% of the total points. A–F grades are then assigned a certain range of points. To receive a grade of "A," a students must have between 91% and 100% of the total points; a "B" grade, between 81% and 90% of the total points; and a "C" grade, between 71% and 80% of the total points.

FIGURE 7-9

Evaluation

A due date will be given for each assignment. If the assignment is late, only partial credit or no credit will be given for the assignment. ALL outside assignments (see below) must be completed to pass the course.

Major tests will be announced in advance. If missed, they must be made up within two (2) days after you return to class. You will also be given some assignments that require processing with your assigned group before you come to class. In essence, you must do the assignment and bring it to class. At times there will be assignments given in class. If missed, these cannot be made up. Short unit tests, if missed, cannot be made up unless a valid reason for the absence is made evident.

A. Points are assigned to each assignment, midterm, and final exam.

B. Your final grade is weighted according to the following formula:

1. Exams	29%
a. midterm exam	14.5%
b. final exam	14.5%
2. Assignments 71%	
a. homework assignments and class discussions	16%
b. experiential assignments	55%
Total	100%

C. Grades will be distributed as follows:

A = 91 – 100% total points
B = 81 – 90% total points
C = 71 – 80% total points
D = 61 – 70% total points
F = below 60% total points

The evaluation section of a syllabus provides information on how students will be evaluated.

Another evaluation example might be, "Develop a plan/strategy for dealing with on-shift emergency situations and employee performance issues, following plant/department guidelines." In this example, each participant must write a plan to deal with shift emergency situations consistent with their own plan and/or department guidelines. This seems reasonable and useful for a half-day workshop on dealing with emergency situations.

Each evaluation will vary depending on the expected outcomes. If an OSHA certification program is being conducted, then it would be a reasonable expectation that the participants take and complete the certification exam. If the purpose of the training session is only awareness, then participation in the training session may be a reasonable expectation. Frequently, feedback from supervisors of trained participants will yield valuable data on what was learned.

As instructors continue with their course development and refine their syllabuses, another layer of breaking down the course into manageable chunks is a unit of instruction. The next section will detail considerations for designing units of instruction.

Units of Instruction

An effective method of organizing content is to use units of instruction. The content is chunked or arranged under various headings, usually corresponding to tasks, duties, general areas of responsibility, or a combination of these three. This content is then grouped into units of instruction that may be centered around a job, problem, or project. Similar content, time and the number of training or education sessions, or past experience may also be used to place content into units. Frequently, instructors organize content around meeting times. For example, a training course may meet for three days and have three units of instruction, or one each day. The course can also be broken down into half days, each with six units of instruction. Again, the level of content, activities, and expectations of learners may dictate the unit organization. The advantages of using units of instruction are as follows:

- All resources are focused toward a measurable goal.
- Programs and offerings become uniform.
- Instructional materials are more easily managed.
- Standards are established for programs, employment, and the job.
- Individual needs of students are more easily identified.
- The instructor can focus on in-service opportunities.
- Students are more highly motivated.

With the unit of instruction, all resources noted are directed toward the particular content. It becomes easier for the instructor to manage the content and activities associated with one unit. Standards can be easily developed, with focus on the real world or job setting. Students become more motivated because uniformity is established, and the instructor can more easily respond to students' needs.

The unit of instruction also requires the course developer to devote time to creating materials that are consistent. A template is helpful in establishing consistency. A template for the units of instruction may consist of the following: (1) unit objectives, (2) unit content outline, (3) student activities, (4) resources and visuals, (5) instructor-developed resources, and (6) unit evaluation

Unit Objectives. Objectives may be written at many levels. Course objectives tend to be written very broadly. Unit objectives, however, are written like performance objectives. A performance objective is based on a task and has three parts: the performance component, condition component, and criteria component.

A unit objective might be written as, "In an appropriate laboratory setting, demonstrate local anesthesia techniques on peer and clinical patients to acceptable competency according to checklist criteria." In this objective, the performance component is "demonstrate local anesthesia techniques on peer and clinical patients"; the condition component is "in an appropriate laboratory setting"; and the criteria component is "to acceptable competency, according to checklist criteria."

Another example of a unit objective might be, "In a group setting, describe the components of the communications model, scoring five out of five on the product checklist." In this example, the performance component is "describe the components of the communications model"; the condition component is "in a group setting"; and the criteria component is "scoring five out of five on the product checklist."

Objectives written in this manner are excellent for a unit of instruction. They let students know precisely the expectations of the instruction and provide an excellent planning guide for the instructor. Students know, for example, that they will be tested in a group setting, and they must describe the five components of the communications model. The instructor must not only provide information on the communications model, but must structure a setting through reading and questions to ensure a student's success in a group setting. Selecting activities to reinforce the five components of the communications model would be required. Structuring the group setting to ensure full student participation becomes a basic requirement.

Typically, objectives may be grouped into three domains: cognitive, psychomotor, and affective. Course developers and instructors often consider these domains when stating unit or specific objectives. The cognitive domain, developed by American educator Benjamin Bloom, is the most common and covers (1) knowledge, or the recall of specific information, (2) comprehension, or the lowest level of understanding, (3) application, or the use of information, (4) analysis, or breaking apart and observing patterns, (5) synthesis, or putting the parts together to form something entirely new, and (6) evaluation, or the use of judgment, to compare, discriminate, and recognize. See Figure 7-10.

The psychomotor domain covers skills or the coordination of physical activities used to perform, manipulate, or construct. The psychomotor domain can be divided into two separate categories: process or product, depending on which the instructor is interested in viewing. In some cases, both are desired. See Figure 7-11.

FIGURE
7-10

COGNITIVE DOMAIN

Categories	Possible Objectives	Appropriate Verbs
1. **Knowledge**—Identifying and recalling specific information: dates, events, places, etc.	Identify common terms. List milling machine parts. Match name with tool. Describe customer service procedures.	Identify, list, match, label, describe outline, show, examine, tabulate, name.
2. **Comprehension**—Grasping the meaning of facts and ideas by interpretation or translation; using descriptors to state the ideas.	Explain in own words the common terms. Predict problems with missing machine parts. Classify the different machine tools. Rephrase customer service procedures.	Explain, classify, translate, discuss, interpret, predict, distinguish, convert, infer.
3. **Application**—Using learned material in new situations; applying facts and techniques in different ways.	Apply terms to new situations. Modify milling machine parts. Develop new classification of tools. Demonstrate customer service procedures.	Apply, build, develop, solve, modify, produce, compute, operate.
4. **Analysis**—Breaking down into meaningful parts, interpreting elements; distinguishing between fact and inferences; recognizing hidden meaning.	Distinguish term usage. Compare different milling machine parts. Examine tools and their possible uses. Contrast different customer service procedures.	Break down, distinguish, discriminate, analyze, compare, classify, examine, diagram, contrast, subdivide.
5. **Synthesis**—Combining parts to make a new whole; developing new structures and system models; relating knowledge from several areas; predicting.	Develop new usage of terms. Create different milling machine parts. Design unique tools. Formulate state-of-the-art customer service procedures.	Develop, build, create, design, invent, modify, order, explain, rewrite, compose, formulate, generalize.
6. **Evaluation**—Judging the value or worth of information and the validity of ideas; strategically comparing and reviewing based on external criteria.	Assess usage of new terms. Contrast different milling machine parts. Evaluate unique tools. Critique state-of-the-art customer service procedures.	Assess, compare, conclude, decide, grade, defend, contrast, justify, investigate, summarize, critique.

This cognitive domain encompasses thinking skills. (Adapted from Gronlund, 2000.)

FIGURE 7-11

PSYCHOMOTOR DOMAIN

Categories	Possible Objectives	Appropriate Verbs
1. **Perception**—Use of sense organs to guide motor activity. Requires intake and reaction.	Recognize problem sounds on machine. Identify that heat needs to be adjusted. Detect nonverbal communication.	Accept, describe, identify, recognize, differentiate, relate, pick, separate.
2. **Set**—Readiness to take focused action. Includes mental and physical preparedness.	Assemble tools to correct problem. Adjust heat based on outdoor temp. Check company service procedures manual.	Arrange, prepare, get set, begin, respond, react, start, volunteer.
3. **Guided Response**—Early stages in learning a complex skill that includes reproduction and trial and error. Requires practice.	Follow manual to correct problem. Modify temperature setting several times. Diagram possible customer service procedures.	Copy, duplicate, follow, trace, modify, produce, dismantle, fix, manipulate, diagram.
4. **Mechanism**—Guided response has become more automatic and the skill can now be performed with confidence and proficiency.	Use the volt-amp meter. Diagnose temperature sensing unit. Present customer service procedures to an outside agency.	Break down, distinguish, discriminate, analyze, compare, classify, examine, diagram, contrast, subdivide.
5. **Complex Overt Response**—Skillful action that may require more complex movement. Performance is more accurate and automatic.	Repair problem beating flat-rate manual. Recalibrate temperature sensing unit. Build and display a customer service diorama.	Develop, build, create, design, invent, modify, order, calibrate, construct, display, redo, compose, formulate.
6. **Adaption**—Developed skill can now be altered to meet different requirements or settings.	Use new repair technique. Contrast different vendor sensing units. Develop a comprehensive program to train customer service personnel.	Assess, adapt, compare, conclude, grade, defend, justify, change, reorganize revise, critique.
7. **Origination**—Creation based on highly developed skills. Creating new movement patterns to fit a particular situation or specific problem.	Construct original tool to perform repair. Design new sensing unit. Develop a self-paced customer service training program.	Create, design, organize, combine, incorporate, mix, construct, develop.

The psychomotor domain encompasses "doing" skills. (Adapted from Gronlund, 2000.)

The affective domain deals with a person's attitudes and behaviors in terms of how they receive, value, and internalize value systems. A person's affect is important when dealing with customers or working with other people in a job setting. See Figure 7-12. Understanding these taxonomies can help technical trainers, instructors, and course developers select the appropriate verb when writing performance objectives, which are covered later in this chapter.

FIGURE 7-12

AFFECTIVE DOMAIN

Categories	Possible Objectives	Appropriate Verbs
1. **Receiving**—Being open to new information and paying attention to something in the environment.	Listen to others with respect. List names of new people in class. Take notes in class.	Ask, acknowledge, describe identify, listen, respond, select, commit, permit.
2. **Responding**—Grasping the meaning of facts and ideas by interpretation or translation; giving descriptors and stating the main idea.	Answer question in a textbook. Raise hand in class discussion. Sign up for special tasks.	Answer, engage, assemble, discuss, assist, act, practice, demonstrate, detail, inform.
3. **Valuing**—Demonstrating definite involvement and commitment based on the worth or value placed on an object, phenomenon, or behavior.	Demonstrate concern for classmates. Display a plan for social improvement. Appreciate the role of science in engineering class.	Present, produce, start, plan, design, read, reveal, justify, propose, report, volunteer.
4. **Organization**—Developing a unique value system based on different views and conflicts. Focus is on comparing, relating, and analytical thinking.	Accept responsibilty for own behavior. Distinguish between instructor's views and own. Prioritize time effectively between family, work, and self.	Break down, distinguish, discriminate, analyze, compare, classify, examine, diagram, contrast, subdivide.
5. **Internalizing Value**—Internalizing value system and demonstrating behavior that is consistent with personal, social, and emotional construct.	Change judgment and behavior in light of new evidence. Join a professional organization because of their values. Formulate and follow ethical practices.	Arrange, comply, define, defend, create, formulate, illustrate, share, explain, generalize, prepare.

The affective domain encompasses attitudes and behaviors. (Adapted from Gronlund, 2000.)

Unit Content Outline. Similar to the course outline, the unit content outline goes more deeply into the subject matter and outlines, in great detail, the content to be delivered. This outline is developed by a content expert and defines the scope and sequence of the unit of instruction. It cannot be developed by someone who does not know and understand the content. The unit content outline is frequently based on the task analysis. Standard outlining procedures are followed but may be aided by wordprocessing computer software.

Once documented, the unit content outline provides the basis for changing the content as it evolves in business or industry, and is an excellent communication tool. The unit content outline is also an excellent guide for the development of appropriate activities and the selection and use of resources. One of the greatest values of a course outline is for evaluation. A unit content outline would be simple to follow in developing test questions for a unit exam. Only the essentials of the course should be included in the unit content outline. See Figure 7-13. As in the course content outline, a first-, second-, and third-order outline should be developed.

FIGURE 7-13

Sample Outline—Units of Instruction

1. Units of Instruction
    - A. Introduction
    - B. Advantages of using a unit of instruction
        - 1) All resources are focused toward a measurable goal.
        - 2) Programs and offerings become uniform.
        - 3) Instructional materials are more easily managed.
        - 4) Standards are established for program, employment, and the job.
        - 5) Individual needs of students are more easily identified.
        - 6) The instructor can focus on in-service opportunities.
        - 7) Students are more highly motivated.
2. Unit Objectives
    - A. Written at many levels
    - B. Examples
    - C. Three objective domains
        - 1) Cognitive
            - a. Definition
            - b. Figure—description, appropriate verbs
        - 2) Psychomotor
            - a. Definition
            - b. Figure—description, appropriate verbs
        - 3) Affective
            - a. Definition
            - b. Figure—description, appropriate verbs
3. Unit Content Outline

The unit content outline should include only the essentials of the course.

As can be seen, this is the outline used to develop this section of the chapter. Another example is taken from the course outline section in Figure 7-14. Section A, Philosophy of education, can be one unit, but can also be broken down further as noted in the section headed "Breakdown."

As seen in this example, a more thorough content analysis has been made to come up with the unit content outline for Section A, Philosophy of education. This detail is sometimes essential for instructors to see the amount of content being shared with students. This outline also provides the course developer many possibilities for facilitating learning by applying a variety of methodologies that enhance learning.

Student Activities. Student activities are those that will engage students to accomplish the objectives. By providing a number of activities or teaching methods, the course developer is taking into account individuals' different learning styles and will assist all students to learn. Listening, reading, planning cooperative learning groups, viewing a CD, developing a simulation exercise, dealing with a case study, project-based learning, researching, and oral reporting are just a few examples of activities that could be planned by the instructor to help meet the unit objectives.

Students spend most of their time outside of class, where much learning takes place. Activities are provided to promote learning and to assist students in achieving competency levels. Thus, decisions about activities should be made as part of the course development. What students do outside class is related to what occurs in class. What is required outside of the training session may also have great utility in the work setting.

Deciding between synchronous (real-time) and asynchronous (at different times) communications to deal with the activity is another decision the instructor will have to make.

Two performance objectives for a unit of instruction are written in the following manner:

1. In the classroom setting, identify the characteristics of the different philosophies of education by scoring 10 out of 10 on a matching quiz.
2. In the classroom setting, discuss the implications of the different philosophies of education for the curriculum and teaching setting, and write a paper indicating the strengths and weaknesses of an educational philosophy, scoring 35 out of 45 on a product rating scale.

An activity that could address the first objective is to first have students read the handout on the characteristics of the different philosophies of education. Students could then take a preference quiz, which would indicate where they stood on each. Students could then be put into groups (inside or outside of class) and provided with a guide sheet that they would complete as part of the discussion to identify the characteristics of the different philosophies of education.

FIGURE 7-14

Sample Course Outline

1. Introduction to Curriculum
   - A. Philosophy of education
     - 1) Types
     - 2) Characteristics
     - 3) Implications for curriculum and teaching
   - B. CTE philosophy and mission
     - 1) History of philosophy
     - 2) Changes over the years
     - 3) Present philosophy
   - C. Philosophy and mission of technical college
     - 1) Early mission
     - 2) Changes affecting mission

Breakdown

- A. Philosophy of education
  - 1) Types
    - a. Perennialism
    - b. Idealism
    - c. Realism
    - d. Experimentalism
    - e. Existentialism
  - 2) Characteristics
    - a. Perennialism
      - (1) Most conservative, traditional, or inflexible
      - (2) Education and training are constant
      - (3) Focus is on developing rationality
      - (4) Goodness is found in rationality itself
    - b. Idealism
      - (1) Reality is in the person's mind
      - (2) Truth is found in ideas and the focus of mind and learning or intellectual processes
      - (3) Goodness is an ideal state, something striven for
    - c. Realism
      - (1) Accept the world as it is and teaches students about the world
      - (2) Goodness is the law of nature
    - d. Experimentalism
      - (1) The world is ever-changing
      - (2) Reality is what is actually experienced
      - (3) Goodness is what is accepted by public test
    - e. Existentialism
      - (1) World is personal subjectivity—individually defined
      - (2) Truth and goodness are a matter of freedom
      - (3) Schools exists to help students know themselves and place in society
  - 3) Implications for curriculum and teaching
    - a. Perennialism
      - (1) Curriculum—constant subjects and doctrine
      - (2) Taught through drill and behavior control
      - (3) Teacher tells and student is passive
    - b. Idealism

A section of a course outline can be one unit or it can be broken down further as shown in the section labeled "Breakdown."

In the second objective, the instructor would set up discussion groups that would review the range of educational philosophies. Each student would take a position, defend their philosophy, and receive feedback from the other students. A rating scale for the written assignment could then be shared with the students and the criteria discussed. Students would then be required to submit a report using the rating scale criteria.

Other activities could be envisioned based on the instructor's perspective. For example, using the Internet to accomplish the preference quiz and discussion might be very desirable, depending on the skills and access of the instructor and students.

What about a training session that deals with management skills? Participants need an opportunity to develop management skills, practice them, and obtain feedback. Thus, an activity that accomplishes the development, practice, and feedback should be provided with follow-up. If a face-to-face follow-up session is not possible, then a chat room on the Internet may suffice. Basically, the development of activities supports the unit objectives and is consistent with the knowledge, skill, and availability of resources and tools.

Resources and Visuals. In this portion of the syllabus, the instructor identifies resources that are used by students to master the content or performance objectives. Resources and visuals might include textbooks, assignment sheets, pamphlets, brochures, audiovisual materials, transparencies, slides, computer sites, and web pages that would be used by the instructor to teach the unit and accessed by students when appropriate.

For example, when addressing the first objective, the instructor may have to assemble a number of resources to support the different educational philosophies and their characteristics. Text or web resources that provide additional information on the five philosophy types should be identified to assist students.

Selecting and developing one of the five philosophies and behaving consistently would require research by the students as they address the second objective. Position papers require use of resources. While it may be an expectation that students research their own resources, it would be helpful to supply items that the instructor has already reviewed.

Filing course materials by unit title or topic offers advantages. This provides a growing resource file for the instructor and provides a flexible way to retrieve information and materials for planning new courses or training seminars. For example, a unit on planning might be used in several different courses or seminars. The folders would contain the basic information on planning, and the instructor would adapt the materials to the specific application at hand. Also, as more experience is gained with this system, the instructor gains new insights into how to focus and develop instructional units so they can be used in other settings, such as an on-line course.

In this section, the instructor is researching and documenting resources already available. In the next section, the instructor develops appropriate resources to meet the performance objectives where existing resources are not available.

Instructor-Developed Resources. In this phase of course development, the instructor develops appropriate resources to meet the performance objectives that cannot be found or do not exist. In some cases, resources are available, but the match is poor with the changing content. Instructor-developed resources may take the form of instruction sheets (Bartel, 1976) or visuals required for instruction. These may take the form of paper handouts, a PDF posting on the web, or a CD-ROM supplied to students. Again, the purpose here is to supplement the instructional resources already available with more focused resources to assist students in accomplishing each performance objective and mastering the content.

Instructor-developed resources in the form of instruction sheets may be developed to meet specific situations. They support the curriculum by clarifying concepts and providing a means to rapidly make changes in the curriculum. They are an excellent source of up-to-date information and help reduce misinterpretation by students. However, instruction sheets may be time-consuming to prepare and, like all materials, the reading level may affect comprehension. There are basically three types of instruction sheets: information, procedure, and assignment (Bartel, 1976). Instruction sheets can be used effectively in any classroom or training setting.

An information sheet is usually written by the instructor and provides the students with information that they could not have found elsewhere. Information sheets supplement or expand on lectures and tend to be concise and to the point. An instructor may choose to develop an information sheet as a handout when commercial materials are not available. A procedure sheet provides the student with the step-by-step process to complete a task, such as changing a tire or preparing a salad. An assignment sheet is designed with a performance objective, tells the students what to do, and provides criteria for evaluation. (Chapter 8 covers these three instructor-developed resources in more detail.) The assignment may be written or performed.

There were two performance objectives provided previously:

1. In the classroom setting, identify the characteristics of the different philosophies of education by scoring 10 out of 10 on a matching quiz.
2. In the classroom setting, discuss the implications of the different philosophies of education for the curriculum and the teaching setting, and write a paper indicating the strengths and weaknesses of an educational philosophy scoring 35 out of 45 on a product rating scale. See Figure 7-15.

FIGURE
7-15

Assignment/Procedure Sheet

Education/Training Philosophy Paper Name ____________________

Objective: Research, select, and defend an educational/training philosophy position.

Rationale: As a technical/training instructor, you might be required to share your educational philosophy during a job interview or with other staff members and students. The purpose of this assignment, then, is to adequately research and write a 5–10 page paper that explains your position and provides a sound rationale for the position. Strengths and weakness of the education/training philosophy should also be included. The paper must be written in a scholarly manner and properly referenced.

You will be required to write a rationale of your reason for the particular philosophy, a description of the philosophy, the strengths and weaknesses of the philosophy, how it applies to your area of expertise. Also, outline how the research was conducted before selection, including influences on the decision, and include list of references used to develop the paper. Items 1-5 and 8 are headings for the 5-10 page paper.

Criteria for Evaluation:

1. **Rationale:** (Explain the rationale for selecting the particular philosophy)

Not Well Explained — Anyone Can Understand

0 1 2 3 4 5 6 7

2. **Description of Philosophy:** (Description covers all key elements of philosophy)

None Noted — Key Elements Noted

0 1 2 3 4 5 6 7

3. **Strengths and Weaknesses** (A balanced perspective of strengths and weaknesses noted)

Incomplete — Balanced Perspective of Strengths and Weaknesses

0 1 2 3 4 5 6 7

4. **Application to Technical Area:** (Case made for applicability of philosophy to technical area)

No Duties Listed/ Not Stated as Duties — All Duties Identified and Well Stated

0 1 2 3 4 5 6 7

5. **Research Process:** (Describes the research process used to uncover information for paper)

None Described — Process Identified– Anyone Can Duplicate

0 1 2 3 4 5 6 7

6. **Paper Conforms to Style Manual:** (APA, 5th edition is followed)

Did Not — Paper is Consistent with Style Manual

0 1 2 3 4 5 6 7

7. **References Noted:** (References are integrated appropriately into the paper. Significant points are cited)

Not Clear — Consists of Three Components

0 1 2 3 4 5 6 7

8. **Reference List:** (Reference list is noted at the end of the paper)

None Used — All References Used in Paper Are Listed

0 1 2 3 4 5 6 7

Total Possible Points: 45 Your score:________

An assignment/procedure sheet includes an objective and rationale for the assignment.

A course developer may decide that the best way to address the first objective is to develop a specific information sheet dealing with the different philosophies of education. It may be organized in such a fashion that the characteristics are also listed for the student. This may take the form of a paper handout or a CD-ROM, or be developed into a PDF file and posted on the Internet. Of course, if existing resources are found (textbooks, articles, web sites) that address the same, the instructor may select those resources instead.

Sometimes questions that guide a student's learning can also be developed. These questions can be part of the syllabus or may be handed out to students for a response. These questions would have to be developed by the instructor. In a training setting, an information sheet can be designed for use in the training seminar and also used to provide a guide at the work site.

In the second objective, the course developer might decide to develop an assignment sheet that outlines the assignment and identifies the criteria. The objective also states that a product rating scale would be used and, thus, would have to be developed as an assignment/procedure sheet.

In Figure 7-12, the assignment includes an objective and rationale for the assignment. Criteria for evaluation are noted along with a rating scale. Students now have an idea of what is to be expected for their paper. Criteria for the assignment are noted for the students and would also be used by the instructor for grading the assignment, which is returned to the student. After the assignment has been graded, the instructor might consider other criteria or the refinement of the existing criteria. The development of instructional resources assists the instructor as well as the students.

Unit Evaluation. A unit evaluation measures students' knowledge of the unit of instruction, skills, and attitudes. One of the ways to determine success is to measure students' learning. This can be assessed in a number of ways, such as a quiz or test, product or process assignments, portfolios, or some other creative means. Measuring students' cognitive knowledge, having students perform, or determining students' attitudes about the unit are all acceptable.

The instructor's success is another reason for evaluation. Did the students learn the material it was intended for them to learn? Getting feedback about how students felt about the unit of instruction would provide important feedback for possible changes.

Performance Objectives

Performance objectives are developed by the trainer/instructor during the design stage to document expected performance. The performance objective is based on the identified task for training or education and indicates the conditions for performing the task and the criteria of performance. Performance objectives indicate what the student will be able to do upon completion of the instruction and activity episode.

Characteristics

Performance objectives provide direction for instruction, including content, procedures, and activities to reinforce learning. They describe the behavior or performance of the student (task, outcome, or performance statement) and the conditions under which the student will be performing the terminal behavior (condition statement). Performance objectives include information about the criteria of performance that will be considered acceptable success standards or criteria (criteria statement).

Components

A performance objective consist of three distinct parts:

1. performance component (the task or behavior)
2. condition component (what is provided to the student during the performance)
3. criteria component (the level of performance or standard)

Performance Component. The performance component is nothing more than the task statement. However, it may be expanded or modified to describe the performance accepted in the training setting. See Figure 7-16. The performance component identifies, in behavioral terms, precisely what it is that the students will be able to do upon completion of some specified segment of instruction. Developmental tips for performance components include the following:

- The performance is the main focus of the objective.
- Another professional should be able to read the performance component and describe exactly what the trainee should be able to do to demonstrate competency in the task.
- This is the performance that will be required of the trainee in the final (terminal) testing situation to be considered competent.
- The performance component refers to student performance and not instructor performance. Do not use "will teach," "will demonstrate," "will present," or other instructor behaviors. Performance objectives describe what the trainee should be able to do.
- Avoid terms which are hard to measure such as "know," "understand," "learn," "demonstrate knowledge of," "be familiar with," or other such phrases.

- Keep away from "the student will be able to . . . ."
- The performance component of an objective may only sample the ways in which the trainee will have to perform the task on the job. Simply require a performance that is representative of how the task is typically performed.

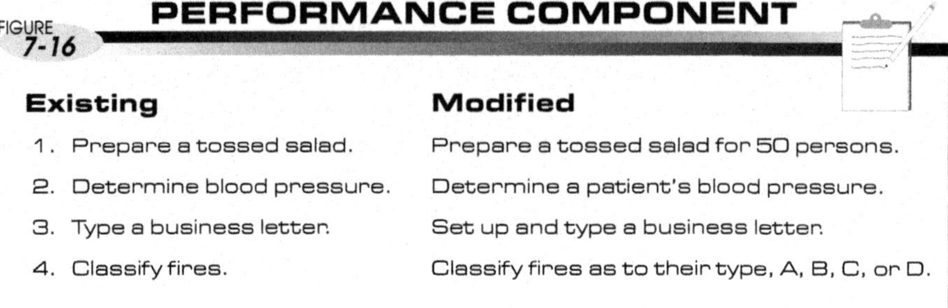

FIGURE 7-16 PERFORMANCE COMPONENT

Existing	Modified
1. Prepare a tossed salad.	Prepare a tossed salad for 50 persons.
2. Determine blood pressure.	Determine a patient's blood pressure.
3. Type a business letter.	Set up and type a business letter.
4. Classify fires.	Classify fires as to their type, A, B, C, or D.

The performance component is nothing more than the task statement, but the task statement may be expanded or modified to describe the performance accepted in the training setting.

Condition Component. The condition component of the objective describes the setting in which the trainee will be required to perform the task to demonstrate mastery. The condition is often referred to as the given. See Figure 7-17. Following are tips for developing condition components:

- Avoid a long list of specific tools, equipment, etc. The objective may become quite lengthy and of little use.
- Do not list items, situations, or restrictions that are obvious to students/instructor, such as "given a workstation, welding rods, and torch."
- Avoid prompting the student in the objective. If the student must determine what tools are needed or must locate the correct replacement parts before performing a service, do not list these tools and parts in the condition. Mention any special restrictions under which the students will have to perform.
- Avoid specifying any reference to how the student will learn the task, such as, "given a lecture on," "given the required reading material," and so on. The focus is on the testing and not the learning.
- Avoid conditions too specific. For example, "given two pieces of metal 4″ × 4″," might be too restrictive. "Given two pieces of material" may be reasonable.
- The condition stated in the objective should resemble the conditions under which the trainee must perform the task on the job. If the worker must be able to perform a weld when given a blueprint, then "given a blueprint . . . " should be specified in the condition portion of the objective.

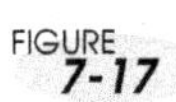

FIGURE 7-17

CONDITION COMPONENT

Things	Situations	Restrictions
• Given certain tools • Using test instruments • Using manuals, specifications, etc. • Provided with mock-ups, devices, etc. • Given consumable supplies or materials	• Given a field situation • Under some simulated situation • Given lists of terms, parts, tools, etc. • Given numbers, figures, or problems • Provided with results of a diagnostic test • Using actual customer's car or other live work	• Without help • Without calculator, special tools, tables, charts, etc. • Without the use of references, texts, books, or manuals

The condition component of the objective describes the setting in which the trainee will be required to perform the task to demonstrate mastery.

Each performance component identified will be expanded to include the condition component. The condition component defines the conditions under which the student will be expected to perform the task. See Figure 7-18. The condition components are listed first, then the performance component, then the criteria component.

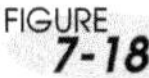

FIGURE 7-18

CONDITION AND PERFORMANCE COMPONENTS

1. Given an appropriate recipe and access to the necessary utensils and ingredients, prepare a tossed salad for 50 persons.
2. In an appropriate clinical setting, determine a patient's blood pressure.
3. Given the appropriate equipment, supplies, format, and copy, set up and type a business letter.
4. When shown color pictures of fires, classify fires as to their type, A, B, C, or D.

Legend: ——— = Condition components
- - - - - - = Performance components

Each performance component can be expanded to include the condition component.

Criteria Component. The criteria component describes how well the learner will perform the task for the instructor to conclude that the task has been mastered. A trainee can master almost all key indicators of competence except, perhaps, speed. The criteria component generally specifies process and/or product performance. Process deals with the observations by the instructor as the trainee demonstrates mastery of the task, while product generally only looks at the product of the process. See Figure 7-19. Tips for developing the criteria component are as follows:

- Keep the acceptable criteria the same for all students in the training program.
- All the important competency indicators should be included in the criteria.
- Include the typical errors made by trainees in the criteria.
- Keep the criteria at a high enough level to ensure appropriate entry-level needs.
- Avoid "to instructor's satisfaction," "to industry standards," "correctly," as these tend to be vague criteria.
- Avoid including instruction in the criteria. "According to specs in the manual" or "criteria in the handout" should be avoided. These resources will change, while criteria are more constant.
- Keep criteria dealing with speed not as high as would be required for an experienced worker performing the task on the job.
- If speed is important for a task, consider a reasonable time limit in the criteria (or include time as an item on the performance test).

When the criteria component is added, the objective is complete. See Figure 7-20.

FIGURE 7-19

CRITERIA COMPONENT

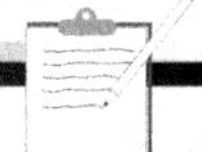

Process Criteria	Product Criteria
• Within 30 minutes	• ±2
• Following safety practices	• Salable
• Performing all steps in sequence	• With 100% accuracy
• Using proper tools and equipment	• No visible cracks or pits
• Not exceeding flat-rate time by more than 25%	• To customer's satisfaction
• Following manufacturer's maintenance procedures	
• Conforms to local building code	
• Within 10% of instructor reading	
• Engine must be tuned to manufacturer's specifications	

The criteria component describes how well the learner will perform the task for the instructor, thus indicating that the task has been mastered.

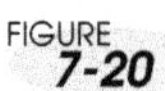

COMPLETE OBJECTIVE

1. Given an appropriate recipe and access to the necessary utensils and ingredients, prepare a tossed salad for 50 persons, per the recipe, and having the residual smaller than 3% weight after serving.
2. In an appropriate clinical setting, determine a patient's blood pressure, with an accuracy of ±6 mm of that recorded for the same patient by the instructor.
3. Given the appropriate equipment, supplies, format, and copy, set up and type a business letter, in mailable form, as defined by the instruction sheet, within 10 minutes.
4. When shown color pictures of fires, classify fires as to their type, A, B, C, or D, per the IFSTA Training Manual, without error.

When the criteria component is added, the objective is complete.

Distance Education Courses

Technology is impacting every aspect of education. New learning technologies are constantly being developed. Distance education, or e-learning, has increased significantly, as has global education. Instructors are being asked to convert their regular, face-to-face classes into distance education courses to serve the needs of working adults or for just-in-time purposes within companies. Course development now requires a more interactive learning environment for both face-to-face and distance education.

Blended education, or the use of a combination of distance education with face-to-face instruction, has also gained popularity. With blended instruction, the facilitator might meet with the students only two to three times per semester. The rest of the class is handled via distance education. All materials are placed on the Internet for easy access.

To address this increased demand, the *Guidelines for the Evaluation of Distance Education (On-line Learning)* is a document that has been developed by the Higher Learning Commission in response to the changing distance-education needs of colleges and universities (Higher Learning Commission, 2009). The following standards represent the expectations of colleges and universities and are applicable to business and industry as well:

1. On-line learning is appropriate to the institution's mission and purpose.

2. The institution's plan for developing, sustaining, and if appropriate, expanding on-line learning offerings are integrated into its regular planning and evaluation process.
3. On-line learning is incorporated into the institution's system of governance and academic oversight.
4. Curricula for the institution's on-line learning are coherent, cohesive, and comparable in academic rigor to the programs offered in traditional instructional formats.
5. The institution evaluates the effectiveness of its on-line learning offerings, including the extent to which the on-line learning goals are achieved, and uses the results of its evaluation to enhance the attainment of the goals.
6. Faculty responsible for delivering the on-line learning curricula and evaluating the students' success in achieving the on-line learning goals are appropriately qualified and effectively supported.
7. The institution provides effective student and academic services to support students enrolled in on-line learning offerings.
8. The institution provides sufficient resources to support and, if appropriate, expand its on-line learning offerings
9. The institution assures the integrity of its on-line learning offerings. (pp. 2–5)

Educational entities should also consider student support in the following areas:

- registration
- financial aid
- library resources
- counseling
- tutoring
- ADA services
- career services
- technical support

Many administrators and instructors are feeling increased pressure to move more courses online. With the increased number of students holding down full-time jobs, e-learning may assist these students in balancing their time demands. Many entities have limited resources and moving courses to online delivery can alleviate classroom space concerns. Using online strategies can also expose faculty to new tools and techniques.

While there may be student learning preferences with online education, motivating students to online environments is about engagement and being organized. Peer and student feedback is still essential with e-learning. Using blogs, wikis (web sites in which content can be modified by users), and other social tools has proved to be an effective method for engaging students.

Most learning management systems (LMSs) include the following tools:

- A *course home page* supplies information, announcements, and contact information.
- A *course calendar* informs users when content should be viewed, resources are addressed, and assignments and quizzes are due.
- The *learning path* provides tools to create and manage lists of tasks for users to complete.
- The *course content* area provides students with instruction sheets and any other information pertinent to the course.
- The *assignments* section lists activities students are expected to complete for the course.
- The *evaluations* section supplies quizzes or exams.
- *Feedback* includes surveys for students to take to provide feedback to the instructor on units/assignments.
- *Grades* allow students to check their progress in the course.
- The *drop box* provides a place where completed assignments can be deposited.
- A list of *links* identifies additional resources, such as PDFs, videos, articles, etc.
- A *discussion* section provides a list of discussion questions so students can respond.
- *Chat areas* allow students to list a topic so all students can respond.
- The *groups* section allows students who are assigned to cooperative learning groups to conduct their own business.
- *Email* provides an area where instructor can email one or all students.

Almost any effective strategy used in a regular classroom can be used in distance education or e-learning courses. Some of the following elements are especially essential to distance education courses.

Signing Up

A frequent concern with distance courses is the student's preparation and whether the student has the appropriate prerequisite knowledge and skills for success. A concerted effort should be made at the time of enrollment to identify the knowledge, skills, and expectations of the students. Distance education students frequently work full time and may not realize the amount of time required each week to complete their assignments. Hardware and software requirements should also be noted.

Some distance education students may have inadequate equipment or software and may not be able to use some of the resources. Also, students should be made aware of where they can get technical assistance.

Organization

Organization is key in any distance education course. A student guide or syllabus should be developed ahead of time identifying all essential information, such as course description, course goals, course objectives, required textbooks, units of instruction, content outline, assignments and how they will be graded, evaluation, course grading, academic misconduct (if applicable), and other course expectations. Absolute deadlines for all assignments should be developed based on the length of the course. The more explicit the expectations, the easier it will be for the instructor and student. It is essential to communicate all policies and procedures in order to reduce the number of student questions and the email traffic that frequently occur with distance courses.

Assignments

All assignments should be developed and posted on the LMS site. A performance objective should be developed and noted for each assignment. Evaluation criteria, such as checklists or rubrics, should also be developed and posted in advance. This will assist students in understanding the criteria of the assignment, reduce questions, and assist instructors in grading.

Resources

All essential resources required for students to successfully complete their assignments should be identified. Any DVD, graphics, multimedia, web sites, and reference sources should be noted, along with any special requirements needed to view them. Reserved resources held in a library should be noted, along with access rules. Specific links to Internet resources should also be noted and periodically checked to ensure that they are still active and accurate. All other possible resources to best accomplish the learning objectives must be employed. For example what resources could be provided to enhance students' exploration of each topic? Streaming video, field trips, podcasts, guest speakers, eportfolios, simulations, games, case studies, and concept mapping are all possibilities.

Activities

At times the instructor might want to involve students in an audio conference, group work, or interactive exercises. Groups may engage in specific problem-solving activities that require constant communication and the development of a product. Most LMSs have a place where groups of students can engage with each other without involving the rest of the class. For example, if students are competing with other groups for the best strategy, they will be able to work with anonymity. The instructor can still have access to each group and can monitor and provide feedback. The instructor or trainer must consider activities that would best assist student learning. Other activities to engage students might include the following:

- written reports
- oral presentations
- multimedia presentations
- product development
- scenarios and simulations
- critical analyses
- field trips
- case studies
- role playing
- self-assessment inventories
- portfolios
- interviews
- research assignments
- capstone project

Discussion and Chat Areas

To keep students engaged and motivated, the instructor can post a series of discussion questions, either by units of instruction or by general questions. Students can then monitor the discussion area by responding to questions and commenting on what other students have posted. Chat areas can also be established through which students can initiate their own questions, soliciting responses from other students in the course. With email, students have the opportunity to build a learning community outside of the LMS to initiate discussions, share ideas, and get feedback. With LMS software, a printed record of the frequency and duration of engagements, including a summary, is available.

Tests and Quizzes

Tests and quizzes can be developed and posted on the LMS site when the course is first developed. A calendar listing dates and times to take a particular test or quiz is part of the system. Using this calendar, students will know when a test or quiz will be available for them to take, along with its time limit. When the instructor first records a test or quiz, decisions are made as to the kinds of possible feedback that can be given to correct and incorrect responses. A final score/grade on each test or quiz provides immediate feedback to students.

Evaluation

Assessments should be integrated into each unit and part of each assignment as a method to ensure students have completed readings, viewed presentations, reviewed concepts, and responded to questions. The assessments could be graded or not, but there should be something to check for understanding. Providing student feedback throughout the course is critical. Developing and using rubrics, checklists, or a set of questions for each assignment will provide students with essential feedback and let them know if they have met the criteria for learning.

Students' achievements in the course must also be assessed. Additionally, students should evaluate the effectiveness of the course at regular intervals, and every opportunity should be given to students to evaluate their online experience. Peer and supervisor reviews should also be conducted.

Review Questions

1. Identify the advantages of a course outline.
2. Identify the advantages of a content outline.
3. Explain how the course and unit content outline differ.
4. What are the differences between a course description and course goal?
5. When should a class schedule be developed? What are its advantages for students?
6. Describe the components of a unit of instruction.
7. Why are student activities so critical?
8. Under what conditions should the instructor develop resources?
9. What are the three components of a performance objective?
10. How do course objectives and unit objectives differ?

References

Bartel, C. R. (1976). *Instructional analysis and materials development.* Homewood, IL: American Technical Publishers.

Carnevale, A. P., Gainer, L. J., & Meltzer, A. S. (1990). *Workplace Basics Training Manual.* San Francisco: Jossey-Bass.

Continuing education and lifelong learning trends. (2009). Retrieved October 21, 2014, from http://www.encyclopedia.com/doc/1G2-3273100056.html

Dean, C. B., Hubbell, E. R., Pitler, H., & Stone B. (2012). *Classroom instruction that works: Research-based strategies for increasing student achievement* (2nd ed.). Alexandria, VA: ASCD.

Finch, C. R., & Crunkilton, J. R. (1999). *Curriculum development in vocational and technical education.* Boston: Allyn & Bacon.

Gronlund, N. E. (2000). *How to write and use instructional objectives* (6th ed.). Upper Saddle River, NJ: Prentice-Hall.

Grunert O'Brien, J. G., Millis, B. J., & Cohen, M. W. (2008). *The Course Syllabus: A Learning-Centered Approach* (2nd ed.). San Francisco: Jossey-Bass.

Heiman, M., & Slomianko, J. (1998). *Learning to learn: Thinking skills for the 21st Century.* Cambridge, MA: Learning to Learn.

Higher Learning Commission. (2009). *Guidelines for evaluation of distance education (on-line learning*). Retrieved October 27, 2014, from http://www.ncahlc.org/Document-Library/publications.html

Kurfiss, J. G. (1988). *Critical thinking: Theory, research, practice and possibilities.* (ASHE-ERIC Higher Education Report No. 2). Washington, DC: Association for the Study of Higher Education.

Mentkowski, M. (2000). *Learning that lasts: Integrating learning, development, and performance in college and beyond.* San Francisco: Jossey-Bass.

Pascarella, E. T., & Terenzini, P. T. (2005). *How college affects students: A third decade of research.* San Francisco: Jossey-Bass.

Rothwell, W. J., & Kazanas, H. C. (2008). *Mastering the instructional design process: A systematic approach* (4th ed.). San Francisco: Pfieffer.

Weimer, M. (1993). *Improve your classroom teaching*. Thousand Oaks, CA: Sage Publications.

Instructional Development

INTRODUCTION

Good training and instruction requires comprehensive planning and preparation. Once the instructional developer, instructor, or trainer has laid out the training program, developed performance objectives, and defined content, instructional development is the next appropriate step.

Instructional development covers both student and instructor activities. Student activities are activities the instructor plans for the students to help them master the material, such as reading, discussing, writing, completing a checklist, role-playing, or using interactive media on the Internet. Activities may take place in the classroom or outside of the classroom. Instructor activities are those things that the instructor does to enhance learning, such as developing objectives, preparing a lecture, developing questions to ask in class, monitoring student progress, or preparing a quiz or exam. These activities may occur before the instruction, during the instruction or lesson, and after the lesson is complete.

Whatever the case, activities need to be structured and planned for as part of instructional development, thus, instructional development includes developing lesson plans and acquiring or developing materials.

OBJECTIVES

After completing this chapter, the reader should be able to do the following:

1. Identify the advantages of using lesson plans.
2. Describe the seven-stage model of lesson planning.
3. Explain the need for lesson plan preliminaries.
4. Develop a lesson plan for a given lesson.
5. Write a performance objective consisting of three parts.
6. Discuss the difference between an information and assignment handout.
7. Recognize the important elements of a learning activity packet (LAP).

LESSON PLANS

Lesson planning is a process of planning and development that results in a road map for the actual instruction. It consists of a series of steps that, if taken, will result in student learning. The key outcome of lesson planning is the lesson plan itself. Lesson plans are usually developed by the instructor to map out the instruction for themselves and learning activities for the student for a particular day or session. They are a tool to assist the instructor in organizing content and focusing on methodology, student activities, and resources for a given presentation.

Every time an instructor plans on presenting information, whether for 5 minutes or 60 minutes, face-to face or over the Internet, a lesson plan should be developed. A trainer might be scheduled for a four-day training session, and during that time frame, seven different topics may be presented. In this case, there should be seven separate lesson plans.

Lesson plans should be developed directly from the content outline and reflect previous decisions made about instructional strategies, media, and the sequence of performance objectives. They should be organized into distinct parts, each reflecting a learning event. Lesson plans should indicate the instructional resources, equipment and materials, and anything else required for instruction.

In some cases, timelines, a checklist of equipment and supplies, correspondence, seating charts, attendance sheets, and the development of instructional resources such as audiovisual materials and instructional handouts are required to complete the lesson plan. Good lesson planning increases the probability that students will learn what is intended. Knowing the ins and outs of lesson planning is critical for any instructor or trainer. Some of what lesson plans provide include the following:

- a detailed content outline
- objectives for the lesson/session
- resources and materials for delivering and reinforcing the content
- activities and/or active participation strategies to reinforce learning
- a focused introduction to prime students for learning
- specific questions for students
- a specific time frame assigned to each item, such as lecture, demonstration, practice, questions, assessment, etc.
- room planning/arrangement information
- an assessment for determining if the objectives have been met
- an opportunity to frame the lesson
- an opportunity to consider the abilities, interests, and motivations of the students
- time to consider the last lesson and where the next lesson is headed
- a guideline for a substitute instructors and supervisor
- a record for revisions

The amount of information contained in a lesson plan will vary by individual trainer or instructor and depending on the setting or lesson. Some companies or educational institutions may require the completion of a standard lesson plan template. If the content of the lesson consists of completely new material, then a more detailed lesson plan may be required. The lesson plan is the blueprint for organizing the information required to adequately deliver a lesson. Good lesson plans not only give direction, they let the instructor know how they are doing and when the student has learned the material.

Some lesson plans are very simple, listing objectives, content outline, and resources. A comprehensive lesson plan includes all of these, as well as delivery method, student and instructor activities, media/resources, timelines, evaluation, and assignments.

Lesson plans should reflect the outcomes desired of students or participants. They can be based on a task, but may be further broken down because of the many steps involved in completing the task. Lesson plans are used by the instructor to structure a lesson. Brunn (2010) noted five steps to effective lesson planning:

1. Establish the lesson's purpose.
2. Create a plan for introducing the lesson.
3. Make decisions regarding how the lesson will be facilitated.
4. Decide how students will share and reflect on their work.
5. Review and revise your teaching plan.

Lesson plans can be developed for a one-half-day or a one-week training session, or a course across the whole semester. Keep in mind that no lesson plan is set in concrete; many things that occur during the course will affect the delivery.

The seven-stage model developed by Madeline Hunter (1976) is frequently used in public schools and incorporates behavioral, cognitive, and constructive psychology approach elements. A study by Steward, Martin, Burns, and Bush (2010) used the Madeline Hunter lesson design and found that with this design, students obtained higher achievement than with a more traditional lesson design. The model consists of (1) the anticipatory set, (2) input, (3) modeling, (4) checking for understanding, (5) guided practice, (6) independent practice, and (7) closure.

The assumption when using the lesson plan model is that a learner objective, which indicates what the student is to know, care about, and be able to do, is first indicated. Furthermore, specific criteria for meeting the objectives are indicated and shared with students. With this in mind, Hunter's lesson plan can be implemented.

The first step in the plan is the anticipatory set. In this stage, bringing students up to speed with the instructor is the focus. Gaining students' attention with a specific task to focus on the upcoming lesson is paramount. Thus, focusing students' attention on the lesson and creating a framework so students can hook into the lesson is the main goal of the anticipatory set. This step is especially important in that it creates an eagerness or reason for students to want to pay attention. According to Hunter, any lesson should include an anticipatory set.

The next stage in the Hunter lesson plan model is input. In this stage, the teacher plans how the content will be delivered. It is assumed that an objective is written and shared with students. Will the content delivered be a standup lecture, video, reading assignment, discussion, or some other means of input to students? Whatever the input, knowledge and skill are passed on to students and must be identified within the lesson plan.

Stage 3 is modeling. The teacher models, demonstrates, shows, and provides examples of what is to be expected after the student acquires the new knowledge or skills. The critical attributes of the expectations are pointed out so that students can have a clear picture. This is a critical stage of lesson planning because the instructor must clearly demonstrate to students what their end product should look like and show them the criteria used for grading.

In stage 4, the instructor checks for understanding. What will the instructor do to determine if students understand the content or have learned the objectives? What will the students do to demonstrate that they understand? There is nothing worse than having students learn things incorrectly. The instructor's job in this stage is to determine if the students have learned the material. If they have, then the instructor can move on; if they have not, then the instructor must have a plan to reteach the lesson.

Stage 5 is guided practice. Once students learn something new, they need an opportunity to demonstrate a grasp of new learning by working through an activity or exercise to practice it. This increases the probability that they will retain the information. Guided practice implies that the students practice under some kind of supervision. If mistakes are made, then feedback can be provided as the mistakes are occurring. This, of course, needs to be anticipated, and the lesson plan provides the opportunity for the instructor to prepare for this.

In stage 6, Hunter considers independent practice a critical part of any lesson. This is reinforcement, and it may be additional assignments involving group or individual work that provide an opportunity for the student to apply the knowledge and practice the new skill without the instructor's monitoring and guidance. Applying the knowledge and skills to other situations is essential.

The last stage in Hunter's lesson plan development is closure. Closure is a review or wrap-up of the lesson. The teacher solicits input from the students to confirm they have a command of the subject matter. This part of the lesson assists students in bringing knowledge and skills together in their own minds. Simply asking students if there are any questions is not closure. Closure involves the students clarifying the essential points of a lesson and attempting to tie them together so that they can see the whole.

The Hunter lesson plan lets students know what instructors are going to tell them with the anticipatory set and objectives, tells them with the presentation, and checks for understanding. It provides opportunity to practice, both with guidance and independently, and then ties everything together in the students' minds with closure.

Another model for lesson plans is noted by Van Wart, Cayer, and Cook (1993) who divide lesson plans into four main stages: (1) course parameters, (2) objectives and performance measures, (3) lesson plan overview, and (4) detailed lesson frames. Course parameters consist of basic information needed to organize the course. Title, contact time, participants' numbers, location, prerequisites, and instructor are noted in this stage. In the second stage, learning objectives, instructional input, practice exercises, and performance measures are noted. Stage 3 provides a specific time frame (minutes or hours) when content is addressed. The last stage further refines the time element in relationship to the objectives, content outline, method of delivery, and any resources used.

In this chapter, three stages of lesson planning are used: (1) lesson plan preliminaries, (2) lesson plan organization, (3) and lesson plan delivery. In stage 1, organization data in terms of where the lesson fits in the schema of other lessons is recorded. This is the major organizational piece and helps instructors track the number of lessons in a unit of instruction or the number of lessons in a course. In stage 2, lesson plan organization, objectives, methods, and evaluation measures are noted. The last stage, lesson plan delivery, ties the lesson to a specific timetable for delivery. Each stage is important, with details to provide a definite structure to the lesson and thus ensure learning.

Lesson Plan Preliminaries

Lesson plan preliminaries include course parameters consisting of basic information, such as course title, dates, instructor, location, prerequisites, and other information determined to be necessary to prepare for the course or session. Lesson plan preliminaries are an integral organizational piece and assist the instructor in knowing where each lesson fits within the larger course. See Figure 8-1.

FIGURE 8-1

Lesson Plan

Department ______________________ Date ______________

Course Title ______________ Lesson Title ______________

Unit Number__________ Lesson No. ______ Time Required ________

Location ______________________ Instructor ______________

Prerequisites ____

A lesson plan preliminaries form includes course parameters consisting of basic information such as course title, dates, instructor, location, and prerequisites.

In the example shown in Figure 8-1, the lesson plan preliminaries consist of the department name, date, course title, lesson title, unit number, lesson number, time required, location, instructor, and prerequisites. Lesson plan preliminaries help organize basic information and offer a way lesson plans can be organized, especially if a course structure includes many lessons over a period of time. In some cases, lesson plan goals may be identified. Also, trainers and instructors may modify the lesson plan preliminaries as needed.

When completing the lesson plan preliminaries, instructors can use folders to help organize the lesson plans, especially if there are several lessons for a unit of instruction and it takes several days to complete them. Using color-coded folders or markings may assist in the organization by keeping lesson plans with units of instruction. Trainers may use a colored marker to highlight the unit or session headings, which would help keep them together. This is very useful if a trainer or instructor is absent and helpful to a supervisor as well.

Lesson Plan Organization

The second stage of lesson planning, lesson plan organization, encompasses learning objectives and performance measures. A learning objective, or performance objective, is developed; a set, or introduction, is established and instructional methods that match the objective are identified. Practice and reinforcement are included in the method. A performance measure, or how the instructor will know that learning has occurred, is identified for each performance objective. The main components of the lesson plan organization are the performance objective, method of delivery, and how practice will be planned, implemented, and evaluated.

Performance Objective. A performance objective may be broken down into three parts: condition, performance, and criteria. See Figure 8-2. Consider the following two performance objectives:

1. In the classroom setting, identify the characteristics of the different philosophies of education by scoring 10 out of 10 on a matching quiz.
2. In the classroom setting, discuss the implications of the different philosophies of education for the curriculum and teaching setting, and write a paper indicating the strengths and weaknesses of one educational philosophy scoring 35 out of 45 on a product rating scale.

FIGURE 8-2

Objective Parts

Condition	Performance	Criterion
1. In a classroom setting	Identify characteristics of the different philosophies of education	Score 10 out of 10 on a matching quiz
2. In a classroom setting	Discuss the implications of the different philosophies of education for the curriculum and teaching setting, and write a paper indicating the strengths and weaknesses of an education philosophy	Score 35 out of 45 on a product rating scale

Performance objectives are broken down into condition, performance, and criteria.

The condition, in both cases, is the classroom setting. The performance in the first objective is to identify the characteristics of the different philosophies of education, and the criterion for evaluation is that the student must score 10 out of 10 on a matching quiz. The criterion not only provides the score they must achieve, but also indicates the method (matching quiz) that will be used to indicate an acceptable level of performance.

In the second objective, the performance level includes discussing the implications of the different philosophies of education for the curriculum and teaching setting and writing a paper indicating the strengths and weakness of an educational philosophy. The student must be engaged with discussion and writing a paper. The paper will be graded by using a product checklist, and passing is a score of 35 out of 45.

The performance objective is thus the foundation of the lesson plan. It clarifies the intent of the instructor and the instruction that will result. Without a performance objective, the rest of the lesson is a guessing game.

Performance components are listed under each performance objective. See Figure 8-3. Depending on the lesson plan design, the complete performance objective may be listed as part of the lesson. In this example, only the performance portion is listed. As the model unfolds, the method, practice, and evaluation will be included.

Set. This is where the instructor plans an introduction to the lesson that helps with buy-in by the students. The instructor must consider how to connect students' prior knowledge and experience to help them focus on the present lesson. In the first objective, the set might be to ask students to think about their own philosophy for teaching or the philosophy of their favorite teacher or trainer and how that resulted in the way they taught. With the second objective, the students might consider all the possible philosophies and which they liked the best and why. In both examples this should get students thinking about what the instructor plans for the lesson.

Method. The method section in the lesson plan deals with input, or how the instructor plans to convey the performance content information to transform students' knowledge and skills. Will it be by reading, group discussion, lecture, video, computer-aided instruction, or some other means for participants to acquire the information? A method requires advanced preparation. For example, if students need to read a handout, then a handout must be prepared. Instructors also need to consider if they want to use an advance organizer (vocabulary list, mini lecture) or a prereading activity to ensure success when reading. Likewise, when reading, the instructor might develop a reading guide (series of questions to which students respond when reading) for a during-reading activity to ensure that students obtain a specific level of knowledge.

This is where the instructor or trainer can be creative and provide multiple paths of input for students. The method selected should be consistent with the content and expectations. For example, if the performance objective requires a test or quiz, then the method should reinforce cognitive information. If the performance objective requires some psychomotor skill, then the input should reflect performance or psychomotor skill.

Items under the method are added for each performance objective. See Figure 8-4. The methods noted are consistent with the conditions for the performance objective and the performance component. A number of different methods can be used. See Appendix I. In many of the methods, content can be delivered via the computer using synchronous or asynchronous strategies. The methods selected greatly depend on the creativity of the instructor.

FIGURE 8-3

Performance Objective	Method	Practice	Evaluation
1. Identify characteristics of the different philosophies of education.			
2. Discuss implications of the educational philosophy for curriculum and teaching.			

Performance components are listed under a given performance objective.

FIGURE 8-4

Performance Objective	Method	Practice	Evaluation
1. Identify characteristics of the different philosophies of education.	A. Lecture and read handouts B. Group discussion		
2. Discuss implications of the educational philosophy for curriculum and teaching.	A. Group discussion B. Distribute and review criteria for paper C. Show samples		

In lesson plan organization, the performance objective is defined and the method is chosen.

Objective 1, "identify characteristics of the different philosophies of education," is supported by two methods—lecture and group discussion. In objective 2, the methods identified are group discussion, review of criteria, and showing samples. Another instructor may use the same objective but decide to use methods other than these.

Practice. Another category in the lesson plan is practice. See Figure 8-5. The purpose of practice is the reinforcement of content and skill. Practice will increase the probability that students will retain the information. However, practice must be correct and should be scheduled. Correct practice means that the instructor monitors the students to make sure they are following the steps and provides feedback along the way. Scheduled practice refers to breaking down the task so that each phase is practiced before the phases are pulled together into a whole. At some point, students will require another practice session to ensure the retention of the information or skill. Practice provides the opportunity for the transfer of knowledge into behavior.

Practice may include completing a reading guide with a series of questions, a small group discussion, a self-assessment, a paper, or some other means of having students use and apply what they have learned. Again, the performance objective dictates the type of reinforcement and practice required. If students are required to complete a task to demonstrate competency, then students need the opportunity to practice it with feedback before they are evaluated.

FIGURE
8-5

Performance Objective	Method	Practice	Evaluation
1. Identify characteristics of the different philosophies of education.	A. Read handouts	A. Complete individual exercise (monitor)	
	B. Group discussion	B. Share philosophies with group members (monitor)	
2. Discuss implications of the educational philosophy for curriculum and teaching.	A. Group discussion	A. Participate in group discussion (guide sheet with instructor monitor)	
	B. Review criteria for paper	B. Write outline to address criteria (monitor)	
	C. Show samples	C. Write paper	

Practice reinforces content and skill.

Following through with objective number 1, the practice portion of the lesson plan includes having participants practice identifying the characteristics of the different philosophies of education by completing an individual exercise and participating in a group discussion. The instructor would monitor students as they complete the individual exercise. Furthermore, the instructor would also monitor the group discussion and provide feedback to individual students.

For the second objective, the instructor has planned for the participants to practice by participating in a group discussion, writing an outline to address criteria, and writing a paper. The instructor would monitor the group discussion and provide feedback on the outline.

Evaluation. The last portion of lesson planning organization is evaluation, or how the instructor determines whether students have mastered the knowledge and skill. See Figure 8-6. Evaluation is the instructor's plans on how to evaluate the students. The evaluation tests whether the participants and instructor have been successful in reaching the targeted outcome. In the performance measure, the students are asked to demonstrate what they learned, consistent with the learning objective. This is directly related to the criteria portion of the performance objective, which indicates the quality and quantity levels required to demonstrate mastery. The criteria for the instruments need to be established and validated.

Again, when dealing with objective number 1, the performance objective deals with the identification of characteristics of the different philosophies of education. For the evaluation portion, students will complete the self-inventory and quiz. In terms of preparation, the instructor must have a handout for the students to complete, and a quiz that measures whether students can indeed identify the characteristics of the different philosophies.

In the second objective, the performance is to discuss implications for curriculum and teaching. Students will thus participate in a discussion with feedback, develop a paper outline, and write a paper. In this example, the instructor should have three items prepared: group participants' guide sheet, criteria for an outline, and criteria for grading the students' papers. This is just an example. Other instructors could select from a number of options for evaluating student outcomes. In essence, the three-part performance objective (condition, performance, and criterion) shown in Figure 8-2 guides the whole process of lesson plan organization.

Lesson Plan Delivery

The third stage, or lesson plan delivery, overviews the methods, practice, and evaluation activities identified in the previous step as they are mapped out against time and activities. Thus, as each activity is assigned a starting and stopping time, this becomes the tentative schedule for the lesson plan. The timing may occur over a week, a few days, or just a day, depending on the lesson. The time also reflects the schedule of the training activity. In a business and industry setting, the training may be delivered over one hour or several days. In a technical college setting, the course may be for one quarter or semester and meet every other day or each day for 55 minutes.

FIGURE 8-6

Performance Objective	Method	Practice	Evaluation
1. Identify characteristics of the different philosophies of education.	A. Read handouts	A. Complete individual exercise (monitor)	A. Individual exercise turned in
	B. Group discussion	B. Share philosophies with group members (monitor)	B. Take quiz on characteristics of the different philosophies of education
2. Discuss implications of the educational philosophy for curriculum and teaching.	A. Group discussion	A. Participate in group discussion (guide sheet with instructor monitor)	A. Read, comment, and return guide sheet
	B. Review criteria for paper	B. Write outline to address criteria (monitor)	B. Provide feedback on outline
	C. Show samples	C. Write paper	C. Grade paper using product checklist

Evaluation is used to determine whether students have acquired new knowledge and skills.

In objective 1, three topics or activities are planned. See Figure 8-7. Each is assigned the number of minutes it will take to complete it. Instructor preparation is dealt with in the last column. This is a reminder that certain things must be prepared if they are to be shared with students or used in the classroom. Objective 2 provides several more steps to complete its objective. Each topic or activity requires the instructor to plan and have something developed. This detail of planning is often required to ensure that everything is prepared for delivery.

FIGURE 8-7

Topic or Activity	Class Time	Instructor Preparation
Objective #1: In the classroom setting, identify the characteristics of the different philosophies of education by scoring 10 out of 10 on a matching quiz.		
A. Lecture on characteristics of the different philosophies of education	20 minutes	Content outline
B. Complete individual exercise	10 minutes	Develop questionnaire
C. Group discussion	20 minutes	Develop discussion guide and participation rating scale
Objective #2: In the classroom setting, discuss the implications of the different philosophies of education for the curriculum and teaching setting and write a paper indicating the strengths and weakness of an educational philosophy scoring 35 out of 45 on a product rating scale.		
A. Group discussion	30 minutes	Develop discussion guide and participant rating scale
B. Complete individual exercise	5 minutes	Develop rating scale for content outline
C. Students write outline, monitor students	20 minutes	Anticipate questions and problems
D. Show samples of completed papers	5 minutes	Make transparencies of samples
E. Share paper rating scale with students	10 minutes	Develop proper rating scale

Topic or activity, class time, and instructor preparation are shown for each objective.

Some instructors share their lesson plans with their students. This might be as a handout or as an overhead. This provides a big picture and lets students know what the trainer or instructor is covering. If participants are absent, the lesson plan information lets them know what has to be done to make up missed course work. Lesson plans are also frequently shared with supervisors, who may use them for evaluation.

Media/Resources

Resources are things the instructor uses to plan and deliver the instruction. While it would be easy to use existing resources, there may be a need to develop new materials depending on the situation. Resources may consist of hardware and software, multimedia tools, articles, research papers, textbooks, web-based materials, speakers, business and industry, field trips, handouts, mock-ups, or items developed by the instructor for use in preparing or delivering the lesson. There are many textbooks and web pages devoted to classroom resources.

There are many models available for selecting resources based on a number of factors. Authors such as Romiszowski (1992) have developed models for media selection. Most of the models include factors such as the following:

- instructional method
- learning task
- characteristics of the learner
- instructor preference
- environment
- available equipment and resources

With today's technology, the notion of synchronous and asynchronous learning needs and media also need to be considered. Synchronous learning is real-time and instructor-led, where all participants are available at the same time. The instructor can communicate with all students, and they with each other, directly. Asynchronous learning is time-delayed, where interaction between the instructor and students occurs intermittently. Interaction among students is also time-delayed.

Synchronous media examples are regular classroom, video and audio conferencing, chat sessions, and anything with live sessions. Synchronous media provides two-way communication with virtually no time delay, permitting all students to immediately interact and work together. Asynchronous media uses various technologies to communicate and complete course activities anytime and anywhere, but not necessarily at the same time. Examples include LMS instruction, media recordings, problem-based learning, collaboration and simulations, to name a few. Asynchronous media requires careful planning, with sufficient interaction to keep students on task (Simonson, Smaldino, Albright, & Zvacek, 2012).

Instructor-Developed Media/Resources

Instructor-developed materials that utilize graphic and audio media to deliver content can be an effective tool for distance education students, especially for those with different learning styles. Educational technology may be classified as media and resources. Media may be a PowerPoint® presentation, transparencies, video CD-ROM, computer-aided instruction, and web-based instruction. Resources include handouts produced by the instructor, textbooks, articles, and visual aids such as mock-ups, bulletin boards, packets, or tests.

The computer has been a significant force in the development of media and resources. However the development of all the possible media and resources is beyond the scope of this text. The focus, instead, will be on a few instructor-developed resources commonly used in technical schools and in business and industry/training settings. Instructor-developed information sheets, procedure sheets, assignment sheets, task and job sheets, and rating sheets will be discussed.

Information Sheet. An information sheet is a handout developed by the instructor to convey concepts and facts deemed essential to learn or essential for supporting content knowledge. It is prepared when sufficient information is not available through other resources and the instructor needs to supplement/reinforce content. Information sheets do not replace content presented by the instructor, but the additional information can enhance the content provided by the instructor. Instructors must be careful to introduce the information sheet during the lesson, explain its purpose and students' responsibilities, and set a time limit for written responses. The information sheet can also be used for future reference. An information sheet has the following characteristics:

- conveys information considered essential for a lesson
- is self-contained; all the information necessary is included
- includes resources
- may include questions to respond to at the end
- may include an evaluation component
- is integrated into the lesson

An information sheet template provides basic information. See Figure 8-8. Not every information sheet could or should include all of the elements identified. Besides the basic information, the template can call for directions, performance objective, content, resources, questions, and evaluation. The most important element may be the implementation of the information sheet. See Figure 8-9. The information sheet is tied to performance objective 2 in Figure 8-7: "In the classroom setting, discuss the implications of the different philosophies of education for the curriculum and teaching setting, and write a paper indicating the strengths and weaknesses of an educational philosophy scoring 35 out of 45 on a product rating scale." This example supplements the content delivered by the instructor and helps students consider implications of the different philosophies for curriculum and teaching.

FIGURE **8-8**

Information Sheet

Course Title ____________

Instructor ____________ Student Name ____________

Course ____________ Sheet Code ____________

Division ____________ Class ____________ Date ____________

Title ____________

Directions: This section covers subject importance and general directions for what is expected.

Performance Objective: The objective is written in three parts.

Content: Content is outlined.

Resources: Resources that include media and support the content are noted in this section.

Questions: In this section the instructor notes questions to ask students.

Evaluation: This is where the instructor will gauge students' learning of the information.

The information sheet template calls for basic information plus a number of different elements.

The main text deals with content related to performance objective 2, which asks students to consider which educational philosophy might be most appropriate to them. The objective relates to the information sheet, and the questions relate to the text of the handout. The evaluation shows that students must first take a position in relation to the four questions, discuss their position in relation to the questions, and reflect on what they would change. Handouts like this provide students with information related to the topic and questions, which reinforces their reading.

FIGURE 8-9

CTE 438-638 Course Construction

Information Sheet: Philosophy
November 20__

Objective: Identify Philosphy of an Institution

Information:

Philosophy is a set of assumptions used in viewing the world. It represents a statement of the basic presuppositions upon which one's view of certain phenomena is based. Having a way of viewing the world allows us to describe how that world operates in human experience.

A philosophy of technical education or training can account for the activities surrounding human learning and how the activities may be projected, explained, or managed. Philosophy becomes the master plan and the foundation for solving problems, answering questions, responding to critics, and guiding rational behavior.

Philosophy guides the alignment of theory and practice. "If you don't know where you are going, it does not matter how you get there." If theory and practice are rooted in philosophy, then a level of coherence should be evident. Educational philosophy asks three fundamental questions: What is real? What is true? What is good?

You can begin to conceptualize your educational philosophy by answering the following four questions:

1. What is the nature of the learner?
2. What is the role of the instructor?
3. How do you determine whether what is taught is the truth?
4. What is the purpose of schooling/training?

Philosophical systems and their generally accepted corresponding educational philosophies help in focusing responses to the four questions posed. Essentialist, perennialist, progressivist, and existentialist philosophies would all present their different positions.

The essential questions to which you must respond are the four identified above. If you select an eclectic approach, the responses to the four questions will be filled with conflict. Your goal is to develop coherent and harmonizing statements to the four questions posed.

Philosophical System	Educational Philosophy
Idealism Realism	Essentialism
Neo-Thomism	Perennialism
Experimentalism	Progessivism
Existentialism	Existentialism

(continued)

FIGURE 8-9

CTE 438-638 Course Construction (continued)

As you begin your search through career, technical, and adult education or training philosophy, terminology may get a little confusing. It may be helpful to define several terms that might be encountered.

Vision: This is what an organization wants to be. This is usually the overriding view. It also takes into account how the organization measures success, how it compares with competitors, how the organization is run on a daily basis, its beliefs and values, how it serves customers, and a review of its strengths, weaknesses, external opportunities, and threats.

Mission Statement: This is why the organization is in business. This includes the laws or legislative acts that were passed that started the organization.

Goals: These are the things that the organization will accomplish. They can be long-term or short-term goals.

Objectives: How the goals will be accomplished in measurable terms.

By reviewing the vision, mission, goals, and objectives of an institution, you begin to get a feel for the organization and can see how it views the nature of the learner, the role of the instructor, the purpose of schooling, and how it determines if what is taught is the truth.

References/Resources:

Peters, M. (2002).

Questions:

1. Consider where you might place yourself within the different philosophical systems. With which educational philosophy does it correspond?
2. Based on the educational philosophy selected, indicate the following:
   A. What is the nature of the learner?
   B. What is the role of the instructor?
   C. How do you determine whether what is taught is the truth?
   D. What is the purpose of schooling/training?

Evaluation:

1. In your group discussion, share your educational philosophy and responses to the four questions.
2. Based on the group discussion feedback, indicate what you plan to change in question 2 (above).

An information handout is tied to a particular objective.

Procedure Sheet. A procedure sheet is another type of handout designed with a specific structure to follow. A procedure sheet may be a set of directions for a task, job, project, or experiment. It is frequently used to explain or reinforce a procedure after an instructor's demonstration or when visual aids are used. Appropriate resources, tools, and materials necessary to complete the procedure are identified. Students can use the procedure sheet as a guide. See Figure 8-10.

FIGURE 8-10

Procedure Sheet: Steps in Writing Procedure Sheets — **CTE 638 Course Construction**

Objective: Identify steps to develop a procedure sheet handout.

Directions: Use the following eight steps when developing procedure sheets for students.

No.	Step	Explanation of Step
1.	Complete identification data.	This ties the handout to a particular unit of instruction. If there are several procedure sheets, then they are also numbered. For example: Unit VIII #4.
2.	Develop title for the procedure sheet.	Each procedure sheet should have a title.
3.	Write performance objective.	What will be learned and accomplished as a result of completing the procedure sheet?
4.	Identify appropriate resources.	These are resources needed to complete the procedure, such as textbooks, audiovisual aids, Internet sources (these should be active links for online courses), and other reference materials.
5.	Identify the tools, equipment, and materials needed for the procedure.	If the procedure is a laboratory assignment, then it is important to identify all equipment, tools, and materials necessary to complete the procedure.
6.	List all the procedure steps.	Number each procedure step in the order it is to be completed.
7.	Develop appropriate illustrations.	It might be helpful to add any appropriate pictures or drawings that highlight key points in the procedure.
8.	Develop a self-evaluation procedure.	It may be necessary to develop a checklist or rubric to assist students in evaluating how to complete the procedure.

A procedure sheet is a set of directions for completing a task.

Assignment Sheet. An assignment sheet is developed by the instructor and provides the requirements for an assignment. See Figure 8-11. Usually the assignment is to be turned in for grading, but the assignment could be participation in fieldwork, a group, or a focused field trip. It could be an activity in or out of class that is made to reinforce some information or presentation, or to develop or refine some psychomotor skill. It is similar to the information sheet in that an objective is provided and is accompanied by questions and evaluation.

FIGURE 8-11

Assignment Sheet Course Title ____________

Instructor ____________ Student Name ____________

Course ____________ Sheet Code ____________

Division ____________ Class ____________ Date ____________

Title ____________

Directions: Lets the student know what is expected and how they are to proceed.

Performance Objective: Three-part objective.

Assignment: Specific statement of assignment to accomplish the performance objective. May be covered in the directions.

Special Tools, Equipment, and Materials: List any special tools, equipment, and materials needed to complete the assignment.

Procedural Steps: List the specific steps to follow to complete the procedure. Indicate critical points where students need to pay particular attention. Any illustrations to assist the student should also be included in this section.

References/Resources: Include any references, resources, and media used to answer questions and to complete the assignment.

Questions: Indicate any questions that require application.

Evaluation: Include what students will do to demonstrate mastery of the assignments. A checklist for students to use to gauge where they are in the assignment would be valuable.

Due Date: Provide a date when the assignment is to be turned in.

An assignment sheet provides a framework for the assignment.

An assignment sheet differs from an information sheet in that the information sheet's purpose is to convey information, while the assignment sheet's main purpose is to provide the framework for the assignment. An assignment sheet is frequently called a task or job sheet and enables the students to complete something. In some cases, the procedure and assignment sheet may be combined.

The assignment sheet has the same preliminary information as an information sheet. The main difference appears in the body of the assignment sheet. Notice that there is a "directions" section that provides sufficient information about the assignment so students can follow. The performance objective states the performance expectations, conditions, and criteria for evaluation. The assignment section provides additional detail, such as when the assignment is due and in what form it should be submitted. Any special tools and equipment needed to accomplish the assignment may be noted along with procedural steps.

References and resources to assist students in completing the assignment are indicated, along with questions to which students should respond and an explanation of how the students will be evaluated. This does not mean that all of these elements need to be present when planning a lesson. Sometimes an instructor has been working with students on completing a specific task and completing steps along the way. When students get to this stage they may have to tie a number of smaller steps together to complete this assignment.

For example, students are required to graph their responses based on their assessment scores. See Figure 8-12. The directions, performance objective, and assignment are all related. References/resources are handouts developed by the instructor. Questions help the student review the process. Evaluation, in this example, is a product checklist and is listed under references/resources.

In another example, students are required to complete an assessment and record their scores. See Figure 8-13. Determining the time to allocate to such an assignment is frequently based on a guess for the first administration. It may not be possible for an instructor to pilot test the assignment, so the best estimate will be sufficient. After it has been administered a few times, the instructor will have a more accurate assessment of the amount of time to provide for students to complete the assignment.

To determine where students find themselves on the philosophy preference, another handout needs to be completed. See Figure 8-14. Students must now graph their responses to the 40 statements. Based on their scores, students can plot where they are on the scale. Thus, there are a number of activities to reinforce the objective. Planning must occur for these activities, which means the instructor or teacher must spend time developing and refining these handouts.

FIGURE 8-12

Assignment Sheet
Philosophy Assessment

CTE 438 Course Construction

Instructor________________ Student Name________________

Course________________ Sheet Code________________

Division________________ Class________ Date________

Title________________________________

Directions: This assignment builds on the class presentation and group discussion from the information handout on philosophy. The assignment is to complete the philosophy assessment inventory. The Philosophy Preference Information and Philosophy Assessment Scoring handouts will be provided in class.

Performance Objective: In the classroom setting, complete the Philosophy Preference Inventory handout, calculate and plot scores of each philosophy, following directions on the Philosophy Assessment Scoring handout and scoring 100% on the product checklist.

Assignment: Read and follow the directions in the Philosophy Preference Information handout. Follow the directions in the Philosophy Assessment Scoring handout to graph your results. Use the self-assessment product checklist to check your results.

References/Resources:

1. Philosophy Preference Information handout
2. Philosophy Assessment Scoring handout
3. Philosophy Information handout

Questions: Upon completing the assignment, respond to the following:

1. How can you explain how you scored on the inventory?
2. Explain whether your placement on the inventory is consistent with an educational institution in which you aspire to work.

Evaluation: Complete product checklist on the back of Philosophy Assessment Scoring handout.

In this assignment handout, students are required to graph their responses based on their assessment scores.

FIGURE 8-13

CTE 438-638
Course Construction

Information Sheet: Philosophy Preference Assessment
November 20__

Directions: For each item below, respond according to the strength of your belief. A **one (1) indicates strong disagreement,** a **five (5) strong agreement.** Record your score to the left of each item.

STRONG DISAGREEMENT → 1; STRONG AGREEMENT → 5

1 2 3 4 5 ___ 1. Ideal teachers are constant questioners.
1 2 3 4 5 ___ 2. Schools exist for societal improvement.
1 2 3 4 5 ___ 3. Teaching should center on the inquiry technique.
1 2 3 4 5 ___ 4. Demonstration and recitation are essential components for learning.
1 2 3 4 5 ___ 5. Students should always be permitted to determine their own rules in the educational process.
1 2 3 4 5 ___ 6. Reality is spiritual and rational.
1 2 3 4 5 ___ 7. Curriculum should be based on the laws of natural science.
1 2 3 4 5 ___ 8. The teacher should be a strong authority figure in the classroom.
1 2 3 4 5 ___ 9. The student is a receiver of knowledge.
1 2 3 4 5 ___ 10. Ideal teachers interpret knowledge.
1 2 3 4 5 ___ 11. Lecture-discussion is the most effective teaching technique.
1 2 3 4 5 ___ 12. Institutions should seek avenues toward self-improvement through an orderly process.
1 2 3 4 5 ___ 13. Schools are obligated to teach moral truths.
1 2 3 4 5 ___ 14. School programs should focus on social problems and issues.
1 2 3 4 5 ___ 15. Institutions exist to preserve and strengthen spiritual and social values.
1 2 3 4 5 ___ 16. Subjective opinion reveals truth.
1 2 3 4 5 ___ 17. Teachers are seen as facilitators of learning.
1 2 3 4 5 ___ 18. Schools should be educational "smorgasbords."
1 2 3 4 5 ___ 19. Memorization is the key to process skills.
1 2 3 4 5 ___ 20. Reality consists of objects.
1 2 3 4 5 ___ 21. Schools exist to foster the intellectual process.
1 2 3 4 5 ___ 22. Schools foster an orderly means for change.
1 2 3 4 5 ___ 23. There are essential skills everyone must learn.
1 2 3 4 5 ___ 24. Teaching by subject area is the most effective approach.
1 2 3 4 5 ___ 25. Students should play an active part in program design and evaluation.
1 2 3 4 5 ___ 26. A functioning member of society follows rules of conduct.
1 2 3 4 5 ___ 27. Reality is rational.
1 2 3 4 5 ___ 28. Schools should reflect the society they serve.
1 2 3 4 5 ___ 29. The teacher should set an example for the students.
1 2 3 4 5 ___ 30. The most effective learning does not take place in a highly structured, strictly disciplined environment.
1 2 3 4 5 ___ 31. The curriculum should be based on unchanging spiritual truths.
1 2 3 4 5 ___ 32. The most effective learning is nonstructured.
1 2 3 4 5 ___ 33. Truth is a constant expressed through ideas.
1 2 3 4 5 ___ 34. Drill and factual knowledge are important components of any learning environment.
1 2 3 4 5 ___ 35. Societal consensus determines morality.
1 2 3 4 5 ___ 36. Knowledge is gained primarily through the senses.
1 2 3 4 5 ___ 37. There are essential pieces of knowledge that everyone should know.
1 2 3 4 5 ___ 38. The school exists to facilitate self-awareness.
1 2 3 4 5 ___ 39. Change is an ever-present process.
1 2 3 4 5 ___ 40. Truths are best taught through the inquiry process.

Students are required to complete the assessment and record their scores to the left of each item.

FIGURE 8-14

Philosophy Assessment Scoring **CTE 438-638 Course Construction**

Sets of test questions by five standard philosophies		Total Numerical Value	Score
Perennialist	6, 8, 10, 13, 15, 31, 34, 37		
Idealist	9, 11, 19, 21, 24, 27, 29, 33		
Realist	4, 7, 12, 20, 22, 23, 26, 28		
Experimentalist	2, 3, 14, 17, 25, 35, 39, 40		
Existentialist	1, 5, 16, 18, 30, 32, 36, 38		

Scoring Steps by Sets:

1. Using the sets provided above, record the value of each answer given (strongly disagree = 1, strongly agree = 5) for each of the five sets.
2. Total the numerical value of each set (score for each set will be between 8 and 40). Record under the Total Numerical Value above.
3. Divide the total numerical value for each set by 5 (example: 20 ÷ 5 = 4). Record under Score above.
4. Plot your score in the middle of each philosophy in the grid and connect the points.

8					
7					
6					
5					
4					
3					
2					
1					
	Perennialist	Idealist	Realist	Experimentalist	Existentialist

Students must complete another handout to determine their philosophy preference. Students graph their response to the 40 statements and plot where they are on the scale. (Adapted from Wiles and Bondi, 2014.)

To assist the instructor in evaluating information sheets, a rating scale can be used. See Figure 8-15. While this rating scale covers 18 possible areas, this is only an example. Instructors may choose to use one of their own rating scales or adopt this example to their own setting.

FIGURE 8-15

Evaluation of Instruction Sheets **Course Construction**

Evaluation of Written Instruction Sheets

Evaluator ______________________ Date ______________

Kind of Sheet ______________ Title ______________

Prepared by______________ Prepared for______________

Ratings

4 High 3 Above Average 2 Below Average 1 Missing
(Draw a line through those items not applicable.)

Circle the number to indicate your rating of the handout.

Criterion	Rating			
	M	BA	AA	HI
1. Language is appropriate to students' level	1	2	3	4
2. Format is simple, complete, and easily understood	1	2	3	4
3. Only relevant material is included	1	2	3	4
4. Adequate and appropriate illustrations are included	1	2	3	4
5. Adequate directions are provided	1	2	3	4
6. Is clear, legible, and attractive	1	2	3	4
7. Is coded to course, unit, etc.	1	2	3	4
8. Contains appropriate heading and subheading	1	2	3	4
9. Contains instruction sheet identification and title	1	2	3	4
10. Includes a set of performance objectives	1	2	3	4
11. Contains text and reference listing	1	2	3	4
12. Lists aids and supporting devices	1	2	3	4
13. Lists tools, equipment, materials, etc.	1	2	3	4
14. Includes procedural steps	1	2	3	4
15. Provides for evaluation of students' progress	1	2	3	4
16. Content contained is current	1	2	3	4
17. Seems to have motivating qualities	1	2	3	4
18. Content is valid	1	2	3	4

Total Possible Points ________ Your Score ________ Percent ________

Instructors can evaluate handouts with a rating scale.

Another possible instructor-developed rating scale is one used to evaluate assignments. With this type of rating scale, the students see immediately the instructor's plan for evaluation. Figure 8-16 shows the assignment objective and the criteria used with corresponding numerical rating scales. These scales are often called performance rating scales. Checking each criterion when evaluating the assignment makes grading more consistent, saves the instructor time during evaluation, and communicates to students the criteria used for evaluation.

FIGURE 8-16

Assignment #1 Curriculum Philosophy and Mode

CTE-438/638 Course Construction in Career and Technical Education

Objective: Explain your philosophy of career, technical, and adult education or training as it applies to your area of expertise, the philosophy of your CTE district, and the relationship of this philosophy to the program you teach. Develop your philosophy into a curriculum model.

Criteria for Evaluation

1. Philosophy (Answer the four questions in Philosophy #2-08.pdf (see slide #10). Citations used and references to support philosophy are present. Ideas flow, and rationale noted. Connection made to CTE or training in B & I.)

Rambles — Rationale is Strong & Connection Made to CTE

0 1 2 3 4 5 6 7

2. Relationship of Philosophy to Content Area (Explain how your philosophy relates to the content area that you are or may be teaching.)

Weak Relationship Made — Strong Relationship

0 1 2 3 4

3. Curriculum Model (Indicate how and why this particular model is effective. The setting or where the model will be used is explained. Relationship to the institution philosophy, mission, and curriculum is established.)

No or Little Rationale — Strong Rationale

0 1 2 3 4 5

4. Visual Representation (A drawing showing the relationship of all the different parts of model is represented.)

Visual is Confusing — Easy to Follow

0 1 2 3 4

5. Narrative on Model (Each different part of the model and its relationship to the other parts is explained.)

Missing or Minimal Information — Complete Description of Each Item

0 1 2 3 4

6. Philosophy Preference Assessment (Take the assessment, plot out your philosophy, and turn in with assignment and reflect on it. Is it consistent with your own philosophy? How is it different? What are some implications?)

Did not Complete — Completed and Reflected

0 1 2 3 4

Total Points Possible 28 — Your Score ________

Instructors can use rating scales to evaluate assignment sheets.

Learning Activity Packets. A learning activity packet (LAP) is another example of an instructor-developed resource. It can, however, be developed by an instructor, an instructional developer working with an SME, and/or an advisory committee. A complete LAP can be found in Appendix L, which uses "Select Sample Technique and Size," as the desired task or competency. The following are representative steps for developing an LAP:

1. Write a short purpose for learning the competency. Consider where it might apply and be used. See Figure 8-17.

FIGURE 8-17

Learning Activity Packet

Select Sample Technique and Size

PURPOSE: When using the survey method for collecting information for a needs assessment or task analysis, sampling techniques are usually employed. The use of appropriate techniques requires knowledge about the target population, sample, different sampling techniques, sample size, and dealing with non-respondents.

PERFORMANCE OBJECTIVE: Given information involving a needs assessment, select appropriate sample technique and size and a procedure to deal with non-respondents. To master this module, a score of 8 out of 10 (80%) must be achieved on Activity 3.2.

ENABLING OBJECTIVES:

1. Identify characteristics of a population and sample.
2. Differentiate between simple random sample, systematic sample, stratified sample, and cluster sample.
3. Select sample size and explain a strategy for dealing with non-respondents.

A learning activity packet (LAP) is an instructor-developed resource that helps students move toward a terminal performance objective.

2. Write a terminal performance objective (TPO) based on the competency. This is a brief statement that describes exactly what the student should be able to do in a training program to demonstrate mastery of a competency after completing all the learning steps. If an instructor knows what students have to do to master a competency, it becomes easier to develop appropriate learning resources to help them get there. As can be seen in Figure 8-17, writing a TPO is the same as writing a complete performance objective. (See Chapter 7.)
3. Identify the enabling objectives. Break down the TPO into manageable learning steps termed enabling objectives (EOs). By completing the EOs, the student will accomplish the TPO. As seen in Figure 8-17, each EO begins with an action verb, is in the present tense, and is observable. There are no conditions or standards in the EO. In this example, the competency has been divided into three EOs. After all of this has been developed, the purpose, TPOs, and EOs can be consolidated and written on the cover of the LAP.
4. Develop a content outline and note any references used.
5. Break each EO into learning steps (LSs) by considering what it will take to complete the EO. There are usually 3–5 specific learning steps. See Figure 8-18.

FIGURE **8-18**

ENABLING OBJECTIVE #1:

Identify characteristics of a population and sample.

Learning Step	Resources
1. Read Resource #1.1 to identify the characteristics of a population and sample.	1. Information Sheet #1.1 "Population and Sample" in this packet.
2. Complete Resource #1.2 to help you identify characteritics of a population and sample.	2. Activity Sheet: #1.2 "Population and Sample" in this packet.
3. Check your responses with Resource #1.3 to see if you can identify characteristics of a population and sample.	3. Activity Sheet: #1.3 "Answer Sheet: Population and Sample" in this packet.

Enabling objectives throughout the LAP are broken down into learning steps. Each enabling objective supports the terminal objective.

6. Develop a resource for each LS. The resource can be an information sheet or an existing resource that students can access, such as a textbook, manual, or CD ROM, or they can observe an advanced student doing a task. Media resources can also be produced using support personnel. See Figure 8-19.

FIGURE 8-19

Information Sheet #1.1: Population and Sample

Introduction:

Sampling is usually used when utilizing a survey technique, such as interviewing, focus groups, questionnaires, or formal research, to gather information for a needs assessment or task analysis. All of these involve, in one way or another, the selection of a given number of people from a defined population as representative of that population.

Sampling involves the selection of a representative subset of people, agencies, industries, businesses, events, or objects for which we wish to generalize results. You may be a trainer determining if the machinists on the production line need statistical process control training. One of the ways of determining this is to ask all of the machinists. If you are working in a large company and have over 100 machinists, would you interview or survey everyone? Interviewing may prove to be very time-consuming. The alternative is to identify a representative sample and use the time and resources available to obtain the information about the total group from a sample of workers. Research has shown that statistics from a representative sample are often more accurate than those from the total population. This is based on the notion that it is usually possible to do a better job of contacting each individual in the sample and thus of obtaining the information requested.

Sampling is used because it will save you time and the expense of studying the entire population. If sampling is correctly done, you can make conclusions about the total population that are likely to

Information sheets in an LAP support the learning steps in an enabling objective.

7. Provide an opportunity to practice or apply the knowledge or skill that was presented in the LS by developing activity sheets, if desired. See Figure 8-20.

FIGURE
8-20

Activity Sheet #1.2: Population and Sample

Check your progress on learning about the characteristics of population and sample by answering the following questions.

1. Explain each in your own words:

   A. Population:

   B. Sample:

2. What are the symbols for population and sample?

   Population: Sample:

Activity sheets in an LAP also support the learning steps in an enabling objective.

8. Provide immediate feedback on the success of any practice activity, along with any correction if needed. Having students check their own answers with an answer key, checking the finished product or procedure with a checklist, or having the instructor evaluate a product or critique a performance would be examples of feedback.

LSs list either presentations, practice, or feedback. LSs do not teach; they simply inform the student on what to do next. Lastly, practice called for in an LS requires students to attempt the exact performance called for in the EO.

The instructional developer or instructor requires extensive training in developing competency-based instruction of this type. In theory, students can move through an LAP at their own pace, and learning and mastery can be significant if the LAP is well-developed and resources are available for support. The LAP can also be placed within a learning management system (LMS) and used for distance education.

Review Questions

1. What are the essential parts of a lesson plan?
2. Explain why a lesson plan is essential for good teaching.
3. What is the relationship of a performance objective to lesson planning?
4. How can a lesson plan help a student that has been ill?
5. Explain why putting a time element in a lesson plan may be important.
6. What should an information sheet handout be based on?
7. Explain the difference between student and instructor activities.
8. Under what conditions could a commercial handout be used with students?
9. What are the advantages and disadvantages of using an LAP?

References

Brunn, P. (2010). *The lesson planning handbook: Essential strategies that inspire thinking and learning*. New York: Scholastic.

Hunter, M. (1976). *Rx for improved instruction*. El Segundo, CA: TIP Publications.

Romiszowski, A. J. (1992). *The selection and use of instructional media* (2nd ed.). London, UK: Kogan Page.

Simonson, M., Smaldino. S., Albright, M., & Zvacek, S. (Eds.). (2012). *Teaching and learning at a distance: Foundations of distance education* (5th ed.). Boston, MA: Pearson Education, Inc.

Steward, M. D., Martin, G. S., Burns, A. C., & Bush, R. F. (2010). Using the Madeline Hunter direct instruction model to improve outcomes assessments in marketing programs. *Journal of Marketing Education. 32,* 128–139.

Van Wart, M., Cayer, N. J., & Cook, S. (1993). *Handbook of training and development for the public sector*. San Francisco: Jossey-Bass.

Wiles, J. W., & Bondi, J. C. (2014). *Curriculum development: A guide to practice* (9th ed.). Upper Saddle River, NJ: Pearson.

Program Evaluation 9

Review Needs • Assess Program Mission and Objectives • Identify Critical Inputs • Identify Critical Processes • Identify Output Measures • Identify Context Factors • Identify Data Collection Points • Develop Instruments and Data Collection Techniques • Review Evaluation Plan • Conduct the Evaluation • Provide Feedback • Evaluate the System

REVIEW QUESTIONS

REFERENCES

INTRODUCTION

Program evaluation is an important element in program development and improvement. It provides data on outcomes and the processes used to develop and implement the course or program. When evaluation is initiated in the first phase of program development, it can provide valuable data for a variety of decisions as development activities progress.

This chapter presents a brief history of the evolution of program evaluation from measurement used to determine grades to a comprehensive systems approach. This review provides a context for the functional program evaluation described. A detailed set of steps for planning and conducting a program evaluation accompany the model. The model and processes presented in this chapter will focus on program evaluation.

OBJECTIVES

After completing this chapter, the reader should be able to do the following:

1. List three roles of program evaluation.
2. Define and describe benchmarking.
3. Identify and describe the four levels of evaluation in Kirkpatrick's evaluation model.
4. Identify the components of the CIPP evaluation model.
5. Sketch the evaluation model presented in this chapter and define each component.

6. Define stakeholders and give three examples.
7. Identify three research designs used in program evaluation that will identify how much a student learned.
8. Describe what is meant when it is said that a program evaluation must be manageable.
9. Describe three ways to gain more utilization of program evaluation results.

Roles of Program Evaluation

Program evaluation plays several important roles in creating and maintaining quality programs. Evaluation data identify the competency levels of program graduates and the degree to which the graduates meet business, industry, and societal needs. Evaluation data can also be used for benchmarking, or for identifying how effectively and efficiently the program is operating. In addition, evaluation data will help to isolate program development processes and components that need to be improved.

Program Outcomes

When evaluation is mentioned, the first thought is often about assessing students' knowledge and skills. This is certainly an important part of program evaluation. However, evaluating program outcomes also includes an assessment of the degree to which students' competencies match course and program objectives. In addition, students' competencies and program objectives must be compared with organizational and community needs. For example, a program may be graduating students who have the competencies specified in course and program objectives, but lack some of the skills needed in the job market. Thus, it is important that the evaluation of program outcomes be multidimensional.

Benchmarking

Benchmarking is a process of comparing a course or program with the best in the region, country, or world to identify educational processes that can be improved. Comparisons are usually made with similar courses and programs.

Some organizations find that it is helpful to compare themselves with different types of companies or organizations that have related processes. For example, a training program that wants to shorten its course planning and development time might study newspaper and TV news programs to determine how they identify and prepare news stories in a brief period of time.

Benchmarking usually starts with selecting processes to study. These will be processes that are important to the performance of the program. They may be processes that have proven to be problem areas, such as identifying relevant content, responding to educational needs in a timely manner, or retaining students. The next step is measuring and documenting these processes. As this is being done, organizations that are leaders in these areas are identified. Information is collected from these organizations to determine what processes they use, how effectively their processes perform, and why they perform this way.

This information is used to identify gaps in performance and priorities for process improvement. The information collected on process design can then be used for program improvement. Other sources of benchmark data are the Baldrige criteria and benchmarking forums. Baldrige has criteria for business, education, and health care. (National Institute of Standards and Technology [NIST], n.d.).

Program evaluations are designed to collect data on important program components and outcomes and make judgments about them. Comparing a program evaluation design with benchmarked programs, best practices, and other evaluations will help to refine the evaluation model and identify the types of data to collect. In turn, the program evaluation will establish a baseline for the current program. This baseline can then be compared to the benchmarks to identify gaps and strengths. The gaps will identify areas for program improvement.

Program Improvement

One of the reasons for conducting a program evaluation is to provide data to plan program improvement. Since program improvement needs to be an ongoing process, program evaluation also needs to be continuous. Evaluation needs to be integrated with program development and improvement processes. Evaluation activities must be carried out on a schedule that provides relevant data when program decisions have to be made.

Program design, development, and improvement processes should be documented. This will facilitate evaluating their effectiveness and identifying areas that need to be improved. Also, this documentation will be useful in any benchmarking studies done.

Approaches to Program Evaluation

Program evaluation is a relatively new concept in education. With the advent of large-scale curriculum projects in the 1960s, program evaluation became more important and developed rapidly. New models were designed, applied, and refined. Information and research on educational program evaluation expanded significantly. College courses and programs were initiated to prepare program evaluators. More and more educational programs were evaluated.

Although program evaluation expanded rapidly in the 1960s and 1970s, educators had been collecting information on students and courses for many decades. Guba and Lincoln identified several antecedents to program evaluation as practiced today. They grouped these into three phases—measurement, description, and judgment. It is worthwhile to briefly review these phases since elements of them are used in modern program evaluation systems, and they give perspective to current systems (Mathison, 2005).

Measurement dates back to the 1800s with student testing used to determine grades. In the late 19th century and the early part of the 20th century, intelligence and aptitude testing was added. Standardized achievement tests came next. For the most part, measurement was done to provide data for grading, graduation, and admissions decisions pertaining to individuals.

The need for curriculum improvement in the 1930s established a need for educational program evaluation. In the measurement phase, course and program content was not questioned. The "basics" formed the content base for the curriculum. An exception to this would be vocational and technical programs that maintained links to competency requirements in business and industry.

However, with pressure to expand the high school curriculum to make it attractive to a wider range of students came the need to question the validity of course and curriculum content. Objectives became an accepted way to identify what students should know. Evaluation in this phase described what students knew in relation to course and curriculum objectives and described the nature of their educational experiences. Measurement became a tool in the description phase.

The large-scale national curriculum projects stimulated by Russia's launching of Sputnik in 1957 created stresses for descriptive evaluation systems. These systems did not have protocols for determining the validity and relevance of course and program objectives. Thus, there was no appropriate process for making judgments about the relevance of objectives, content, and outcomes. In addition, descriptive evaluations provided data at the end of courses and programs.

Now, however, curriculum developers were asking for evaluation data during the design and implementation of new courses. Thus, process or formative data became an important part of program evaluation. Moreover, judgments required standards and someone to do the judging. Professionals in academic disciplines identified academic standards, and employers specified vocational and technical program standards. Evaluators were frequently placed in the role of judge.

In the judgment phase, program evaluation was expanded to look at the role of a program in a larger context, whether the role was to produce future scientists, competent technicians, or citizens who were scientifically literate. Program and course objectives were evaluated and judged against the needs of our society, government, and labor market.

Kirkpatrick's Four Levels

The most popular evaluation model in the training field is the four-level model developed by Donald Kirkpatrick. The four levels are reaction, learning, behavior, and results (Kirkpatrick & Kirkpatrick, 2006). The focus of these levels is on the products or outputs of training, and they provide ideas for the product evaluation. However, the four levels do not provide as much information for process evaluation. Kirkpatrick noted that all of the levels are important, and data collected at one level have an impact on the next level.

Level I—Reaction. Students' or participants' reactions to a course or program are collected at the first level, reaction. This provides a measurement of customer satisfaction that Kirkpatrick thought was important. Courses or training workshops that generate negative feelings do not continue to receive support from supervisors and managers. See Figure 9-1. The Statistics and Process Control Program Evaluation form was designed to collect the training program participants' perceptions of the value of the course content, quality of instruction, and appropriateness of classroom activities. This form collects process evaluation data in the areas of learning activities, instructional pace, and suggestions for improvement. The authors have used this in many different settings and have found that participant feedback is very helpful and important. Supervisors in the contracting companies also found the information valuable.

Level II—Learning. Kirkpatrick defines Level II, learning, as the "extent to which participants change attitudes, improve knowledge, and/or increase skill as a result of attending the program" (Kirkpatrick & Kirkpatrick, 2006, p. 22). The nature of the evaluation in each of these three areas will depend upon the objectives of the training program. In some programs, skill increase may be the primary objective. Although attitudes may not appear to be an objective in many training courses, attitudes are involved when trainers want the participants to adopt and use new knowledge and processes. The Statistics and Process Control Evaluation form included items that assessed the participants' intent to use the statistics and quality assurance techniques covered in the training program. Workshop activities and instruction were designed to build the participants' confidence in using statistics and process control techniques and to illustrate the usefulness of statistics and process control techniques in practical applications.

FIGURE 9-1

Statistics and Process Control
Program Evaluation

Directions: Respond to each of the following statements based on your experiences in this training program.

1 = SD = Strongly Disagree
2 = D = Disagree
3 = U = Undecided
4 = A = Agree
5 = SA = Strongly Agree

Characteristics of the Training Program	Responses SD 1	D 2	U 3	A 4	SA 5
1. This program was worthwhile	1	2	3	4	5
2. I enjoyed using MINITAB®	1	2	3	4	5
3. MINITAB® can be helpful in my work	1	2	3	4	5
4. I gained a better understanding of statistics	1	2	3	4	5
5. I will be able to use the contents of this training program	1	2	3	4	5
6. I liked the opportunity to work with my own data	1	2	3	4	5
7. There should be more opportunity to apply the contents to practical problems related to my work	1	2	3	4	5
8. I knew most of the content of this training program before we started the sessions	1	2	3	4	5
9. I learned a lot	1	2	3	4	5
10. The instructors' explanations were clear	1	2	3	4	5
11. The instructors effectively answered questions	1	2	3	4	5
12. The instructors were able to relate the content of this training program to practical problems	1	2	3	4	5
13. The instructors were well prepared	1	2	3	4	5
14. I plan to use some of the techniques presented	1	2	3	4	5
15. Too many topics were included in the program	1	2	3	4	5
16. Too few topics were included in the program	1	2	3	4	5
17. The visuals were helpful	1	2	3	4	5
18. The handouts were helpful	1	2	3	4	5

19. How could training be improved? ______________________

20. What did you like best about the training program? ______________________

Participants' reactions to a course or program can provide helpful feedback for program evaluation.

Usually it is necessary to use a preassessment in order to measure individual change. The Statistics and Process Control training program used a pretest and a posttest. The same test was used for both. Participants were not alerted to this fact when they completed the pretest or during the workshop in order to reduce the amount of interaction between the pretest content and the students' learning strategies. The test was designed to provide data for each of the course objectives. Pretest results were reviewed to fine-tune instruction in order to start at an appropriate level and move at an effective pace. The difference between each participant's post- and pretest scores was the score change and reflected the amount learned. In a course or program that included skill development, a performance test would be included. This would require the participants to demonstrate their skills.

Level III—Behavior. Level III, behavior, is concerned with the extent to which students use and apply what they have learned in their work. Level II provides information on what the students have learned. Level III generates information on the extent to which this learning is applied and the impacts on the participants' job performance.

Kirkpatrick cautioned that the "right climate" was needed for participants to use their new knowledge, skills, and attitudes in their work (Kirkpatrick & Kirkpatrick, 2006, p. 23). He concluded that the immediate supervisor was the most important element in creating this climate. It is important that students be encouraged and facilitated in applying their new competencies. Any evaluation at this level will need to assess the nature of this climate and its potential impacts on participants in the training program.

Level IV—Results. At Level IV, results, the focus is on the impacts on the organization. These might include impacts on productivity, costs, quality, safety, or sales, depending on the nature of the training course. In fact, there may be other organizational impacts that are important, depending on the objectives of the training. Measuring results usually takes a longer time frame. There has to be enough time for the participants to apply what they learned and for these changes in behavior to have an impact on the organization.

An organization's program and production data may provide a ready-made baseline for measuring results. Also, an organization's human resource data can provide a baseline for measuring impacts on safety, absences, and turnover. However, these databases need to be reviewed to determine if they are accurate and up-to-date. Also, it must be determined whether the data will be affected by the outcomes of an educational or training program. For example, if the data on absences does not differentiate by reason for the absence, it will hard to determine the impact of an improved safety program on absences. If these databases do not meet these criteria, new or additional measures will have to be developed.

Phillips, Wayne, and Phillips (2012) have suggested that a fifth level, return on investment (ROI), be added to Kirkpatrick's model. Return on investment is the ratio of the dollar value of the results to the organization to the cost of the training. ROI is widely used in companies and would provide a comparison with other functional areas. However, many practitioners are reluctant to use ROI because it is relatively easy to quantify training costs, but it is much more difficult to place a dollar value on many of the results and on behavior changes.

CIPP Evaluation Model

The CIPP evaluation model is a third-generation evaluation system. *C* represents the context, or environment, within which a course, program, or organization operates and provides a means to judge the relevance and validity of goals and objectives. *I* represents the inputs to the system. In training and educational programs, students are the inputs. Their knowledge and skill levels will be changed by the educational activities and processes (*P*) provided in the system. The second *P* stands for products or outputs. In educational and training systems, students with new skill and knowledge levels are the outputs.

Modified CIPP Model

The authors have successfully used the CIPP model to design and conduct several large-scale evaluation projects. These included three statewide evaluation projects. As the CIPP model was used in different situations, it became apparent that it could be improved. These improvements included the following:

- using stakeholder input
- adding program criteria to use in making judgments
- collecting qualitative and quantitative data
- using benchmark data and time-series data for comparisons
- adding an implementation workshop to help educators use the evaluation results

Stakeholder input was solicited to reduce bias in selecting evaluation questions and criteria and to expand the viewpoints used to design the evaluation systems. Care was taken to obtain input from all stakeholder groups.

Stakeholders and experts were requested to identify program characteristics and products that were related to quality courses and programs. This information was used to establish criteria that could be used when making judgments. Benchmark and time-series data were also used in establishing criteria. Using a time-series design in program evaluation provides an opportunity to assess the impacts of course and program changes with less cost and disruption.

Creating a true experimental design in educational settings is usually difficult and can create a variety of problems. A time-series design in which data are collected before a change is made and again after the change is fully operational is less disruptive and can usually be done with a moderate amount of preplanning. Benchmarks provide data on quality programs and are useful in establishing evaluation criteria and planning program improvements.

Qualitative data collection was added to gain flexibility and provide a wider variety of data. This provided an opportunity for stakeholders to give feedback on all of their perceptions, ideas, and concerns about the program being evaluated. It provided the evaluators flexibility to pursue new ideas and venues that had not been identified at the beginning of the evaluation. Adding qualitative data also allowed the evaluators to focus the quantitative data collection in areas where it was more appropriate, required, or useful in comparisons with other programs.

Program evaluations often satisfy funding, accountability, and accreditation requirements. However, many times the evaluation report is filed and has little or no impact on improving the program. As a result of these experiences, the authors added an implementation workshop and modified the program evaluation report to contain more specific recommendations pertaining to program revisions. The implementation workshop included sessions on interpreting and using evaluation data in program improvement, change strategies, and planning techniques. Participants used their program evaluation data to outline a program improvement plan in the last session of the workshop. An evaluation model evolved out of these experiences. See Figure 9-2.

A systems approach provides a structured technique for analyzing a course or program and determining the essential elements to include in the evaluation. The basic concept behind using a systems approach in designing and conducting a program evaluation is to understand the needs and objectives that drive the program and identify the critical inputs, processes, products, and contextual factors related to it. Involving stakeholders in the design of the evaluation and evaluation processes helps to ensure that all of the important facets are reviewed and evaluated. The model shown in Figure 9-2 draws upon the CIPP evaluation system (Stufflebeam, Madaus, & Kellaghan, 2000). This system was expanded to include purpose, stakeholders, and program improvement.

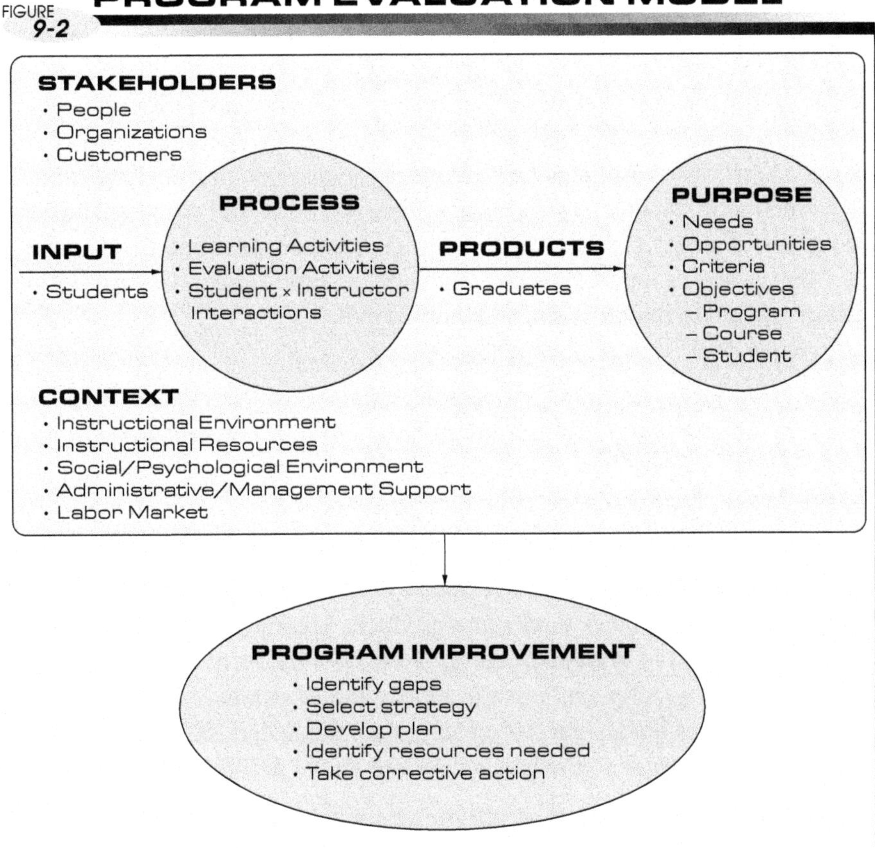

This program evaluation model evolved out of a workshop on implementing the evaluation report.

Stakeholders. In this evaluation system, stakeholders give input on the evaluation questions that need to be answered and provide data that is used in the evaluation. They may provide data that partially answers their own questions, but will also provide responses to questions asked by other stakeholders. Stakeholders are people, groups, and organizations that can impact and/or are impacted by a program. Stakeholders include students, instructors, employers, and community. School programs also have board members, parents, and administrators as stakeholders. Training programs have supervisors, managers, and customers included in their stakeholder groups.

Context. Systems operate within a context, or environment. For education and training programs, this context includes the instructional environment and resources, management support, status of the labor market, organizational culture, and societal expectations. The quality of classrooms, labs, and support areas are a part of the instructional environment. Also, instructors' skills and their expectations of students help to create the instructional environment.

Instructional resources include hardware, software, and course materials. Management support is often a factor in creating or obtaining these materials. Management support can also influence the time assigned to instruction, visibility given to the program, and staff morale.

Input. Inputs are raw material that will be processed into outputs or products. In an educational system, students are the inputs. Each one enters with a specific level of knowledge, skills, and attitudes. A group of students will have varied levels of these. These levels need to be assessed and documented if changes due to instruction are to be measured and used in the evaluation. The exact types of skills, knowledge, and attitudes to measure will depend upon the objectives of the system.

Process. Processes change inputs into products. Learning activities, class discussions, interactions with instructors, and assessment activities are included in this area. Mentorships, internships, and apprenticeships are also included. Processes need to be designed to change the knowledge, skills, and attitude levels on the input side to the levels required on the product side.

Product. Products are course or program completers. They are students who have completed the course or program and have specific levels of knowledge, skills, and attitudes. The extent to which these levels are better than the input levels will be one indicator of the impact of the educational experience. In order for a program to be successful, the product competency levels must match those specified in the objectives listed in the program purpose. Also, the purpose may identify the number of graduates required to fulfill a need. For example, a community may need 20 registered nurses each year. If a number is given, the program is evaluated on this criterion also.

In many instances, stakeholders are concerned about the proportion of entering students that complete the course or program. High dropout levels may signal problems in program design and instruction. Also, many career preparation programs follow up with dropouts to determine program impacts and reasons for leaving the program.

Product evaluation data is usually collected at the end of a course or program. However, consideration should also be given to short- and long-term follow-up assessments. Some competencies, such as the ability to apply knowledge and skills in a job setting, are difficult to evaluate without following up with graduates and their employers.

Purpose. Purpose is a very important part of the evaluation system. It identifies the criteria that will be used to evaluate the end products and the processes used to create them. This component includes the needs statement, program mission and objectives, course objectives, and criteria to be used in making evaluation decisions. During an evaluation, evaluators will look at the processes used to identify needs and distill objectives, as well as the final need, mission, and objective statements.

Program Improvement. Program improvement is one of the major goals of program evaluation. It has been the authors' experience that the link between program evaluation and program improvement must be established during the time the program evaluation is being planned. The staff members responsible for program improvement are stakeholders in the program evaluation. Their input is needed to determine what process and products to evaluate.

After evaluation data have been collected, evaluators need to run the analyses needed by the program improvement staff and report the results in a functional format. In addition, evaluators should help them use the results to identify areas that need improvement and develop improvement plans.

Program evaluation should be an ongoing activity. Needs change as society, business, and organizations change. Instructional strategies and technology change and different groups of students have unique capabilities. The individuals responsible for program evaluation need to communicate with program managers to determine when they need process and product evaluation results to make program decisions.

RESEARCH DESIGNS

One important reason to conduct a program evaluation is to determine the program's impacts on students. In order to do this, an appropriate research design must be selected. This design will be used to establish valid comparisons to determine program impacts. This needs to be done at the beginning of the program development or improvement process because it may be essential to have baseline data to contrast with final outcomes.

The following designs are a sample of those that can be used to determine impacts. The following symbols are used to illustrate the evaluation designs.

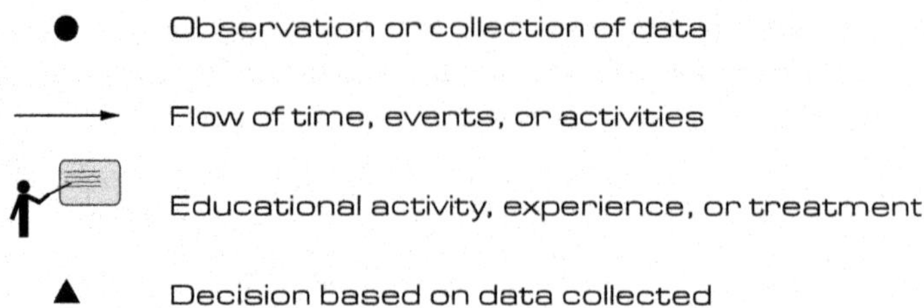

One Group, Posttest Only Design

In this design, the educational activity or experience is offered first, and then data are collected. Decisions are made based on the data. See Figure 9-3.

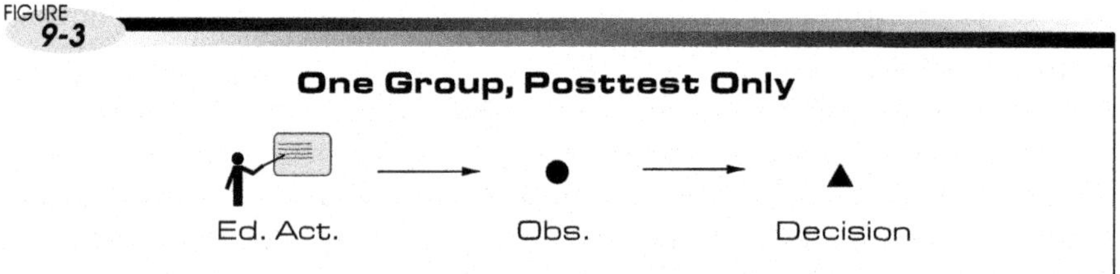

FIGURE 9-3

This design should only be used when it is not feasible to use any other design.

Strengths. This design involves only the group to which the educational experience was presented. The posttest-only design involves a minimum of time on the part of students. If the instrument(s) used are valid, one can determine if the goals of the program have been accomplished. If the objectives of the educational activity are not attained, information will be available on the objectives not met.

Weaknesses. There is no assurance with this design that there was a change in the participants as a result of exposure to the educational activity. No data are available to indicate their entering level of competency. Even if there was some evidence of the changes that occurred, it is not absolutely clear that these changes would not have occurred through the process of maturation or exposure to other activities and information typically in the students' environment. Some of this weakness may be overcome by asking the participants to indicate the changes they perceived as a result of the experience. This would not work for assigning grades, but it can provide insights into impacts and deficiencies.

Types of Decisions. All decisions made with this evaluation design must be carefully tempered to account for the weaknesses noted. Some weak decisions related to the achievement of the objectives of the educational experience may be made. However, they should be carefully labeled as being tentative.

When to Use. This design should only be used in those situations in which none of the other designs are feasible. For example, if an educational experience has been offered and no pretest data is available, this would be the only viable alternative. It would be better to collect post data than none at all. The post data may also include some reactions to the educational experience. This information could be very helpful in redesigning the experience. Also, if the post data indicate that the objectives of the educational program have not been achieved, the evaluator would know that the educational experience has to be redesigned.

One Group, Pre- and Posttest Design

In this design, the evaluator collects data before and after the educational program is conducted. See Figure 9-4.

FIGURE 9-4

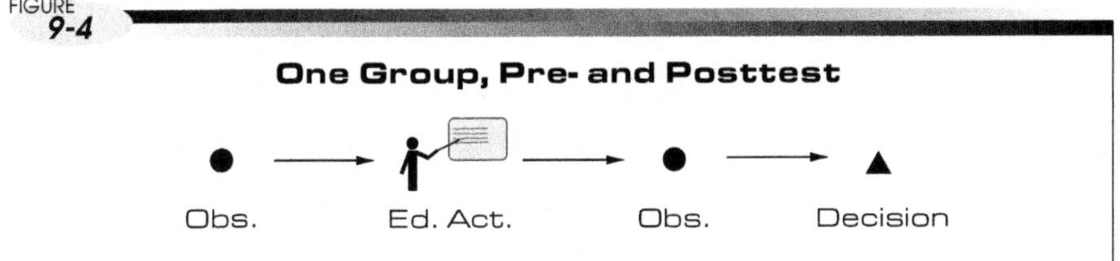

This design can be used when time is available to develop a preassessment and a more sophisticated design cannot be used.

Strengths. The one group design with pre- and posttest data has the same strengths indicated for the prior design, plus the availability of pretest data. The pretest data provide a basis for identifying changes that took place during the educational activity or experience.

Weaknesses. Although changes during the educational experience can be identified with this design, the evaluator cannot be absolutely sure that all changes were the result of the educational program. The growth observed during the activity may be the result of maturation or other experiences in which the participants were involved. This weakness is not as significant a problem for training programs or courses that are intensive and short-term. In these cases the opportunity for other experiences and maturation to have an impact is reduced. Also, if the course content is very technical, there is less chance that it could be learned from other courses or general experiences. If this design is used, information should be collected on the out-of-class experiences students are having.

Types of Decisions. With the use of this design, stronger decisions can be made related to the changes that took place during the educational experience. However, the fact that no control group is available makes it necessary to indicate that these decisions are somewhat tentative. If the objectives of the educational activity are not attained, this design will identify the areas in which student performance does not achieve criterion levels. This, of course, assumes that the tests or instruments used for the observation are valid and designed to measure the objectives for the educational activity. Obviously, this assumption pertains to all of the designs.

When to Use. This design should be used when it is not possible to apply a more sophisticated design and when time is available to develop a preassessment. The pretest and posttest may be the same instrument. The pretest should at least be a subpart or a parallel form of the instrument used at the end of the experience. Use of the same instrument as a pre- and postmeasure may lead to the participants doing better on the postmeasure than ordinarily would be observed because of their experience with it as a pretest. However, unless a parallel form of the instrument is available, there is no other alternative than to use it both times. It should also be noted that the pretest data could be used to assess needs.

Control Group/Experimental Group Design (Parallel Groups)

In this design, an experimental group receives the educational experience while the control group does not. Individuals are assigned to the two groups by a random process. Also, more than one experimental or control group can be used. See Figure 9-5.

Strengths. This design has the strengths noted for the previous design and, in addition, provides a control or contrast group against which the impacts observed in the experimental group can be compared. Use of this design will allow the evaluator to account for changes that might take place through maturation and exposure to other events and activities in the educational environment that are not a part of the specific educational activity provided for the experimental group. As a result, any differences that are found in the experimental group can be assigned to the educational activity.

FIGURE 9-5

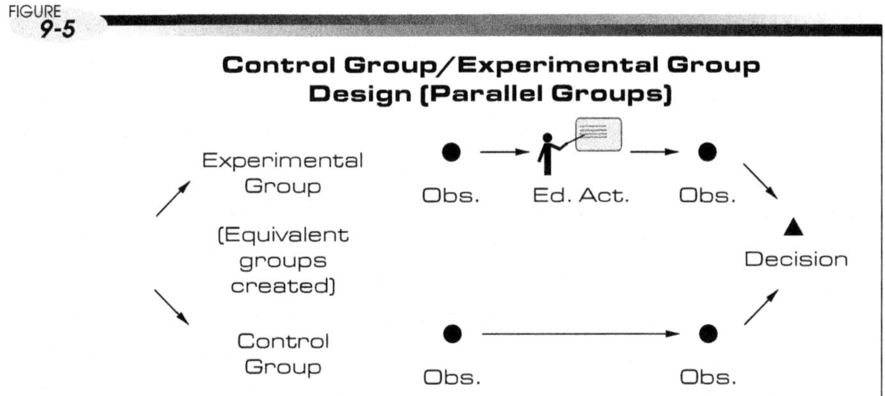

This design should be used when intact groups that can serve as experimental and control groups can be identified.

This design is strongest when students can be randomly assigned to the two groups. However, this is often not possible in the typical school or training setting. Usually, it will be necessary to work with intact groups and the evaluator will need to determine the starting competency level. Any differences in initial capabilities can be statistically treated if they are significant. When the groups are assigned randomly, it would not be absolutely necessary to conduct a pretest.

Weaknesses. Theoretically, this is the strongest evaluation design. Practically, however, it has several problems. First, it is usually difficult to randomly assign students to classroom groups. Therefore, intact classes or groups have to be used and the design becomes quasi-experimental. Frequently, these groups are not equivalent in interests, capabilities, and achievement. As a result, the data collected have to be statistically adjusted in order to make valid comparisons. This increases the level of statistical sophistication required in order to utilize this design and interpret the results.

Another problem that is associated with this design is the assumption that the experimental group will be the only group receiving the educational experience or treatment. Usually, it is not possible to control the treatment to the degree required to meet this assumption. Individuals in the control group will obtain information from individuals in the experimental group. Similarly, staff involved with the control group will pick up ideas of what is going on in the experimental group. And in some instances it is not possible to omit one group of persons from an effective or attractive educational experience.

Types of Decisions. With the control/experimental group design, it is possible to make decisions with a fair level of certainty concerning the impacts of the educational activity or experience. Much of the tentativeness in decision making that was noted for the first two designs will not have to be used when this design is involved in the evaluation. However, it is still necessary to be sure that the educational activity was carried out as designed and that the control group was not exposed to some or much of this treatment as well.

When to Use. If it is possible to identify intact groups that can serve as experimental and control groups for educational treatment, this design should be used. Also, if it is possible to randomly assign students to classroom groups, this design should be used. However, if it would be disruptive or very difficult to identify two parallel groups, then this design should not be used.

Rotational Design

In the rotational design, one group receives the educational program or experience first, and the second group first serves as a comparison group and then becomes the experimental group. In this design, both groups are evaluated three times—before the group 1 receives the treatment, after group 1 completes the treatment, and after group 2 completes the treatment.

This design is most functional when the treatment is not longer than one semester. The authors have successfully used this design to evaluate a series of quality training workshops. The workshops were two weeks long and offered at different plant sites. A pretest was used in all workshops to determine entry-level knowledge. This test was used again at the end of the workshop. No doubt taking the same test twice had some positive impact on posttest scores. However, each group benefited from the same testing process. See Figure 9-6.

Strengths. The rotational design has the strengths identified for the control/experimental group design described in the previous section. In addition, it provides an indication of the repeatability of the educational outcomes associated with the activity. Moreover, it provides the same educational treatment to both groups involved in the study. Often, this can be a concern for educators since, if the educational activity is worthwhile, there is little reason not to provide it for all persons rather than to only a selected experimental group.

Weaknesses. With the exception of providing the treatment to all persons involved, this design has the same weaknesses as the control/experimental group design. In addition, it requires that the educational activity or treatment be provided a second time in order to expose the original control group

(group 2). This means that additional time and resources will be required in order to carry out the design. Also, the time required to complete the evaluation will be almost double. In order to be effective, this design must include a pretest before the educational activity is initiated with group 1.

FIGURE 9-6

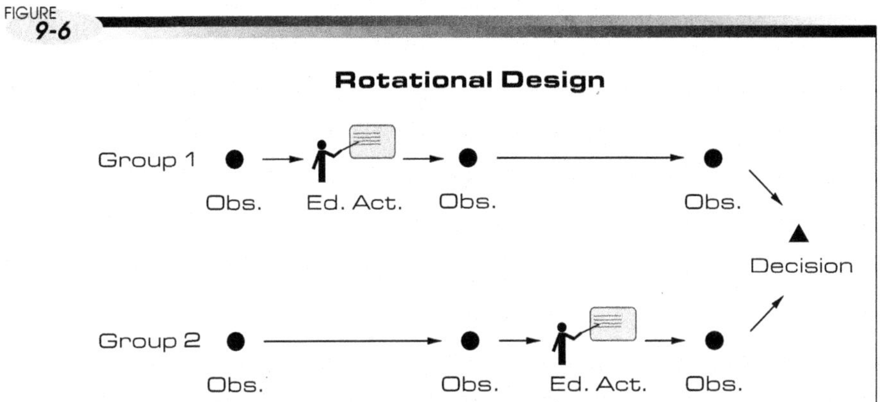

This design can be used when intact classroom groups must be involved in the evaluation and when sufficient time is available to educate or provide activities for both groups.

Types of Decisions. The same decisions as identified for the control/experimental group design can be made. In addition, decisions related to the repeatability of the outcomes can be made. When analyzing the last set of observations, the evaluator must keep in mind that the performance of group 1 may decrease between the second and third observations. This will be more likely to happen if the treatment results in relatively large changes, since forgetting will have a larger impact in this situation.

When to Use. This design should be used when intact classroom groups must be involved in the evaluation. Also, sufficient time must be available to provide the educational experience or activity for both groups. This design can also be used for training workshops that are offered at different times.

Time-Series Design

Many times it is not possible to obtain experimental and control groups that are parallel to each other or to use a rotational design. The time-series design provides a method for evaluating the impacts of an educational experience or activity under these conditions. This design involves several pre-observations to establish a baseline of data. These pre-observations might be standardized test scores, certification exam results, or job performance data at the end of several school years or training periods. This baseline will give the performance level and trends of the capability being measured. Introduction of the instructional activity during the next time period followed by another observation with the same test or measure would allow one to assess the impacts of this activity.

This design can also be used within a school year by collecting data through several observations during the year prior to the introduction of the educational experience. The students would be tested again after the educational experience to determine changes in their levels of performance. See Figure 9-7.

FIGURE 9-7

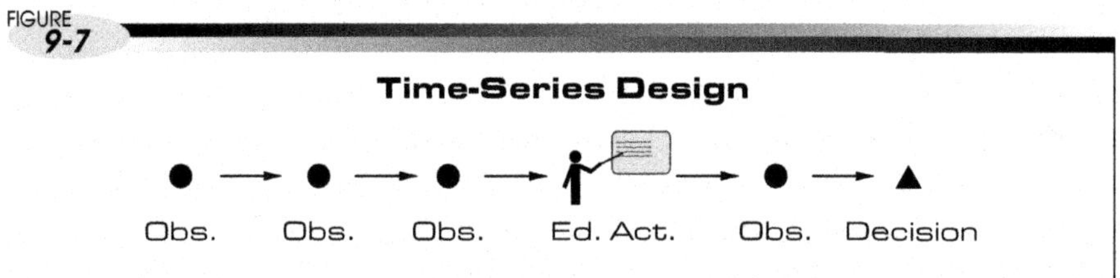

This design can be used if adequate baseline data are available. The implementation of this design requires more time than any of the others.

Strengths. This design is efficient when existing standardized test data, such as math skills and performance testing, professional certification test results, or quality data can be used to establish baselines and to measure the impacts of the educational or training program. This design is least disruptive to the educational setting. The pre-observations provide a valid contrast or control to use in assessing the impacts of an instructional activity.

Weaknesses. This design requires considerable planning and data collection prior to the introduction of the educational activity. Therefore, it may take several months or years before the needed baseline data is available. This may be a serious deterrent in the evaluation of an educational innovation. However, this design is effective for knowledge and core skills that have considerable continuity from year to year. In the case of training, a baseline of quality or job performance data is available in many companies.

Types of Decisions. If the environment and the characteristics of the participants are relatively similar to those from whom the baseline or pretest data were collected, decisions can be made on the impacts of the educational experience with a fair level of confidence. The level of confidence in the decision would be similar to that for the rotational design.

When to Use. This design should be used when adequate baseline data are available. Frequently, a school will have a consistent evaluation program related to basic skills and achievement scores. If these data are generated by the same testing program year after year, a good baseline is available for assessing impacts on these capabilities. Similarly, if a company has a consistent and valid set of baseline data, this information can be used to evaluate the effects of a training program. One caution needs to be mentioned: time-series data will reflect all changes, instructional programs, and events that take place during the time period studied. This design requires careful planning over a longer period of time than any of the other designs described. It is, however, the least disruptive.

Planning a Program Evaluation

The processes covered in this section are based on the program evaluation model given in Figure 9-2. This model includes the collection and use of process and product data. In addition, it is based on systems concepts. The elements in the model interact to achieve a purpose. Inputs, processes, and context all have an impact on the outcomes. Process evaluation is also referred to as formative evaluation and product evaluation is also termed summative evaluation.

The first major goal of the evaluation system is program improvement. A second major goal is defining program impacts and determining the merit of the program. Program evaluation needs to be woven into the curriculum design, development, and implementation processes. It should be designed to provide data for design, development, implementation, and improvement decisions. Evaluation data not only are useful in making decisions in these areas, but will also help improve the curriculum development process used.

When it is necessary to evaluate an existing program, the model is still appropriate. It provides a valid framework for evaluating the products or outputs from an educational program and determining their relevance to the program's purpose. Information on program development processes will be collected in retrospect, and some may not be available. The resulting evaluation data are still very useful as the main loss is the lack of data during the curriculum development phases.

Program evaluation must be manageable. It must provide valid data in time for decision making. Priorities need to be established to guide what data are collected and when they are reported. It is not effective or efficient to collect a large volume of data and not be able to process it in a timely manner.

Another important concept in program evaluation is the use of multiple sources of data for critical elements in the evaluation. Frequently, this is called triangulation. To illustrate this, consider graduate competencies. These are critical to the success of the graduates and the program. Graduates must have the competencies specified in the program objectives, and these objectives must match role requirements on the job and in society. Therefore, evaluation should include data on the degree to which students attained course objectives, graduates' perceptions of the adequacy of their competencies, and employers' feedback on their performance.

Finally, consideration must be given to how the evaluation results can be used for improving the program. The evaluation system should be designed to facilitate utilization. The individuals who will make decisions on revising and improving the program should be involved as early as possible. They can help to identify the data needed and the schedule for data collection. Data collection should be scheduled so that the information is available at decision making time. Instructors and curriculum developers should be given help in interpreting and using the evaluation results. They should also be encouraged to make relevant changes.

Steps in the Program Evaluation

The following steps are recommended for designing a program evaluation. They are presented in the usual sequence in which they would be done. It may be necessary to go back and revisit some of the steps as the evaluation is designed and conducted.

Step 1. Review Program Design. The purpose of this step is to become familiar with the program objectives and the processes used to develop the program. If the program is in operation, there should be considerable data available on both of these. However, it is often the case that there is little documentation on them. The evaluator may have to clarify the program objectives as a part of the evaluation. If the program is in the planning stage, the evaluator can provide input on the types of documentation needed. (Additional information on program and course design can be found in Chapter 7.)

Important decision points and dates need to be identified during this review. This information will guide the design of the evaluation. Also, the nature of these decisions will help to identify the stakeholders who should be included in the evaluation process.

Step 2. Obtain Stakeholder Input. At this point stakeholders should be contacted to determine what types of questions they have about the program and the types of evaluation data they want. Also, it is important to determine when they need this data.

Stakeholders are people, groups, or organizations that are or will be affected by, or can have an influence on the program. For example, students are and employers of graduates are stakeholders. Employers who are not served by an educational or training program may be stakeholders if they feel that they should be served.

A review of the evaluation model presented in Figure 9-2 will facilitate identifying stakeholders. In this step, stakeholders are asked what questions they want answered. As the evaluation progresses, they may be contacted again for input on selected questions. In addition, as stakeholders are contacted, they should be asked to identify additional stakeholders.

Step 3. Review Needs. The goal of this step is to clearly identify and understand the needs that stimulated the development of the program. The needs assessment process should be reviewed to determine if it is valid and functional. If needs have been identified, a determination of what sources were used, when the data were collected, and how they were analyzed to isolate the needs must be made. A variety of data sources should have been used, and the data must reflect current conditions. (Additional information on needs assessment can be found in Chapter 3.)

Step 4. Assess Program Mission and Objectives. The intent of this step is to ascertain if the program's mission and objectives match the needs identified. Quality and clarity of the mission statement and objectives will also be assessed. The validity of the mission and objectives will be determined by comparing them with the needs used to justify the program. This comparison will include a check for contents that do not have a basis in the needs statements, as well as for omissions.

Program objectives will identify knowledge, skills, and attitudes students need to develop in the program. These must be verified by checking them against the identified needs and the results of the task analysis used. There may also be program-level objectives that are concerned with the number of graduates and percent of dropouts from the program. For instance, if area labor market data indicate the need for 20 additional nurses each year, one of the program's objectives should relate to this number.

Input from stakeholders may suggest additional data that should be collected and analyzed in this step. Graduates, for example, may relate that they lack certain competencies that are important in their jobs. This would direct the evaluator to look at the needs assessment, task analysis, and objectives-writing processes to determine where the omission occurred.

Step 5. Identify Critical Inputs. Inputs are things that will be changed by the processes used in the instructional system. Students are the typical inputs in educational and training systems. Their knowledge, skills, and/or attitudes are changed as a result of their experiences in these systems. Students have many characteristics that can be measured. The task of the evaluator is to determine which characteristics are relevant to the instructional program and evaluation.

Program and course objectives define the knowledge, skills, and attitudes that are to be changed. These objectives need to be reviewed to determine what student data should be collected prior to instruction and the most appropriate processes to use in acquiring these data. In some instances, school or company data may provide a baseline that can be used to determine changes or gain scores that reflect the impacts of instruction. In many instances it will be necessary to develop assessment instruments to use as pre- and post measures. In fact, it is usually worthwhile to use both existing baseline data and specific assessment instruments. Baseline data will help to assess long-term impacts. Specific instruments are more focused and more sensitive to competency changes that take place in a course. This is especially true in the short term.

The characteristics of students entering the program should also be used in selecting the comparison group for the evaluation. Individuals in the comparison group need to have similar knowledge, skills, and experience. Depending on the evaluation design used, it may be necessary to pretest the comparison group.

Step 6. Identify Critical Processes. Processes transform inputs into products. In a learning environment, these are activities that affect learners. These processes include learning activities, student-instructor interactions, and evaluation activities. It is important to look at how the learning activities and their content relate to the program objectives and the students' characteristics. Does instruction start at the students' level of knowledge? Do learning activities involve students in using content when application is one of the competencies listed in the objectives? Pace of instruction also needs to be reviewed to determine if it matches the students' capacity to acquire new competencies. (Additional information on instructional design can be found in Chapter 6.)

The quality of instructor-student interactions is critical to a positive and supportive learning environment. A variety of studies have found that instructors who have a sound understanding of their subject and can communicate their knowledge in a coherent manner provide more effective instruction. Teachers who have high expectations of their students and anticipate that they will do well foster a more productive learning environment. Also, student involvement in planning class activities and applying course content often leads to more effective learning.

Usually a program evaluation will review the scope and sequence of the program and the courses in it to determine if they are valid and complete. The evaluator would look for and review the program plan and course outlines to ascertain this. However, it is important to also determine if these plans were carried out. Many content areas have established guides, models, or standards that can be used to evaluate content, scope, and sequence. Stakeholders may also have questions and concerns that will influence the types of data collected in the processes area.

Step 7. Identify Output Measures. Measures of the students' knowledge, skills, and attitudes at the end of the program will determine their competency levels and the degree to which the program objectives have been achieved. These measures must match the knowledge, skills, and attitudes specified in the course and program objectives. In other words, they must be valid. Thus, this step starts with a review of these objectives, the program description, and the course outlines. Most of this work may already have been completed when the critical input characteristics were identified.

Kirkpatrick's evaluation model does an effective job of identifying four levels of product measurement that are important: reaction, learning, behavior, and results. Reaction and learning are measured at the end of the course or program. Reaction is concerned with what the student thinks about the program. Measures of knowledge, skills, and relevant attitudes are used to assess learning.

Measures of behavioral changes are done when students have an opportunity to apply what they learned. For students in a training program, behavioral changes might be measured in two weeks or two months after the training program. Results, which are longer-term impacts on the organization, might take as long as several years to assess. For students in college programs, results might be measured in one-year and five-year follow-up studies. When behavior and results are measured, it is also very important to look at the constraints in the environment.

Application of new knowledge, techniques, and processes may be significantly hampered if the work environment is hostile to change or lacks the resources needed to implement new techniques and processes. A separate assessment of these constraints may be needed. If pretests were used, it is important to administer these again at the end of the program. Any comparison groups will also take the posttests. Dropouts and early leavers are also a part of program output. Their experiences in the program, competencies gained, and use of these competencies need to be accessed. In addition, their reasons for leaving early should be identified.

Step 8. Identify Context Factors. Context includes the elements in the system environment that can influence the impacts, processes, products, and purpose. One of the most efficient ways to identify these factors is to review the purpose, products, processes, and inputs to identify what context factors influence them. Since there are many factors that could have an impact, it will probably be necessary to prioritize them based on the extent to which they will influence the system. Stakeholders can help identify and prioritize these. The program evaluation model in Figure 9-2 lists five major areas to review: (1) instructional environment, (2) instructional resources, (3) social/psychological environment, (4) administrative/management support, and (5) labor market conditions.

Instructional environment encompasses the facilities and major equipment used by the program. To the extent that the quality and condition of classrooms and laboratories influence results, they should be included in the evaluation. This factor may also include the campus if it has a potential impact.

Instructional resources include the items that are consumed in the instructional process or have a relatively short life span. Textbooks, manuals, handouts, and lab supplies are a part of this area. Also, computer software can be included here since it changes frequently.

The social and psychological environment is concerned with the extent to which peers, instructors, and family members support students' participation in the program. Is the program perceived to be worthwhile? Do students enter the program because they want to, or are they forced into it? Are the students in the program supportive of each other, and do students in other programs respect them? Do instructors provide positive feedback? See Appendix D.

Administrative and management support can be demonstrated in several ways. Some of these are reflected in the factors already described. In addition, as Kirkpatrick and Kirkpatrick (2006) noted, management must be willing to allow students and graduates to use their new knowledge and skills if there is to be a change in behavior and an impact on results. Also, the level of management support evident in written and verbal communications will have a significant impact on students' and staff's perceptions of a program.

The status of the labor market has a significant impact on career, technical, and training programs. Two facets of the labor market, demand and competency, are especially important. If demand for graduates is increasing, students will be more interested in enrolling and placement will be improved. A shortage of graduates from college programs may stimulate more training courses to upgrade incumbent workers. In contrast, a decrease in demand may cause students to switch to other programs.

Changes in the skill content of a job, especially if they are rapid, can have significant impacts on a program. For example, the development of the personal computer and office software produced significant changes in the competencies needed by secretaries and accountants. In addition, this led to the demise of keypunch jobs. Thus, it is important to determine whether the program has a process in place to monitor skill changes in the labor market and whether this process is used consistently.

Step 9. Identify Data Collection Points. The purpose of this step is to enhance the usefulness of these process and product evaluation data in program development, management, and improvement. In order to do this, the major decision points in curriculum development and instruction must be identified, and what data is needed at each point. Also, an appropriate data collection schedule must be established in order to provide evaluation reports ahead of the decision points.

The evaluator needs to talk with the major decision makers to determine when they need data and what data are required. For example, when a program is being designed or revised, data on needs, labor market changes, and previous program performance are needed.

The end result of this step should be a chart that lists the major decision points, a time schedule for each point, and the data required for each decision. If the program developers have an activity schedule, evaluation activities and report points can be entered into it.

Step 10. Develop Instruments and Data Collection Techniques. An analysis of the decisions that need to be made and a review of the purpose, inputs, processes, products, and context data required will provide a good basis for selecting or developing the instruments and procedures to be used in collecting data. Also, the data sources will have an impact on the techniques used. For example, it may be feasible to conduct personal interviews with stakeholders in local areas. However, it may be necessary to conduct telephone interviews or use a survey with stakeholders who are not in the local area.

One of the major concerns in developing or selecting an instrument is validity. The data collection technique must collect the right data. Each measure used must be reviewed to determine if it is valid. This is done by comparing the nature of the data collected with the data needed to assess the characteristic being evaluated.

Some measures and data may already be available. Classroom tests and performance measures may provide the data required to assess students' competencies. Their validity should be checked to ensure they provide the appropriate data. Certification tests may provide a valid way to measure the impacts a program has on students' competencies. For longer term results, an organization's quality and productivity data are potential measures of impacts on behavior and results.

When possible, it is good practice to have multiple sources of data to assess a specific element in the system. For instance, student and instructor feedback, plus the evaluator's observations, can be used to assess the quality of the learning environment. Each data source has its strengths and biases. The composite picture generated by the three sources will give a more valid and detailed description of the learning environment. An additional reason for using the evaluator's observations and interviews is to enhance the evaluator's understanding of the system and to gain a better feel for what is happening in the system.

It is often a challenge to reduce data collection activities to a manageable set. There is usually a tendency to want to collect a large amount of data so nothing is missed. However, to be functional, the evaluation must not only collect, but must also process, analyze, and report the results in a timely manner. Priorities must be established and applied to ensure that the evaluation is manageable.

Step 11. Review Evaluation Plan. At this point the evaluation plan needs to be reviewed to determine if it is complete and valid. The evaluator should do a cognitive walk-through of the plan to ascertain whether it provides valid process and product data for the decisions that need to be made relating to the program. The following characteristics should be checked:

- validity (Do the data collected relate to the decisions that must be made?)
- scope (Are the data needed collected?)
- timeliness (Are data available when decisions must be made?)
- manageability (Can evaluation activities be completed with the time and resources available?)

After the evaluator has reviewed the evaluation system, it should be discussed with major stakeholders of the program being evaluated. These stakeholders usually include the program manager, curriculum developers, instructors, students, and administrators or managers associated with the program. Other stakeholders should be involved as appropriate. Stakeholders should be asked to respond to the following questions:

- Does this evaluation system collect the data you need?
- Does the evaluation collect the data other stakeholders need?
- Is the data collection schedule appropriate?

- Can the evaluation activities be carried out as planned?
- Are there any problem areas?

Responses to these questions provide the basis for final revisions and modifications to the evaluation system.

Step 12. Conduct the Evaluation. The evaluation plan has been carefully developed, reviewed, and refined. Now it is time to implement that plan. The evaluation plan should be carried out as designed unless there are compelling reasons to change it as the evaluation progresses. The more complex the program being evaluated, the more likely it is that there will be a need to make some modifications.

Modifications should be carefully designed and reviewed with appropriate stakeholders. Also, the impacts of these changes on other aspects of the evaluation must be considered. Any modifications implemented must be documented.

During the course of the evaluation, the evaluator will be interacting with a variety of people involved in the program. Evaluation may not be their main interest and it may be somewhat threatening to them. Thus, it is important to be relaxed and calm when interacting with them.

Data collected needs to be processed on a timely basis. It is very important that results are shared with appropriate stakeholders when the information is needed for decision making. This will help to solidify their cooperation and support for the evaluation.

During this stage, data from students, instructors, and others will be collected. These data need to be handled in a secure manner. This is especially true of any data that include an identifier for a specific person. The evaluation will need to conform to the human subjects regulations that apply to it, and it may be necessary to have a signed release form in order to use some types of data.

As the evaluation is carried out, the evaluator will gain a number of insights and ideas for improving the instruments and evaluation processes. These should be recorded and saved for use in revising the evaluation system. Some things to look for are the following:

- scope (Were sufficient data available for use in decision making?)
- schedule (Were results ready when decision makers needed them?)
- instruments (Are the data collection techniques valid, efficient, and sensitive enough to measure important characteristics?)

Step 13. Provide Feedback. It is important to provide feedback to each stakeholder group. Their information needs should be reviewed and reports designed for each group. Also, stakeholders should have access to all reports. These reports must be relevant, timely, sufficient, and functional.

Since decisions are made throughout the program development and implementation process, several reports will be needed. Usually, it is important to have a written report, even if it is in a brief memo format. This provides documentation for the evaluation. There will be times, however, when it is important to give an oral presentation of the results. This is especially true when it is imperative that decision makers make use of the data in their work. Also, there are some people who process information more effectively when they hear and see it. (Additional information on report writing can be found in Chapter 5.)

Providing feedback on a timely schedule is very important. Curriculum developers, instructors, and other stakeholders must have the data before they need to make decisions. For example, an evaluation and validation of the competency list must be completed before these competencies are used to design a program. If the evaluation data are not presented in time, decisions will be made without a complete set of data and stakeholders will not rely on the evaluation results as they make decisions.

To the degree possible, decision makers should receive all of the data they need in order to make informed decisions. However, the evaluator usually does not control all of the data needed. The evaluator's first concern should be to provide the information generated by the evaluation. In addition, the evaluator should help decision makers identify other data they need and suggest ways they might access it. It is also important that decision makers not be inundated with data that has little relevance to the decisions at hand.

The data provided to stakeholders must be functional. They should be concise and easy to interpret. Jargon should be avoided and all acronyms defined. Many readers find graphs easier to interpret than tables and narrative. Statistics that the stakeholders understand should be used. When possible, the analysis and conclusions should be made to relate to the decisions that need to be made.

Step 14. Evaluate the System. There are two main reasons for evaluating the evaluation system used. First, the evaluator needs to know the strengths and weaknesses of the system used. Some of the weaknesses can be corrected as the evaluation is in progress. Others will remain and have some impact on the results; however, the evaluator will know what they are and their likely impacts on the evaluation results. The second reason for evaluating the system is to learn how to design better evaluation systems and processes. One of the best ways to expand one's program evaluation skills is to design and conduct an evaluation and obtain input on its quality.

As the evaluation system is implemented, ideas for changes, questions, and problems will arise. These need to be handled as they arise. In addition, these should be documented as to their nature and resolution. Also, any ideas on how the problems could be avoided should be noted. At the end of the evaluation, stakeholders should be asked to identify what they like about the system and for suggestions on how the system could be improved.

Once all of the input has been assembled, it should be carefully analyzed to determine how the evaluation could have been improved. Also, this information should be used to ascertain how the evaluation system design process can be improved. Some of the specific characteristics that need to checked are the following:

- validity of the results
- reliability of the data
- sensitivity to changes in outcomes
- adequacy of the scope of the data
- appropriate timing
- efficiency

The first concern should be the validity of the results. Evaluation results should reflect the actual impacts, positive and negative, of the program. Results from the evaluation can be compared with other indicators of program performance. Some of these, such as performance on the job, will require longer-term follow-up. More immediate feedback can be obtained from changes in students' performance levels, their achievement on certificate tests, and stakeholder feedback.

Reliability refers to the amount of error in the data collected. Errors occur for a variety of reasons. For example, a test key may be inaccurate, survey directions may not be clear, comments may be misinterpreted, or data may be incorrectly recorded. Also, some respondents may want to present a false picture. Data need to be checked for consistency, and multiple sources of information should be used whenever possible.

Many programs and classes have an impact, but the tests used to measure these impacts are not sensitive to the changes in knowledge or skills involved. For example, the competencies acquired in a statistics workshop probably would not have an effect on performance on a standardized math test. However, the competencies learned may be essential when interpreting quality data. The instruments used need to be focused on the competencies, processes, and decisions that are relevant to the program that is being evaluated.

Typically, a program evaluation will require a variety of process and product data. The program evaluation model presented in Figure 9-2 and input from stakeholders will help to ensure that the data collected have an adequate scope. One factor that often threatens the scope of information is the difficulty encountered in measuring some phenomenon. Attitudes, for example, are often more difficult to measure. Extra effort must be made to include these areas in the evaluation.

One sure indicator that an evaluation lacks appropriate scope is when there are not enough data to adequately determine if a project objective has been attained or important processes are effective. As the evaluation progresses, the evaluator should note areas where additional data are needed. In some instances it may be possible to obtain some of this information. In any case, the notes will be useful when the final evaluation report is written and when planning future program evaluations.

Appropriate timing of data collection and reporting is important to an effective evaluation. Evaluation results can be an important input into program decision making. A note should be made of any problems in timing. These notes should be reviewed at the end of the evaluation to determine how the problems can be avoided in future evaluations.

An effective evaluation should also be efficient. The main goal of curriculum and program development is to create effective and efficient learning experiences, courses, and programs. The program evaluation must not detract from these efforts. Efficient and cost-effective data collection techniques need to be used. Existing records and the data generated by the curriculum development and instructional processes should be used.

Obviously, efficiency is a balancing act with the other criteria. Reducing data collection can create problems with the scope of the evaluation. Using existing data may reduce validity and sensitivity. Evaluators always need to ask themselves, "Can I do this more efficiently and still retain validity, scope, and sensitivity?"

Review Questions

1. Briefly describe the three roles of program evaluation.
2. What three phases has program evaluation gone through according to Guba and Lincoln?
3. What are the four levels in Kirkpatrick's evaluation model?
4. Which one of Kirkpatrick's levels requires a long-term follow-up?
5. What are the main components of the CIPP evaluation system?
6. Sketch the CIPP evaluation system.
7. How often should a program evaluation be done?
8. Describe how a time-series design would be used in evaluating a new math program.
9. Describe how an experimental design could be used in the evaluation of a one-week workshop on communication skills.
10. What is the first step in planning a program evaluation?
11. List three typical stakeholders in a program evaluation.
12. What are three criteria to use when selecting or developing an instrument to use in an evaluation?
13. Give two examples of product or formative data in a program evaluation.
14. List two types of input data that might be collected in a program evaluation.
15. What are two reasons for evaluating the evaluation system?

REFERENCES

Kirkpatrick, D. L., & Kirkpatrick J. D. (2006). *Evaluating training programs: The four levels* (3rd ed). San Francisco, CA: Berrett-Koehler.

Mathison, S. (Ed.). (2005) Models of evaluation: Mining evaluation models. In *Encyclopedia of evaluation* (pp. 256–257). Thousand Oaks, CA: Sage Publications.

National Institute of Standards and Technology (NIST). (n.d.). *Baldrige national quality program*. Retrieved September 30, 2014, from http://www.nist.gov/baldrige/index.cfm

Stufflebeam, D. L., Madaus, G. F., and Kellaghan, T. (Eds.). (2000). *Evaluation models: Viewpoints on educational and human services evaluation* (2nd ed). Boston: Kluwer Academic Publishers.

Phillips, J. J., Wayne, B., & Phillips, P. F. (2012). *Project management ROI: A step-by-step guide for measuring the impact and ROI for projects.* Hoboken, NJ: John Wiley & Sons.

Appendix

APPENDIX A

Task Validation and Needs Assessment Instruments

The purpose of these two surveys was to validate the task list for the Customer Service Representative (CSR) position and identify training needs. The task list was developed in two DACUM sessions (see Chapter 2 for more information on DACUM). One session obtained input from CSRs and the second session collected feedback from their supervisors. The curriculum developers wanted to be able to compare the survey results from the CSRs and supervisors. Also, they wanted to be able to be able to quantify the level of importance and training need for each task. Thus, a numerical rating scale was selected for the surveys. Two scales are included in the survey: importance and need. Five levels are included in each scale to give respondents enough "response space" to record their judgments. The response choices on both scales are the same for CSRs and supervisors. However, on the Training Need scale, the CSRs are asked to rate themselves and the supervisors are instructed to rate the training needs of the CSRs they supervise.

The tasks are listed by general area of competency (GAC) to simplify the respondents' work and to facilitate the use of the results. Space is provided under each GAC for additional tasks to be listed. Although a formal process was used to develop the task list (DACUM), there is always a possibility that a task was missed. The surveys also include a section on future competencies. These were identified at the end of the DACUM session with each group.

In the last section, respondents were asked to identify the site where they worked, their experience on the job, and their educational level. Responses on these items were used to sub-divide each group for more detailed analyses (cross-tabulations).

CSR Survey

Directions: Use your experiences as a CSR to rate the following items. The column on the left contains the competencies identified for CSRs. We need your input on the importance of each competency and the amount of training you feel that you need for each one. In *Column A,* rate the *importance* of each competency. Base your response on the frequency that you use the competency and how critical it is to doing your work correctly. The more frequent and critical, the more important the competency is. In *Column B,* rate the extent to which you feel a *need for training* related to the competency. There is space at the end of each section to add competencies. Use the following ratings:

A: Importance	**B: Training Need**
1 = NI = Not Important	1 = N = None/No Need
2 = MI = Moderately important	2 = S = Slight Need
3 = I = Important	3 = M = Moderate Need
4 = VI = Very Important	4 = H = High Need
5 = E = Essential	5 = VH = Very High Need

Competency	**A. Importance** NI 1	MI 2	I 3	VI 4	E 5	**B. Training Need** N 1	S 2	M 3	H 4	VH 5
Using computers										
1. Use software	1	2	3	4	5	1	2	3	4	5
2. Use keyboard skills	1	2	3	4	5	1	2	3	4	5
3. Troubleshoot software	1	2	3	4	5	1	2	3	4	5
4. Troubleshoot computer	1	2	3	4	5	1	2	3	4	5
5. Other ______	1	2	3	4	5	1	2	3	4	5
Using soft skills										
6. Apply interpersonal skills	1	2	3	4	5	1	2	3	4	5
7. Use appropriate language and terminology	1	2	3	4	5	1	2	3	4	5
8. Resolve conflicts	1	2	3	4	5	1	2	3	4	5
9. Communicate with supervisor	1	2	3	4	5	1	2	3	4	5
10. Use correct spelling and grammar	1	2	3	4	5	1	2	3	4	5
11. Record and interpret comments	1	2	3	4	5	1	2	3	4	5
12. Other ______	1	2	3	4	5	1	2	3	4	5
Assisting with customers										
13. Control call conversations	1	2	3	4	5	1	2	3	4	5
14. Provide customer service	1	2	3	4	5	1	2	3	4	5
15. Resolve complaints	1	2	3	4	5	1	2	3	4	5
16. Direct customers to appropriate resource	1	2	3	4	5	1	2	3	4	5
17. Take messages	1	2	3	4	5	1	2	3	4	5
18. Diffuse volatile situations	1	2	3	4	5	1	2	3	4	5
19. Other ______	1	2	3	4	5	1	2	3	4	5
Processing claims										
20. Identify insurance company requirements	1	2	3	4	5	1	2	3	4	5
21. Use profile book	1	2	3	4	5	1	2	3	4	5
22. Process order	1	2	3	4	5	1	2	3	4	5

CSR Survey (continued)

Competency	A. Importance NI 1	MI 2	I 3	VI 4	E 5	B. Training Need N 1	S 2	M 3	H 4	VH 5
Processing claims (continued)										
23. Ask appropriate questions	1	2	3	4	5	1	2	3	4	5
24. Respond to questions	1	2	3	4	5	1	2	3	4	5
25. Call shops with order information	1	2	3	4	5	1	2	3	4	5
26. Communicate with insurance companies	1	2	3	4	5	1	2	3	4	5
27. Communicate with other departments	1	2	3	4	5	1	2	3	4	5
28. Perform claim inquiries	1	2	3	4	5	1	2	3	4	5
29. Resolve claim issues	1	2	3	4	5	1	2	3	4	5
30. Other ______________	1	2	3	4	5	1	2	3	4	5
Maintaining company standards										
31. Follow policy and procedures	1	2	3	4	5	1	2	3	4	5
32. Adapt to new policies	1	2	3	4	5	1	2	3	4	5
33. Meet required expectations	1	2	3	4	5	1	2	3	4	5
34. Adapt to changing work environment	1	2	3	4	5	1	2	3	4	5
35. Participate in training	1	2	3	4	5	1	2	3	4	5
36. Other ______________	1	2	3	4	5	1	2	3	4	5
Performing additional responsibilities										
37. Assist other workers	1	2	3	4	5	1	2	3	4	5
38. Perform CSR coach responsibilities	1	2	3	4	5	1	2	3	4	5
39. Use office equipment	1	2	3	4	5	1	2	3	4	5
40. Distribute information	1	2	3	4	5	1	2	3	4	5
41. Update profile books	1	2	3	4	5	1	2	3	4	5
42. Other ______________	1	2	3	4	5	1	2	3	4	5

Future Competencies

Directions: Several competencies that may have more importance in the future are listed below. Rate the importance of each one in *column A*. The more likely a competency is to be needed in the future and the more impact it will have on your work, the more important it will be. In *column B*, rate the amount of training you need for each one.

A: Importance

1 = NI = Not Important
2 = MI = Moderately important
3 = I = Important
4 = VI = Very Important
5 = E = Essential

B: Training Need

1 = N = None/No Need
2 = S = Slight Need
3 = M = Moderate Need
4 = H = High Need
5 = VH = Very High Need

Competency	A. Importance NI 1	MI 2	I 3	VI 4	E 5	B. Training Need N 1	S 2	M 3	H 4	VH 5
43. Process property claims	1	2	3	4	5	1	2	3	4	5
44. Process vehicle claims	1	2	3	4	5	1	2	3	4	5
45. Advanced computer skills	1	2	3	4	5	1	2	3	4	5
46. Work with a larger number of business terms and regulations	1	2	3	4	5	1	2	3	4	5

CSR Survey (continued)

Competency	A. Importance					B. Training Need				
	NI	MI	I	VI	E	N	S	M	H	VH
	1	2	3	4	5	1	2	3	4	5
(continued)										
47. Become more involved in managing our work	1	2	3	4	5	1	2	3	4	5
48. Other ______________________________	1	2	3	4	5	1	2	3	4	5

49. At which site do you work?

_____ 1. Twin Cities
_____ 2. Orlando

50. How long have you worked as a CSR?

_____ 1. 3 months or less
_____ 2. 4–12 months
_____ 3. 1–3 years
_____ 4. 3 years or more

51. Do you have other work experience related to this job (CSR)?

_____ 1. Yes (Please list.)

____

____

_____ 2. No

52. What is your educational level?

_____ 1. Less than high school diploma
_____ 2. High school diploma
_____ 3. Some college (technical college or university)
_____ 4. Technical college or associate degree
_____ 5. Four-year college degree

Thank you for responding.

Please return as directed.

CSR Survey—Supervisor Form

Directions: Use your experiences as a supervisor of CSRs to rate the following items. The column on the left contains the competencies identified for CSRs. We need your input on the importance of each competency and the amount of training you feel that CSRs need for each one. In *Column A,* rate the *importance* of each competency. Base your response on the frequency that CSRs use the competency and how critical it is to doing their work correctly. The more frequent and critical, the more important the competency is. In *Column B,* rate the extent to which you feel there is a *need for training* related to the competency. There is space at the end of each section to add competencies. Use the following ratings:

A: Importance	**B: Training Need**
1 = NI = Not Important	1 = N = None/No Need
2 = MI = Moderately important	2 = S = Slight Need
3 = I = Important	3 = M = Moderate Need
4 = VI = Very Important	4 = H = High Need
5 = E = Essential	5 = VH = Very High Need

Competency	**A. Importance** NI 1	MI 2	I 3	VI 4	E 5	**B. Training Need** N 1	S 2	M 3	H 4	VH 5
Using computers										
1. Use software	1	2	3	4	5	1	2	3	4	5
2. Use keyboard skills	1	2	3	4	5	1	2	3	4	5
3. Troubleshoot software	1	2	3	4	5	1	2	3	4	5
4. Troubleshoot computer	1	2	3	4	5	1	2	3	4	5
5. Other ________	1	2	3	4	5	1	2	3	4	5
Using soft skills										
6. Apply interpersonal skills	1	2	3	4	5	1	2	3	4	5
7. Use appropriate language and terminology	1	2	3	4	5	1	2	3	4	5
8. Resolve conflicts	1	2	3	4	5	1	2	3	4	5
9. Communicate with supervisor	1	2	3	4	5	1	2	3	4	5
10. Use correct spelling and grammar	1	2	3	4	5	1	2	3	4	5
11. Record and interpret comments	1	2	3	4	5	1	2	3	4	5
12. Other ________	1	2	3	4	5	1	2	3	4	5
Assisting with customers										
13. Control call conversations	1	2	3	4	5	1	2	3	4	5
14. Provide customer service	1	2	3	4	5	1	2	3	4	5
15. Resolve complaints	1	2	3	4	5	1	2	3	4	5
16. Direct customers to appropriate resource	1	2	3	4	5	1	2	3	4	5
17. Take messages	1	2	3	4	5	1	2	3	4	5
18. Diffuse volatile situations	1	2	3	4	5	1	2	3	4	5
19. Other ________	1	2	3	4	5	1	2	3	4	5
Processing claims										
20. Identify insurance company requirements	1	2	3	4	5	1	2	3	4	5
21. Use profile book	1	2	3	4	5	1	2	3	4	5
22. Process order	1	2	3	4	5	1	2	3	4	5

CSR Survey—Supervisor Form (continued)

Competency	A. Importance NI 1	MI 2	I 3	VI 4	E 5	B. Training Need N 1	S 2	M 3	H 4	VH 5
Processing claims (continued)										
23. Ask appropriate questions	1	2	3	4	5	1	2	3	4	5
24. Respond to questions	1	2	3	4	5	1	2	3	4	5
25. Call shops with order information	1	2	3	4	5	1	2	3	4	5
26. Communicate with insurance companies	1	2	3	4	5	1	2	3	4	5
27. Communicate with other departments	1	2	3	4	5	1	2	3	4	5
28. Perform claim inquiries	1	2	3	4	5	1	2	3	4	5
29. Resolve claim issues	1	2	3	4	5	1	2	3	4	5
30. Other ______	1	2	3	4	5	1	2	3	4	5
Maintaining company standards										
31. Follow policy and procedures	1	2	3	4	5	1	2	3	4	5
32. Adapt to new policies	1	2	3	4	5	1	2	3	4	5
33. Meet required expectations	1	2	3	4	5	1	2	3	4	5
34. Adapt to changing work environment	1	2	3	4	5	1	2	3	4	5
35. Participate in training	1	2	3	4	5	1	2	3	4	5
36. Other ______	1	2	3	4	5	1	2	3	4	5
Performing additional responsibilities										
37. Assist other workers	1	2	3	4	5	1	2	3	4	5
38. Perform CSR coach responsibilities	1	2	3	4	5	1	2	3	4	5
39. Use office equipment	1	2	3	4	5	1	2	3	4	5
40. Distribute information	1	2	3	4	5	1	2	3	4	5
41. Update profile books	1	2	3	4	5	1	2	3	4	5
42. Other ______	1	2	3	4	5	1	2	3	4	5

Future Competencies

Directions: Several competencies that may have more importance in the future are listed below. Rate the importance of each one in *column A.* The more likely a competency is to be needed in the future and the more impact it will have on the work of CSRs, the more important it will be. In *column B,* rate the amount of training CSRs will need for each one.

A: Importance

1 = NI = Not Important
2 = MI = Moderately important
3 = I = Important
4 = VI = Very Important
5 = E = Essential

B: Training Need

1 = N = None/No Need
2 = S = Slight Need
3 = M = Moderate Need
4 = H = High Need
5 = VH = Very High Need

Competency	A. Importance NI 1	MI 2	I 3	VI 4	E 5	B. Training Need N 1	S 2	M 3	H 4	VH 5
43. Process property claims	1	2	3	4	5	1	2	3	4	5
44. Process vehicle claims	1	2	3	4	5	1	2	3	4	5
45. Advanced computer skills	1	2	3	4	5	1	2	3	4	5
46. Work with a larger number of business terms and regulations	1	2	3	4	5	1	2	3	4	5

CSR Survey—Supervisor Form (continued)

Competency	A. Importance NI 1	MI 2	I 3	VI 4	E 5	B. Training Need N 1	S 2	M 3	H 4	VH 5
(continued)										
47. Become more involved in managing our work	1	2	3	4	5	1	2	3	4	5
48. Other ______________	1	2	3	4	5	1	2	3	4	5

49. At which site do you work?
____ 1. Twin Cities
____ 2. Orlando

50. How long have you worked as a supervisor?
____ 1. 3 months or less
____ 2. 4–12 months
____ 3. 1–3 years
____ 4. 3 years or more

51. Have you worked as a CSR?
____ 1. Yes
____ 2. No

52. What is your educational level?
____ 1. Less than high school diploma
____ 2. High school diploma
____ 3. Some college (technical college or university)
____ 4. Technical college or associate degree
____ 5. Four-year college degree

Thank you for responding.

Please return as directed.

APPENDIX B

Delphi Technique

This example was adapted from a survey performed by the authors. The purpose was to collect projections of trends over a 10-year period. The study was concerned with identifying trends that would affect business and industry and would thus have ramifications for training programs. The Delphi technique was selected because it was designed for situations like this. Also, the curriculum developers had successfully used it for similar studies.

The panel of experts was comprised of individuals from business and industry. Recommendations for panel members were received from technical college faculty and advisory committee members. Prior to mailing the round 1 survey, potential panel members were contacted to determine if they were willing to participate in the Delphi survey. They were informed of the tasks involved and the importance of the results. They were also assured that they would receive a copy of the results. Those who agreed to participate received the three rounds of the Delphi survey used in this study. Samples of these materials follow.

Round 1 was used to identify potential trends and changes that would influence business and industry. The responses to this survey were used to develop the trend and change statements for the round 2 survey. Panel members' responses to round 2 indicated how likely the change would happen by the end of the next ten years (the year 2010). Responses to round 2 were summarized, and the area of consensus was identified for each item. For round 3, each panel member received his/her round 2 survey back along with a summary of round 2 results and a listing of consensus areas for each item. They then had their choice of moving out-of-consensus responses to the consensus areas for these items or writing a justification for retaining an out-of-consensus response.

The following pages provide examples of the round 1 and 2 surveys, summary of results, and justifications for out-of-consensus responses. (Chapter 2 contains more information on designing and conducting a Delphi study.)

Delphi Survey — Round 1

These open-ended questions were used to gather input on changes that would occur over the next 10 years. They were mailed to a panel of experts with a cover letter that reviewed the purpose of the study and their role in it. The panel members were also informed that they could respond based on their experiences.

Trends Survey

Directions: Identify the major changes and trends that will occur by the year 2010 in each of the areas noted below. List the changes/trends that come to mind as you read each question. You do not need to do any special research to complete this survey.

1. What changes/trends will occur in the technology used in business and industry by the year 2010?

2. What changes/trends will occur in work and management systems by the year 2010?

3. What changes will occur in society by the year 2010 that will have significant impacts on business and industry?

4. What other changes will occur by the year 2010 that will have significant impacts on business and industry?

Delphi Survey — Round 2

The comments on the round 1 survey were used to develop the statements for the round 2 survey. This survey was sent to the panel members and each survey had a code number that identified the panel member who received it. This was done so the completed surveys could be returned to the appropriate panel members in Round 3.

Delphi Survey

Directions: Round 2 of the Delphi survey is conducted to determine the major changes in technology by the year 2010. The statements that appear below have been synthesized because several of you submitted statements that were similar. They have been grouped according to eleven general categories.

In round 2, we ask that you rate each of the statements on a scale of 1 to 7. The ratings should indicate your judgment of the likelihood that each event will occur by the year 2010. The percentage probability for each response is given in parentheses. Circle your response.

1 = Will not happen (0%)
2 = Very unlikely will happen (1–20%)
3 = Unlikely will happen (21–40%)
4 = Moderate chance will happen (41–60%)
5 = Likely will happen (61–80%)
6 = Very likely will happen (81–99%)
7 = Definitely will happen (100%)

Notes: Following each statement you are invited to make a comment if you wish to clarify or specify your rating.

7 = Definitely will happen (100%)
6 = Very likely will happen (81–99%)
5 = Likely will happen (61–80%)
4 = Moderate chance will happen (41–60%)
3 = Unlikely will happen (21–40%)
2 = Very unlikely will happen (1–20%)
1 = Will not happen (0%)

Artificial Intelligence/Expert Systems

1. Expert systems with systematic rules for decision making will decrease the need for technical experts. 1 2 3 4 5 6 7
   Comments: ______________________
2. User friendly, expert systems will be used in most industry and business fields by 2010. 1 2 3 4 5 6 7
   Comments: ______________________

Automated Office/Datamation

3. The use of electronic databases with controlled access will replace conventional record systems in 40% or more of the businesses and industries. 1 2 3 4 5 6 7
   Comments: ______________________
4. Administration support staff members will utilize integrated electronic workstations as part of their everyday functions. 1 2 3 4 5 6 7
   Comments: ______________________

(continued . . .)

7 = Definitely will happen (100%)
6 = Very likely will happen (81–99%)
5 = Likely will happen (61–80%)
4 = Moderate chance will happen (41–60%)
3 = Unlikely will happen (21–40%)
2 = Very unlikely will happen (1–20%)
1 = Will not happen (0%)

Automated Office/Datamation (continued)

5. Impact printers will reach obsolescence by 2010. 1 2 3 4 5 6 7
   Comments: ______
6. Words-per-minute and keyboarding skills will be abolished as the standard used to identify a person's clerical proficiency. 1 2 3 4 5 6 7
   Comments: ______
7. At least 50% of the computers on the market will include voice actuation as a standard feature.
   Comments: ______

Biotechnology

8. Genetically engineered products to cure AIDS and some cancers will be on the market. 1 2 3 4 5 6 7
   Comments: ______
9. There will be a 50% increase in the availability of federal support for biotechnology research to develop cures for disabling and life threatening diseases. 1 2 3 4 5 6 7
   Comments: ______
10. Of the technological advances in science, genetic engineering will be the most controversial. 1 2 3 4 5 6 7
    Comments: ______
11. Computer assisted design (CAD) will be used for more than 90% of all drafting and design tasks in business and industry. 1 2 3 4 5 6 7
    Comments: ______

Composite Materials

12. Sixty percent or more of automobile components will be manufactured of composite materials. 1 2 3 4 5 6 7
    Comments: ______
13. By the year 2010, 20% or more of the structural steel requirements will be met with composite materials. 1 2 3 4 5 6 7
    Comments: ______

Consensus Summary

The responses to the previous survey, round 2, were summarized, and the consensus area for each item was determined. This completed round 2. The consensus areas were marked on each respondent's survey. For round 3 of the Delphi process, each respondent received his/her own round 2 survey back with the following instructions: Review all of the items and if your response is not in the consensus area for an item, you can (1) change your response to the consensus area, or (2) keep your response from round 2 and write a justification for responding outside of the consensus area.

The consensus areas listed in the next pages were attained after round 3. A similar summary was developed for round 2. Comments justifying non-consensus responses are given after consensus results. The boxes in the summary identify the consensus areas. The lines indicate the span of response choices selected by the respondents. Also, a brief summary of the arguments for out-of-consensus responses is listed under each item.

Trends Forecasting Survey Results

Note: Respondents' comments for non-consensus

+ indicates comment of respondent rating item above consensus area
– indicates comment of respondent rating item below consensus area

7 = Definitely will happen (100%)
6 = Very likely will happen (81–99%)
5 = Likely will happen (61–80%)
4 = Moderate chance will happen (41–60%)
3 = Unlikely will happen (21–40%)
2 = Very unlikely will happen (1–20%)
1 = Will not happen (0%)

Artificial Intelligence/Expert Systems 0 20 40 60 80 100

1. Expert systems with systematic rules for decision making will decrease the need for technical experts. 1 2 3 4 5 6 7

   28% 55% 17%

   Respondent's comments for non-consensus:
   + Reduced role with employee involvement.
   – Increase before decrease.
   – Yes, but not in 10 years.

2. User friendly, expert systems will be used in most industry and business fields by 2010. 1 2 3 4 5 6 7

   34% 66%

   Respondent's comments for non-consensus:
   – Change most to many.
   – Yes, but not in 10 years.

Automated Office/Datamation

3. The use of electronic databases with controlled access will replace conventional record systems in 40% or more of the businesses and industries. 1 2 3 4 5 6 7

   6% 94%

   Respondent's comments for non-consensus:
   – Cost factor is a problem for small businesses.

4. Administration support staff members will utilize integrated electronic workstations as part of their everyday functions. 1 2 3 4 5 6 7

   12% 88%

   Respondent's comments for non-consensus:
   – Administrators (now in 40s) won't know how to connect.

(continued . . .)

Automated Office/Datamation (continued)

5. Impact printers will reach obsolescence by 2010. — 1 2 3 4 5 6 7

   Respondent's comments for non-consensus:
   – Technically obsolete, but many will still be in use.

   17% 83%

6. Words-per-minute and keyboarding skills will be abolished as the standard used to identify a person's clerical proficiency. — 1 2 3 4 5 6 7

   Respondent's comments for non-consensus:
   + More likely.
   – Never was the standard.

   17% 60% 23%

7. At least 50% of the computers on the market will include voice actuation as a standard feature. — 1 2 3 4 5 6 7

   Respondent's comments for non-consensus:
   + Closer than we think.
   – Will still be add on.
   – % is too high.

   17% 72% 11%

Biotechnology

8. Genetically engineered products to cure AIDS and some cancers will be on the market. — 1 2 3 4 5 6 7

   Respondent's comments for non-consensus:
   + Higher likelihood based on scientific progress.
   – Prevention not cure.

   17% 72% 11%

9. There will be a 50% increase in the availability of federal support for biotechnology research to develop cures for disabling and life threatening diseases. — 1 2 3 4 5 6 7

   Respondent's comments for non-consensus:
   + 50% increase is a small $ amount.

   6% 88% 6%

10. Of the technological advances in science, genetic engineering will be the most controversial. — 1 2 3 4 5 6 7

    100%

11. Computer-assisted design (CAD) will be used for more than 90% of all drafting and design tasks in business and industry. — 1 2 3 4 5 6 7

    Respondent's comments for non-consensus:
    + Without it, companies cannot subcontract.

    6% 88% 6%

Composite Materials

12. Sixty percent or more of automobile components will be manufactured of composite materials. — 1 2 3 4 5 6 7

    Respondent's comments for non-consensus:
    – % is too high.

    12% 88%

13. By the year 2010, 20% or more of the structural steel requirements will be met with composite materials. — 1 2 3 4 5 6 7

    Respondent's comments for non-consensus:
    – 20% is too low.
    – Depends on one's definition of structural steel.

    34% 66%

Technological Trends Forecast
Comments (Non-consensus)

#1:
- – The need for technical experts will increase before decreasing.
- – Too soon (2010) to make any impact on numbers of experts needed.
- \+ A lot of information has been crossing my desk that leads me to believe that AI/Expert Systems will be very impactful. Also, organizationally, I am seeing a reduced role for the technical "expert" as employee involvement and teamwork increase.
- – From my perspective in biological sciences, I see a tremendous human input for many processes. These would have to be automated first; then, made "intelligent."
- \+ Will explore decisions further.

#2:
- – If the word "most" was changed to "many," I would tend to agree with the level 5.
- – Seldom used now; can't move that fast in ten years.
- – Time is too short to be in most industries.
- – Communicating artificial intelligence systems could be a large handicap.

#3:
- – TOO many small businesses included in the 40% for them to afford capital outlay.

#4:
- – Unclear as to the number/percent of involvement.
- – Many individuals in their 40s will be administrative staff in the year 2010 (10 yrs.), and they still won't know how to use the CONNECT system on their desk!

#5: (Consensus) But there will still be many in use.
- – While impact printers may be considered technologically obsolete by 2010 their use will still be substantial. The same kinds of predictions for typewriters was made with the movement of computers and word processing... And it was also nonsense... witness the work place. Also, recognize the proliferation of small businesses which are less likely to go high-tech due to loss and other considerations.

#6:
- – Never was "the" standard, but will still be important.
- \+ Where computers are in use by both professional and clerical persons, these standards have already been de-emphasized... But not removed. Clerical work in automated/computerized settings is becoming more focused on system knowledge and such things as accuracy checks. Speed as a major factor is giving way to quality.
- \+ Voice activated electronics will offset current clerical.
- \+ I'm much more knowledgeable in this area, because I do test development and validation for a living. Words-per-minute is scientifically invalid for the evaluation of a person's proficiency on electronic editing equipment. Words-per-minute is a terribly outdated measure designed in the early 1900s to determine stroking speed on a traditional typewriter. This outdated measure is not only invalid for use on an automated/electronic keyboard, but would also be illegal to use as a screening device for job applicants because it is not sufficiently job related. Because I am the Director of test research and development for a major corporation, and develop and validate employee selection tools in accordance with both professional (the American Psychological Association) and legal (the EEOC) standards, I feel I'm more knowledgeable in this area than other members of your research panel. In conjunction with the proliferation of automated equipment in all business (and manufacturing) environments as well as the heightened emphasis on the civil Rights Act as it relates to Employee section Procedures (Civil Rights Act of 1990), it is inevitable that a method much more accurate than a words-per-minute timed writing will be established for the evaluation of productivity in the automated business environment.
- – Will still exist to some extent by 2010.
- – There will always be routine production that needs such work.

(continued . . .)

(. . . continued)

#7: + We have it this month (v. act.) on telephones by US Sprint; it will be a common feature in addition to the keyboard.
- – If at all, it will still be an added extra.
- – Percentage is too high.

#8: – Emphasis will be on prevention, not cure.
- + I base this on the views of a friend who is a biologist, chemist, and physician working in medical research.
- + Progress in science leads me to this belief.

#9: + I base this on the views of a friend who is a biologist, chemist, and physician working in medical research.

#11: + Even the small shops of 5–10 people are rapidly putting it in. If you don't have this capability, you may not get any subcontract work.

#12: – They have not changed that fast in the past ten years. Why should they in the next ten?

(Consensus) I still doubt it, but have no idea...Therefore will change my position towards the group's view.
- – Percentage is too high.

#13: – Depends on what is considered to be "structural steel." My definition is probably narrow in relation to the group.
- – Look at the use of carbon fiber in current high stress areas, free standing, i.e., sailboat masts.
- – The movement to alternative composites has lagged because consumers want cars, refrigerators, etc. that are "tough" i.e. made of steel.

APPENDIX C

Coordinating and Supervising Youth Apprenticeship Programs

The purpose of this study was to identify additional competencies the directors of high school career and technical education programs had to develop in order to administer youth apprenticeship programs. When the State of Wisconsin made a thrust to significantly increase the number of youth apprentice programs in Wisconsin high schools, there was a need to determine what program administration skills these directors needed to develop.

A number of high school administrators had been working with their programs for about one year. Thus, the decision was made to use a two-stage survey design process. The first stage was comprised of a brief survey with three open-ended questions (see the sample that follows). The questions were used to stimulate ideas. The third question was used to obtain input for a teacher survey. All administrators of high school youth apprenticeship programs received this survey.

Responses to the first two questions were used to write the competency statements that appear in the second survey. This survey was sent to all educators who were administering youth apprenticeship programs in Wisconsin. They were asked to identify the importance and their current skill level for each competency. A numeric rating scale format was selected for this survey in order to have quantitative data available for determining importance and competency levels and for identifying areas where training was needed.

The demographic items were included to provide information on the experiences of the respondents. Many of the program administrators had been employed in high schools for several years. However, some were from industry and were new to the high school setting or employed by an organization other than a high school. These items were also used to run summaries for subgroups of respondents.

The response confirmation form was included to provide a way for respondents to identify that they had mailed their survey. This provides a means of identifying nonrespondents without having people place their names on the surveys.

Coordinating and Supervising Youth Apprenticeship Programs

Directions: Use your experiences working with youth apprenticeship programs to respond to the following questions. You do not need to spend a lot of time on each question. Record the two or three things that come to mind first after you read each question.

1. What knowledge, skills, and competencies did you need to develop as you initiated and implemented your youth apprenticeship program?

2. What knowledge, skills, and competencies did you need to refine or expand as you initiated your youth apprenticeship program?

3. What competencies did teachers who worked with apprentices need to develop?

Thank you for responding. Please return in the enclosed envelope, or fax to (715) 555-1985.

Wisconsin University

Menomonie, Wisconsin 54751

Dr. John James
Director of South School Education
351 South St.
Plainfield, WI 54444

Dear Dr. James:

Recently you received a brief survey on the competencies needed by coordinators of youth apprenticeship programs. The responses to this survey have been used to identify a list of competencies. These competencies are included in the enclosed survey.

You can provide valuable information that will help teacher educators develop courses and workshops related to these competencies. Please use your experiences with your youth apprenticeship program to respond to the enclosed survey. It should take no longer than ten minutes to complete this survey. The results will be shared with teacher education departments in Wisconsin, DPI, Department of Workforce Development, and the State Technical College Board Staff.

All responses will be anonymous. Return the enclosed form to confirm that you have mailed the completed survey. A separate business reply envelope is provided for this form. Also, if you would like to receive a summary of the results, indicate this on the form.

Your participation in this survey is appreciated. If you have any questions, you can contact me at (715) 555-1382.

Sincerely yours,

Oskar Nelson, Director
Center for Career and Technical Education
WU
Center Building
100 3rd Ave.
Menomonie, WI 54751

mw

Enclosures:

Survey (1)
Business Reply Envelopes (2)

Youth Apprenticeship Program Management Skills

Directions: Use your experience with youth apprenticeship programs as the basis for answering the following questions. Respond twice to each question. In column A indicate how important each competency is to a person who directs, or coordinates a youth apprenticeship program. In column B, indicate your current level of skill in each competency area.

A: Importance

1 = NI = Not Important
2 = SI = Slightly Important
3 = MI = Moderately important
4 = I = Important
5 = VI = Very Important

B: Your Current Level of Skill

1 = L = Low
2 = NI = Needs Improvement
3 = A = Adequate
4 = G = Good
5 = E = Excellent

Competency	A. Importance NI 1	SI 2	MI 3	I 4	VI 5	B. Skill Level L 1	NI 2	A 3	G 4	E 5
The ability to										
1. complete the Wisconsin Youth Apprenticeship program process	1	2	3	4	5	1	2	3	4	5
2. apply child labor laws (knowledge of child labor laws)	1	2	3	4	5	1	2	3	4	5
3. apply youth apprenticeship program guidelines and goals to our program	1	2	3	4	5	1	2	3	4	5
4. revise our current program to meet youth apprenticeship requirements	1	2	3	4	5	1	2	3	4	5
5. promote program to students	1	2	3	4	5	1	2	3	4	5
6. promote the program to our teachers, counselors, and administrators	1	2	3	4	5	1	2	3	4	5
7. promote the program to parents	1	2	3	4	5	1	2	3	4	5
8. sell or recruit employers to participate in a youth apprenticeship program........	1	2	3	4	5	1	2	3	4	5
9. take initiative in contacting and asking businesses to participate (make cold calls)	1	2	3	4	5	1	2	3	4	5
10. understand the terms and language used *in* business and industry..............	1	2	3	4	5	1	2	3	4	5
11. learn the technical terms used in my youth apprenticeship areas	1	2	3	4	5	1	2	3	4	5
12. understand how business operates.......	1	2	3	4	5	1	2	3	4	5
13. balance what the state expects with what the worksite can provide	1	2	3	4	5	1	2	3	4	5
14. train/develop job site mentors	1	2	3	4	5	1	2	3	4	5
15. manage my time effectively	1	2	3	4	5	1	2	3	4	5
16. effectively organize activities (apply organizational skills)	1	2	3	4	5	1	2	3	4	5
17. lead or facilitate a group (meeting)	1	2	3	4	5	1	2	3	4	5
18. budget financial resources	1	2	3	4	5	1	2	3	4	5

Youth Apprenticeship
Program Management Skills (continued)

Competency	A. Importance NI 1	SI 2	MI 3	I 4	VI 5	B. Your Competency Level L 1	NI 2	A 3	G 4	E 5
The ability to										
19. network with other school districts, businesses, and organizations	1	2	3	4	5	1	2	3	4	5
20. work with technical college faculty and staff to deliver coursework, articulate credits, etc	1	2	3	4	5	1	2	3	4	5
21. interpret local labor market statistics to determine employer needs	1	2	3	4	5	1	2	3	4	5
22. develop a vocational curriculum	1	2	3	4	5	1	2	3	4	5
23 involve an advisory committee in making curriculum and program decisions	1	2	3	4	5	1	2	3	4	5
24. evaluate the effectiveness of the program	1	2	3	4	5	1	2	3	4	5
25. work with people who have different interests and goals	1	2	3	4	5	1	2	3	4	5
26. Other ____________________	1	2	3	4	5	1	2	3	4	5

Some demographic information—

Which of the following best decribes your employer?

____ 1. Business/Industry
____ 2. CESA
____ 3. Chamber of Commerce
____ 4. School District
____ 5. Technical College
____ 6. Other ______________________________

What job, or work experience, do you have in education?
(check all that apply)

____ 1. Administrator
____ 2. Counselor
____ 3. Local Vocational Education Coordinator (LVEC and/or STW Coordinator
____ 4. Teacher—Academic Area
____ 5. Teacher—Vocational Area
____ 6. Other ______________________________

How many years have you worked in education?

____ 1. Less than 1 Year
____ 2. 1–2 Years
____ 3. 3–5 Years
____ 4. 6–10 Years
____ 5. 11–20 Years
____ 6. 21 or More Years

Thank you for responding.
Please return to:
Oskar Nelson
Wisconsin University
Menomonie, WI 54751

Youth Apprenticeship Survey

Response Confirmation Form

Directions: After you have mailed your completed survey, complete this form and return it in a separate business reply envelope or fax to the number noted below.

Name ______________________________ Date ______________

Address ____

School/Organization __________________________________

City ____________________ State __________ Zip __________

If you want a summary of the results, check the box below.

☐ check for summary report

Return to: Oskar Nelson
WU
Menomonie, WI 54751

or fax to: (715) 555-1985

APPENDIX D

Likert Instrument

The following Likert instrument was developed to measure the school climate experienced by high school students who participated in a project that enrolled them in courses at a two-year technical college campus for part of the school day. The Likert technique was selected because it provided information on specific aspects of the students' experiences and also gave a total score that could be used to assess their overall experiences in the project and at the technical college. Also, the Likert format is familiar to most high school students and relatively easy for them to complete.

Items 1–24 are the Likert items. The responses to these items were scored with a computer program that weighted the responses based on how positive or negative they were and gave a total weighted score. A response summary was also generated for each item. Item 27 was included to obtain the students' overall perceptions of the climate. Responses to this item were correlated with the students' total scores to provide a concurrent validity check for the total scores. Item 29, distance traveled to the technical college campus, was included so that the impacts of commuting distances could be determined.

Health Program Survey

Directions: Please respond to the following items based on your experiences this school year. There are no right or wrong answers. Select the response that best represents your feelings. TC is used to identify our Technical College. If you have comments related to an item, write them under the item.

Use the following responses for the next section. Circle your responses.

1 = SD = Strongly Disagree
2 = D = Disagree
3 = U = Undecided
4 = A = Agree
5 = SA = Strongly Agree

Statements	SD 1	D 2	U 3	A 4	SA 5
1. I enjoy my classes at TC	1	2	3	4	5
2. The courses I am taking at TC relate directly to my career plans	1	2	3	4	5
3. My parents are supportive of my participation in the Health Academy	1	2	3	4	5
4. My TC instructors expect that I will do good work in their courses	1	2	3	4	5
5. My high school instructors feel that the Health Academy is worthwhile	1	2	3	4	5
6. Transportation from TC to my high school is a problem at times	1	2	3	4	5
7. Parking is often a problem at TC	1	2	3	4	5
8. Parking is often a problem at high school	1	2	3	4	5
9. My enrollment in the Health Academy program has created some significant problems in scheduling the high school classes I need	1	2	3	4	5
10. If I have a question about my courses or schedule at TC, I can get help from TC instructors and/or staff	1	2	3	4	5
11. Participating in the Health Academy at TC this year has caused me to reduce my participation in the music, art, and/or drama programs at my high school	1	2	3	4	5
12. Participating in the Health Academy has caused me to reduce my participation in extracurricular activities (sports, student clubs, etc.) this year	1	2	3	4	5
13. I have opportunities to interact with college students enrolled in other programs at TC	1	2	3	4	5
14. I feel at ease on the TC campus	1	2	3	4	5
15. I think that the Health Academy is a good program	1	2	3	4	5
16. Students in my TC classes are friendly	1	2	3	4	5
17. My instructors at TC encourage me to do good work in my classes	1	2	3	4	5
18. I am concerned about my grades in my health care courses at TC	1	2	3	4	5
19. My friends think that the Health Academy is a good program	1	2	3	4	5
20. My high school classmates are supportive of my participation in the Health Academy program	1	2	3	4	5

Health Program Survey (continued)

Statements	SD 1	D 2	U 3	A 4	SA 5
21. I will encourage students to enroll in the Health Academy program	1	2	3	4	5
22. The Health Academy Student Handbook was useful	1	2	3	4	5
23. I plan to continue in the Health Academy program next term	1	2	3	4	5
24. Participating in the Health Academy courses at TC this year has improved my study habits	1	2	3	4	5

25. Since beginning the Health Academy program last fall, my grade point average for my classes at my high school has:
    _______ 1. Improved
    _______ 2. Stayed the same
    _______ 3. Dropped

26. Since beginning the Health Academy program last fall, my school attendance has:
    _______ 1. Improved
    _______ 2. Stayed the same
    _______ 3. Dropped

27. What rating do you give to your experiences during this school year? Circle the number that represents your response.

Very Bad			**OK**			**Excellent**
1	2	3	4	5	6	7

28. How do your experiences this school year compare to those you had last year?

Much Worse			**Same**			**Much Better**
1	2	3	4	5	6	7

29. How far is your high school from the TC campus?
    _______ 1. 10 miles or less
    _______ 2. 11–20 miles
    _______ 3. 21–30 miles
    _______ 4. 31–40 miles
    _______ 5. 41 or more miles

30. When did you first enroll in the Health Academy program? _______________

31. What year/grade are you in school? _______________

32. How many classes did you take at your high school this term? _______________

Thank you for responding.

Please turn in your completed survey.

APPENDIX E

Sampling

Sampling involves selecting a representative subset of people, agencies, or businesses from the total group available. Sampling is used for a variety of reasons. It may be very expensive to contact the total population or group or it may be too time-consuming to attempt to contact everyone. The alternative is to identify a representative sample and use the time and resources available to obtain information from members of the sample. Research has shown that statistics from a sample are often more accurate than those from a survey of the total population. This results from the fact that it is usually possible to do a better job of contacting each person or organization involved in the sample and obtaining the information requested.

Sampling can be a complex process. However, for the types of samples used in needs assessment and task analysis studies, the sampling processes used are logical and relatively simple. This section will define essential concepts, discuss various types of samples, and present a sampling procedure.

Definitions

It is important to understand the main terms used in the discussion of sampling. Thus, the following definitions are offered to facilitate interpretation and use of the content of this section.

Population. A population is comprised of all the people, organizations, or companies that meet the criteria for the total group. For a follow-up study of one-year graduates in a program evaluation, the population would be all of the individuals who had graduated from the program one year ago. A needs assessment study to ascertain the need for improved computer skills in the workplace would use a population that included all of the companies and organizations in the region served by the school. This could include profit and non-profit organizations, depending on the focus of the study.

Criteria for selecting the appropriate population come from the purpose and objectives of the study. In the follow-up study example, if the purpose is to determine the effectiveness of the program, there is a need to obtain data from people who can provide insights on its impacts. If the study is concerned with graduates' transitions into the workplace, there will be an objective to this effect and one of the criteria for the population will be that it include recent graduates. In order to make an appropriate selection of graduates, "recent" will have to be defined in operational terms. Selecting "one-year" graduates would be a step toward an operational definition. However, the criterion should be further defined in terms of completion or graduation dates.

This study might also want to have input from the graduates' employers. If this is the case, another objective needs to specify this. From this, a second population of company managers and/or supervisors would be identified.

If there are problems in identifying the appropriate population(s) for a study, the purpose and objectives need to be reviewed and refined. The population must be an appropriate source of data for the study. The purpose and objectives must be clearly stated in order to make this judgment.

Sample. A sample is a subset or portion of the population. It is usually taken to determine the nature of the population.

Sampling Error. Survey results published in newspapers, journals, and reports usually carry a note on the size of the sampling error associated with the statistics reported. Readers often interpret this to mean that results from the surveys that use samples are not accurate. or not as accurate as those from a census in which everyone in the population is contacted. However, this is not true. Unless there is a 100% response in a census study, there are errors in the results. The challenges and complaints about the U.S. Census results attest to this fact.

Sampling error, as used in a scientific context, refers to the likely range within which the actual population value will fall. Usually, survey research reports identify a range within which the population value would fall if the entire population were surveyed and responded. This is typically stated as plus or minus a specific percent. For example, national opinion surveys often present results that have a sampling error of ±3%.

Sampling errors are normally distributed and the error is typically reported as plus or minus one standard deviation (one sampling error) from the value or percent found in the survey. There are approximately two chances in three that the population value will be within + or – one sampling error of the sample value. To illustrate this, consider the case of a national survey of public opinion on education. If 60% respond that there is enough emphasis on math in the school curriculum, and the sampling error is 3%, there are two chances out of three the population value is between 57% and 63%. In other words, if the entire population in the United States were surveyed, there are two chances in three that the population value will be somewhere between 57% to 63%.

The size of the sampling error is primarily determined by the size of the sample. Population size also has some impact. Larger sample sizes have smaller sampling errors. However, sample sizes are not determined as a percentage of population size. The section on sample sizes discusses this in more detail and presents a sample size chart.

It is also important to note that sampling error is not the same as the bias that may occur in the results because of low response rates. Low response rates are a problem when sampling or doing a census. Those responding may not be representative of the entire group. It is important to make an effort to contact at least a sample of nonrespondents to acquire their input and determine how it differs from that of the initial respondents. Including demographic items on the survey will also help to define the characteristics of those who have responded.

Types of Samples

Several types of samples are used in research studies. The objectives of the study and characteristics of the population guide the selection of the types of sample. The nature of the sampling frame may also have an impact on this choice. A sampling frame lists all of the members of a population.

Random Sample. The process of selecting a random sample ensures that each person or element in the population has an equal chance of being selected. In other words, being selected as a member of a random sample is based purely on chance. One random sampling method that many have observed is placing names in a hat and randomly selecting the number of names needed. In the age of the computer, software is often used to generate a random sample from a given population. If the names or identification labels for the members of the population are stored in a computer databank, it is relatively easy to obtain or write a program that will randomly select members from the population and print a list of names, addresses, and/or other data on the members of the sample. The names and addresses may be printed directly on mailing labels to facilitate a mail survey. A table of random numbers may also be used to select the members of a random sample. Tables of random numbers or digits are given in most statistics and research books.

Stratified Random Sample. In some instances it may be important to ensure that certain groups are adequately represented in the sample. For example, in a survey of local business and industry, in which only one or two companies are large, these companies could be omitted from a pure random sample. In order to ensure that one or more of these large companies would appear, the original population can be stratified by size of the business or industry and the companies can be randomly selected within each of these categories. In general, this is the process for selecting a stratified random sample. The purpose of the study will dictate what categories or groupings (strata) are important to be represented in the sample. If there is a possibility that a random sampling process might not select a person or element from that group within the population, a stratified random sampling process should be used.

The first step in selecting a stratified random sample is to identify the strata or groupings of interest within the population. After these have been identified, a random selection of members from within each stratum or group can be made. If there are a very small number of members within any given stratum, a proportionately larger sample can be selected from that group in order to have enough data to develop meaningful statistics. If a statewide sample of high school seniors is being selected, it would probably not be necessary to stratify the population on gender. This population is relatively large and the proportion of males and females is very similar. Therefore, it is likely that a sample drawn from this population would have an almost equal proportion of males and females. In fact, if the number of males and females was too disproportionate in the sample selected, one would probably question the outcome of the sampling technique. In contrast, if a needs assessment of college freshmen wants to determine the stresses faced by traditional and nontraditional students, the population should be stratified on this factor if the proportion of nontraditional students is relatively small.

Systematic Sample. This sample is selected by taking every Kth name or entry from a list of names. The value of K could be 5, 15, 20, 100 or more depending on the sample size needed and the size of the population. The formula for determining the value of K is K = N/n where N is the population size and n is the sample size needed. For example, if the population for a needs assessment is 800 and the sample size is 260, then the value of K is 3.07 (800 ÷ 260 = 3.07). Since a fraction of a person cannot be selected, K would be set at 3 and the sample would be slightly larger than 260. To identify the sample, the starting point would be randomly selected. A number between one and three would be identified with a table of random numbers or by drawing the number from a hat. After the starting point has been identified, every third name would be selected. If the number three, for example, were drawn as the starting point, the next names selected for the sample would be numbers 6, 9, 12, 15 and so forth.

This process works efficiently when there is a list or sampling frame from which to select the sample. The sampling frame is the complete list of the members of the population. It could be a phone book, employee roster, or a map that identifies and locates the companies in an area.

Systematic sampling is an efficient alternative when the sampling frame is not in a computer database or it is not possible to access this database. This is especially true when the population is relatively large. Also, it is a functional process for field research when there is limited access to computer databases or decisions must be made quickly.

The potential problems encountered when using systematic sampling need to be considered before using this sampling technique. When the sampling frame is ordered from large to small or small to large, some members of the list may be undersampled or left out depending on the starting point and the number of members with specific characteristics. For example, if the sampling frame for a needs assessment survey is organized by the size of annual sales and there are only a few companies with large annual sales, systematic sampling might fail to include any of these companies. In this situation it would be better to use a stratified random sample to ensure that companies with small, medium, and large sales are appropriately represented.

A problem can also be encountered when there is a periodic order or pattern in the sampling frame. For instance, some nationalities have last names that cluster under certain letters of the alphabet. It is possible to under or oversample a nationality depending on the starting point selected and the size of K. Another example would be when the sampling frame or list of names is structured by department. It would be possible to miss some departments, especially if some departments are small and K is larger than the size of these departments.

It is always a good idea to review the sample selected with any sampling technique. However, it is especially important to do this when systematic sampling is used to identify the sample. Check to see if these patterns and/or omissions cause the sample to not be representative of the population.

Cluster Sample. In cluster sampling, groups rather than individuals are selected for the sample. Groups are selected to provide a representative cross section of individuals. An example of an application of cluster sampling is the process used by the authors to select students for a college climate survey. The purpose of the study was to determine UW-Stout's students' perceptions of the academic and social climate at the university. Cluster sampling was selected to reduce costs, improve response rates, and save time. A random sample could have been selected, but is would have involved extensive labor and postage costs to prepare and mail the surveys. In addition, the anticipated response rate was low. In the cluster sampling process, subject matter areas that enrolled a representative cross section of the students were identified.

For example, almost all freshmen students take an English course. In order to make the freshmen sample representative, remedial, regular, and honors classes were selected for the sample. The number of each type reflected the number of students enrolled in each. Also, morning, midday, and afternoon classes were selected for the sample. There were no evening classes scheduled. Department heads in the subject matter areas involved agreed to ask the instructors of the classes in the sample to administer the survey at the beginning of a class session. This process worked very effectively. The response rate was very high, costs were moderate, and the survey study was completed in a relatively short period of time.

Judgmental Sample. Another type of sampling process sometimes used is one in which the researchers select people or elements from the population that they feel are appropriate for the sample needed in the study. In some instances, this may be a valid sample. If it is necessary to have people who are knowledgeable of a new technology or a particular problem area in order to identify needs related to the area, then a judgmental sample would be appropriate. If, however, the purpose of the study is to obtain data that can be generalized to the total population, then the judgmental sample is not appropriate. It is usually difficult to prove that a judgmental sample does not have some type of a bias. In addition, it is usually impossible to identify the exact nature and impacts of these biases.

The Delphi technique described in Chapter 2 uses a judgmental sample. Experts are selected to serve on the Delphi panel and provide input. Several years ago, the authors designed a Delphi study on the technological and social trends that would drive changes in Wisconsin. Because of the broad scope of the study, several panels of experts were selected. In each case, people who were very knowledgeable and aware of the trends in the area were selected. An effort was made to have people with a variety of perspectives on each panel.

Focus groups and case studies usually use judgmental samples. An advisory committee is also a judgmental sample.

Politics of Sampling

Sometimes there are considerations outside of the research or survey design realm that influence the sampling process. Some of these factors affect "buy-in" to the results. For instance, if the results from a sample of department members identify the need for a staff development program, the department members who were not surveyed might say "the survey results do not reflect my needs, I was never surveyed." If this is a potential problem, and it is not too difficult to include everyone, the survey should be given to all of the department members. In other situations there may be an attempt to "stack" the sample with people who have a specific point of view. If this is a problem, it would be better to design the study with a 100% sample as a sampling process.

Sample Sizes

Factors that influence sample size are the type of study, population size and diversity, degree of precision needed, and level of confidence desired. In addition, survey response rates may have an influence in some studies.

Minimum sample sizes of 25 to 30 are recommended for experimental and correlational research. These types of designs might be used in evaluating a program or a new curriculum. For example, one group might use a new approach to study statistical analysis, and the performance of students in this group would be compared with the performance of another group that used the traditional approach. Each group should have 25 to 30 students.

Sample sizes for survey studies are determined by the population size, degree of precision needed, and the level of confidence selected. In most cases the population size is known or a good estimate is available. If the population is relatively large, 2000 or more, a change of 300 to 500 in its size will not have a major impact on sample size.

Sample Sizes (*S*) Required for Given Population Sizes (*N*) with 5% Precision

N	*S*	*N*	*S*	*N*	*S*	*N*	*S*	*N*	*S*
10	10	100	80	280	162	800	260	2800	338
15	14	110	86	290	165	850	265	3000	341
20	19	120	92	300	169	900	269	3500	346
25	24	130	97	320	175	950	274	4000	351
30	28	140	103	340	181	1000	278	4500	354
35	32	150	108	360	186	1100	285	5000	357
40	36	160	113	380	191	1200	291	6000	361
45	40	170	118	400	196	1300	297	7000	364
50	44	180	123	420	201	1400	302	8000	367
55	48	190	127	440	205	1500	306	9000	368
60	52	200	132	460	210	1600	310	10,000	370
65	56	210	136	480	214	1700	313	15,000	375
70	59	220	140	500	217	1800	317	20,000	377
75	63	230	144	550	226	1900	320	30,000	379
80	66	240	148	600	234	2000	322	40,000	380
85	70	250	152	650	242	2200	327	50,000	381
90	73	260	155	700	248	2400	331	75,000	382
95	76	270	159	750	254	2600	335	100,000	384

Precision refers to the size of the sampling error that is acceptable for the study. This factor is termed "accuracy" in some books. For most training and educational decisions, 5% is an acceptable level of precision. When this is applied to actual results, it is ±5%.

Thus, if a survey found that 70% of the respondents wanted training and the precision level was ±5%, there are two chances in three that 70% ±5%, or 65% to 75% of the population, want training.

Some national opinion surveys use a ±3% precision level. The higher the precision level, the smaller the sampling error, the larger the sample needed. For a population of 50,000, a sample of 381 is needed to achieve a precision level of ±5%. To increase the precision level to ±3%, a sample of 1,045 is required.

Confidence level refers to the likelihood that the factors and outcomes previously discussed will hold true in an actual study. To illustrate this, consider a study of 300 instructors. According to the table, the sample size for this group with ±5% precision is 169. The sample of 169 instructors is surveyed and the results are tabulated. A question now arises, how certain are the researchers that the resulting ±5% will include the population values two times out of three?

This is a confidence question. The sample sizes in the table are based on 95% confidence. In other words, in 19 of 20 studies of this type, the population values will be included. Common confidence levels are 90%, 95%, and 99%. The higher the confidence level, the larger the sample required.

Other Factors. Other factors also can influence the choice of sample sizes. If the population is diverse and/or the opinions surveyed vary over a wide range, the sample size should be increased.

A decision must also be made at what analysis level the precision value will be applied. The previous example of 300 instructors required a sample of 169 for ±5% precision for the total sample. However, if it is important to distinguish between the opinions of beginning and continuing instructors, it may be necessary to set the sample sizes based on the size of each subgroup. If there are 50 new instructors and 250 continuing instructors, attaining ±5% precision for each group would require a sample of 44 new instructors and a sample of 152 continuing instructors. In this situation, a random sample stratified on tenure level (new/continuing) would be appropriate. Also, since the sample of 44 includes almost 90% of the new instructors, it would be logical to survey all of these instructors. Given the fact that there have been more contacts and interaction with the continuing instructors, this 100% sample of new instructors should not pose a public relations or political problem.

Another factor to consider when establishing sample sizes is the anticipated response rate. Increasing the sample size because response rates are projected to be low will *not* overcome the possible bias introduced by low response rates. However, it will provide more data and make it easier to detect patterns in the data. It would be appropriate to increase sample sizes to ensure that the number of respondents equals the sample size specified in the table (30 to 40 responses). If the number of respondents is equal to the required sample size, the precision level selected when determining the sample size will apply to the results. However, this will not remove the problem of the potential bias caused by the nonrespondents. The amount of bias in these results will need to be ascertained by other means, such as an intensive follow-up of a sample of nonrespondents.

Sampling Process

The following steps provide a general procedure for selecting a sample. In some steps, it may be necessary to refer back to the discussion of the related concepts in order to make the decisions required.

1. Review the purpose, objectives, and design of the study to determine the appropriate population.

2. Determine the best type of sample to select—random, stratified random, etc. The nature and availability of the sampling frame, time constraints, study design, and cost will all be factors in this decision.

3. Determine the degree of precision needed in the study and to what data analysis level, total group or subgroup, this degree of precision applies. Use the information on the table to select the sample size.

4. Select or construct the sampling frame for the population.

5. Use the sampling process selected to identify the sample.

6. Review the sample to see if there are any patterns or problems that would cause the sample and data from it to be challenged. If there are questions, resample from the population.

7. Use the sample in conducting the study.

APPENDIX F
DACUM Maps

In this appendix, two examples of a DACUM (developing a curriculum) map are provided.

In the first example, the Customer Service Representatives (CSR) DACUM map shows the duties and tasks performed for someone in the CSR occupation. The duties are identified on the left column and the tasks associated with each duty are identified in the adjacent row. A group of CSRs and supervisors participated in the development of this DACUM map.

In the second example, the Finance Youth Apprenticeship DACUM map shows the duties and tasks associated with the finance occupation. Basic skills related to general education and employable skills are also identified. The second portion of the map shows the four courses, their titles, and course objectives. The panel of experts from business and industry are listed at the end of the document.

Customer Service Representatives

Duties	Tasks/Competencies									
A. Using Computers	A.1 Use software	A.2 Use keyboard skills	A.3 Troubleshoot software	A.4 Troubleshoot computers						
B. Using Soft Skills	B.1 Apply interpersonal skills	B.2 Use appropriate language and terminology	B.3 Resolve conflicts	B.4 Communicate with supervisor	B.5 Use correct spelling and grammar	B.6 Record and interpret comments				
C. Assisting with Customers	C.1 Control call conversations	C.2 Provide customer service	C.3 Resolve complaints	C.4 Direct customers to appropriate resource	C.5 Take messages	C.6 Diffuse volatile situations				
D. Processing Claims	D.1 Identify insurance company requirements	D.2 Use profile book	D.3 Ask appropriate questions	D.4 Process orders	D.5 Respond to questions	D.6 Call shops with order information	D.7 Communicate with insurance company	D.8 Communicate with other departments	D.9 Perform claim inquiries	D.10 Resolve claim issues
E. Maintaining Company Standards	E.1 Follow policy and procedures	E.2 Adapt to new policies	E.3 Meet required expectations	E.4 Adapt to changing work environment	E.5 Participate in training					
F. Performing Additional Responsibilities	F.1 Assist other workers	F.2 Perform CSR coach responsibilities	F.3 Use office equipment	F.4 Distribute information	F.5 Update profile books					

Future Skills:

- Property
- Vehicle
- Computer
- Administration
- Business Terms and Regulations
- Claims

FINANCE YOUTH APPRENTICESHIP—DACUM
Finance Occupation Skills

Duties	Tasks/Competencies							
Perform Teller-Related Functions	Process incoming mail and respond to inquiries.*	Perform customer account inquries.*	Use filing system and technical devices for transactions.*	Use proper check endorsements and cashing policies.	Cross-sell products and services appropriately.*	Process personal depository and withdrawal functions.*	Process business depository and withdrawal functions.*	Process loan payments*
	Use security and compliance regulations in transactions.*	Process cash, noncash, and other negotiable items.*	Perform end-of-day cash balance.*	Follow appropriate security policies and procedures.*				
Perform New Accounts and Related Service Functions	Provide complete information on depository products to customer.*	Explain account options and assist customer in selecting appropriately.*	Explain regulatory requirements and ramifications of accounts to customer.	Complete documentation to open and close accounts.*	Process decedent accounts.*	Cross-sell products and services appropriately.*	Follow security and regulatory compliance procedures.*	
Perform Lending Functions	Explain various forms of credit and their importance.*	Explain loan policy.	Explain credit options.*	Explain appropriate credit contract to customer.	Complete documentation for loan requests.*	Order and evaluate credit reports properly.*	Evaluate credit (worthiness) and make loan recommendation.*	Use credit records to process payments and payoffs.*
	Complete loan closing.*	Process and perform collection functions.*	Follow security and regulatory compliance procedures.*	Cross-sell products and service appropriately.*				
Perform Customer Support Functions	Respond to customer account inquiries.*	Produce and analyze simple statistics.*	Explain and perform check clearing process.*	Post items to account. (item posting)*	Process return items. (return item posting)*	Retrieve and apply data from data storage system.*	Cross-sell products and services appropriately.*	Follow security and regulatory compliance procedures.*
Perform Accounting Operations and Functions	Explain general ledger and accounting structure.*	Produce accounting documentation.*	Identify costs and profits of employer.*	Determine profitability of customer relationship.*	Identify reports that must be filed. (federal/ state)*	Produce and analyze simple statistics.*	Post items to account. (item posting)*	Process accounts payable.*
	Retrieve and apply data from data storage system.*	Follow security and regulatory compliance procedures.*						

* Indicates tasks/functions that could invovle computer applications

FINANCE YOUTH APPRENTICESHIP—DACUM

Basic Skills

Duties	Tasks				
Communication Skills	Listen to interpreters	Listen to questions in order to respond appropriately.	Write organized,concise, and grammatically correct memos and letters.	Present information orally in an organized manner.	Ability to work in teams.
Mathematics Skills	Calculate percentages.	Solve basic interest problems.	Solve basic linear equations.		
Computer Skills	Use proper keyboarding techniques.	Operate computer keyboard.	Operate ten-key calculator.		

Employability Skills

Duties	Tasks				
Skills	Prepare a resume.	Write a cover letter applying for a finance job.	Produce a business letter using the appropriate margins, indents, tabs, etc.	Identify strategies for locating job openings including networking.	Complete a job application form.
	Demonstrate job interview skills.	Follow up job interview with a letter or phone call promptly.	Evaluate employment benefit packages.	Assess/compare job offers.	

FINANCE YOUTH APPRENTICESHIP—DACUM
Coursework Related to Identified Duties & Tasks

Course Title	Course Objectives							
Principles of Depository Institutions	Illustrate understanding of American evolution of banking.[2]	Differentiate between depository institutions.[2]	Use negotiable instruments.[1]	Identify different types of endorsements and ramifications of each.[1]	Interrelate deposit payment and credit functions and their importance.[1]	Identify and properly handle counterfeit currency.[1]	Understand the money supply and how it affects the ecomomy.[2]	List products and services offered by depository institutions.[2]
	Choose appropriate services for customer.[1]	Illustrate an understanding of government regulation of industry.[1]	Identify regulators responsible for various financial institutions.[2]	Differentiate between demand and time deposits.[1]	Explain the concepts of liquidity safety and profitability.[1]	Define and use industry terminology.[1]	Recognize the need for confidentiality.[1]	
Marketing for Depository Institutions	Understand need for marketing in depository institutions.[1]	Illustrate interrelationship between management and marketing philosophy.[2]	Give examples of market segmentation applicable to depository institutions.[1]	Discuss impact of environment issues of firm's marketing plan.[2]	Illustrate basic pricing strategies.[1]	Illustrate impact of direct marketing and public relations.[1]	Describe relationship between cross-selling and good customer service.[1]	Describe services offered by firm in customer orientation fashion.[1]
	Apply basic selling techniques to financial products.[1]	Market self through professional image.[1]						
The Law and Depository Institutions	Recognize significance of contract between firm and account holder.[1]	List requirements of negotiability.[1]	Explain protections of holder in due course.[1]	Understand application of agency law to firm/customer and firm/employee.[1]	Apply credit protection laws to retail lending situations.[1]	Differentiate between real and personal property and forms of concurrent ownership.[1]	Be familiar with impact of bankruptcy law on depository institutions.[2]	Understand concepts of APR and APY.[1]
	Research impact of current regulations on industry.[2]	Be familiar with basic torts and crimes that affect financial institutions.[1]						
Depository Institutions Operations	Define regulatory framework of various institutions.[2]	Explain the U.S. payment system.[1]	Describe the check collection process.[1]	Identify rules and practices that govern demand deposit activities.[1]	Describe electronic components of U.S. payment system.[1]	Illustrate how depository institutions create money.[2]	List cash management services that might be offered to customers.[2]	Explain importance of internal controls in cash and check processing.[1]
	Explain income statement and balance sheet of institution.[1]	Reconcile checking account statement.[1]	Identify risks involved in check processing.[1]					

[1] Need to know [2] Nice to know

APPENDIX G

Program Evaluation Instruments

Two surveys designed to obtain feedback on programs are included in this appendix. Designing the two instruments posed different challenges. The mine safety group was interested in determining the face validity and value of their certification examination. Also, the group wanted suggestions for improving their examination. The Wisconsin Career Counseling Center Workshop Survey was designed to assess the impacts of a workshop conducted for the counseling center staff.

The Certified Mine Safety Examination was administered to a group of experienced mine safety specialists. They had received their test results before the survey was mailed. The committee of mine safety professionals that developed the certification examination was interested in the examinees' perceptions of the face validity, accuracy, value of the test, and test results. The following Certified Mine Safety Examination Survey was based on the measurement concepts of validity and reliability. Examinees were asked to indicate if the test contents were relevant, had covered all important knowledge areas, and had placed appropriate emphasis on each area. They were also asked if their scores were appropriate to their competency levels. Space was provided after each question to encourage written comments and suggestions.

The design of the Wisconsin Career Counseling Center Workshop Survey was based on the objectives and the content of a workshop offered for center staff and secondary school educators. The career counseling centers were housed in a regional facility and provided services to middle schools and high schools in the region. The first section of the survey was concerned with the various ways educators at the school level could develop stronger working relationships with the center in their region. The second section was focused on the extent to which educators had increased their discussion of career development concepts and had used more activities related to this area. The items in this section were given a rating scale that indicated five levels of use. In the last section, educators were asked to identify the career counseling center and community resources they used. Workshop participants were asked to identify what had helped or hindered their career development work during the school year.

Certified Mine Safety Examination Survey

Directions: Use your experience sitting for the Certified Mine Safety Examination (CMSE) to answer the following statements and questions. Use the following responses. Also, space has been provided for comments.

1 = SD = Strongly Disagree
2 = D = Disagree
3 = SID = Slightly Disagree
4 = ? = Undecided, or Not Enough Information to Answer
5 = SIA = Slightly Agree
6 = A = Agree
7 = SA = Strongly Agree

Certified Mine Safety Exam Characteristics	Responses SD 1	D 2	SID 3	? 4	SIA 5	A 6	SA 7
1. The exam (CMSE) tests relevant information and knowledge...... Comments:	1	2	3	4	5	6	7
2. The CMSE covered all topics/areas of knowledge that mine safety professionals need to know...... Comments: (If you disagree, identify the changes needed)	1	2	3	4	5	6	7
3. Some areas of knowledge were emphasized *too* much... Comments: (If you agree, please identify the area.)	1	2	3	4	5	6	7
4. There was an appropriate balance between the areas/topics contained in the exam. (In other words, the number of questions and test points assigned to each topic were appropriate.)...... Comments:(If you disagree, identify the changes needed.)	1	2	3	4	5	6	7
5. My test score was an accurate indicator of my knowledge...... Comments:	1	2	3	4	5	6	7
6. Sitting for the CMSE was a worthwhile experience for me...... Comments:	1	2	3	4	5	6	7

(continued . . .)

(. . . continued)

7. How much time did you spend preparing for the CMSE?

____ 1. None	____ 5. 11–20 hours
____ 2. 2 hours or less	____ 6. 21–30 hours
____ 3. 3–5 hours	____ 7. 31–40 hours
____ 4. 6–10 hours	____ 8. 41 hours or more

8. What level of certification did you achieve as a result of your performance on the CMSE?
   ____ 1. Mine Safety Trainee
   ____ 2. Mine Safety Technician
   ____ 3. Assoc. MSP
   ____ 4. CMSP

9. How many times did you sit for the CMSE? ________

10. How could the CMSE examination and test process be improved?

11. What follow-up activities have you undertaken as a result of taking the CMSE?

12. Any other suggestions for improving the CMSE?

Thank you for responding. Please return this form to:

Oskar Nelson
CTE/WU
Menomonie, WI 54751

Also, return the enclosed Survey Return Confirmation Card in the second envelope.

CMSE Survey Return Confirmation

I have completed and returned the CMSE Survey.

Name: ______________________________ Date: ______________

Your response is appreciated. Please return this form in the second business reply envelope provided.

Oskar Nelson
CTE/WU
Menomonie, WI 54751

Wisconsin Career Counseling Center
Workshop Survey

A. List the last four digits of your social security number ________.
(NOTE: This will help us correlate the information collected on this survey with the information collected at the end of the workshop last fall. No names will be used in our analyses and the last four digits will not compromise the security of your social security number.)

B. Reinforcement of state-level guidelines in development of local plans. Indicate what types of activities you used during this school year. (Check all that apply.)

Resources	**Response** (Check all that apply)
Helping to build bridges between the Career Center and our school district.	
1. Include Career Center staff in local planning of district career development program	______
2. Work with Career Center staff in development of non-duplicative local service for students. (Develop provisions for coordination of referrals, assessment results, etc.)	______
3. Use resources to mutually benefit Career Centers and school career development program (e.g., form consortia for licensing fees, making joint purchases, etc.)........	______
4. Develop electronic linkages with Career Center. (e.g., e-mail, connect to Center Web Site, etc.)	______
5. Other: ____________________	______

C. Career Development Topics

Directions: To what extent did you increase the use of the following topics/concepts in your educational activities during 2003–2004? You can add more topics at the end of this section. Use one of the following responses.

1 = NO = No/Did Not Use
2 = NOI = Did Not Increase Use
3 = S = Some Increase
4 = M = Much
5 = E = Extensive Increase

Career Development Topics/Concepts	**Responses** NO 1	NOI 2	S 3	M 4	E 5
Help students learn how to:					
6. Relate school courses and experiences to work/jobs........	1	2	3	4	5
7. Understand the education requirements for various jobs in our community	1	2	3	4	5
8. Measure and identify interests and aptitudes	1	2	3	4	5
9. Relate (connect) their interests and aptitudes to job requirements	1	2	3	4	5
10. Use a variety of resources, such as WCIS, DISCOVER, and the Internet, to obtain information on jobs, careers and educational programs........	1	2	3	4	5

(continued . . .)

Career Development Topics/Concepts	**Responses** NO 1	NOI 2	S 3	M 4	E 5
Help students learn how to: (continued)					
11. Relate the content in various courses to jobs that are related to their career plans	1	2	3	4	5
12. Develop career goals	1	2	3	4	5
13. Select a career path	1	2	3	4	5
14. Develop a career plan	1	2	3	4	5
15. Select courses that relate to their career goals	1	2	3	4	5
16. Prepare a resume	1	2	3	4	5
17. Obtain work experience in business or industry	1	2	3	4	5
18. Identify the post-high-school education and training they need	1	2	3	4	5
19. Other: ______	1	2	3	4	5
20. Other: ______	1	2	3	4	5

Resources	**Response** (Check all that apply)
21–30. What type of resources did you use this year to carry out the activities you noted above? (Check all that apply)	
21. Take students to the Career Center	______
22. Take teachers and other staff to the Career Center	______
23. Have Career Center staff visit our school and present to students	______
24. Have Career Center staff visit our school and present to staff members	______
25. Borrow Career Center materials for use in our school	______
26. Involve more people from business and industry in our career development program	______
27. Construct more career development experiences for our students	______
28. Involve parents more in our career planning activities	______
29. Other: ______	______
30. Other: ______	______

31. What helped your career development work this year?

32. What hindered your career development work this year?

33. Which of the following best describes your position? (Check one.)

____ 1. Teacher

____ 2. Counselor

____ 3. Administrator

____ 4. STW Coordinator

____ 5. Other ______

(continued . . .)

(. . . continued)

34. Which of the following best describes your use of Career Center resources *last year* (2003–2004)?

____ 1. I did not use them

____ 2. I made some use of them

____ 3. I made extensive use of them

____ 4. I made very extensive use of them

35. Which of the following best describes your use of Career Center resources *this year* (2004–2005)?

____ 1. I did not use them

____ 2. I made some use of them

____ 3. I made extensive use of them

____ 4. I made very extensive use of them

Thank you for responding.

Please return to:

Oskar Nelson
WU
Center Building
Menomonie, WI 54751

APPENDIX H
Occupational Analysis Sources

Several sources are identified in this appendix for instructors and trainers to research existing occupational analyses.

Occupational Analysis Sources
American Society for Training & Development Members may use the research services for occupational and job analyses. This is an especially effective source for industrial trainers. (www.astd.org/ASTD.html)
Career and Technical Education Homepage The office of Vocational and Adult Education is a rich resource of government publications in occupations. (www.ed.gov/about/offices/list/ovae/index.html)
Center for Occupational Research and Development The Center for Occupational Research and Development (CORD) is a resource of occupational analyses in selected areas mainly dealing with education. (www.cord.org/)
Colleges and Universities Most colleges and universities have sections within their libraries that house curriculum guides that, in some cases, contain occupational analyses.
Curriculum Coordination Centers There are federally funded curriculum coordination centers designed to provide technical assistance for people providing training programs. To locate the curriculum center for your state, call the vocational education division of your state department of education for the address and telephone number of the curriculum coordination center.
DACUM Information System The DACUM Information System site catalogs DACUM charts. These are used primarily for education and training programs in Canada and the United States.
Education Resources Information Center (ERIC) System Occupational and task analyses are available on-line or on microfiche. Requesting an ERIC (available on EDSCOHost) search will result in job analyses, occupational analyses, or task analyses for the job or jobs being analyzed.
International Society for Performance Improvement This is another professional training and development association that will perform selected occupational and task analysis searches if you are a member. (www.ispi.org/) (continued . . .)

(. . . continued)

Internet
The Internet has many excellent examples of task analyses. A search of the term "task analysis" using any of the search engines will produce excellent results.

The National Research Center in Career and Technical Education
The national center, funded by federal dollars, researches and catalogs occupational analyses.
(www.nccte.org)

O*NET Online
O*Net is an online occupational information network.
(http://online.onetcenter.org/)

Publications of the American Association of Community Colleges
This publication lists guidelines for program planners, facility guides, and curriculum guides. (www.aacc.nche.edu)

U.S. Department of Commerce, National Technical Information Service
The U.S. Department of Commerce uses occupational analyses for training.
(www.ntis.gov)

The U.S. Military
The U.S. Military has developed and used task inventories for training. They are available from the following:

- Personnel Research Laboratory
  Lackland Air Force Base, Texas 78236
- Headquarters, U.S. Marine Corps, Office of Manpower Utilization
  Marine Corps Development and Education Command
  Quantico, Virginia, 22314.
- The Human Resources Research Organization (HumRRO)
  66 Canal Center Plaza, Suite 400
  Alexandria, VA, 22314
  (source of military and civilian inventories and analyses)
  (www.humrro.org)

Vocational Consortium
This group of states works cooperatively with member states to develop occupational analyses. These analyses are developed into curriculum guides that can be purchased.

- MAVC
  1515 W. 6th Avenue
  Stillwater, OK 74074

The Vocational-Technical Education Consortium of States (VTECS)
VTECS has developed several task analysis handbooks of duties, tasks, procedures for instruction, and criterion reference measures.
(www.v-tecs.org/)

APPENDIX I

Methods for Lesson Plan Organization

The following chart should be helpful to any instructor or trainer considering different types of teaching methods. The possible teaching methods are listed in the left column. The next two columns identify advantages and disadvantages of each teaching method. The last column to the right lists lesson plan considerations to use with each type of teaching method. All of these should be considered when planning and implementing instruction.

Methods for Lesson Plan Organization

Teaching Method	Advantages	Disadvantages	Lesson Planning
Lecture	• Presents factual material in direct, logical manner • Contains experience that inspires • Stimulates thinking to open discussion • Is useful for large groups	• Experts are not always good teachers • Audience is passive • Learning is difficult to gauge • Communication is one-way	• Needs clear introduction and summary • Need time and content limit to be effective • Should include examples, anecdotes
Lecture with discussion	• Involves audience after the lecture • Audience can question, clarify, and challenge	• Time may limit discussion period • Quality is limited to quality of questions and discussion	• Requires that questions be prepared prior to discussion
Panel of experts	• Allows experts to present different opinions • Can provide better discussion than a one-person discussion • Frequent change of speaker keeps attention from lagging	• Experts may not be good speakers • Personalities may overshadow content • Subject may not be in logical order	• Facilitator coordinates focus of panel, introduces, and summarizes • Panel is briefed
Brainstorming	• Is listening exercise that allows creative thinking for new ideas • Encourages full participation because all ideas equally recorded • Draws on group's knowledge and experience • Spirit of congeniality is created • One idea can spark off other ideas	• Can be unfocused • Needs to be limited to 5–7 minutes • People may have difficulty getting away from known reality • If not facilitated well, criticism and evaluation may occur	• Facilitator selects issue • Must have some ideas if group needs to be stimulated
Videotapes	• Entertaining way of teaching content and raising issues • *Keep group's attention* • Looks professional • Stimulates discussion	• Can raise too many issues to have a focused discussion • *Discussion may not have full participation* • Is only as effective as following discussion	• Trainer needs to set up equipment • Effective only if facilitator prepares *questions to discuss after viewing*
Class discussion	• Pools ideas and experiences from group • Is effective after a presentation, film, or experience that needs to be analyzed • Allows everyone to participate in an active process	• Not practical with more than 20 people • A few people can dominate • Others may not participate • Is time-consuming • Can get off track	• Requires careful planning by facilitator to guide discussion • Requires question outline

Small group discussion	• Allows participation of everyone • People often more comfortable in small groups • Can reach group consensus	• Needs careful thought as to purpose of group • Groups may get sidetracked	• Facilitator needs to prepare specific tasks or questions for group to answer
Case studies	• Develops analytic and problem-solving skills • Allows for exploration of solutions for complex issues • Allows student to apply new knowledge and skills	• People may not see relevance to their own situation • Insufficient information can lead to inappropriate results	• Case must be clearly defined in some cases • Case study must be prepared
Role playing	• Introduces problem situation dramatically • Provides opportunity for people to assume roles of others and thus appreciate another point of view • Allows for exploration of solutions • Provides opportunity to practice skills	• People may be too self-conscious • Not appropriate for large groups • People may feel threatened	• Trainer has to define problem situation and roles clearly • Trainer must give very clear instructions
Report-back sessions	• Allows for large group discussion of role plays, case studies, and small group exercise • Gives people a chance to reflect on experience • Each group takes responsibility for its operation	• Can be repetitive if each small group says the same thing	• Trainer has to prepare questions for groups to discuss
Worksheets/ surveys	• Allows people to think for themselves without being influenced by others • Individual thoughts can then be shared in large group	• Can be used for only a short period of time	• Facilitator has to prepare handouts
Index card exercise	• Opportunity to explore different and complex issues	• People may not do exercise	• Facilitator must prepare questions
Guest speaker	• Personalizes topic • Breaks down audience's stereotypes	• May not be a good speaker	• Contact speakers and coordinate • Introduce speaker appropriately
Values clarification exercise	• Opportunity to explore values and beliefs • Allows people to discuss values in a safe environment • Gives structure to discussion	• People may not be honest • People may be too self-conscious	• Facilitator must carefully prepare exercise • Must give clear instructions • Facilitator must prepare discussion questions

APPENDIX J

Level I Evaluation Instrument

The purpose of this form was to collect evaluation feedback from participants in a two-week workshop on statistics and process control. The results were used to assess the participants' reactions to the workshop and to improve the design of the future workshops in the series.

A Likert-type response format was selected because it permitted a mix of items that would not have fit as well with another type of rating scale. Also, most participants were familiar with this format.

This instrument is typical of those that would be used in Level I of Kirkpatrick's evaluation model. It collects the participants' opinions, thoughts, and conclusions about the training workshop. The workshop instructors designed this instrument to provide information that would help them improve the design of the workshop and the quality of instruction. For example, responses to item 8 indicated whether the workshop started at the right level and contained new content. The pace of instruction is assessed in items 15 and 16. Applications of workshop content to practical problems and the participants' plans to use some of the techniques presented are covered in items 5, 6, 7, and 14. The open-ended questions at the end of the survey give the participants an opportunity to comment on any aspect of the workshop. The suggestions given to improve the workshop were especially helpful.

Statistics and Process Control Program Evaluation

Directions: Respond to each of the following statements based on your experiences in this training program.

1 = SD = Strongly Disagree
2 = D = Disagree
3 = U = Undecided
4 = A = Agree
5 = SA = Strongly Agree

Characteristics of the Training Program	Responses SD 1	D 2	U 3	A 4	SA 5
1. This program was enjoyable	1	2	3	4	5
2. I enjoyed using MINITAB®	1	2	3	4	5
3. MINITAB® can be helpful in my work	1	2	3	4	5
4. I gained a better understanding of statistics	1	2	3	4	5
5. I will be able to use the contents of this training program	1	2	3	4	5
6. I liked the opportunity to work with my own data	1	2	3	4	5
7. There should be more opportunity to apply the contents to practical problems related to my work	1	2	3	4	5
8. I knew most of the content of this training program before we started the sessions	1	2	3	4	5
9. I learned a lot	1	2	3	4	5
10. The instructors' explanations were clear	1	2	3	4	5
11. The instructors effectively answered questions	1	2	3	4	5
12. The instructors were able to relate the content of this training program to practical problems	1	2	3	4	5
13. The instuctors were well prepared	1	2	3	4	5
14. I plan to use some of the techniques presented	1	2	3	4	5
15. Too many topics were included in the program	1	2	3	4	5
16. Too few topics were included in the program	1	2	3	4	5
17. The visuals were helpful	1	2	3	4	5
18. The handouts were helpful	1	2	3	4	5

19. How could this training be improved? ____________________

____

20. What did you like best about the training program? ____________________

____

APPENDIX K
Analyzing Needs and Performance Data

This appendix focuses on strategies and techniques that can be used to select appropriate analysis procedures and develop information for decision making. Common descriptive statistics are defined, discussed, and linked with appropriate measurement levels. The discussions in this appendix are general and are oriented to appropriate use and interpretation of data. For more detailed information, the reader should refer to the research methods referenced at the end of this appendix. Specific statistical and survey software are not listed. There are several packages that will work effectively and some readers will find that a spreadsheet will be adequate.

Significance and hypothesis testing are not discussed, although they may be appropriate when pre/post and group comparisons are done. Information on these types of tests is given in the references. Also, the assistance of a statistician would be appropriate.

This appendix includes several activities for the preprocessing review. These include suggestions for survey design and a final quality check prior to distributing the survey. Techniques for reviewing and editing the completed survey are also included.

MEASUREMENT LEVELS

The type of data collected by a needs assessment, occupational survey, or program-evaluation instrument has a direct influence on the type of data analysis used. A question that asks respondents to indicate at what location they work generates different data than a question that asks them to rate their skill level in performing a task. An effective way to determine the appropriate analysis type is to determine the measurement level used in the question and the type of statistics needed to meet the objectives of the study. (Note: If the measurement level and statistical data needed are not congruent, the question will need to be revised.)

Four levels of measurement are commonly identified by statisticians: nominal, ordinal, interval, and ratio. These four levels and related sample survey items are discussed in more detail in the pages that follow. Also, a table that identifies appropriate statistics for each measurement level is presented at the end of this section.

Nominal

At the nominal level of measurement, numbers are used as labels for discrete groups or categories. An example would be a question that identifies the site or location at which respondents work. In the example below, the numbers represent four distinct sites. The individuals conducting the study are interested in the number responding at each site and what percent of the total respondents come from each site.

- At which of the following sites do you work?

  _____ (1) Day
  _____ (2) Mytown
  _____ (3) Prosper
  _____ (4) Twin Cities

This item might also be used to run a cross-tabulation or breakout by site. Often, survey analysis software will generate summaries based on how people respond to a given item. In this case, a cross-tabulation would give a summary for each of the four sites. These summaries can be used to tailor educational programs for each site if there are major differences.

Ordinal

An ordinal scale places categories or objects in an ordered sequence from high to low, or vice versa. However, the categories or intervals are not the same size. An item that is often used in needs and performance assessment studies that produces ordinal level data is one that requests educational level. In the sample item below, six levels of education are sequenced from lower to higher levels of attainment.

- Which of the following best identifies the highest education level you have attained? (Select only one response.)

  _____ (1) Less than high school diploma
  _____ (2) High school diploma or equivalent
  _____ (3) Technical service/trade school
  _____ (4) Some college
  _____ (5) Two-year degree/diploma
  _____ (6) Bachelor's degree
  _____ (7) Graduate degree

In this example, the amount of study required at each level varies; thus, the interval or category sizes vary. However, the sequence does represent lower to higher levels of educational attainment.

For this scale, the median can be used to describe the typical level of education of a sample group. (The median and other statistical measures are discussed in more detail later in this appendix.) It may also be useful to report the number and percentage in each educational level.

Interval

At the interval level of measurement, the intervals are the same size. A weather reporter commonly uses interval level measurement when reporting the daily temperatures. Each degree unit is the same size, and zero is an arbitrary point on the scale. This is true of both the Fahrenheit and Celsius scales. Test scores are also frequently treated as interval level measurements.

Figure K-1 presents a DACUM scale for an occupational analysis. Most curriculum developers and researchers assume that this is an interval scale.

FIGURE K-1

Tasks	Performance Level N 1	MA 2	SA 3	DO 4	SK 5	T 6
(1) Upload photo from camera to computer...	1	2	3	4	5	6
(2) Crop photo with software......................	1	2	3	4	5	6

Scale

1 = N = cannot do
2 = MA = can do with much assistance
3 = SA = can do with some assistance
4 = DO = can do without assistance
5 = SK = can do skillfully/quickly
6 = T = can teach to others

The mean, or arithmetic average, can be used to depict the typical response or score on an interval scale. In the example, it is assumed that each increase in skill level, or each interval, is the same size. Variability in the responses can be described with the standard deviation. All of the statistics used at the lower levels of measurement can also be used to describe the results.

Ratio

A ratio level measurement scale has an ordered sequence of equal-sized intervals and a point that represents the absence of the entity being measured. Some examples of interval measures are weight, time, and length. Any of the statistics used at the previous levels of measurement can be used with interval data. In addition, ratios can be calculated and used. For example, consider the following item that is often included in needs and occupational assessments. The possible responses to this item are ratio level data since the time unit (year) is the same amount of time per unit and zero indicates no instructional experience.

- How many years have you worked as an instructor? ___ years.

A mean and standard deviation can be calculated for the responses from a group to indicate the group members' typical level of instructional experience and the variation in the length of their experience. In addition, ratios can be calculated. For example, the instructor with four years of teaching experience has twice as much experience as the instructor with two years of experience.

Much of the data collected for needs and performance assessments will be interval level or lower. However, several criteria used to evaluate the technical education and training are measured at the ratio level. Time required to complete a task, unit costs, cycle time, and sales volume are all examples.

Measurement Levels and Statistics

Various types of questions or survey items generate different types of data. Each of these item types are valid if they provide useful data. Each higher level of measurement provides more information, thus the level selected should match the information needs of the study. Also, appropriate data analysis techniques must be used.

The information in Figure K-2 will help in selecting appropriate statistical analysis processes. Measurement levels are given in the left-hand column. The center column lists the statistics used to denote the typical value of a set of responses. These are also called measures of central tendency. Appropriate indicators of variability for each measurement level are listed in the right-hand column.

To illustrate the use of this information, consider the development of the survey item designed to identify education level from the previous section. The first step is to determine that this information is relevant to the needs assessment or occupational analysis being conducted. Next, the amount of data needed on educational attainment must be determined. Is it adequate to only know if the respondents are high school or college graduates? In the example used, it was decided to request more specific data by listing response choices that range from less than a high school diploma to graduate school. These response choices and the resulting scale are ordinal. When compared to the measurement levels in Figure K-2, it is apparent that the useful statistics are the median and range. It may be helpful to report the number (frequency) and percent of respondents in each educational category.

FIGURE
K-2

Measurement Level	Statistics For: Typical Value	Statistics For: Variability
Nominal	mode, *f*, *p*, %	% in each category
Ordinal	median	range or IQR
Interval	mean ($\overline{X}$)	standard deviation (*s*)
Ratio	mean ($\overline{X}$)	standard deviation (*s*)

Key to symbols:

f = frequency
IQR = interquartile range
p = proportion
% = percent
s = standard deviation
X = individual score or response value
$\overline{X}$ = average score or value

The final step in this review process is to answer the question, "Does this survey question provide data needed for this study and the curriculum decisions that need to be made?" If the answer is no, the item will have to be redesigned or omitted.

DESCRIPTIVE STATISTICS

The emphasis in this section is on selecting appropriate statistics and interpreting them correctly. Procedures for calculating statistical values will not receive much attention. Software is available that will efficiently handle the calculations and processing needed. Also, there are many statistics books that go into detail in presenting formulas for these statistics and discussing calculation processes. Several statistics books are referenced at the end of this appendix.

One of the purposes of statistics is to synthesize the information in a set of data to facilitate understanding and help make decisions. Several statistics commonly used in curriculum development and evaluation studies are discussed in this section with examples to demonstrate their use.

Frequency (*f*)

Frequency is the number of responses made in a specific category. It is sometimes referred to as a tally. Figure K-3 presents data related to the survey item in the discussion of nominal level measurement.

The column labeled *n* contains the frequency counts for each response. Sometimes frequency (*f*) will be used in place of *n*. However, *n* is more commonly used. Also, *n* will appear again in later parts of this discussion.

FIGURE
K-3

Facility Site	*n*	%
(1) Day	2	10
(2) Mytown	6	30
(3) Prosper	2	10
(4) Twin Cities	10	50
Total	N = 20	100

A lowercase n is used to identify the number in a sample or subpart of a larger group. For example, in Figure K-3, the n for Day is 2. An uppercase N is used to denote the size of a population or total group, in this case, 20. The n, or frequency, for each site in Figure K-3 indicates the groups or sites represented in the survey data and the number of people responding from each site. Since the Twin Cities and Mytown sites have 16 of the 20 respondents, they have the most impact on the outcome of the survey.

Proportion (p) and Percent (%)

Proportion (p) is determined by dividing the number in the subgroup by the total group size ($p = n \div N$). In Figure K-3, the proportion of respondents from the Twin Cities is 0.5 ($p = 10 \div 20$).

The percentage is calculated by multiplying the proportion by 100 ($\% = p100$ or $[n \div N]100$). The percentage of respondents from the Twin Cities is 50% ($[10 \div 20]100$).

Either proportion or percentage can be used in analyzing and reporting results. Percentages tend to be used more frequently, and as a result, people are more familiar with them. Also, it is easier to discuss numbers in the form of percentages than proportions; for example, 50% of the respondents are from the Twin Cities versus 0.5 of the respondents are from the Twin Cities.

Percentages and proportions are useful in identifying the relative size of subgroups, as shown in the site data from Figure K-3. In addition, they are very helpful when comparing sets of data from groups that have different numbers of people.

Measures of Central Tendency

In a needs assessment or occupational analysis it is necessary to compare the results to an established performance criterion. It is also necessary to contrast the importance of tasks in the study in order to make decisions on what content to include in a course, what emphasis to place on various content elements, and what sequence to use. This decision making process is easier if there is a summary statistic that represents the typical value of the responses. The measures of central tendency provide representative or typical values for a set of data. The three measures of central tendency are mean, median, and mode.

Mean. The mean is the arithmetic average of the values or scores in a set of data. To obtain the mean for a set of data, add the individual scores and divide by the number of scores in the set. The formula for calculating the mean is:

$$\bar{X} = \frac{\Sigma X}{n}$$

An individual score or value in the data set is represented by *X*. The Greek letter sigma (Σ) indicates that all of the individual scores (*X*s) in the set are added together. This sum is divided by the group size (*n*) to obtain the mean ($\bar{X}$).

The data in the response column of Figure K-4 is listed in the sequence in which it was collected. It is hard to discern a pattern in these values, and it is even more difficult when the data set is larger. After the mean is calculated ($\bar{X} = 2.625$), it becomes apparent that members of the group need some assistance to a lot of assistance to do this task. This interpretation is based on the fact that the mean falls between "can do with a lot of assistance (2)" and "can do with some assistance (3)" on the response scale. Since the numbers used to calculate the mean are whole numbers, this value should be rounded to 2.6 or 2.63.

This mean can be used to contrast the performance level on this task with performance levels for other tasks in the list. Are respondents more or less skilled on this task than other tasks on the list? A review of the means for the tasks will answer this question.

This mean can also be compared with the performance level needed on this task. If instructors need to be able to do this without help (response level 4), the group has to improve.

Median. Another measure of central tendency is the median. The median divides a distribution in half based on the responses or score values in the data set. To calculate the median without software, the data needs to be ordered by score value. The median is the point where one-half of the responses are below and one-half are above. This is demonstrated in the right-hand column in Figure K-4. The data has been ordered and the median is 2.5. There are four responses smaller than this value, and four larger. The median has been calculated by adding the two middle numbers and dividing by 2.

The median of 2.5 in Figure K-4 indicates that one-half of the responses are ones and twos. When this result is interpreted with the response scale, it indicates that one-half of the instructors responding either cannot do this task or must have a lot of help as they perform it.

FIGURE
K-4

This data set is comprised of the responses to the following needs assessment survey item task:

- Upload photo from camera to computer

Data

Respondent	Response	Ordered#
1	4	5
2	1	4
3	3	3
4	2	3
	mean = 2.6	median = 2.5
5	1	2
6	5	2
7	2	1
8	3	1

Response Key

1 = cannot do
2 = can do with much assistance
3 = can do with some assistance
4 = can do without assistance
5 = can do skillfully/quickly
6 = can teach to others

#NOTE: The data in this column are sequenced by size and no longer represent the responses of specific individuals.

The median for this example is smaller than the mean. Since the numeric values of the responses are used, means are influenced by very high or very low values in a set of responses. Medians are not influenced as much by these values. Also, medians indicate the exact point at which one-half of the responses are below, which can be useful. On the other hand, an advantage of using means is that they are easier to compare with statistical formulas to determine if there are significant differences.

Mode. Another measure of central tendency is the mode. The mode is the most common response or score. An example of a data set with a single mode is found in Figure K-3. The Twin Cities, with ten respondents, is the mode. A set of data can have only one mean and median. However, it can have more than one mode. The data in Figure K-4 has three modes: responses 1, 2, and 3. All of these responses were given by two people. Multiple modes can make it difficult to compare items or to compare one group to another. However, the mode can be useful in discerning the nature of the group, especially when there are one or two modes that represent a large majority of the respondents.

Measures of Variability

Measures of variability indicate how much the scores in a set of data differ from each other. A quick review of the data in Figure K-4 reveals that the responses vary from one to five. This represents a difference in skill level from "cannot do" to "can do skillfully/quickly." This variation needs to be recognized and taken into account when program development and instructional design decisions are made.

There are three common measures of variability: range (*R*), interquartile range (*IQR*), and standard deviation (*s*). The range can be used with all three measures of central tendency. IQR is used with the median. Standard deviation is used with the mean.

Range (*R*). Range (*R*) is the difference between the high and low values in a data set ($R = H - L$). Weather reports typically give high and low temperature readings for the day. The larger this range, the more noticeable the change in temperature throughout the day.

The range for responses in Figure K-4 is 5 – 1 ($R = H - L$), or 4 points. This range indicates that there is considerable variability in the skill levels reported. The median for this set of responses is 2.5, and denotes that one-half of the respondents cannot do the task or need considerable assistance to do the task. However, the range suggests that there are some who may not need much assistance. A review of the individual response summary reveals how many may not need further instruction.

The range indicates the total span of responses or values in a data set. Thus, it is useful in making program and instructional design decisions. Larger values indicate more variability and the potential need for more flexible instruction systems.

The range is not as stable as the other two measures of variability. It is directly affected by a change in either the high or low values. The smallest value the range can have is zero. This occurs when all of the values in the data set are the same.

Interquartile Range (*IQR*). The interquartile range (*IQR*) is the difference between the value of quartile 3 and quartile 1 ($IQR = Q_3 - Q_1$). A quartile is one of any three points that divides an ordered distribution in four parts, each containing one quarter of the scores. Quartile 3 is the point at which 75% of scores are below. In the example in Figure K-4, 75% of the scores are below the score of 4. Six scores or responses are below this point. The point on the distribution of scores at which six scores are below is 3.5. Twenty-five percent of the scores are below quartile one. In the example, the value of the first quartile is 1.5. The *IQR* for this set of data is 2 (3.5 – 1.5 = 2). This indicates that the respondents have reported differing skill levels.

An *IQR* is not affected by changes in the high or low scores in a distribution. Thus, it is more stable than the range. An *IQR* gives the range of scores for the middle 50% of the responses. For the data in Figure K-4, the *IQR* is 2, which indicates that one-half of the responses are within a 2-point range. Since the median is 2.5, 50% of the responses are encompassed in the "can do with a lot of assistance" and "can do with some assistance" response choices.

Since the median is the same as the second quartile, the *IQR* is the appropriate measure of variability to go along with the median. The range can also be used as a measure of variability if its sensitivity to extreme scores is not a problem.

Standard Deviation (*s*). Standard deviation (*s*) is a measure of how much the individual values in a data set vary from the mean of that set. The more the scores vary from the mean, the larger the value of *s*. When all responses in a set are the same, the value of *s* is zero. The maximum value a standard deviation can have is approximately one-half the range of possible scores.

The general formula for the standard deviation is

$$s = \sqrt{\frac{\Sigma(X - \bar{X})^2}{n}}$$

Usually, computer software is used to calculate standard deviations. The value of the standard deviation for the data in Figure K-4 is 1.41. This value may indicate that the skill levels in the group vary enough to merit a further review of the number of responses in each of the response choices. When the standard deviation is less than one, 70% to 80% of the responses will be within plus or minus one point of the mean, and would indicate that the skill levels reported are very similar.

To briefly review, the measures of central tendency, mean, median, and mode, indicate the typical value of the responses in a data set. In the example in Figure K-4, these measures indicate that the typical skill level reported by the group is in the "can do with a lot of assistance" to "can do with some assistance" range. The measures of variability, range, *IQR*, and standard deviation, indicate how similar the responses are. In the example, they reflect the differences in skill levels reported, which range from "cannot do" to "can do skillfully/quickly."

The interpretation of these statistics depends on the length of the response scale and the definition of the responses on the scale. For example, the scale used in Figure K-4 has six response categories and measures different levels of skill. A median of 2.5 on this scale indicates that one-half of the respondents cannot do the task or can only do it if they have a lot of assistance. If the *IQR* is less than or equal to 1, then the variability is considered to be small, meaning the group members have very similar skills and probably need the same training. If the *IQR* is larger than 1, the response pattern on the item should be reviewed to determine if different levels of training are needed. In the example, the *IQR* is 2 and the individuals who can do the task proficiently and without assistance do not need training.

One activity that helps to interpret statistics is to review the results for a sample of items and relate them to the response scale. The first step is to select the type of statistics to be used. (See Figure K-2.) Assuming the data is from an interval scale, the mean and standard deviation will be used in this example. The next step is to select items with both low and high means, and items with small, medium, and large standard deviations. For each of the items selected, review the response pattern results. See Figure K-5. Notice how these patterns vary for a standard deviation of 0 versus a standard deviation of 1.0 versus a standard deviation of 2.0. After several items have been reviewed, the means and standard deviations will have more meaning and will be more connected to the training/curriculum decisions that need to be made.

Rank Order

Rank order places observations, scores, or responses in order by their size. Ranking can be done from small to large, or large to small, depending on the nature of the values being ranked. The data in the right-hand column in Figure K-4 is rank ordered from the smallest value to the largest. Many statistical software packages have a command, such as "rank" or "order" that will rank the data.

Various values can be used to rank data. In Figure K-4, individual response values are ranked. Mean or median values can be ranked to compare skill levels on various tasks and identify instructional priorities.

Placing data in rank order helps identify and communicate priorities. Items with high priority will be listed at the end of the distribution of values, and those with similar ratings placed next to each other. Ranking also facilitates decision making. Decision rules or cut points can be applied to the distribution to determine the consequences and adjustments that need to be made to arrive at logical curriculum decisions.

GRAPHIC ANALYSIS OF DATA

For many, a graphic analysis of data helps improve their understanding of results. Also, graphic presentation of results usually facilitates communication and understanding. This is especially true when comparisons are being made. This section will present some basic concepts on distributions, visual comparisons, and graphic comparisons.

FIGURE K-5

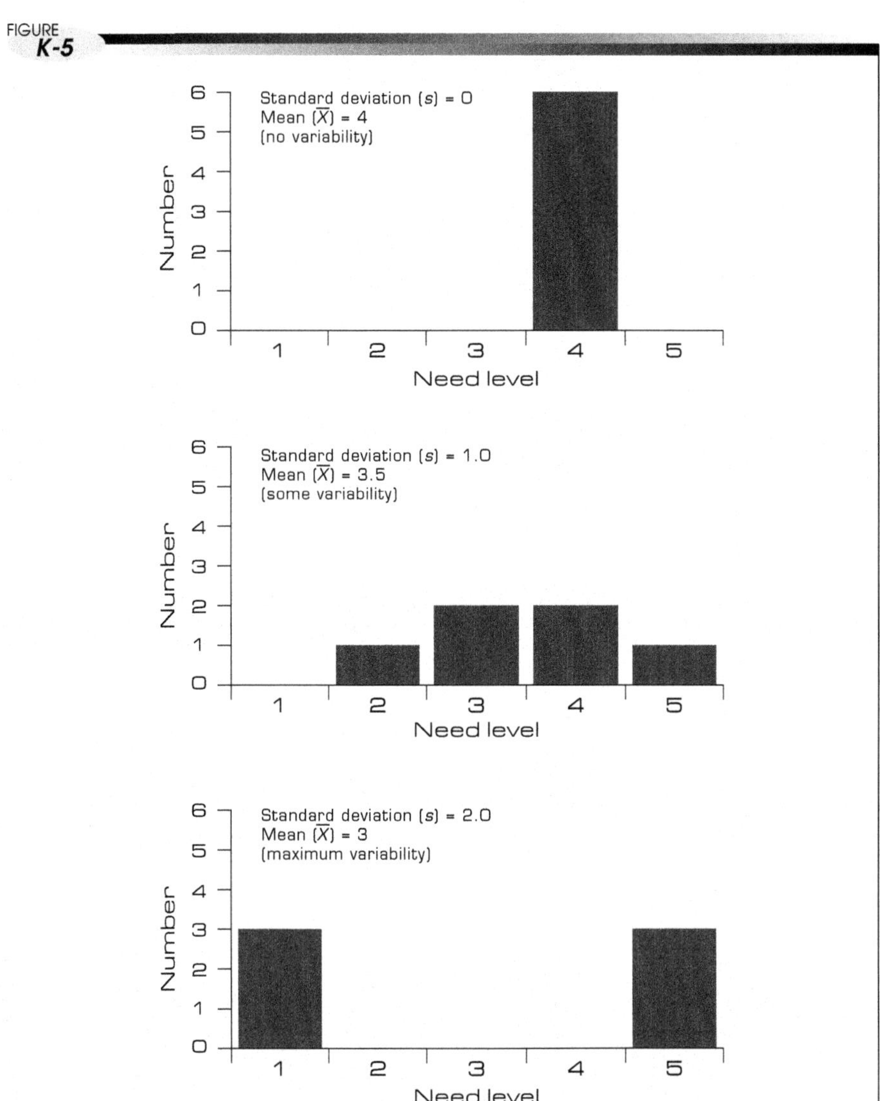

Distributions

Distributions can be presented in tabular or graphic form. Here, the graphic form will be discussed. A graphic distribution shows the frequency or percent of responses chosen to each response choice on an ordinal, interval, or ratio scale. Graphic distributions display the typical response, variability of the responses, and the shape of the distribution.

One of the most common distributions used in statistics is the normal distribution. This section will present the general characteristics of the normal curve and will be used in defining several terms related to distributions. More detailed information on the normal distribution can be found in the reference works listed at the end of this appendix.

The normal distribution is a bell-shaped curve as depicted in Figure K-6. Most of the observations are in the center of the distribution. Variability is denoted by the spread of scores or values from the midpoint of the distribution. The standard deviations on the baseline are one way to scale variability. Almost all of the area (99.74%) under the normal curve falls within ±3 standard deviations from the mean. The area between the curve and the baseline is equal to 100% or 1.0. The area encompassed by each standard deviation is given in Figure K-6.

FIGURE K-6

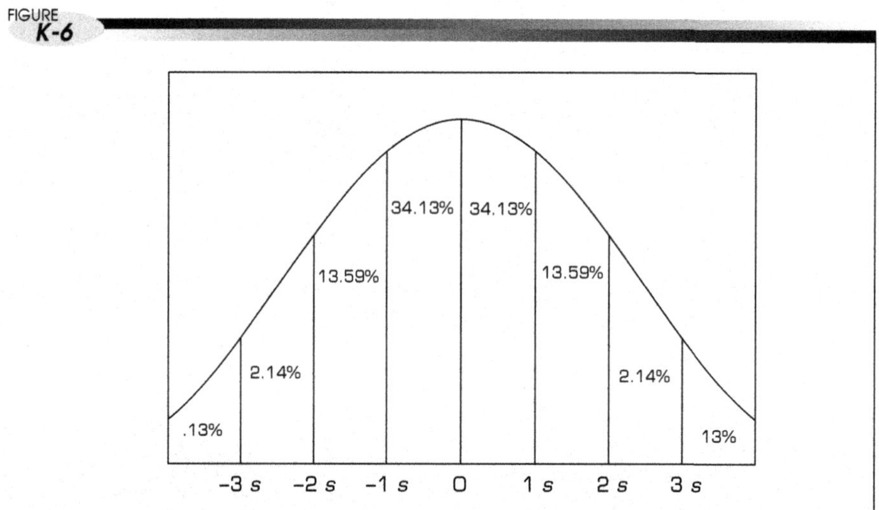

Responses on a survey are not always normally distributed. For example, the responses listed in Figure K-4 are not normally distributed. As shown in Figure K-6, most of the responses are clustered on the lower end of the distribution. In terms of the survey question, this distribution indicates that three-fourths of the respondents need assistance to complete this task. See Figure K-7.

Specific terms are used to describe distributions that vary from normal. Figure K-8 illustrates common terms used and their related distributions. When there are a few very high scores, such as the distribution of incomes in the U.S., the distribution is skewed to the right. When the extreme scores are on the lower end, the distribution is skewed to the left.

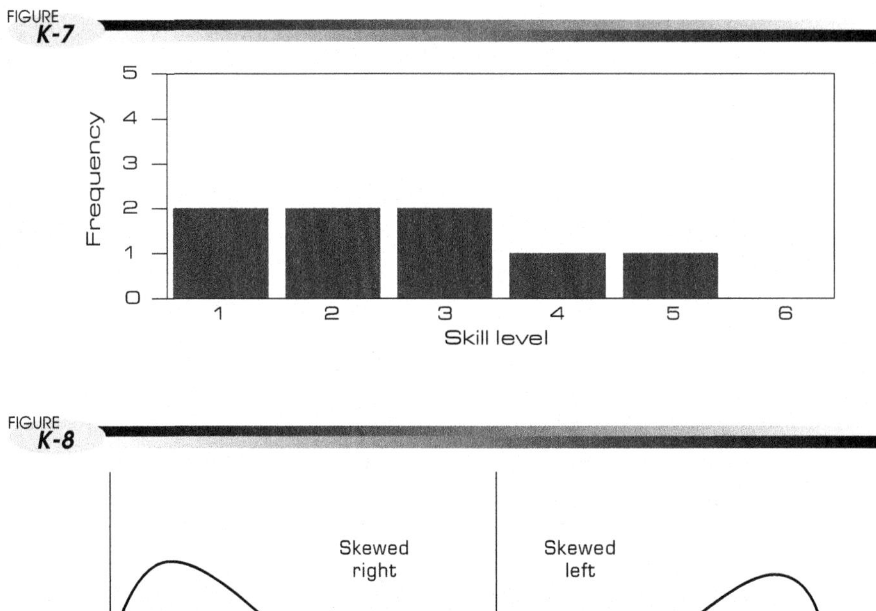

Other distributions, such as the binominal distribution for nominal data, are also used in statistics. When a distribution is used as a model to identify precise probabilities, it is important that the appropriate distribution is selected. More information on distributions is contained in the statistical references listed at the end of this appendix. The information on the normal distribution given in this section should be sufficient for the curriculum development applications discussed in this book.

Why Do a Visual Analysis?

A visual analysis can add better understanding to the statistics generated in a statistical analysis. The shape and spread of the response values in a graphic distribution depict how knowledge, needs, and skills are distributed among respondents who completed the survey. Also, charts are useful in comparing the response distributions of two or more groups. Applications of graphic analysis are described in more detail in the paragraphs that follow.

Shape of the Distribution. The shape of the distribution is helpful in interpreting the data. For example, if skills are being evaluated it identifies the number of people at each skill level. A normal distribution has a few people at the low and high ends with most of the people in the middle. A normal distribution may signify the need for three training approaches for students. Skewed distributions indicate that a few people have very low or very high skill levels depending on the direction that the distribution is skewed. Skewed distributions suggest the need for at least two training approaches. These needs are explained in more detail in the section on variability. The histogram command in statistical software will generate a graph for a set of data.

Typical Responses. In a normal distribution, the mean, median, and mode have the same value. In a skewed or nonsymmetrical distribution, they have different values. See Figure K-9. In a skewed distribution, the mode is the response with the highest frequency. The mean will fall more toward the long tail or extreme values in the distribution. The median is not influenced as much by extreme scores since their specific numeric value is not used to determine it. If response distributions are skewed to an extreme, the mean will overestimate or underestimate the level of need or skill in the responding group. In this situation, the median may be a more useful tool in decision making. In addition, the mode can be used along with the median to identify the most common skill level in the group.

Variability. Typical statistics program printouts will include measures of variability such as standard deviation (s), range (R), and interquartile range (IQR). A graphic distribution is very helpful in interpreting these statistics. The distributions in Figure K-5 illustrate this.

FIGURE K-9

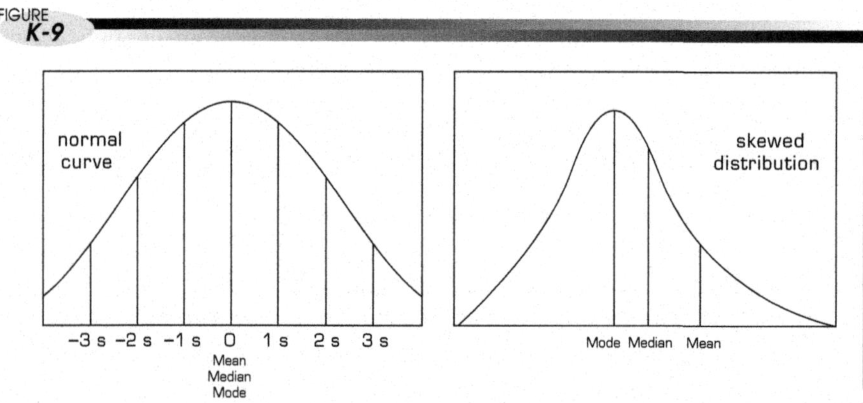

The first histogram or graphic distribution represents a distribution that has no variability. All of the responses are the same, and the standard deviation (s) and range (R) are zero. In this case, one course design can be used for the group, and the mean, median, or mode can be used to determine the emphasis to be used.

The second histogram has a more normal distribution with responses that vary from 2 to 5. In other words, members of the group have skills that range from high (5) to low (2). This range of differences in skill levels is reflected in the values of the standard deviation (0.96), range (3.0), and *IQR* (1.0). An analysis of these statistics and the histogram suggest that one course design will not fit the needs of all of these people.

The third histogram illustrates the maximum variability possible in a distribution. One-half of the respondents have selected 1, and the other half have selected 5. The standard deviation, range, and *IQR* are the highest possible for a 5-point rating scale. These values indicate the need for a course for those who have no skill with the task (response 1). Those who selected response 5 may be candidates to be mentors.

Making Comparisons. There are numerous types of charts and graphs that can be used. A chart or graph that accurately presents the data and communicates effectively should be chosen carefully. Color and special symbols can be effective, but they can also detract, and, in some instances, make the chart difficult to read. Newspapers, magazines, and journals use a number of charts and graphs and can be a good source of ideas. This section will focus on three basic types of charts: bar, pie, and line.

Bar charts can be used to present a variety of data and to give group comparisons. The variable values are placed on one axis of the chart and outcomes on the other axis. The example in Figure K-7 presents the six possible responses on the horizontal axis (x-axis). All six responses are included even though only five were selected. It is important to communicate to the reader that no one was at level six. The vertical axis (y-axis) identifies the median skill level in this example.

Bar charts are effective in presenting the results for one group on an item. They are also effective in presenting comparisons as shown in Figure K-10. The bars for instructors represent the data from Figure K-4 and their perceived level of skill in uploading photos from a camera to a computer. The perceived competency levels of the new and experienced teachers in the group are also graphed. It is easy to determine that new teachers gave somewhat lower ratings than experienced teachers did.

There are limits to the number of groups that can be compared in one chart. Four or five groups is the maximum number of groups that should be used in most situations. If more groups are added, the chart becomes cluttered and the reader is forced to make too many comparisons.

FIGURE K-10

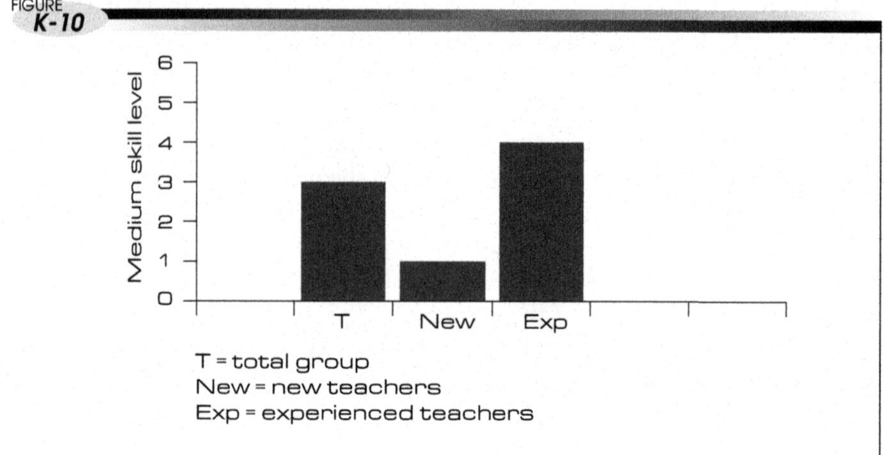

Pie charts are very popular in the general media. They are effective in conveying the proportion or percent of respondents who have selected various responses. Figure K-11 presents the same data as the bar chart in Figure K-7. Using the pie chart, it is easy to identify the percentage of instructors at each skill level. It is also easy to see that no one selected item 6.

FIGURE K-11

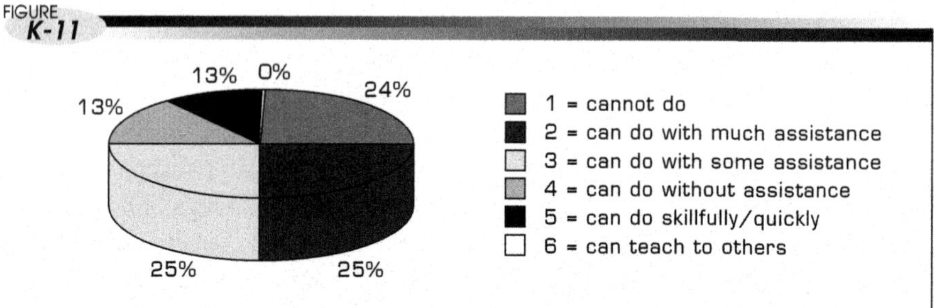

Pie charts are not as effective in presenting comparisons. The reader has to review multiple pie charts to obtain the comparison data and may have a difficult time remembering the appropriate data. Also, pie charts should not be used when there are many categories. When there are many slices in the pie, it is difficult to select shading or colors that accurately differentiate each slice. Five to seven slices is probably the limit.

Line charts are useful in depicting trends. The line chart in Figure K-12 describes improvement in performance over time. Comparisons can be given on line charts. As with bar charts, no more than four or five comparisons or groups should be listed.

FIGURE K-12

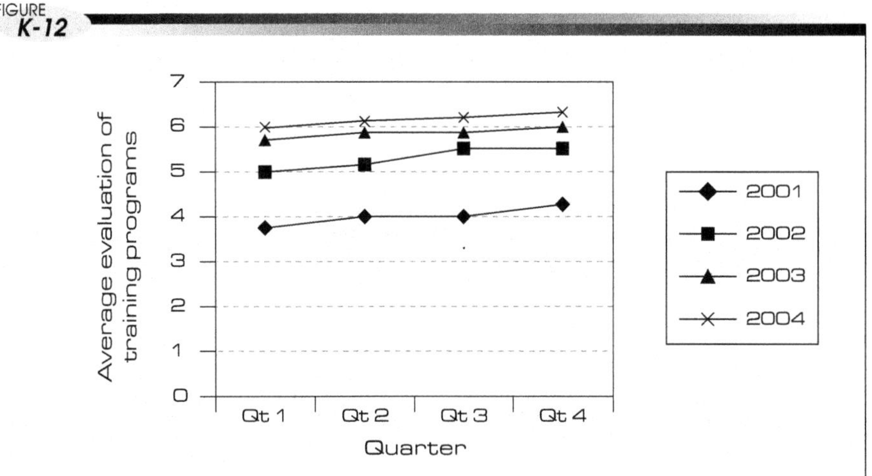

PREPROCESSING REVIEW

The preprocessing review is an important step in attaining accurate data summaries. This process includes preplanning, instrument design, and editing.

Plan and Design Instruments to Minimize Problems and Facilitate Processing

Creative and sophisticated analysis techniques cannot overcome poor instrument design. Proper instrument design is essential to effective data analysis. Items must be relevant to the study objectives and structured to facilitate data processing. Data processing and analysis can be facilitated by using the following guidelines:

- Use rating scales and fixed response or multiple choice items when feasible.
- Precode or number response choices (See Appendix A for sample surveys).
- Design response choices so respondents can check (√) or circle responses.
- Number questions so they are easy to identify.
- Place rating scale responses in the same place on the survey. For example, place them in a column on the right-hand side of the page.
- Place open-ended questions at the end of the survey when possible.

More detailed information on instrument development is given in Chapter 2.

It is also important that problems in data collection are minimized. No amount of editing and coding will overcome mistakes made by respondents because directions were unclear and ambiguous or because part of the survey was left out during duplicating or entering the text in a web survey. The following suggestions will help to minimize these problems:

- Write clear and concise directions that will communicate with the intended respondents.
- Use simple and familiar question types and response formats.
- Avoid formatting responses in an unusual way.
- Use as few item types or formats as possible.
- Be consistent within the survey. Use terms the same way and run all rating scales from low to high or vice versa.
- Do not overcrowd a page with text, and leave adequate room for responses.
- Tell the reader to "see other side" when questions are printed on both sides of the survey paper.
- Pilot test the survey. Have one or two colleagues review it.

Quality Check

Even with the precautions and checks noted above, it is important to do a quality check. The following checks need to be made on the master copy of the instrument:

- Proof the copy. A spell check program should be run, but it is not sufficient to catch all errors. For example, it will not identify a "t" missing from "the." Also, check for missing words and grammar.
- Check type, font size, and clarity. Avoid the use of italics and script. Complete this review on a practice copy on the color of paper to be used for the survey. If it is an internet survey, check the contrast between the background and the print.
- Check to see how the survey appears on the printed page if it is going to be duplicated on paper. Do not try to place too much text on a page. The questions and responses should be easy to find and read. There must be enough space for written responses.
- Contrast text margins with print/copier margins. Run sample copies to ensure that the survey text is not lost in the margins.

After the surveys have been printed, select at least a small sample of copies to determine if there were any duplicating problems. Check for light or smeared print, missing pages, and incorrect collating if the survey contains multiple pages.

Review Completed Surveys

Even the most efficiently designed survey instruments have some problems. Thus, it is important to review the completed surveys before the responses are processed. Those that have minor problems can be edited. The surveys with major problems can be removed from the set.

General guidelines for reviewing and editing the surveys should be established before initiating the review. The amount of editing that will be done should be defined. For example, will any responses be edited or will an "omit" be entered instead? Also, a guideline needs to be set for removing a survey from the study. This can be done by specifying the number of items that must be completed on the survey or the set of items that must be completed in order for it to qualify.

These general guidelines provide direction and a basis for consistent decision making during the preprocessing review. However, decisions will need to be made as the surveys are reviewed. As specific decisions are made, record and use them for all surveys. This may make it necessary to go back and rescan some surveys that have already been reviewed.

If there is a significant error in the survey instrument, its impact will show up quickly in the completed surveys. For instance, if instructions are not clear, respondents may not respond correctly. Multiple responses may appear on items in which single responses were desired. Or some people check between the numbers or responses on a rating scale when it was intended that only the numbers listed be used.

As soon as a problem is detected, make a decision/rule for it and apply this to all of the surveys. This may require rechecking some of the surveys. If the data has been compromised too much by an error or problem, the instrument will have to be revised and the survey will need to be run again. The following are some common problems and how they might be handled in the preprocessing process.

- Surveys may be blank. Remove these surveys from the set. If the surveys are coded, record the survey code number.
- Surveys may only be partly completed. Determine how many responses are needed to retain the question in the study. Usually this decision will depend on the number of needs or task statements completed in a needs assessment or task analysis. If the individual has responded to many of the most relevant items, the decision probably would be to include the survey in the study. This is especially true if the group surveyed is small.
- Pages may be missing. Sometimes a page is left out in the printing and assembly process. If this is not detected in the quality check, it will show up in the data summary as a significant increase in omitted responses starting with the first item on the missing page. If this happens, the scope of the data missing and the number of survey forms involved will need to be considered in making the decision to proceed or start over.

- Respondents may show a lack of interest. Some indicators of lack of interest are when respondents draw a vertical line through, or make a rectangle around, the same response choice for all of the needs assessment items in a rating scale. Negative comments and the neatness of the responses are also indicators. If the purpose of the survey is to assess interest in a seminar or workshop, the survey is valid. If the purpose is to assess skill levels of the respondents, the survey probably has little value, especially if the responses selected all indicate skill levels that are much higher or lower than expected.
- Multiple responses are sometimes made on items that require only one response. Poor directions, respondents failing to read the directions, or the fact that there are two "best responses" from which the respondent should "select the best response" may be the cause. For example, when individuals are asked to check the highest level of education they have attained on a list that includes high school diploma, some college, and bachelor's degree some will check both high school diploma and bachelor's degree. If it is known that most of the people surveyed have a bachelor's degree, this response could be used and the diploma response could be disregarded. Also, responses to other items can be checked, such as job title, for clues to the appropriate response.

  As these decisions are made they need to be recorded. In some circumstances, both responses may be appropriate. For instance, a person may be both an instructor and an administrator. If this is true, both responses can be entered if the database will take multiple responses. If only one response can be used, the survey director will need to decide which one is most appropriate or decide to eliminate the question from the study.
- Respondents may give in-between responses on rating scales. Usually rating scales are designed so the respondent will circle one response on the scale. Sometimes, however, respondents will mark their responses between those listed. When this happens a decision will have to be made on what response or value to enter. A conservative approach would be to select the nearest number on the rating that indicates lower interest, need, or skill levels.

  Multiple responses like this may indicate that the rating scale does not have enough response choices. Review the response choices, especially those in the area where the in-between responses are being marked, and determine if one or more responses should be added.

Coding Written Responses

If open-ended questions are included in the survey or comments are requested, decisions will have to be made on how to process and analyze this data.

Coding these responses and entering the codes in the database will make it possible to compare the written responses to other responses to the survey. The process of coding involves two steps. The first is to identify appropriate categories for the responses. After that has been done, numbers can be selected to represent these categories.

If it is not important to have open-ended responses in the database, they can be analyzed separately. However, this analysis will also involve categorizing the responses based on their conceptual content.

Several approaches can be used to categorize the responses. If the number of comments is small, the comments can be listed on paper and then reviewed for common themes or topics. One possible technique is to place a different geometric shape next to each unique idea. The first idea or theme would be identified with a triangle, the next with a square, and so on. When the first idea comes up again in the list, a triangle is placed next to it. After the list of comments has been reviewed, the number of triangles, squares, circles, and other shapes can be tallied.

If the number of comments is large, it will be more efficient to select the comments from a sample of surveys and place them on 3 × 5 cards for sorting. One comment is placed on each card. The cards are then sorted into piles based on the contents of the statements. All cards with statements related to one idea or concept go into the same pile. After the individual cards have been placed in piles, each pile can be reviewed and a label selected for each. It is also a good idea to write a brief description of the concept or idea reflected by the cards in a pile.

The next step is to give a code number, letter, or word label to each category (pile). Numbers are usually easier to process with software. If there is a sequence or hierarchy in the categories, this should be reflected in the number sequence. The purpose of the categorization process is to identify unique ideas or themes in the comments and to compress the data. Compressing the comments or data into several useful and meaningful categories facilitates analysis.

The following are factors to consider when coding written responses:

- Review the study objectives before starting the coding process. Identify what data is relevant to the objectives.
- Determine if valid categories are available from previous studies.
- Make sure the categories established are mutually exclusive (a response can fit into only one category), comprehensive (all of the responses fit into one of the categories established), and meaningful (categories must be relevant to the study objectives).

APPENDIX L

Learning Activity Packet

A useful instructor-developed resource is the learning activity packet (LAP). An LAP is a self-paced resource consisting of a terminal performance objective, with enabling objectives and resources provided in each section to help reach the terminal objective. The instructor develops an LAP to address a competency or task. Students use an LAP in a competency-based setting or as an instructional aid for learning and demonstrating competency of subject matter. This example of an LAP uses "Select Sample Technique and Size" as the desired competency to be acquired after accomplishing the performance objective.

Learning Activity Packet

Select Sample Technique and Size

PURPOSE: When using the survey method for collecting information for a needs assessment or task analysis, sampling techniques are usually employed. The use of appropriate techniques requires knowledge about the target population, sample, different sampling techniques, sample size, and dealing with non-respondents.

PERFORMANCE OBJECTIVE: Given information involving a needs assessment, select appropriate sample technique and size and a procedure to deal with non-respondents. To master this module, a score of 8 out of 10 (80%) must be achieved on Activity 3.2.

ENABLING OBJECTIVES:

1. Identify characteristics of a population and sample.

2. Differentiate between simple random sample, systematic sample, stratified sample, and cluster sample.

3. Select sample size and explain a strategy for dealing with non-respondents.

CTE-334/534 Performance Analysis

Howard D. Lee

School of Education
University of Wisconsin-Stout

Content Outline

1. Population
   A. Definition of Population
   B. Criteria for Population
2. Sample
   A. Definition of Sample
   B. Purpose of Sample
   C. When to Select Sample
3. Types of Samples
   A. Simple Random Sample
   B. Systematic Sample
   C. Stratified Sample
   D. Cluster Sample
4. Sample Size
   A. Level of Precision
   B. Level of Confidence
   C. Sample Size Chart
5. Steps in Sample Design
6. Non-respondents

References

1. Blank, W.E. (1982). *Handbook for developing competency-based training programs.* Englewood Cliffs, NJ: Prentice-Hall, Inc.

2. Lee, H., & Nelson O. (2006). *Instructional analysis and course development.* American Technical Publishers, Homewood, IL.

3. Northeast Metro Technical College. (1994). *Writing course modules.* White Bear Lake, MN.

ENABLING OBJECTIVE #1:

Identify characteristics of a population and sample.

Learning Step	Resources
1. Read Resource #1.1 to identify the characteristics of a population and sample.	1. Information Sheet #1.1 "Population and Sample" in this packet.
2. Complete Resource #1.2 to help you identify characteritics of a population and sample.	2. Activity Sheet: #1.2 "Population and Sample" in this packet.
3. Check your responses with Resource #1.3 to see if you can identify characteristics of a population and sample.	3. Activity Sheet: #1.3 "Answer Sheet: Population and Sample" in this packet.

Information Sheet #1.1: **Population and Sample**

Introduction:

Sampling is usually used when utilizing a survey technique, interviewing, observation, questionnaires, or formal research to gather information for a needs assessment or task analysis. All of these involve, in one way or another, the selection of a given number of people from a defined population as representative of that population.

Sampling involves the selection of a representative sub-set of people, agencies, industries, businesses, events, or objects to which we wish to generalize the results to. You may be a trainer determining if the machinist on the production line needs statistical process control training. One of the ways of determining this is to ask all of the machinists. If you are working in a large company and have over 100 machinists, would you interview or survey everyone? Interviewing may prove to be very time consuming. The alternative is to identify a representative sample and use the time and resources available to obtain the information about the total group from a sample of workers. Research has shown that statistics from a representative sample are often more accurate than those from the total population. This is based on the notion that it is usually possible to do a better job of contacting each individual in the sample and thus obtaining the information requested.

Sampling is used because it will save you time and the expense of studying the entire population. If sampling is correctly done, you can make conclusions about the total population that are likely to be correct. Sampling is a very important tool in the educators/trainers toolbox. While sampling can be very sophisticated, the basic rules are reasonable and may be applied to many situations besides needs assessment and task analysis. Let's take a look as some important concepts in sampling by looking at some definitions.

Population:

The first step in sampling is to define the target population. The population is all the people in the study. All of the workers in the United States who operate a drill press, or all of the workers in the company who operate a drill press. Both of these could be the population depending on the scope of the study. Are you concerned with the needs of all the drill press operators across the United States, or just the ones in a company or a geographic region? The population depends on the scope, objectives, and criteria of the target group involved in the needs assessment or task analysis.

If you are interested in the needs of the students who use the learning resource center at a university, then all 7,000 students enrolled at the university are the population. These 7,000 students are the "N" (number) of the population. Keep in mind that the population is really made up of many subgroups such as age, year in school, on campus, off campus, males, females, etc. Depending on the objects of the study, you may want to further define these subgroups.

What if you are doing a needs assessment for the state's department of education, and you wish to establish a program for in-service teachers on the very latest research in learning theory? What would your population be? Learning theory pertains to all teachers, but depending on the research, you may define the population as only secondary school teachers in state. The scope and objectives of the research in learning theory will help you establish the criteria for the target population.

Now suppose you are interested in the training needs of all the sales representatives who sell a new copy machine. What kinds of factors might determine the population? The company that produces the copy machine is an international company. Would you define the population as only the North American sales force, or would you include the international sales force? What would help you determine this?

Defining the population is very important to educators and trainers. It is the first step in dealing with sampling.

Sample:

Once you have the population defined, you need to begin thinking about obtaining a sample of the population (which is a proportion). To help achieve a representative group, a random sample from the target population is needed. A random sample simply means that everyone in the target population has an equal chance of being selected. The main purpose of a random sample is that the results yield data that can be generalized to larger populations. If the population is 25–30 or more, or the survey is complicated, a sample is generally used. A sample is no more than a representative group of individuals or elements from the total population. The actual sample size (number) is frequently referred to as the "n" of the study.

The sample selection process occurs prior to the construction and validation of the data gathering instrument or procedure. The sampling selection and instrument development are interrelated. You might determine that it is necessary to develop an instrument containing some items to be answered only by members of certain subgroups, or that it would be more effective to survey a smaller population more than once. These would have an impact on sample selection and instrument construction.

Since samples are used to draw inferences about a population, the population must be clearly defined. Many people new to surveying think that the sample is not a problem. But **procedures that are not representative of the population bring into question the confidence in their response and the survey.**

Activity Sheet #1.2: **Population and Sample**

Check your progress on learning about the characteristics of population and sample by answering the following questions.

1. Explain each in your own words:
   A. Population:

   B. Sample:

2. What are the symbols for population and sample?

   Population: Sample:

3. Explain under what conditions the following would be the population or sample.
   A. All the students at UW-Stout:

   B. Students in the freshman class at Stout:

   C. All the students who walk through the union on Wednesday:

   D. All the business and industry in the northeast Wisconsin area that have trainers:

Activity Sheet #1.3: Answer Sheet: Population and Sample

Check your progress on learning about the characteristics of population and sample by answering the following questions.

1. Explain the following in your own words:

   A. Population: Target group defined by the scope and objectives of the study. Criteria may have to be identified to select people, agencies, industries, business events or objects for a study. First step in dealing with sampling.

   B. Sample: A representative group of the target population.

2. What is the usual symbol for population and sample?

   Population: Sample:

3. Explain under what conditions the following would be the population or sample.

   A. All the students at UW-Stout: Population: if the scope and objectives of study are only concerned with all the students at Stout. The generalizations to be made only pertain to all the students at Stout. Sample: would be a sample if the students at Stout are only a subgroup of the total population. For example, someone is interested in all the students in the UW system.

   B. Students in the freshmen class at Stout: The freshmen students would be the population if the study were only interested in issues pertaining to freshmen students. The study may determine if the freshmen students enjoyed their experience in the dorm, how registration went, or what their needs were during the first semester. If a study were conducted that looked at needs of all students during registration, then the freshmen class would be a sample because they would be a subgroup of all the students.

   C. All the students who walk through the union on Wednesday: This would be the total population for a researcher who was only interested in the activities of the union on Wednesday and not the other days of the week. It would be a sample if the researcher was interested in all the traffic through the union.

   D. All the business and industry in the northeast area of the state that have trainers: This would be the population if the scope of the study just entailed northeast area of the state. It would be a sample when looking at the whole state and dividing the state into regions.

ENABLING OBJECTIVE #2:

Differentiate between simple random sample, systematic sample, stratified sample, and cluster sample.

Learning Step	Resources
1. Read Resource #2.1 to differentiate between simple random sample, systematic sample, stratified sample, and cluster sample.	1. Information Sheet #2.1 "Types of Samples" in this packet.
2. Complete Resource #2.2 to help you differentiate between simple random sample, systematic sample, stratified sample, and cluster sample.	2. Activity Sheet: #2.2 "Types of Samples" in this packet.
3. Check your responses with Resource #2.3 to see if you can differentiate between simple random sample, systematic sample, stratified sample, and cluster sample.	3. Activity Sheet: #2.3 "Answer Sheet: Types of Samples" in this packet.

Information Sheet #2.1: **Types of Samples**

There are basically four types of probability sampling types.

Simple Random Sample:

In this type of sample, every person in the population has an equal and independent chance of being selected. Independent means that the selection of one individual does not affect the selection of another individual. Being selected as a member of a random sample is based purely on chance.

One way to draw names is to place names of the students in a hat and randomly draw the number of names needed. Bingo and lottery machines utilize air and ping-pong balls with numbers and letters on them. Each ball has an equal chance of being selected when the drawing tube is opened.

This method has its limitations, especially with larger populations. The hats and machines can only accommodate so many pieces of paper or ping pong balls. Let's say you want to take a random population of the students at a university of 7,000. What would you have to do to ensure that everyone has an equal chance of being selected? You could put each name on a slip of paper and put the names in a big rotary drum and spin it. Or you could buy 7,000 ping-pong balls, put the names on them, and purchase an air machine. However, there are a couple of easier ways.

In larger populations like 7,000, a sample size of 362 may be appropriate. A traditional method of selecting a simple random sample is to use of a table of random numbers. In this method, each person in the target population is assigned a number. The educator or trainer then selects a row or column (randomly of course) as a starting point from a table of random numbers. The numbers that follow are then selected until the sample size is completed.

Suppose you are interested in the needs of the 7,000 students at UW-Stout. An appropriate sample size might be 362. You would assign each student a number and use a table of random numbers like that on the next page. You would then close your eyes, place your pencil on the table, and begin at that point. Suppose your pencil hit Column 2, Row 2, and landed on 22164. The researcher would work starting down that column using the last four digits with the numbers 7,000 or smaller (since the population is 7,000) and pick every number until 362 numbers have been selected. For example: 2164, 4133, 4486, 2584, 5665, 5454, 4508, 5642, etc.

Software programs are available that can generate a random sample for a given population. If the names or identification labels for the members of the population are stored in a database, it is relatively easy to obtain or write a program that will randomly select members from the population and print a list of names, addresses, and/or other data pertaining to members of the sample. The names and addresses may be printed directly on mailing labels to facilitate a mail survey.

This procedure gives everyone in the population an equal chance of being selected, which is the basic requirement of a simple random sample. However, it is rarely possible to achieve a true simple random sample because subjects may not cooperate and others will be lost through attrition.

Table of Random Numbers (partial table shown)

Row	Column 1	2	3	4	5	6	7	8	9	10
1	32388	52390	16815	69298	82732	38480	73817	32523	41961	44437
2	05300	22164	24369	54224	35983	19687	11052	91491	60383	19746
3	66523	44133	00697	35552	35970	19124	63318	29686	03387	59846
4	44167	64486	64758	75366	76554	31601	12614	33072	60332	92325
5	47914	02584	37680	20801	72152	39339	34806	08930	85001	87820
6	63445	17361	62825	39908	05607	91284	68833	25570	38818	46920
7	89917	15665	52872	73823	73144	88662	88970	74492	51805	99378
8	92648	45454	09552	88815	16553	51125	79375	97596	16296	66092
9	20979	04508	64535	31355	86064	29472	47689	05974	52468	16834
10	81959	65642	74240	56302	00033	67107	77510	70625	28725	34191

Systematic Sample:

This is another version of the simple random sample, and it can be used if all members in the defined population have already been placed on a list in random order. Then, only one out of every 3, 5, 6, 10, etc., is selected. This is a more common procedure. In this procedure, you would take every Kth person from the list when Kth = N/n, where N is the total population and n is the sample size. Example: Let's say we're dealing with a population of 100 people and our sample size is 25. Then what is our Kth person? Simply divide 100 by 25, which equals 4. We would then take every 4th person on the randomized list.

Systematic samples differ from the simple random samples in that each member of the population is not selected independently. Once the first member has been selected, all the other members of the random sample are automatically determined.

Let's look at another example: Let's say we are interested in the needs of all the university students. We know the population, or N = 7,000. If we used a sample size of 362 students, what is the Kth? 7,000/362 = 19. This means that we would pick every 19th student from the randomized list of students.

Trainers and educators frequently have to work from list of names, agencies, businesses, and industries. They are often found in alphabetical order and are not randomized. This brings up a sampling frame. The actual list used in a systematic sample is the sampling frame. A sampling frame for the UW-Stout student populations could be the student directory. In other words the directory is your sampling frame, and you would pick every 19th student to be your sample. A sampling frame may be a printout from the business office where by students are listed by Social Security number. That list becomes the sampling frame. As you can see, the problem with this is that you do not have a true random sample because the sampling frame was not generated in a random fashion. This, then, becomes a limitation of the study.

In 1936, Alf London ran against Franklin Roosevelt for the Presidency. The pollsters picked London to win, but of course, he did not. What was the problem? The pollsters used a systematic random sample with the phone book as their sampling frame. In 1936, many people still did not have phones. This is an example of convenience and not true random selection. The selection of the sampling frame is important.

If your population is all of the student body, you may want to use the university's phone book because you want to call them. However, many students may not have a phone, only use as cell phone, or may have registered late and do not appear in the book. Plus, many students drop out during the year. Also, if you are using the university phone book, or a very long list of names, it's pretty hard to count out every 19th name. It may be easier to select names by using a gauge that measures so many lines per inch.

Stratified Sample:

A sample that takes into account subgroups in the population by sampling a proportion of each subgroup is a stratified random sample. This type of sample assures that certain groups are adequately represented. In this method, the population is divided into strata, or groups of concern to the study.

Let's say you had a layered cake. You could take a bite of only one layer and make generalizations about the whole cake, but that would be another type of sample. If you take a bite of each layer and make generalizations about the whole cake, that's a stratified sample. To stratify, as used in sampling, means to break up the people or things into groups with common characteristics that distinguish them from other groups.

Let's use the university student population again and say we wanted to obtain a stratified sample of students. We would make sure we have students represented from each class plus graduate students. We have to be concerned with the number in each population. If we find that there are twice as many freshmen as seniors, we would want to make sure we sample twice as many freshmen as we do seniors. The proportion of subjects randomly selected from each subgroup is usually the same proportion of that group in the target population. If freshmen make up 35% of the 7,000 students, then they should also make up 35% of the sample.

Let's say you wanted to do a task analysis of all administrative assistants in a town. Where would you find these workers? In what kinds of businesses? Law firms, insurance, government, medical, banks, churches, and the list goes on. The researcher would need to find out the numbers from each type of business or organization that have administrative assistants and establish proportions, then select proportions from each group. If there is a possibility that a random sample will not select a person or element from that group within the population, then a stratified random sample should be used. Stratified samples are particularly useful in a needs assessment and task analysis when you are comparing responses between subgroups in the population.

Cluster Sample:

Another way to sample a population is by cluster sample. With this technique, the individual is not the focus. It is rather a naturally occurring group of individuals. It is used when it is more feasible or convenient to select individuals from a defined population. Let's again say you had a layered cake. If you take a bite of each layer and make generalizations about the whole cake, that's a stratified sample. But if you take a bite of only one layer and make generalizations about a whole cake, that's a cluster sample. Each layer may be different, but by sampling only one and making generalizations about the whole cake, it's cluster sampling.

Cluster sampling is like testing whether grapes are ripe. If you want to determine how ripe the bunch is, you pick one to sample. You don't have to eat a whole bunch, a few will do. You don't even have to sample every bunch of grapes to form an opinion about whether the grapes are ripe.

A cluster sample takes advantage of the existence of natural classes or groups in a population. Subgroups of any population occur everywhere. The cluster may be:

- People clustered in households
- Households clustered in blocks
- Air travelers clustered in flights
- Business customers clustered in sales territories
- Students clustered at the university
- Male students clustered in PE at the university
- A town's community members clustered in the Rotary, Chamber of Commerce, etc.

Let's again take the university population. Can you think of any natural clustering already existing in the population? Classes, courses, resident, eye color, right-handed, have car, live in the dorm, etc. The cluster is selected depending on the data being collected. Once you define the cluster, then you take a sample of that cluster. In cluster sampling, you are only looking at a certain population. You may sample only freshmen male students and make inferences about all the men on campus.

Cluster sampling may save you time and money, but it is less accurate and increases the sampling error.

11

Activity Sheet #2.2 **Types of Samples**

Complete the following:

1. Match the following terms in Column A with the description in Column B by placing the appropriate letter in the blank. Use each item in Column A as many times as necessary, but only one letter per blank.

Column A	Column B
A. Simple Random Sample	___ Taking a proportion of each subgroup.
B. Systematic Sample	___ Everyone has an equal chance of being selected.
C. Stratified Sample	___ Utilize sampling frame.
D. Cluster Sample	___ Sample naturally occurring groups.
	___ Students enrolled in Task Analysis.
	___ Every group is represented.
	___ Lottery is an example.
	___ Every Kth person.
	___ Target population.

2. If you were attempting to determine the training needs of the new employees of AGF Glass Company, what type of survey technique would you use? Justify your decision.

Activity Sheet #2.2 Answer Sheet: Types of Samples

Complete the following:

1. Match the following terms in Column A with the description in Column B by placing the appropriate letter in the blank. Use each item in Column A as many times as necessary, but only one letter per blank.

Column A	Column B
A. Simple Random Sample	C Taking a proportion of each subgroup.
B. Systematic Sample	A Everyone has an equal chance of being selected.
C. Stratified Sample	B Utilize sampling frame.
D. Cluster Sample	D Sample naturally occurring groups.
	D Students enrolled in Task Analysis.
	C Every group is represented.
	A Lottery is an example.
	B Every Kth person.
	___ Target population.

2. If you were attempting to determine the training needs of the new employees of AGF Glass Company, what type of survey technique would you use? Justify your decision.

   There are several possibilities depending on the focus of the study. Because there are many workers with various levels and kinds of experience and many job descriptions, stratified and cluster sampling would seem to work best if you ask general needs questions. Factory floor workers, office workers, and managers are just a few groups who may have specific training needs. Because they can be grouped in these general categories (there may be others), and you are looking at training needs of new employees, a stratified sample would seem to be the best choice. This would ensure the appropriate proportions from each group. The training needs can then be compared by groups.

   The possibilities are many, depending on the scope and objectives of the needs assessment.

ENABLING OBJECTIVE #3:

Select sample size and explain a strategy for dealing with non-respondents

Learning Step	Resources
1. Read Resource #3.1 to select sample size and explain a strategy for dealing with non-respondents.	1. Information Sheet #3.1 "Sample Size and Non-Respondents" in this packet.
2. Complete Resource #3.2 to help you select sample size and explain a strategy for dealing with non-respondents.	2. Activity Sheet: #3.2 "Sample Size and Non-Respondents" in this packet.
3. Check your responses with Resource #3.3 to see if you can select sample size and explain a strategy for dealing with non-respondents.	3. Activity Sheet: #3.3 "Answer Sheet: Sample Size and Non-Respondents" in this packet.

Information Sheet #3.1 **Sample Size and Non-Respondents**

Sample Size:

Several factors may enter into the selection of a sample size. The general rule is the larger the sample size, the better. The larger the sample, the closer it will approach the population mean and standard deviation. Most studies are limited by financial and time restrictions, and the sample sizes are oftentimes smaller.

The sample size may be selected based on the level of accuracy needed for the study. For example, if you were surveying a population of 1000 students and wanted to have + or –5%, you would select a sample size of 278. If, however, you wanted + or –5% accuracy for the statistics for the responses from male and female, you would have to base your sample size on the number of males and females. For the purposes of this illustration, let us assume that there are 500 males and 500 females. To obtain + or –5% accuracy for each of these groups, you would need a sample of 217 males and 217 females. The total sample of 434 would give statistics with more than + or –5% accuracy for the total group. The study would also be more expensive since more people are involved.

When we speak of sample size, we are mainly dealing with the level of probability and the amount of error we can accept. Therefore, we are dealing with two factors:

1. Level of Probability—accuracy + or –5% is considered acceptable
2. Sampling Error—repeatability (if you do it again, will you get the same results)

The probability level (also called the confidence level) is usually set at the 95% (the so-called .05 level or + or –5%). This means there is a 95% chance that the sample is distributed in the same way as the population. The sampling chart takes the .05 level into consideration. The sampling error deals with the extent to which the means of repeatedly drawn random samples deviate from one another and from the population mean. Larger sample size reduces the error and adds stability to the findings.

In 1948, Thomas E. Dewey and Harry S. Truman ran against each other for the Presidency. All of the polls indicated that Dewey would win. The accuracy was very high. Of course, Truman won. The problem was they quit polling the people three weeks before the election and the sampling error had increased because people had changed their minds.

On the next page is a chart used to determine sample size. Find the size of the population under the column labeled "Population Size" and then read across to the sample size in the next column. These sample sizes will provide you with data with + or –5% accuracy in 95 samples out of 100. If you wanted to survey the Stout student population, you would only need a sample of 362 students and your results would be accurate to within + or –5%.

Sample Size

Population Size	Sample Size	Accuracy	Population Size	Sample Size	Accuracy*
25	24	+/–5%	1000	278	+/–5%
50	44	+/–5%	1500	306	+/–5%
75	63	+/–5%	2000	322	+/–5%
100	80	+/–5%	3000	341	+/–5%
150	108	+/–5%	5000	357	+/–5%
200	133	+/–5%	10,000	370	+/–5%
250	152	+/–5%	20,000	377	+/–5%
300	169	+/–5%	50,000	381	+/–5%
400	196	+/–5%	75,000	382	+/–5%
500	217	+/–5%	100,000	384	+/–5%
600	234	+/–5%	Very	250	+/–7%
700	245	+/–5%	Large	1000	+/–4%
800	260	+/–5%	Populations	1500	+/–3%
900	269	+/–5%			+/–5%

For populations between the sizes listed, interpolate from the sample sizes given.
* For values near 50% (this is region of largest error)

Steps in Sample Design:

Follow the steps listed below when selecting a sample:

1. Decide on the target population based on criteria for the study. Consider the cost implications of your population definition for various sample sizes.
2. Decide on how much "error" you can permit. The level of accuracy needed would increase directly as the costs and significance of the impacts of a decision increase.
3. Select or set up a sampling "frame" that is a list of all the "units" in the "population" from which you can make a random selection. If the population is smaller than 25–30, the population is your sample.
4. Consider the various sampling designs you might use.
5. Use a sample size chart and select the sample.
6. Caution: Response rates are not equivalent to a sample. For example, if you need a sample size of 100 and expect a response rate of 40%, it is not valid to increase the sample size to 250 in order to assure 100 responses. The 100 responses would give the statistical accuracy needed, but there would be a potential of significant bias in the responses. The problem of less than 100% response rates must be addressed differenty. Non-respondents must be contacted and data acquired from them. This strategy is discussed in the next section.

Non-Respondents:

A. You always needs to consider following-up with non-respondents. After you get your surveys back, you may need to contact the population and/or non-respondents again through the mail or by phone. This may produce another 12–15% return.

B. You then need to contact a sample of the remaining non-respondents either by interview or by phone. Ask them a sample of the questions or all of the questions in the needs assessment or task analysis.

C. This information from the non-respondent group is processed separately. Summarize the findings and compare them with the other collected data.

D. If the information is different from the regular respondents, the discrepancies indicate potential bias and must be discussed in the analysis of data. Usually the results will be the same, and the information from both groups can be pooled.

E. You cannot just substitute other people for non-respondents because they may be like the people that have already responded. You need to follow-up with the non-respondents.

17

Activity Sheet #3.2: **Sample Size and Non-Respondents**

Complete the following (Note – each question is worth 2 points.):

1. Using the sample size chart on page 16 of this packet, determine the following sample sizes:

   A. N = 100 s =

   B. N = 650 s =

   C. N = Population of Wisconsin s =

2. Determine the sampling size using the stratified sample for each grade level for the university student population.

	Number	Proportion	Sample
Freshman =	2400		
Sophomore =	1800		
Junior =	1500		
Senior =	1750		
Graduate Students =	550		
		n =	

3. When using data from a sample, why is it likely that a sampling error will be present?

4. The larger the sample, the more representative of the population it is likely to be. Explain this statement.

5. Explain a procedure for dealing with non-respondents.

Activity Sheet #3.3: Answer Sheet: Sample Size and Non-Respondents

1. Using the sample size chart on page 16 of this packet, determine the following sample sizes:

A. N = 100	s = 80
B. N = 650	s = 240
C. N = Population of Wisconsin	s = 1500

2. Determine the sampling size using the stratified sample for each grade level for the university student population.

	Number	Proportion	Sample
Freshman =	2400	.300	109
Sophomore =	1800	.225	82
Junior =	1500	.188	69
Senior =	1750	.218	80
Graduate Students =	550	.069	25
	8000	1.0	n = 365

3. When using data from a sample, why is it likely that a sampling error will be present?

   A sampling error is likely due to chance because it is not probable that individuals representing, for example, various ranges of needs (in a needs assessment survey) will be present in the sample in exactly the same percentages as those existing in the population.

4. The larger the sample, the more representative of the population it is likely to be. Explain this statement.

   In a small sample, a disproportionate number of individuals representing either high or low opinions about needs (if doing a needs assessment) may be selected. If this occurred, it would be due to the limited opportunity for the variable to average out in the small sample.

5. Explain a procedure for dealing with non-respondents.

   A. Contact as many non-respondents through the mail or with a phone contact as reasonable two weeks after the initial mailing.

   B. Approximately 4 weeks after the initial survey, contact a sample of the remaining non-respondents and ask them a sample of the questions from the survey.

C. This information from the non-respondent group should be processed separately. Summarize the findings and compare with data from the normal returns.

D. If the information is different from the regular respondents, the discrepancies indicate potential bias and must be discussed in the analysis of the data. If the data is the same from both groups, the data can be pooled.

Bibliography

Allen, E. (Ed.). (1990). *Needs assessment instruments ASTD trainer's toolkit.* Alexandria, VA: American Society for Training and Development.

ASTD (1992). *The best of needs assessment.* Alexandria, VA: ASTD.

Bailey, L., Calderon, R., Gragg, W., & Abate, L. (2008). *Using job and task analysis in a faster-is-better world.* Presentation at the 2008 ASTD International Conference & Exposition, San Diego, CA.

Branch, R. M. (2010). *Instructional design: The ADDIE approach.* New York: Springer Science+Business Media.

Brauer, W. M., & Bensen, M. J. (1997). *Tomorrow's technology: "Know how" for manufacturing and technology leaders of the 21st century* (research report). Bemidji, MN: Bemidji State University.

Briggs, L. J., Gustafson, K. L., & Tellman, M. H. (Eds.) (1991). *Instructional design: Principles and applications* (2nd ed.). Englewood Cliffs, NJ: Educational Technology Publications.

Carnevale, A. P., Gainer, L. J., & Meltzer, A. S. (1990). *Workplace Basics Training Manual.* San Francisco: Jossey-Bass.

Chang, R. Y., & Kelly, P. K. (1994). *Improving through benchmarking.* San Francisco: Jossey Bass/Pfeiffer.

Cooper, D. R., & Schindler, P. S. (2013). *Business research methods* (12th ed.). Boston: McGraw Hill.

Cooper. J. M. (Ed.). (2006). *Classroom teaching skills.* (8th ed.). Beverly, MA: Wadsworth Publishing.

Danielson, C. (2002). *Enhancing student achievement: A framework for school improvement.* Alexandria, VA: ASCD.

Dillman, D. A., Smyth, J. D., & Christian, L. M. (2014). *Internet, phone, mail, and mixed-mode surveys: The tailored design method* (4th ed.). Hoboken, NJ: John Wiley and Sons.

Edmonds, G. S., Branch, R. C., & Mukherjee, P. (1994). A conceptual framework for comparing instructional design models. *Educational Research and Technology, 42*(2), 55–72.

Giachino, J. W., & Gallington, R. I. (1977). *Course construction in industrial arts, vocational and technical education.* Homewood, IL: American Technical Publishers.

Glenn, J. C., & Gordon T. J. (Eds.) (2009). *The millennium project: Futures research methodology version 3.0* (CD-ROM). New York: American Council for the United Nations.

Goetsch, D. L., & Davis, S. B. (2013). *Quality management for organizational excellence: Introduction to total quality* (7th ed.). Boston: Pearson Publishing.

Gordon, S. E. (1994). *Systematic training program design: Maximizing effectiveness and minimizing liability.* Englewood Cliffs, NJ: Prentice Hall.

Gupta, U. G., & Clarke, R. E. (1996). Theory and applications of the Delphi Technique: A bibliography (1975–1994). *Technology Forecasting and Social Change, 53,* 185–211.

Halfin, H., & Nelson, O. (1977). DACUM gives direction. *The Wisconsin Vocational Educator, 6,* 4.

Keeney, S., Hasson, F., & McKenna, H. (2011). *The Delphi Technique in Nursing and Health Research.* Oxford, England: Wiley-Blackwell.

Kirkpatrick, D. L., & Kirkpatrick, J. D. (2006). *Evaluating training programs* (3rd ed.). San Francisco: Berrett-Koehler.

Krueger, R. A., & Casey, M. A. (2009). *Focus groups: A practical guide for applied research* (4th ed.). Thousand Oaks, CA: Sage Publications.

Leatherman, D. (2007). *The training trilogy: Conducting needs assessments, designing programs, training skills* (3rd ed.). Amherst, MA: HRD Press.

McArdle, G. E. H. (1998). *Conducting a needs analysis.* Menlo Park, CA: CPISP Publications.

Morrison, G. R., Ross, S. M., Kemp, J. E., & Kalman, H. K., (2007). *Designing effective instruction* (5th ed.). Hoboken, NJ: John Wiley & Sons, Inc.

Nelson, O. (1982). *Using the Delphi Technique to develop evaluation and research instruments.* Menomonie, WI: Center for VTAE, UW-Stout.

Oliva, P. F., & Gordon, W. R. II (2013). *Developing the curriculum* (8th ed.). Upper Saddle River, NJ: Pearson

Pitler, H., Hubbell, E. R., & Kuhn, M. (2012). *Using technology with classroom instruction that works* (2nd ed.). Denver, CO: McREL.

Posavac, E. J. (2011). *Program evaluation: Methods and case studies* (8th ed.). Upper Saddle River, NJ: Prentice-Hall.

Rothwell, W, J., & Kazanas, H. C. (2008). *Mastering the instructional design process: A systematic approach* (4th ed.). San Francisco: Pfieffer.

Rossi, P. H., Lipsey, M. W., & Freeman, H. E. (2004). *Evaluation: A systematic approach* (7th ed.). Thousand Oaks, CA: Sage Publications.

Royse, D., Staton-Tindall, M., Badger, K., & Webster. J. M. (2009). *Needs assessment.* New York: Oxford University Press.

Richardson, W. (2010). *Blogs, wikis, podcasts, and other powerful web tools for classrooms* (3rd ed.). Thousand Oaks, CA: Corwin Press.

Ruark, B. R. (July, 2008). The year 2012: ARDDIE is IN, ADDIE is OUT. *Training + Development,* (44-49).

Soriano, F. I. (2013). *Conducting needs assessments: A multidiscipline approach* (2nd ed.). Thousand Oaks, CA: Sage Publications.

Stake, R. E. (1995). *The art of case study research.* Thousand Oaks, CA: Sage Publications.

Williams, L. (1999). A simple, thorough approach to training needs assessment. *Corporate University Review, 7*(6), 22.

Yin, R. K. (2014). *Case study research: Design and methods* (5th ed.). Thousand Oaks, CA: Sage Publications.

Index

Page numbers in italic refer to figures.

A

B

C

D

N

O

P

Q

R

S

T

U

V